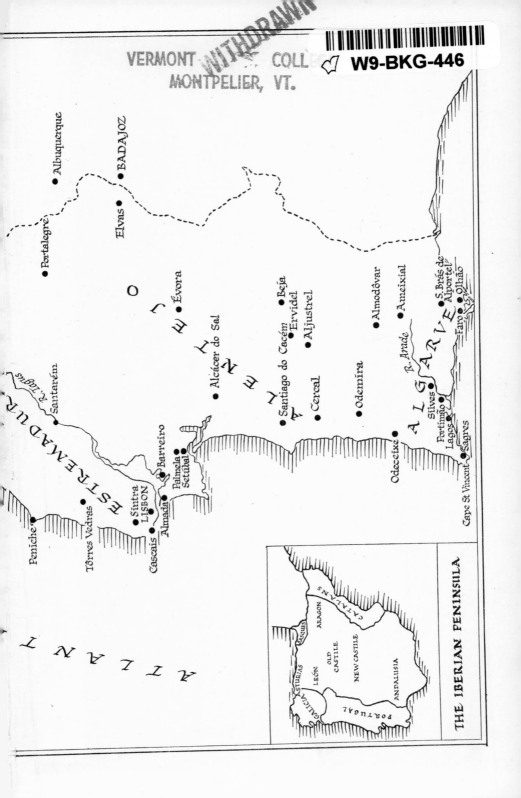

THE IBERIAN PENINSULA

Oldest Ally

A Portrait of Salazar's Portugal

Also by Peter Fryer

Hungarian Tragedy

OLDEST ALLY

A Portrait of Salazar's Portugal

Peter Fryer

&

Patricia McGowan Pinheiro

DENNIS DOBSON

London

First published in 1961 by

DOBSON BOOKS LTD

80 KENSINGTON CHURCH STREET · LONDON · W8

Printed in Great Britain by
Taylor Garnett Evans & Co. Ltd, Watford, Herts

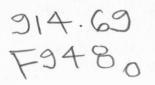

To
A.C.
with love and gratitude

Contents

7

PART THREE

Illustrations

Introduction

THIS account of Portugal today is based partly on our own personal observation, partly on things friends and acquaintances told us while we were there, partly on our reading and research. We have not been to the Portuguese colonies in Africa, yet we have included a chapter about them, since we felt that no serious book on present-day Portugal was complete that did not discuss that country's colonial problem. In this chapter we do not rely solely on the documentation that is available on Angola and Mozambique, but include some first-hand accounts by Portuguese we met who were recently in Portuguese Africa.

In the case of one of us the personal observation of Portugal and things Portuguese extends not merely over the four months of our 1960 visit, but over three and a half decades. Her father is Portuguese, till the age of five Portuguese was her first language, and she visited Portugal every year of her childhood and quite frequently afterwards. So this is not just a book of new impressions, though there are some in it. It is not simply a travel book, though the trips we made and the things we saw are described. It tries also to answer some of the first questions of a British reader just starting to be interested in a little-known but colourful country that he might one day think of visiting: 'Why is Portugal, the first modern empire-building nation, now so backward, so poor, so illiterate, so stagnant—and why has she submitted to a reactionary dictatorship for an entire generation?'

The ordinary British tourist may sometimes wonder about this, but he is so delighted with the welcome he gets and the comfort he lives in that he soon dismisses it from his mind. He basks on the Coast of the Sun, visits the earthly paradise of Sintra, gives coppers to picturesque beggars here and there, chats with retired compatriots who have found that Portugal is a haven for the foreigner ending his days on a fixed income.

13

Yet whoever reads a little history; or learns the language well enough to be able to talk easily with ordinary people; or feels deeply about democracy and free expression; or hates the sight of poverty side by side with ostentatious wealth – whoever does any one of these cannot rest content with a tourist's-eye view of Portugal. Once he meets Portuguese who trust him, once he ventures off the beaten track, he soon discovers that Estoril and Sintra are far from typical of the land that Salazar has ruled for thirty-three years; and that the democratic traditions we take for granted in Britain not merely do not exist in Portugal, but are frankly condemned by the authorities.

He will find people with the lowest standard of living in Europe. He will find people who are hungry, whose intake of calories is the lowest in Europe. He will find the only children in Europe who suffer from pellagra. He will find farm labourers who can get only two months' work in the whole year. He will find an infant mortality rate of 84 per 1,000 live births, compared with over a hundred other countries where it is 50 or less. He will find that almost half the people are illiterate.

And he will find that no effective protest against these conditions is possible, since Portugal has a muzzled Press, only one legal political party (a fascist party) and the rest banned, elections so arranged that opposition elements have no chance of winning, and above all a secret political police modelled on the Gestapo, which arrests, tortures and murders dissenters, and which even has the right to extend their prison sentences indefinitely if it so desires.

When he gets this far in his inquiries he may well reflect that this régime is bound to Britain not merely by a 600-year-old alliance, but also by common membership of the North Atlantic Treaty Organization, which is supposed to be defending a Free World. And when he meets, as we did, Portuguese democrats who point out that by buttressing Salazar with friendly messages and royal visits Britain is helping to perpetuate the kind of régime we fought the war to get rid of, that Britain's real friends in Portugal cannot understand why our country has any truck with Salazar – then he will be saddened and ashamed.

We should have liked to thank by name the many Portuguese friends who not only put up with our harassing inquiries but went to enormous trouble to make our stay both pleasant and fruitful. They found the people we wanted to meet and arranged introductions; they found the books we needed to read and helped us check the facts we needed to check; they fed two impecunious foreigners and lent them money so that the trip could be finished as originally planned; not least, they read large parts of our manuscript, criticized it, saved us from making a number of mistakes and gave us the benefit of a variety of specialist knowledge. Our Portuguese friends are busy people, yet they found the time to do all this, not primarily out of personal regard for us, but because they felt the publication of a book such as this would help the cause of democracy in Portugal. Wherever we have disagreed with their advice on particular matters and clung obstinately to our own views, the responsibility is ours; and the mistakes that no doubt remain are our own doing, too.

Unfortunately we cannot name any of these people to whom we are so indebted. One of Salazar's laws makes it an offence punishable by imprisonment for a Portuguese citizen to criticize his country to a foreigner. Yet it is Salazar and not his critics who defames Portugal, by making that beautiful country a place of oppression and hardship and fear. The critics of Salazar love their country and want to see it a free and happy place.

So do we. That is why we have been very outspoken in this book. Where we thought things were bad we have said so. Salazar's publicists may seize on these criticisms to make out that we are anti-Portuguese. Others will see that we have written about Portugal and her people *não só com justiça, mas também com carinho*.

P.F.

P.McG.P.

PART ONE

I

Lisbon notebook

On the train

'A modern enough town. We drank eighteen cups of wine between us – and nobody beat us up.' The speaker was a red-faced man in a green polo-necked jersey. His dark green suit was almost threadbare, but it was painstakingly brushed and pressed; and his broad hands with their calluses and deeply ingrained grime were a badge. He and a companion helped one another aboard the train with elaborate courtesy and rolled down the central gangway to their seats.

The carriage was filled with Portuguese workers returning from spells of migrant labour in France. We were waiting at Irún station, just over the French frontier, to begin the long journey to Lisbon. The Spanish railway carriages in front of ours and behind it were a dingy brown that might once have been the colour of chocolate. We felt rather superior because our little carriage, built of aluminium, gleamed in their midst like some silver-accoutred pony disdainfully picking its way among a train of Rocinantes – and because, 400 miles from Portugal, it carried the words *Companhia dos Caminhos de Ferro Portugueses* on its flanks like a challenge, for all to see. None of these new-fangled Castilian spellings and lispings for us, but the latter-day Latin of Camões, of which he himself wrote:

Slightly corrupt, 'tis still the Roman tongue.

The Portuguese workers sat nodding gravely as the Portuguese conductor lectured them. This was a first-class carriage on loan to second-class passengers, he said. Therefore its occupants must be on their best behaviour. They must keep the carriage clean, refrain from spitting and not spill food or wine on the floor.

While he spoke the Spanish occupants of the other carriages, which would go their separate ways at Medina del Campo, began to sing and to hammer the doors and wooden seats in time with their sweet,

19

sad songs. The Portuguese were subdued – until an opportunity for banter presented itself. A young Spaniard, perhaps eighteen years old, had taken a seat booked by a Portuguese and refused to give it up until the conductor insisted. The Portuguese had been drinking wine, and he went on grumbling for a long time after he was securely in his place – a place he scarcely sat in the whole of the rest of the journey. The Spanish boy was proud, and rather upset at having been made a fool of, and he showed it, so the Portuguese workers poked fun at him, as workers of all countries poke fun at those who cannot see a joke against themselves. Red-cheeked but silent, pretending not to understand a word, the boy took out a paper-backed book and began to read. He got off the train at Salamanca next day still wrapped in his haughty cloak of silence.

The Portuguese whose 'nobody beat us up' was a jesting reference to this touchiness between two of the five nations that inhabit the Iberian peninsula (the others are the Basques, the Catalans and the Galicians) turned out to be a natural comedian. His clowning might have been boring. But this man was an artist in gentle teasing. As the train got under way he marked down his victim: an expensively dressed and rather plain and rather hoity-toity German woman who was obviously dismayed at finding herself travelling among men with rough hands and rough clothes and rough voices, and who was determined to keep her dignity and her virtue alike intact. The comedian, assuming a ludicrous air of gallantry, sought to strike up a conversation with her. After his first few flirtatious remarks she rose, approached the conductor, paid the excess fare and strode off purposefully to the cloister of a first-class compartment. But the comedian was not daunted. When she came back for her luggage he insisted on carrying it for her, and he made several trips backwards and forwards to report to our carriage her progress in settling down and going to sleep. He told us gaily that he had the number of her seat, and that the coming night would not be dull for him or for her.

*　　　*　　　*

Surely there can be no slower 'rapid' train in the world than this night train that creeps from Irún to San Sebastián, and from San Sebastián to Vitoria, and thence to Burgos and Medina del Campo, till dawn breaks on the gaunt landscape of the Castilian plain and lights up these monotonous fields and poverty-stricken villages. Slowly, as if it too is disconcerted by the scene, the train steams through a brown, bitter semi-desert stretching to the horizon on both sides, with scarcely a tree or a hillock or a wall to ease the eye. In the villages the churches are in decay, the façades crumbling, sockets gaping in the belfries where bells should be swinging. The dingy hovels around them, mud-coloured, are crumbling too. Men live in some, animals in others. Often both share the same quarters. A man on a mule, his cloak drawn tightly around him, waits for the train to pass. Farm labourers trudge by with their feet bound in dirty rags and thrust into some kind of slippers, so that Franco's law against going barefoot shall be obeyed.

Occasionally the monotony is broken by the soft grey-green of olive trees as the train passes through a plantation; and Salamanca's *Catedral nueva* catches and reflects the early sun in a glow of yellow and pink that rivals the sunrise clouds. But it is only for a few moments, and then we are back in the scrubby, all-but-barren bleakness of the ancient kingdom of León. Even the Portuguese workers, and these are men who have tasted poverty and hardship all their lives, are moved by the primitive appearance of these villages. They comment too, on the way locomotives are refuelled at Fuentes de Oñoro, the Spanish frontier town. Here we are not yet in the age of the shovel, let alone the age of the lunik. One man picks slabs of coal from a heap and tosses them to his mate, who manhandles them into the tender.

Once we cross the border into Portugal the scenery changes, and the change is a dramatic one. For many miles the land is still harsh and rocky enough; but the Portuguese peasant proprietors, unlike the landowners of Castile, have not fecklessly stripped their land of trees, and they scratch a living wherever there is an inch of soil over the rock. There are terraces on the steep hillsides, wells, pumps and small, elaborately walled fields. Wherever a piece of ground as big as a sheet can be made to grow maize or oats or cabbages, it is cultivated, down to the last scrap of earth above the blood-red River Noeime.

There is of course another and more serious reason for the smallness of these fields. Primogeniture was abolished by a Liberal administration in the nineteenth century. This apparently progressive measure turned out to be the ruin of the north. From generation to generation the fields are divided and subdivided among the sons and daughters, till holdings dwindle to a bare subsistence level or below. 'No fortune lasts more than three generations,' it is said. The fourth generation mortgages the land to a rich man, who builds up a new estate, and the process begins again. The peasant who inherits only a fraction of his father's land must make it yield as much as he can. So there are furrows or standing crops to be seen in fields so stony that they would break the heart and the ploughshare of any English farmer. The peasant of the Beira Alta calls his region *uma terra fria, feia, forte e farta* – 'a cold, ugly, strong, sated land'. By his sweat he refreshes it each year; each year he challenges the wilderness of rock and, with his labour, brings the beauty of seed and harvest to these mountains. So much for the legend that the peasant of southern Europe is not industrious.

There could be no greater contrast than that between the villages of the Beira Alta and those of Castile a few miles to the east. The Castilian farm labourers seem too poor to buy paint. Between the frontier and the town of Guarda, the highest town in Portugal, where it became too dark to see, scarcely a house, however poor, did not have its doors and window frames pricked out in scarlet or yellow. The meanest of these peasants saves up for an annual repainting and cleaning. There are vines on pergolas and flowers in pots on the doorsteps. This love of colour extends even to the railway stations, where the square, coloured earthenware tiles called *azulejos*, whose use on Portuguese buildings dates back to the end of the fifteenth century, are set in gaudy pictures and elaborate floral designs on the walls of ticket offices, the Customs house, the police office and the lavatories. At first glance the walls resemble the interior of a Victorian gin palace or theatre in England. But look again and you will see that the national motifs save these unexpected decorations from garishness. Their very naïvety, indeed, is a pleasant change from advertisements for brassières and horror films.

*　　　　　*　　　　　*

In the darkness there was little to be seen of the university city of Coimbra. Soon afterwards the train gathered speed and swung south for the run into Lisbon. The last of a long series of ticket inspectors, who generally timed their visits to awaken us out of a doze, examined our tickets with an air of profound suspicion, then coolly and, one would swear, triumphantly demanded an excess payment of 25 *escudos* per person – about 6s 3d. When we objected to this, pointing out that the train was neither the de luxe vehicle nor the express which our tickets warned us might carry such extra payments, the inspector explained blandly that this was a 'velocity tax', payable because the train was an express between Pampilhosa and Lisbon. Savage tearing of receipts from receipt book. Presentation with a flourish. Self-satisfied smile. Exit. The conductor, appealed to, said all was in order. 'But what about when the train was going so slowly through Spain?' we asked. 'We didn't get a refund then.' 'That is a matter between you and the company,' he answered.

To be sure, the train was now going more quickly, but there were frequent stops, the delay at stations was at least as long as it had been before, and we were twenty minutes late at Lisbon's Santa Apolónia station.

The station was clean, light and airy, with tall, graceful windows and a spacious entrance hall crowded – or so it seemed to the weary traveller – with soft-voiced touts in grey uniforms and peaked caps. These persons offered hotels and *pensões* to those foreigners (can there be many?) temeritous enough to arrive in Lisbon at midnight without having booked accommodation. Each carried a closed umbrella on his left arm; with his right hand he proffered a card or a brochure, or deferentially plucked one's sleeve. This occupation seems to pay well: the sleeve-pluckers looked well nourished, their uniforms were neat and clean, their umbrellas were carried with an air. At last we were in a taxi, the crowd of sleeve-pluckers fell away, and we were speeding beside the Tagus, across whose dark waters gleamed the lights of Cacilhas and Almada.

First impressions

After Paris, which looks more sad and more seedy at each visit, the streets of Lisbon are fresh and bright. Paris is like a man who has not bothered to shave for a couple of days. Lisbon washes her face and puts on a clean dress every morning. Almost without exception the façades of houses and blocks of flats and offices are in excellent repair. The common practice is to paint the whole of the outside of the building in a pastel shade: sugar pink, powder blue, dove grey, olive green, apple green, turquoise, biscuit or the yellow of melted butter. Sometimes the window shutters and balconies will be in some contrasting shade, the slabs of luscious, almost edible colour pleasuring the eye like the rectangles of an abstract painting. 'Colour is life,' says a paint firm's poster prominently displayed on a building site in the suburb of Benfica. And Portuguese architects seem to use the palette even before they reach for the T-square. Even the gates and railings of new factories are painted in gay tints.

It is a well-cared-for city. The main streets and squares, all cobbled, are well swept, with broad mosaic pavements of basalt and limestone. Often the pavements are patterned, though in one place the black and white patterns have been done away with recently 'to facilitate traffic' and in another have been torn up in the construction of an underground railway that was opened in 1959 in an attempt to solve the growing traffic problem. Steep hills and bridges where streets climb dizzily over lower streets give unexpected and often beautiful views. In every direction there are to be seen modernity and elegance, the results of vigorous and imaginative town planning.

Of course there are blemishes – we mean obvious architectural blemishes, not the hidden-away slums and shanty towns that – except for the famous Alfama – are rarely seen by the tourist. How in the world do the citizens of Lisbon tolerate the Praça de Touros, that monstrous bullring in the north of the city, a gross and crushingly ugly edifice in neo-Moorish style, raw, red and bulbous? Or the Lys cinema, with its curious nippled cupola, stuck on as if by an after-thought? Still more distasteful is the way the superb and spacious Avenida da Liberdade, nearly a hundred yards broad and nearly a mile long, with tall palm trees and statues of Almeida Garrett, the nine-teenth-century liberal poet and dramatist, and of other great men of that time, is disfigured by sky-signs that tower well above the roof-tops. Certainly the signs make a glittering neon display at night, as if the lights of Piccadilly Circus had been grafted on to more noble buildings and permitted to spread. This may make some Portuguese feel cosmopolitan. It made us feel sad. The same offence against good taste spoils the Rossio, the city's central square, where hideous signs clash with the Ionic columns of the National Theatre that Garrett founded.

Portugal's capital is a striking combination of new and old. Immacu-late lawns in front of the Higher Technical Institute – there are no signs saying 'Keep off the grass', but no one thinks of treading on a single blade of it – are swept clear of autumn leaves by men with besoms. Through the modern traffic, amid buses that are very like London buses, except that these are painted green and designed for keep-to-the-right driving, goes a horse and cart bearing a peasant couple holding up an umbrella against the rain. Amid the business men and elegant shoppers there go fishwives and fruit sellers carrying their wares in baskets on their heads. We saw one who bore thus a plank some fifteen feet long, with all the grace and assurance of an African woman carrying a water-pot. It is not only the women who use their heads in this way. We saw a man walking with an enormous table on his head, and on the table were stacked shoe boxes, three rows deep, nine rows across and ten rows high – 270 boxes in all!

Lisbon's middle class, swollen by the large number of civil servants that a corporate State requires, lives in its cafés. At least, the men do. Most cafés – other than the fashionable *pastelarias*, where rich women go for afternoon tea or to meet their lovers, and where high-class prostitutes meet their clients – are by an unwritten law out of bounds to the female sex, as are the taverns of the workers. In the cafés professional men transact much of their business; often the deal is conducted and clinched in a few words on the pavement after a long gossip over coffee. In the cafés men sit for hours at a time to read the newspapers and write letters. In the cafés many university and secondary school students do a great deal of their reading, since the average Portuguese middle-class home has nowhere for young people to study: their bedrooms have only beds in them and bed sitting-rooms are rare. And in their favourite cafés middle-class opponents of the Salazar régime forgather daily to discuss politics over a *galão*, a 'gallon', as a large milk-and-a-dash is called. Their regular habits must lighten appreciably the duties of the secret police.

Young and old alike, the middle-class men of Lisbon dress to kill, or at any rate to wound. No spark of individuality is allowed in the dress. Dark suits, well pressed and carefully brushed, white collars, dark ties, handkerchiefs peeping out of breast pockets, half an inch of spotless cuff, gleaming black shoes kept clean by the ministrations of the city's army of bootblacks: these are tailors' dummies straight from the windows of that admirable shop in Covent Garden. No English business man was ever so dandified in his everyday costume. All that is lacking is the bowler hat, which has gone out of fashion in the last twenty years. The gap between well-to-do and poor in Portugal is so wide that a man who neglects to adopt the recognized social uniform of the rich, a uniform which proclaims that its wearer could not possibly do any work with his hands, will find himself treated with consistent disrespect. By his dress the Portuguese petty *bourgeois* claims his class position before the world. But his home and his mode of life often belie this keeping up of appearances. He may live in a small and overcrowded flat, very sparsely furnished; he may take home, especially if he works for the government, an embarrassingly small salary, perhaps no more than £25 or £30 a month; there may well be no holidays away from home; there may be no money in the bank; and he may be in debt to a variety of hire-purchase firms and to the pawnshop, and unable to pay the doctor's bill or the hospital bill.

The Portuguese are full of a courtesy that is disarming, if somewhat flowery and formal. Foreigners in their midst are privileged beings, for whom an entire queue at a bus stop will stand aside, who can disobey the traffic policeman at a pedestrian crossing without being fined on the spot, and who can even tread heavily on a man's foot, as one of us did at dusk one day in a crowded street, and be rewarded, after the first involuntary cry of pain and curse, with a delightful smile and an apology. The national sentiment is that the foreigner must be given a good impression of Portugal and its people. Alas, that so many Portuguese men, however smart their suits may be, however engaging their smiles may be, should offend, quite unconsciously, not against some factitious code of 'good manners', but against the elementary rules of social hygiene. We refer to the widespread habit of hawking and spitting which is the continuo to every walk and every bus-ride through the Lisbon streets.

Portuguese men of all classes spit freely and copiously; many doctors have spittoons in their consulting rooms for their own use, and these vessels are to be seen in hospital corridors. Just as some New York streets are carpeted with discarded chewing gum, so some Lisbon streets are coated with discarded mucus. The noise that accompanies these discharges is full of gusto and as frightening to the uninitiated as a pistol-shot. Behind us on the bus one night sat a well-dressed man who every three minutes cleared his throat with a rasping sound like a double-bass played *fortissimo* by inexpert fingers, brought the contents forward on a note a minor third higher, pulled down the window, spat to leeward, and closed the window with a contented grunt. And this was by no means exceptional. No Portuguese would dream of jostling you in a public place, unlike the animal behaviour on the London tube at the rush-hour. But many will cough in your face or on to the back of your neck without a tremor of shame. Still, progress is being made in matters of hygiene. Forty years ago, wash-basins were emptied from windows of upper stories in Braga with a shout of '*Água-vai!*' – 'Water is coming!' – to warn the passer-by, like the 'Gardyloo!' of old Edinburgh. This practice has happily fallen into desuetude, and forty years hence the habit of expectoration may well have followed it.

*   *   *

Craftsmanship is still very much alive in Portugal. You can take a worn-out suit to a tailor and have it turned, and it comes back almost as good as new. Cobblers will make your shoes for you. Cabinet-makers, carpenters and joiners working on their own account will make you furniture to your specification, and if you want a chair upholstered a man comes from his workshop round the corner and does it in your home. Leatherwork, basketwork, metalwork, bookbinding – big books are often bought gradually in parts and sent for binding – all these can be done for you by private craftsmen who often ply their trade in full public view in little workshops in the side-streets and who, so undeveloped is mass production, charge less than the few large shops do for the equivalent ready-made articles. Many middle-class households have a seamstress in once a week, perhaps with a young assistant, to do general household repairs, mend sheets and darn socks. The family's clothing, including that of the children, is run up at the dressmaker's.

Embroidery is a great national tradition. You can go to an embroiderer to have work done to your own design; and there is almost always embroidery on sheets, table linen, bathroom towels and women's underwear. Several shops in the Rossio display some of the best of this embroidery for the tourist trade; but if you know where to go in the countryside you can buy work of the same standard for considerably less. The women who do it are paid very little – a few coppers an hour – and ruin their eyes over the fine needlework. Many of them start their training at the age of three. Various regional designs are handed down from mother to daughter. Since the export of embroidery to the United States has begun on a large scale a system of outwork has developed, with women working for a whole hierarchy of middlemen who reap the profits.

The persistence of the independent craftsman is largely responsible for there being almost no department stores in Lisbon. There are only two, and both are very small by British standards. Instead there is a multitude of small shops displaying both familiar goods and such outlandish commodities as the spidery cousins of crabs, twitching and writhing on the ends of strings, octopuses and other sea food, still weirder in appearance, that we passed with a shudder, bolts of cloth half unfolded hanging down outside the shops, fishermen's nets of different colours, coils of rope of all thicknesses, piles of chamber-pots, boots and shoes in uncured leather, and Portuguese translations of science-fiction and of a recent French book on the thought of Karl

Marx. In some streets almost every third shop is either a cobbler-cum-bootblack's establishment where men sit having their shoes cleaned, or a barber's. The former are open to the street, the latter enclosed merely by a sheet of plain glass, so that one can look in and see a row of men being shaved, like fishes laid out on a slab, while others queue standing behind the chairs. The barbers' shops are generally crowded, for many men do not shave at home.

Discoveries

The first morning of our stay at a village fifty minutes out of Lisbon we were awakened by a sound like Indian music: a soft, random tinkling over about half an octave, without any distinguishable theme, on a scale built of quarter-tones and other strange intervals. Across the ploughed field below the balcony came a flock of sheep with bells round their necks, being driven to pasture. Soon a man began ploughing a field in the middle distance with a pair of oxen, each bearing two bells. Four separate notes, clear and plangent, whose permutations went on the whole morning. Another ploughman in a further field sang to his honey-coloured beasts, the wordless melody carrying across the still, warm air like a song heard in a dream. Whether his song was improvised or traditional it was full of plaintive flourishes and ululations that sounded unmistakably Moorish. It is 700 years since the Moorish rulers were finally driven out of the land and the *Reconquista* was accomplished; but Arabs remained, to be assimilated into the Portuguese nation and to exercise an influence on its culture.

The cock who lived in a big wooden cage next door gave an occasional hoarse *cocorocó* and was answered by his brothers in the distance. A rangy black cat, announcing his presence with a strident cry, came slinking across the field for scraps. Wooden wheels creaked along the rough track at the front of the house. Far from breaking the morning stillness, these sounds enhanced it. An hour from Lisbon's bustle, two days from London's searing decibels, was an anodyne silence that felt, and fitted, like a new skin.

*   *   *

We walked along country roads to the summer palace of the Portuguese kings at Queluz. It is a graceful building in pink and cream with an immense cobbled courtyard in front and, at the back, a formal garden to end all formal gardens, complete with allegorical statues, ponds and urns. The guide conducted us through the rooms in a whirlwind tour, observing sourly that the French had taken away many of the best things at the time of Napoleon.

The walk to Queluz and back was a long and fascinating one, in a terrain where the outermost suburbs of a fast-expanding city meet and mingle with the villages; where blocks of new flats, whose tenants do not hesitate to hang their washing out at the front, stand in the midst of fields and meadows and groves of orange trees. Everywhere are bright red roofs built of pantiles, with overhanging pagoda-like eaves that seem to show the influence of the Discoveries. One soon learns to discern this influence on all sides.

Portugal is very aware of her past greatness, when she was the creator and the centre of a thriving empire. And she is proud – perhaps in too nostalgic a way – of those far-off days. By chance we noticed one morning in an old issue of the *Diário de Notícias* an item, prominently 'boxed', reporting the announcement by a Russian professor, after 'patient study of Spanish, Italian and Portuguese documents, and of exceedingly rare documents in Leningrad and Moscow libraries', that America was discovered, not by Christopher Columbus, but – long before 1492 – by Portuguese navigators. The source of this announcement did not prevent its being received with interest and perhaps a little complacency. After all, Portuguese voyagers rediscovered Madeira, which the Genoese had found and forgotten; they rediscovered the Azores; they discovered Brazil, Labrador and the sea route to India; they were the first to round the Cape of Good Hope and they gave it its name; they were the first to explore the African coast past the Tropic of Cancer, and they set up trading posts all round it; they were the first Europeans to reach Japan, taking there the sponge-cake, Christianity and the smooth-bore musket; and an expedition led by a Portuguese, Fernão de Magalhães (known to British schoolchildren as Magellan) was the first to circumnavigate the globe. It scarcely needed a Russian scholar to confirm what every Portuguese schoolboy already suspected: that they had beaten Columbus to it.

All over Portugal the effects of the Discoveries are still to be seen. The crews sent out in the fifteenth century by John of Gaunt's grandson Henrique (called by non-Portuguese 'the Navigator', though in fact he himself never went on a voyage) consisted of simple seamen commanded by men specially trained by the geographers, cartographers, astronomers, mathematicians and pilots that Henrique assembled.

These crews, even the few noblemen among their officers, left behind, when they set sail in their caravels, carracks and galleons, a way of life not substantially different from the austerity of the rest of medieval Europe. Wall-hangings and carpets were little known; there was little silver and a dearth of gold; the only silk for clothing was borne overland from the east by caravan and was therefore very costly; cooking was simple and monotonous because spices also had to come this long distance by land. There was neither tea, coffee, chocolate nor sugar. The Portuguese explorers found luxury, elaborate art, a voluptuous mode of life. The impression made on them was so great that they brought home, not only finished articles, but also craftsmen to work and to teach. They brought back palm trees, eucalyptus, Bougainvillaea and tropical cactuses, which flourished in the warm climate and go on flourishing today. They brought back monkeys and parrots and macaws, and such pets are still to be seen in cafés, or sunning themselves and chattering in cages fixed to the outside walls of houses. They brought back ideas about design and decoration which led to the making of exotic furniture in mother of pearl and ivory, the weaving of carpets modelled on those of India, the building of churches embellished as oriental temples are, their altars encrusted with silver and gold, lapis lazuli and alabaster – like those in the sumptuous chapels of the Church of São Roque in Lisbon. They brought back a taste for rice and spices and tropical fruits and eastern sweetmeats. These things are still enjoyed in Portugal, where rice dishes, spiced meats and rich sweets are relished by all who can afford them.

It is this remarkable combination of Latin, Moorish, oriental and African influences which makes Portugal such a strange and enchanting country. And, for those who have eyes to see, this combination exists in a modern synthesis in the newest and most up-to-date blocks of flats, just as it does in the physiognomy of the people.

On the far west of Lisbon, on the river bank, stands the Tower of Belém, built by King Manuel I in the early part of the sixteenth century as a welcome to returning navigators; and nearby is the enormous Hieronymite Monastery, begun at the same period in the same exuberant, eastward-looking Manueline style. The architects of the Discoveries made their buildings redolent of the ocean and its fruits, and of the new-found lands across the ocean. You see cables and hawsers tied in monstrous knots, cords running through rings and coiling round pillars, the scales of fish and the fish themselves dancing on the waves, fronds of seaweed, branches of coral tied with chains, fishing floats, pearls. You see foliage, laurel leaves, artichokes, maize-cobs, cork trees and their roots, collars hung with bells, jets of spurting flame. Here are the adventure and mystery of the east and its sea-lanes translated into writhing, buoyant stone in a myriad shapes as varied as the beckoning and minatory seas themselves.

*   *   *

During our explorations of Lisbon and its environs we generally had a light lunch in one of the many little groceries with adjoining taverns. At Belas we ate bread with ham sausage, strongly garlicked, and washed it down with a pleasant white wine, then tried what the woman who served us called a speciality of the region, though we fancy they are made elsewhere: *fofos*, a kind of sponge-cake with custard inside, exceedingly short and delectable. The bill came to less than 2*s* each, but one must remember that 2*s* is a quarter of what many workers earn in a single day. While we ate, two dogs sat gazing mournfully up at us, their eyes following every movement of hand and fork. A woman carrying a flea-bitten and anaemic-looking baby, accompanied by a singularly beautiful little girl, came in to ask how much her grocery bill was. She promised to pay the 100 *escudos* outstanding as soon as she received some money owing to her. We met her again a little way along the road, and when we smiled at her daughter she asked us for money 'to buy the children some bread'. Portuguese friends told us later that the trifling amount we gave her was about ten times the amount one ever gives to a beggar.

Everyone agrees that the more open forms of begging have diminished to some extent in Portugal in the last few years. But there is still much of it, for life is terribly hard for those unable to work for one reason or another. In the Lisbon streets women beg very discreetly, sidling up and whispering in your ear as you walk along. Many of them are gipsies. At railway stations men with deformities will make a regular round of the waiting-rooms or will sit whining on the platform. Begging is not against the law, but the government has been campaigning against it to avoid criticism by foreign tourists. In fact there are in Lisbon fewer beggars operating as street musicians or match sellers than are to be seen in London, where one of us once counted fourteen between Baker Street tube station and Selfridges. In their place is something much worse, and much more revealing: a huge number of persons roaming the streets to sell tickets in the

national lottery. In the centre of Lisbon your ears are assailed from
morning to night by the cries of these venders, exhorting you to try
your luck, waving their sheaves of blue tickets in your face, tugging
your sleeve, or even walking beside you for several paces in a desperate
attempt to coax a few coppers from your pocket into theirs. These are
the poorest of the poor. Among them are old men, their eyes gleaming
above the dirty bristles on their cheeks, cripples on crutches and in
wheel chairs, women carrying babies slung over their shoulders, and
young boys darting backwards and forwards like fish. At the corner
of the Rua do Carmo, Lisbon's Bond Street, stood a boy of about eighteen, quite blind, his beautiful, tortured face turning this way and that,
the features illuminated as though by some inner vision he could see
the crowds that paraded heedlessly past the bunch of lottery tickets
he brandished.

Another form of begging, which the tourist is quite unaware of,
but which every middle-class Portuguese housewife makes provision
for, is the interminable round of callers at houses and flats on Fridays.
Since Friday is a holy day, it is the favourite time for those who practise house-to-house begging. These persons feel – and the results
they get show that they are right – that on such a day the devout
Catholic is not so likely to refuse a hand-out. And so the doorbell
rings every few minutes throughout the day and, singly or in whole
families, beggars ask for alms in the name of Christ.

In the poorer quarters of Lisbon and in the countryside, children
generally ask the stranger for a *tostãozinho*, their name for a tenth of
an *escudo* (though they hope for rather more). On a cold, wet evening
in the suburbs we saw two barefooted girls, aged perhaps nine and six,
who had just come up to us and asked for money, squatting on the
pavement and counting up what they had been given that day. Their
old-young faces were pinched and sly, and the elder wore an
expression of hardness and disillusionment, half-adult, half-animal,
that no child should have to wear. These children were not begging
for themselves. They had been sent out by their mother to eke out the
family budget.

*   *   *

Lisbon's poorest quarter is her most picturesque, and in consequence
so alluring to tourists that the people that live in it tend to be cynical
about the part the rubbernecks who explore its steep, secret alleys

expect them to play. In fact the dwellers in the Alfama are not, for the most part, the gaudy vagabonds of legend, but ordinary *lisboetas* of the working class, who live there only because they cannot find, or cannot afford, anywhere better. The combination of the sinister, the exotic and the bizarre that the tourist hopes to find – or fancies he finds – there exists largely in his imagination. Glasgow has no slums so rancid as the Alfama can show; but Portugal has many that are worse, and that shelter people far less cheerful and buoyant than these who eye foreign visitors with much the same air as do the parrots that adorn their damp-stained, peeling walls.

Churches, stables now inhabited by men, tiny shops, cottages, great stone buildings long ago deserted by the aristocrats and merchants who built them – all are packed together higgledy-piggledy on a precipitous hillside above the quays, the moss-draped roofs of some becoming almost the courtyards of others. Between them twist lanes so narrow that in places the houses almost touch at the top, while at the bottom two persons are only just able to pass. Life teems here. Swarms of flies and children dance and buzz in the small, unexpected squares; cats and babies howl, or bask in the sunshine that manages to squeeze into these stifling stone ravines.

The visitor sees what he has come to see, smells what his fastidious nose translates into the smells of dirt and poverty. But underneath is a seething life the visitor never dreams of. Here was the one place in Lisbon where we found the walls covered with political slogans. And along with the smells of garlic, urine, sweat and decay there comes the scent of rebellion. There are more ways than one of being rebellious. In the Alfama the visitor's gaze is returned with dignity; for once, though the children beg, no one offers to clean his shoes, or guide him, or sell him anything. If Lisbon's middle class on the whole fawns on foreigners, if some of her citizens have forgotten that they too are men, the people of the Alfama are not given to cringing. Crowded in a noisome ghetto that is neither quaint nor colourful if you have to live in it, they bear themselves as human beings. Yet there are many in Portugal who consider them to be little better than animals.

It is dark in the Alfama; in the garden behind the castle that stands on the hill's summit everything in the animal kingdom is white, and the contrast is a piquant one. White peacocks, white ducks, white geese, white swans, white pigeons, cross and recross the lawns self-importantly, chased by delighted children. At dusk, having become grey, these birds go to roost on walls the Visigoths built. On these walls, and on the roofs of houses that descend in terraces beneath them, are kitchen gardens where cabbages grow and chickens are kept.

High above the city and the river, the castle grounds are a place to sit and rest and watch the sunlight slanting through the trees. The whole of Lisbon is laid out at your feet. It shimmers in the heat; from a thousand motor-car and office windows the sun flashes up; the river's vaster mirror blinds you with its brilliance.

*   *   *

Lisbon's glory is her waterfront. You gain access to the chain of quays at its most dramatic point under the Arch of Triumph, through which can be seen from a great way off the green bronze rump of the horse on which sits Dom José I, royal supporter of Portugal's Peter the Great, the Marquis of Pombal. The statue is in the centre of the eighteenth-century Praça do Comércio, said by some to be the finest square in Europe, though it is a pity that motor-cars are now allowed to park on it. On three sides are regular, handsome buildings housing various ministries. On the fourth side a broad marble staircase leads down to the blue waters of the Tagus, in which is reflected a startling sky never seen north of the Pyrenees.

On the river there are sailing boats, battleships, pleasure steamers suggesting miniature Mississippi steamboats, fishing vessels with crescent-shaped prows seeming to echo the design of the Phoenician craft that were the first to creep along the Portuguese shore. And there are ferry boats that for threepence will carry you out over the choppy waves, past gulls bobbing on the water and a three-masted naval training ship riding at anchor, to the Setúbal peninsula. Ahead of you, on the top of the hill, stands a grotesque monument to the present-day power of the Church in Portugal: a gigantic, modernistic statue of Jesus Christ, arms outstretched, towering above the river. The official name of this statue is *Cristo Rei* – 'Christ the King'. But the people of Lisbon, with their customary irreverence, have given it the title '*o sinaleiro*' – 'the traffic cop'. The monument, completed only recently, was paid for by a fund collected from the faithful. It is said by the gossip-loving café-goers that one of the priests responsible for the fund helped himself to 5,000 *contos* (£62,500) and absconded to South America.

You have been looking across the river. Now look to port and, though you are facing eastwards, you cannot see where land begins,

so deep is the bottle-shaped inlet known as the Sea of Straw on whose
north bank, behind you, sit the seven hills of Lisbon. Turn round, and
there along a ten-mile frontage rise tier upon tier of houses and
churches, the Praça do Comércio in the centre constantly drawing the
eye back to its measured colonnades.

It was on the Praça do Comércio, lapped by Atlantic tides and by
waters that flow down from the Spanish Meseta, that there gathered
on VE night, 1945, half a million Lisbon people. The crowd completely filled the great square to celebrate the victory over fascism
which they imagined would result in the disappearance of their own
dictator – Salazar.

II

Southern notebook

Broad plains and narrow lives

We went to the Algarve, Portugal's southernmost province, by bus, not by train, because from the bus there is so much more to see. You pass through villages, and you have a wider variety of travelling companion, for the bus, though a long-distance one, serves also as a local conveyance along much of its route. Crossing the Tagus to Barreiro on the south bank, we watched the early February sun rise over the water, slowly blocking in with colour the outlines of boats and sails. The first few minutes of the bus journey took us through an industrial landscape, with tall, smoking chimneys, little railway tracks crossing the road and disappearing into workshops at frequent intervals, and the letters CUF here and there to remind us of the great and powerful combine that owns a good part of Barreiro, which is the centre of the new steel industry.

Before long a company of gipsies swarmed on board the bus, shouting and laughing without inhibition. None of them, we imagined, had read the editorial in *O Século* a few days before, foreshadowing an effort to make this community lead more sanitary lives and send their children to school. If they had, they showed no inclination to quench their boisterous language, which made our conductor raise his eyebrows and look at us as though we three were the only cultured people on the bus. Certainly few other Portuguese men would address a woman affectionately as 'you big whore', as did one of these gipsies, or shout after their friends who descended at one stop the minimum price they must obtain for the gaudy rolls of cloth they were to sell, or rush down like children leaving school, to search for a missing companion. And yet Portugal would be a poorer and less colourful place if these strange, olive-skinned people, whose womenfolk are immediately identifiable by their long skirts and garish blouses and flamboyant ear-rings, were to be assimilated or otherwise to disappear from the scene. In the north, we found later, some of them have acquired prosperity, perhaps by smuggling things across the Spanish frontier, and drive around the streets of Oporto in enormous Cadillacs and Buicks – and in a richer version of the dress their poorer kinsfolk beg in and sell in and steal in.

Before entering the Algarve we had to pass through two other regions. First the Estremadura, with its ricefields and beanfields. Then the Alentejo: the land beyond the Tagus. This great central province is at once the richest and the poorest part of Portugal: rich because most of it is owned by some of the biggest landowners in the country; poor because most of the population are landless agricultural labourers who work on the big estates, and among whom the introduction of tractors has brought unemployment and uncertainty. Here everything is on a big scale: big plains, big estates, big fields, big plantations of cork-oaks and olive trees, big flocks of sheep and herds of black pigs – one-third of Portugal's sheep and about the same proportion of her pigs are to be found in the Alentejo. Everything, that is, except the wretched dwellings of the landworkers, which are somewhat better looking than those in Castile, certainly, because they are almost always whitewashed, but which are often simply low, one-story boxes with a door and a couple of wooden-shuttered holes in the walls for windows. No glass. The only common decoration is the chimney, which will be ornamented with carvings or lace-like trellis-work in the Moorish style, and painted a vivid blue or yellow. The farther south you go the more decorative the chimneys are, till in the Algarve they are fantastically ornate.

The people dress poorly, the men generally in broad-brimmed black hats, checked shirts, rough sheepskin coats hanging low at the back like the tails of a dress suit (but not divided) – coats cut away at the front to *bolero* length and with overhanging epaulet shoulders – patched and repatched trousers, gumboots and umbrellas. The women wear regional costume, plainer than that worn on feast-days, but still picturesque to English eyes. Its outstanding feature is the black hat, resembling a large trilby, worn over a kerchief that covers the head and the back of the neck, rather like a wimple. The effect is medieval and pleasing. In this head-dress, and in a blouse and long skirt, the women toil in the fields, backs bent low over the furrows, in groups of three or four so that they can sweeten the labour with gossip.

The *alentejanos* lead a narrow life in their villages and even in their towns. We saw no television aerials, and the chief leisure occupation of the men seems to be standing in the street watching people go by. It is hard to imagine the poverty of life in a place where one of the major daily events is the arrival of the bus from Lisbon. In Cercal and Odemira and the curious little village of Odeceixe there were crowds to greet the bus when it pulled in: some meeting people, some seeing people off, some collecting or 'posting' parcels, some selling hot chestnuts, cakes, tangerines and lottery tickets to the passengers, some just curious onlookers.

Neither of us had had much breakfast, and by the time we reached Alcácer do Sal, sixty miles out, we risked being left behind and, the instant the bus stopped, dashed into a café and had coffee. Since we were still not warm after a cold dawn start, we had brandy as well. The total bill was 1s 6d, and the feeling of warmth that small sum brought was worth much more. But by one o'clock, or just before, when the bus stopped at Santiago do Cacém for fifty minutes, we were ravenous. We chose a simple-looking place called the Casa de Pasto Alegria, and were very glad we had done so.

A young woman, buxom and red-cheeked and delighted to find that one of us spoke Portuguese, insisted on putting us in a little room on our own, presumably because we were foreigners. We sat eyeing the inevitable Last Supper on the wall and the equally inevitable Singer sewing machine in the corner. Then the food came, and we concentrated on that. We had a good vegetable soup; a meaty fish called *pargo*, served with boiled potatoes that were plainly cooked but delicious with olive oil and vinegar; and, with chipped potatoes, great slabs of fried pork that had been standing for twenty-four hours in a marinade of white wine, garlic and laurel leaves. With this we drank two carafes of local red wine, which made an admirable accompaniment to a homely meal. It was country fare, but there was plenty of it, and to hungry people it was what the food snobs call a memorable meal. The bill came to 37 *escudos*, or 9s 3d for two. Anyone who follows in our footsteps will probably find when he is really hungry that this genuine Portuguese cooking is more to his taste than the mock-French or pseudo-international cuisine of the big and biggish hotels. It will probably suit his pocket better as well. The Casa de Pasto Alegria is mentioned in no guide book or travel book, as far as we know; but it deserves such a distinction more than many pretentious places do. And if you do not mind entering eating-houses frequented by working people you will find its equivalent in almost every Portuguese town.

Around Alcácer do Sal ('Castle of Salt', from the Sado river's salt deposits) there were dunes, the almost white sand showing through a sprinkling of scrubby little plants. Then acre after acre of cork-oaks, the bottoms of their trunks bare and dark brown where the cork had been stripped off. Sometimes we passed through avenues of fragrant eucalyptus. Nearing Santiago do Cacém we were in a world of Moorish windmills, more nonchalant in appearance than those there are – or used to be – in England. Their canvas sails were spread over a fragile-looking framework of eight spokes, and they leaned back at an angle, more amicable by far than the robot-like metal windpumps that dot the countryside round Lisbon. There is something very mysterious about a real windmill in full possession of its sails; it may be its commanding position on the top of a hill, or the eerie circular motion of its sails, or the deceptive simplicity of the principle on which it works. Whatever it is, windmills have the air of housing intelligences, on the whole mild, reflective and happy, insisting on only one thing: that they go on turning. You can see what Don Quixote had in mind. Windmills give the most ordinary landscape a share of romance, and those around Santiago do Cacém are no exception.

The sad south coast

The road wound round hairpin bends and double bends, with rolling country on either side, and we stopped frequently, where some track from a village hidden behind hills joined the main road, to pick up a little group of travellers. Towards sunset we crossed into the Algarve. On this coast road, unlike the inland road we returned by, there was no startling change. This province is supposed to resemble north Africa in many ways; but there are few Moorish influences here that are not shared to some extent with the rest of Portugal. The women in the Algarve countryside dress in deepest black. They pull their shawls over the bottom half of the face when they are out walking or riding side-saddle on donkey or mule, and we supposed this custom to be a vestige of the veil. But there is nothing in the physical appearance of the people to distinguish them from their northern countrymen, and their speech differs in pronunciation, vocabulary and cadence from that of Lisbon only to the extent, say, that Durham speech differs from that of London.

We reached the coast at Lagos, which saw some of the Portuguese explorers depart for Madeira, the Azores and west Africa five hundred years ago, and which gave its name to the Nigerian Lagos. Today there is little left of its old glories, which included a slave market under the arches of what is now the Customs building. The old port is silted up. It is a dusty, rather dirty town. In the Church of Santo António is a statue of that saint wearing the crimson sash of a field officer. It is said that he was once appointed a major-general in the Portuguese army on full pay, and that a proxy used to sign the pay-roll.

And so we came to Portimão, the Algarve's chief port.

*   *   *

On the whole the Algarve (the name comes from Al-Gharb, meaning 'the west', i.e. the western province of the Moors' Iberian caliphate) was a trifle disappointing. It may be that we did not see it at its best. Perhaps the dull, cold weather was dispiriting, and a few hours of Mediterranean sunshine would have transformed the bleak waterfront of Portimão into a place of southern gaiety and splendour. To be sure, the almond blossom was out, and that was a token of a spring that was creeping its way day by day up the continent. But what of the brochures for tourists that raved about the all-the-year-round sun-shine? In February Portimão was a kind of southern Hull on a small scale: the same flatness and lack of sparkle, the same combination of dourness and hospitality in its people, the same smell of fish along the riverside, the same drab factory belt between the town centre and the seaside, the same spectacle of idle men – here, seasonal workers – killing time on the street corners.

At first therefore we decided to use Portimão as a base and to go for a day to Cape St Vincent, in the far west of the province, and watch the sun set from there. To the Greeks and Romans this, the extreme south-western point of Europe, was the Promontorium Sacrum. The setting sun looked a hundred times bigger than elsewhere, and you could hear the hiss as it met the waves and was extinguished by them. Here, said the Greek explorer Artemidorus, was where the gods slept at night after the labours of the day. And from his workshop at Sagres near here Henrique 'the Navigator' directed the Discoveries. But the taxi-driver to whom we put the project of a trip to Portugal's Ultima Thule told us he could not do it for less than 200 *escudos*.

It was, he said, 150 kilometres there and back, and his *patrão*, called over to confirm this, did so gravely. The maps say it is exactly 112 kilometres. But maps are notoriously unreliable. So we thanked him and went by bus to Praia da Rocha instead.

Of Praia da Rocha, two miles south of Portimão, the brochure issued by the Casa de Portugal in Lower Regent Street – the London branch of the National Secretariat of Information, Tourism and Popular Culture – has this to say:

This seaside resort is internationally known for the beauty of its fine beaches, its spectacular cliffs and rocks and a privileged winter climate which allows bathing all the year round. The temperature of the water in December, January and February averages 63 degrees (9 a.m.) and the following are average air temperatures, for the 24 hours, and monthly hours of sunshine, over the last four years for the month of December.
Temperature: 57 degrees. Sunshine: 190 hours.

We should have liked to cast the author of these lines from one of his spectacular cliffs or push him from one of his fine beaches to test for himself the temperature of the water. It was cold, dull, windy and drizzly; the waves were sinuously menacing, like white treacle oozing up the counterpane in a feverish dream; the only signs of 'privilege' were the villas, some owned by sardine magnates, strung along the cliff top – a choice collection of thirties architecture, with names like 'Weekend' – and, of course, the Hotel Bela Vista. An English acquaintance in Lisbon had just spent a couple of days at this hotel with his small son, and reported that it had set him back 600 *escudos*. So we contented ourselves with looking at the outside and regretting that our hour in Praia da Rocha was not one of the 190 sunny ones.

At one end of the cliff, set on a rock where the Arade river flows into the Atlantic, is the sixteenth-century Fort of St Katherine, where there is a little chapel dedicated to the local patroness of sailors and fishermen. Once a year her image is taken in a procession to the sea-shore so that the waves may be blessed. The Portimão band leads the procession, and St Katherine is escorted by priests and followed by local dignitaries and the members of the guilds carrying their banners. 'To do the ceremony properly the Saint should be carried right into the sea, but in the last few years the weather has not been suitable and the clergy very wisely have remained on dry land. Apparently the

B*—OA

efficacy of the blessing has been in no way impaired by this act of common sense.'[1]

Walking back from Praia da Rocha, we were soon passing sardine-canning factories and blocks of workers' dwellings adjacent to them. These were not houses, but something akin to barracks. There stretched along the main road a series of tiny windows, some with panes missing here and there. No doors were visible, for the entrances are at the back, closer to the factory. Each cell has one or two ill-lit, congested rooms. Rich tourists who speed up and down this road, to and from the fine beaches and the spectacular cliffs, probably think – if they think of it at all – that this building is part of the factory. In a way, of course, it is: it is the place where the animate machines are rested and refuelled, and new ones created.

Farther on were boatyards where fishing vessels were being built and repaired, with planks that the boat-builders themselves were cutting out from tree-trunks to their own requirements. Barefooted men and boys drew heavy saws through the wood, so near their naked toes that we winced.

*   *   *

Six miles north-east of Portimão is Silves, a town built by Yemenite Arabs, who called it Xelb. Under the Moors it was a provincial capital. We wanted to see what had become of a place that was once as important as Lisbon. We found a decaying little town, whose British-owned cork-processing factories, it seems, are what keeps it alive. But there are imposing relics of its ancient greatness: the thirteenth-century Gothic cathedral, built in the local reddish-brown stone, now crumbling but still impressive; and the Moorish castle, which dominates the town and commands a splendid view of the countryside.

We arrived at the castle escorted by a flock of dark-eyed little girls, chattering like birds and giggling at the *estrangeiros* they had captured. They followed us through the massive keep into the courtyard, now ablaze with blossom. But the custodian would not let them climb with us on to the battlements, though they insisted they were our cousins. For a time they skipped and shrieked; but they grew tired of the castle long before we did.

Aloft, treading the red sandstone and peering through the machicolations and embrasures, we marvelled at the feeling of security this

[1] A. H. Stuart, *Algarve* (Lisbon, n.d. [c. 1952]), p. 22.

castle must have given to those who built it and held it. It is said to
have sheltered an army of 30,000 Moors. Yet it fell, and it is 700 years
since these stones were trodden by the Arab princes, who must have
wondered how long their empire would last, the captains and the
soldiers – Berbers and Jews among them – and the slaves; and the
empire of which these were a part, and most of the Portuguese empire
that succeeded it, have both vanished. The reservoirs built by the
Moors inside the castle walls are still in use. In one corner is a well.
There is a legend that at water-level an underground passage led to
open country behind the besiegers' lines, and that in this way the
garrison was provisioned. And there is said to have been a conduit
bringing water from the Arade river, until a traitor told the Portuguese
where it was, so that it was cut, and thirst compelled the garrison to
surrender.

*   *   *

Our first night in Portimão found us so tired after a long bus journey
that we were not disturbed by noise; at least that was the only explanation we could think of for our being able to sleep so soundly. For, the
second night at the Pensão Familiar Grade, there was no peace at all.
Somewhere downstairs men were engaged in a repetitive, apparently
compulsive and sleep-murdering activity.

First there would be strange bangings, slappings, creakings,
hammerings and tongings, accompanied by laughter and lively
conversation. Then several minutes of a whirring noise like an over-
grown vacuum cleaner. Then the banging and talking again. Throughout the night the cycle went on. From 2 a.m. every hour that struck
did so audibly. First the church bells of Portimão, which seemed to
have been moved to new belfries just opposite the *pensão*. A good five
minutes after the last bell's overtones had died away, and one was
dozing off as best one could, the cuckoo clock in the dining-room had
its say too. So loud was this bird that it awoke the Portimão cocks.
At any rate, they began to crow at 3.5 a.m. precisely, and they crowed
from then onwards with the utmost regularity and vainglory. Nor
was this all. It so happened that the bell for the street door and for room
service rang in that very corridor, and it was very loud indeed – so
loud that when you heard it in the daytime, let alone at night, it made
you jump. There was a terrifying peal just before 4 a.m., and it
initiated footsteps and arguments and the slamming of doors. About
6 a.m. the downstairs noise spilled out into the street, and there was

a clattering as of crates being lifted into carts. Then footsteps, car
doors and horns, laughter, cries of '*Ruibarbo! Ruibarbo!*' or something,
schoolchildren's yells, motors being raced: all the cacophony of a new
day.

When, red-eyed and taut-nerved, we groped our way downstairs,
we found that we had spent the night over a bakery. We were in no
condition to resist a bill of appalling dimensions, which charged us for
two meals we had not eaten. We had forgotten that this is customary
at a *pensão* if one does not state categorically at the start that one is
there for bed and breakfast only.

Besides losing sleep, we had not been able to use the lavatory.
This was the only place we found where the lavatory was not clean.

From Portimão we went thirty-eight miles along the south coast
to Faro, the chief town of the Algarve. Some say its name comes from
Haroun, a Moorish nobleman who ruled there; others suggest that it is
derived from φάρος, the Greek word for lighthouse. We had bread,
ham and red wine at a little working-class café and took the bus to
Olhão, another fishing port five miles farther on. Here we had intended
to spend the night, for the old town with its curious one-story buildings like white cubes was said to be worth exploring. But we found a
desolate place, the saddest we had yet encountered. The season had
been poor, and many fishermen were hanging about the streets. Some
were playing marbles in the gutters. There was an atmosphere of
dejection everywhere. At one end of the waterfront we came out on a
vast muddy expanse; at the other there were narrow, cobbled streets
that reeked of poverty. Someone had been slogan-painting. The slogan
was 'Peace', not the demand for bread and work one might have
expected. The smell of fish and the unending drizzle added to the
depression we felt, and we took the bus back to Faro and stayed there
instead. We were told afterwards that Olhão in the moonlight is
transformed into a place of magical silhouettes, black and white and
grey, with overlapping angular shapes and queer shadows.

As we stepped down from the bus at Faro there was a noise, and
we saw a gaunt, blonde woman grinning at us, flapping her arms,
exclaiming gutturally and hailing us as if we were long-lost relatives.
She clutched our arms in the powerful grip of desperate friendliness
and would have hauled us off. But we recognized the mad xenophilic
gleam in her eye and refused to be hauled. She could have been a
German expatriate; whoever she was her manner was alarming, and
we took refuge in the Hotel Aliança.

Faro lived up to its promise of providing encounters. We met an English-speaking priest and a sad little poet, who condemned his contemporaries as insufficiently realistic. But we did not, alas! meet the citizen of Faro who a few years ago was reported as 'still active at the age of 114'. He said he owed his long life to having drunk the milk of a white goat, administered to him by a nurse as she said a 'mystic prayer'. Faro, incidentally, was the first place in Portugal to possess a printing press; the British Museum has a copy of the Pentateuch printed there in 1487. Faro also had a library, which Essex took away with him in 1596 when he sacked the city, then occupied by the Spanish. The library is said to be now in the Bodleian.

Prison and palaces

We turned our faces northwards again and set out for Évora. Twice the countryside changed dramatically. At first we were in the littoral plain, where oranges, tangerines, lemons, figs, peaches, apricots, cherries, medlars, plums, grapes, melons, persimmons, walnuts and almonds abound, as though some colossal cornucopia has been scattered over the land. The almond blossom is deservedly famous, but in 1960 it had been diminished by the winter's heavy rains. Soon we were climbing. Then, almost in the twinkling of an eye, we were among wild, steep hills, with rugged fissures and gulleys, and perilous bends in the road where the wheels of the bus seemed to be hanging over into space. At one point an immense flock of birds rose and circled a precipitous valley far below us. Almost the only trees to be seen on these slopes were cork-oaks and olive trees, the latter with curious flat tops as if they had been sat on when they were little.

At São Brás de Alportel, where this hilly country of the Serra do Caldeirão begins, our bus was escorted from the main square by an odd-looking man blowing a whistle and signalling. The driver said this was a poor fellow who thought he was a traffic policeman responsible for the movements of buses in his town. He did no harm to anyone, and was very happy in his delusion.

On we went, through avenues of mimosa at its brilliant best and past knobbly hills scattered with heather. At last the hills ended and we were suddenly down on the Alentejo plain. No longer did the road double back on itself every few hundred yards. Here was a land of straight roads stretching to the horizon, or to the top of a slight rise beyond which the silver-grey ribbon would run on again, seemingly for ever, with scarcely a curve. On this plain the towns and villages were often visible for miles as patches of gleaming white and red in a sea of green and brown.

When we stretched our legs for a few minutes in the main square of Almodôvar, a small town of 6,000 inhabitants, we saw a barred window on the ground floor of a corner building. Behind the bars, on a broad window-sill, a man was sitting. Outside the window a group of men stood around, and from time to time one or other of them exchanged a few words with the man inside. We thought this was a prison, but we were not sure, so we asked the bus driver. Quickly he crossed two fingers of either hand in an expressive gesture that clearly meant 'prison'.

'Pretty, isn't it?' he said as he started the motor up.

It might be argued that a man who can spend the day talking with his friends while he is serving his sentence is better off than one who is wholly cut off from the outside world. But we did not think this public exhibition of a malefactor was very dignified, either for the man behind bars or for those who saw him there. It used to be much commoner in Portugal than it is now. In Lagos the prisoners used to be seen in the windows of the prison's upper stories, and they would let down baskets for friends to put food in, and tourists cigarettes. Perhaps the poverty of Almodôvar – the decrepit appearance of the hovels and the shabbiness of the people's dress – contributed to our feeling that there was something barbaric and reminiscent of the stocks in this scene on the main square.

We changed buses at Ervidel and before long saw Beja rising from the plain. In such handsome towns as Beja and Évora the wealth of the Alentejo is concentrated. They seem all the more prosperous in contrast with the miserable villages of which they are markets and of which Évora is the administrative centre. The Romans called Beja Pax Julia, and they built a castle there; it was later rebuilt, and a keep was added in 1319, in the reign of Dom Dinis; it now houses a military museum. There is a regional museum, with relics of the Romans, the Visigoths and the Moors, in the Convent of Conceição. It was from this convent that the nun Mariana Alcoforado wrote her love letters to the Marquis de Chamilly, letters which, sad though the story is, now strike us as too lush for comfortable reading. Outside the convent is a statue of Queen Isabel. The legend is told that, distressed by the hardships suffered by the poor, she used to go out with a basket of food and distribute it among them. One day the king, who was a harsh man, met her while she was thus engaged, and demanded to know what was under the cloth which covered her basket.

'Roses, my Lord, that I have been out gathering,' she replied, at the same time praying hard to the Virgin Mary.

And sure enough, when she raised the cloth the food in the basket had been miraculously transformed into roses. The same story is told of a medieval queen of Hungary.

Beja has some interesting churches, one of which dates from before the monarchy, and some other fine buildings. But for a remarkable concentration of architecture spanning eighteen centuries one must go to Évora, the Liberalitas Julia of the Romans and today unquestionably Portugal's most beautiful town. Within a radius of a few hundred yards there stand the Temple of Diana, built by the Romans at the end of the second century A.D.; the cathedral, begun in 1186 and finished in the middle of the succeeding century; the archbishop's palace, which now houses a regional museum; the former choirboys' college, now the public library; the Cadaval Palace; the palace of the Counts of Soure; the sixteenth-century Church of São Mamede; the former monastery of the Lóios, built in the fifteenth century; and the palace of the Counts of Basto, where Catherine of Braganza, wife of King Charles II of England, lived. And these are only a fraction of the historic buildings to be seen in Évora. Along the east side of the Praça do Geraldo, and extending beyond it, is an arcade with the remains of ancient pillars. This is the town's shopping centre. It reminded us a little of Chester, though, unlike the Rows, this arcade has no upper story. The Praça was named after Geraldo Sem-Pavor ('the Fearless'), who liberated Évora from the Moors in 1166 after an occupation that had lasted for over 450 years. Not far from the Praça do Geraldo, near the Palace of the Inquisitors, is the house where Vasco da Gama lived until he was appointed Viceroy of India in 1524. For exactly 200 years Évora was a renowned centre of learning, till the Marquis of Pombal closed its university. But seminary students in their black cloaks can still be seen strolling through the streets and reading in the cafés.

Évora's most spectacular buildings are the cathedral and the Temple of Diana. The former has two immense and rather forbidding granite towers, one tapering into a spire covered with *azulejos*. The temple has been used as a fortress and as a slaughterhouse. Its Corinthian columns, still standing on three sides of the rectangle, were cleared of their accretions in 1870. Their granite shafts and white marble capitals and bases are scarcely beautiful; but they have that haunting air of

nobility and timelessness that compels the attention of even the most
casual and unreflective sightseer. There are few better-preserved
Roman remains in the whole of Portugal and Spain. In comparison
with this large reminder of Rome's dominion the regional museum is
extremely disappointing: a skimpy collection of sculptures and inscrip-
tions, crudely arranged, and an ill-lit room containing highly deriva-
tive Portuguese paintings from the sixteenth and seventeenth centuries.
The library too is rather disappointing. Though it boasts half a million
manuscripts, 200,000 books and 500 *incunabula*, the reading-room
shelves are crammed with volumes of ancient theological controversies,
and even these are securely locked away behind doors of wire netting.

For a town so rich in possessions of cultural interest Évora is singularly lacking in hotels and *pensões*. There is a *pensão* on the Praça do
Geraldo, but it looked as if it would be too noisy for comfort. We went
therefore to the Eborense, on the Largo da Misericórdia, which has
an agreeable entrance up a flight of stone steps and along a balcony
with a good view of the south end of the town and the countryside
beyond. On the principle of 'always put the foreigners in your best
and dearest rooms' we were ushered into superb bedchambers decorated in Moorish style, with rich wall hangings and private sitting-
rooms and bathrooms. The tariff was calamitously high for our
narrow budget, and we asked for something cheaper. This request
was granted. For half the price we had pleasant, plain top-story
rooms with intriguing views.

The manners of the citizens of Évora, sad to say, are surprisingly
rude for people who live surrounded by such beautiful architecture.
In the Algarve the foreigner is stared at hard and his appearance and
behaviour are commented on freely – but the interest is friendly and
dignified. In Évora it is unmistakably hostile, not to say malicious,
particularly among the young men who stand around the streets.
These are the sons of landowners, and their favourite sport used to be
driving their motor-cars up and down the Alentejo's long, straight
roads at ninety miles an hour, heedless of whom they maimed or killed.
They are the kind of person you would expect to find in the rich capital
of an agricultural province: well-to-do, smug, intolerant, utterly
parochial. The Portuguese awakening, when it comes, will not begin
in Évora.

III

Northern notebook

The cradle of Portugal

The 'Rocket' whisked us northwards. It is an afternoon express, two carriages long, which deposits the traveller at Oporto's São Bento station exactly four hours after it purrs out of Lisbon. You have lunch in the capital; you are just beginning to feel hungry again as you cross Eiffel's bridge over the Douro and gaze out at the spectacular view of ravine and town; you leave the train in good time for dinner.

Here, you are in the cradle of the Portuguese nation. Somewhere here – it may have been on the opposite bank of the river, approximately where Vila Nova de Gaia stands today – the Romans had their Portus Cale. Under the Swabians, the German wanderers who in the fifth and sixth centuries A.D. ruled Galicia and what is today Portugal's Minho province, there were, it seems, two Portucales: one on either bank of the river. Early in the eighth century Portucale was destroyed by the Moors as a punishment for its resistance; it was re-established in 868, by which time 'Portugal' had come to mean the lands between the Minho river and the Douro. And the first Portuguese were soon marching southwards, gradually winning the south for Christianity – and trade.

Oporto was one of the earliest *bourgeois* towns in Europe, a town of merchants who sent their ships out to the North Sea and the Mediterranean. And today it is still first and foremost a trading centre. The town has grown out of the wine trade and the fish trade. The river banks are lined with port warehouses, world-famous names like Sandeman sprawling across their roofs to remind you that English traders have been here for centuries.

Do not expect Oporto to be a smaller, provincial edition of Lisbon. Though they are only 215 miles apart, there is more difference between them than between London and, say, Liverpool. Oporto has none of Lisbon's grace and light and aristocratic elegance; its charm is of a

49

different kind. But it bears no resemblance, either, to an industrial town in Britain. There is industry, but it is largely new industry, and mainly on the outskirts.

The Portuguese call it *o Porto*, 'the Port'; the English run the two words together. But it is no longer a seaport today. The harbour has a great sand-bar across it, and only small craft can reach the landing-places on a river narrower than the Thames. Leixões, at the mouth of the Douro, is the port for ocean-going vessels, and now has more than three times as much traffic as Oporto itself – though most of the goods it handles pass through Oporto.

Lisboetas think of Oporto as a sad, dark town, a town of granite and of people with an amusing accent – people whom they call *tripeiros*, 'tripe-eaters', from an incident in a battle long ago. (The *portuenses* return the compliment by calling the people of Lisbon *alfacinhas*, 'lettuce-eaters'.)

But we did not find Oporto gloomy. To be sure, its sky is not so vividly blue as the sky in the south, there is often a mist hanging over the Douro's narrow gorge, and the steep, tortuous streets are often dark, for the tall house-tops seem to meet above your head. Yet these streets teem with life and colour. Here and there throughout the city there are still farms, some mere patches of cultivated land, others full-scale *quintas*, each with its vineyards, orchards and gardens dominated by a great villa in which the rich owners still live as their predecessors have lived for hundreds of years. In the centre of the town the houses have narrow frontages, but are built deep. Behind them there are often gardens whose trees and blossoms peep from behind high stone or *azulejo*-covered walls. The fashionable shops in one or two streets, and the great cubist structure of the *Banco do Atlântico*, remind you that the twentieth century has reached Oporto. But there is nothing like the abundance of smart tea-shops that Lisbon can boast; instead there are street after street where shopkeepers still hang their wares outside in motley confusion. The bustling crowds on the pavements include many country people: men in broad-brimmed black hats, women with huge gold ear-rings, fisherfolk in clogs and shawls. Ox-carts still come into town, though they are far fewer nowadays. Everywhere are men and women carrying everything from fish-baskets to steamer-trunks on their heads. In and out of the traffic they wind their way, jostling the chromium-plated American cars that are the pride and joy of the well-to-do.

*   *   *

These were our first impressions of Oporto as we walked its streets the first few days of our stay. Presently we began to know it better.

Our friends gave us a royal welcome. The hospitality of the north is a byword: so are its lavish meals, and we each gained several pounds before we left. But more memorable than the food they gave us were the people themselves.

Oporto has not many more than a quarter of a million inhabitants. It has its own university, and a lively cultural life. Among the professional classes everyone knows practically everyone else. Now, Lisbon's population is to a great extent made up of people who were born elsewhere; in political matters Lisbon people are cautious and often uncertain where others stand. But Oporto has been a Liberal stronghold since the nineteenth century. It has witnessed many revolts and has been the seat of risings and revolutions. And it probably numbers among its citizens more opponents of the present régime than does the capital, which is to a great extent a city of civil servants. In Oporto everyone knows pretty well where everyone else stands politically. They were at school and university together – or their fathers were. And the sides people have taken in the many battles that have raged have not been forgotten over the years.

In short, Oporto people feel more strongly about politics. We soon had this brought home to us when we learned that the university has no Faculty of Arts. This was closed down by the government in the thirties because the students were too hostile to the régime. Only by abolishing the entire Faculty could the authorities disperse this centre of sedition. And so a young person in Oporto who wants to study languages, literature or philosophy must go to Coimbra or Lisbon, far from the subversive cultural influence of his native town.

Yet this measure seemed to have had little effect on the many young people we met. They were uncompromising in their opposition to Salazar. Our hosts not only introduced us to the political figures whose views and information we have set down elsewhere in this book; they also made it possible for us to see some of the less attractive sights of the place – sights that would greatly surprise most tourists.

House of mercy

A doctor we met offered to take us over Oporto's great hospital, the Misericórdia. This is one of the oldest of the large hospitals in Portugal. It was the largest in the north until the new Oporto teaching hospital was opened, outside the city. We saw only the latter's modern façade; but even our most critical guides assured us that conditions there were better than in the Misericórdia.

They need to be.

The doctor who showed us round the hospital would be called a part-time consultant in Britain. He went there every morning for about three hours' duty before going on to his own surgery. He was a specialist, distinguished in his field and respected by his colleagues. The fee he received for his services was less than £10 a month, and he regarded his activities in the hospital as charitable work. Because of his position he was able to take us to almost every part of the huge building.

Its pretentious columns, we found, hid what was largely a shell. The wards and various other parts of the building were often connected, not by covered corridors, but by external balconies, supported by the pillars we had admired from the street. Along these corridors, which were open to the weather – and it can be quite cold and miserable in Oporto for several months of the year – wandered those patients who could walk. More serious cases were wheeled along on trolleys, protected only by the thinnest of coverlets. The floor was of old, dusty wood. Every few feet there was a large spittoon, obviously in frequent use. Everywhere doctors were to be seen with cigarettes in hand or mouth.

We went into several wards. All were shabby. The bedclothes were patched and darned and very scanty indeed. What were not scanty were the visible signs of fear and superstition. Beside each wretched bed there stood, on a small table, a collection of images of saints and sacred pictures.

One nurse was loud in her complaints of the difficulties that attended her work.

'Look at the floor,' she said. It was made of rough, splintered planks.

'It can only be scrubbed,' she told us. 'We have no vacuum cleaners in the hospital. The floor is too rough to polish. Dust and bacteria just cannot be moved from the crevices in these boards.'

Supplies were so short, she added, and the hospital authorities so parsimonious, that dressings and bandages had to be washed and used over and over again.

There was only one blanket on each bed.

We passed through the casualty department. It was a scene from

Bedlam. No serried rows of benches with people quietly waiting as they do in Britain. No efficient, calm attendants creating an atmosphere in which everyone is confident that emergencies will be dealt with promptly. Instead, a small, airless bulge in a dark corridor, filled with shouting, crying people. At first there did not seem to be an attendant or a nurse in sight. For a few harrowing moments we stood and watched this scene. Some were writhing in agony, others moaning; here and there a stronger one would wave a mutilated limb as he shouted for help. At last someone came. The clamour increased as everybody sought to attract his attention. But he was one and they were many. We gathered that he was little more than an orderly, though he was called a male nurse. The miserable £6 or so a month he earned, coupled with long hours and execrable conditions, cannot have made him very sweet-tempered. He was neither calm nor gentle with the unfortunates who milled and shouted around him. He spoke to them brutally and pushed his way through them without ceremony.

Slowly we walked away. We could not look at each other.

We came to a children's ward. It was not a large room. In it were eight beds. The nurse in charge hurried forward to greet us and we were introduced to her. Our gaze fell on the beds behind her. In three of them lay six children, one at the foot of each bed, one at the head. At the foot of the nearest bed there lay, moaning, a child of about four, with a bandaged head. In the same bed was an eighteen-month-old with a rasping cough that was clearly disturbing its bedfellow.

What was the matter with these two?

The first had a fractured cranium. He had fallen from a bridge while playing. The other had a lung complaint.

Was it a good idea to have these two in the same bed, where they could only disturb each other?

'Oh, no!' the nurse replied. 'But there simply aren't enough beds. Sometimes I have as many as five or six children in one bed, all of them suffering from quite different complaints which should really be kept far apart.'

In the next bed a tiny infant lay without moving. Its little, wrinkled face was puckered and old-looking. Its skin was a bluish grey. Regularly, every few seconds, it uttered a feeble whimper that sounded like the desolate cry of a dying puppy.

'It must be a very new baby,' we said, our voices choking. 'Was it born with something wrong with it?'

'No, it's not so very young,' said the nurse bitterly. 'About fourteen months old. But it *was* born with something wrong with it – poverty. It is dying slowly of a deficiency disease.'

Charity children

We went home to lunch with our friend the doctor. During the meal he was called to the telephone several times. One of the calls was from a children's home not far away. A child was ill. He asked if we would like to go with him.

The home was situated in a large old house in a narrow street. It was administered by a private charity and was not a State enterprise, so we cannot say how typical it was. We have no doubt however that the all-pervading State subjected its affairs to some sort of scrutiny. We were introduced to the warden, a pleasant-looking young woman who told us that she had been a primary schoolteacher before starting her new job only a few weeks earlier. She apologized with an embarrassed air because the children were so inadequately provided for . . . 'We are very poor,' she told us as she led us upstairs to the sick child.

Here and there little cropped-headed boys peeped out at us from behind doors. They all wore the characteristic white pinafore common to Portuguese schoolchildren of both sexes. It is buttoned up to the neck with a high Russian collar and the skirt is rather full.

The sleeping quarters, which were on an upper floor, comprised two very large rooms each containing some forty iron bedsteads. Connecting the two was a kind of lobby leading to a balcony, from which a staircase gave access to a fair-sized garden at the back of the house. The door to the balcony was shut. It was very cold outside.

'I moved the boy here to be away from the others,' we heard the warden tell the doctor as she took him towards a bed in the corner of this lobby. 'He's running a high temperature and is coughing a lot.'

We stood by the door while the child was examined. He was a handsome boy of about ten years old.

'First of all,' said the doctor as he drew the bedclothes around the child, 'this lad needs warmth.'

He fingered the blanket.

'This is quite inadequate – one thin blanket . . .'

He beckoned us over and pointed. It was true. A worn-out blanket covered the bed over clean but heavily darned sheets. On top was a sleazy cotton bedspread. On this floor there was no heating, and we ourselves, warmly clad in woollies and overcoats, had been feeling chilly. The sick child wore thin cotton pyjamas.

The young woman looked bitter.

'Don't I know it, *senhor doutor*,' she retorted. 'Ever since I arrived I've been begging the Board for more bedding. They say there is no money. I don't know how the children keep as well as they do. The only consolation is that they are better off here than they would be in the street.'

After the doctor had given her some instructions about treatment – most of which involved warmth and food, and drugs which could not be paid for, but which he offered to provide himself – the warden took us into the dormitories.

She led us from bed to bed and showed us in detail the condition of each one. Everything was spotlessly clean, and mended and re-mended. But it was all terribly inadequate. On the rail at the foot of every bed hung a towel. Some of them looked new. She picked one up.

'Look at these,' she said. 'They came last week after I had protested every day since I started to work here. Until these arrived one towel was shared by two boys. As it is, there is now one apiece. They are washed, dried and returned to the children the same day. So we do half at a time, and while their own are in the wash the children must dry themselves on shared towels, or else not wash at all for several hours.'

We went down to the floor below to see the dining-room and kitchen. Both were on the simplest possible scale. The former was dark and gloomy, its walls entirely unrelieved except for a dim painting of the usual Last Supper. Nowhere was there a touch of colour.

We asked about the children's diet. Its main components were vegetable soup, bread, 100 grammes or so of fish a day, a little meat once a week, and fruit. There was no mention of milk, butter or eggs.

All the time there were small figures following us at a distance. They were well behaved and silent. Out in the garden the children we had seen from the balcony were making no noise either. But despite their thin clothes and meagre-sounding diet they all – to our surprise – looked reasonably healthy.

Before we said good-bye the warden took us into her office on the ground floor. It was as sparsely furnished and comfortless as the rest of the building. She asked us to sit down and then addressed us as much as the doctor.

'You have seen how we manage,' she said. 'None of the children is starving, and we get along somehow. But it is all so cheerless and so mean. The children are never really warm in the winter. There isn't a penny to brighten the place up with curtains or paint. I have to make the most careful calculations to see that they get the food we are giving them now. Not a copper can be spared for the slightest luxury.'

We asked her whether the children were orphans.

'Not necessarily. In fact some of them have one parent, others both parents, living. They have been taken in here, for the most part, not because there was no one to look after them, but because whoever there was couldn't. They are children of the poorest of the poor, who have been living in the street and snatching whatever crusts they could. Many of them were sent out begging because their parents had no work and no money. Most of them have been brought here by parents or relatives who pleaded with us to take them in because they could no longer feed them.'

The young woman spoke with emotion in her voice, and we felt that in one thing these waifs were fortunate – to have someone to look after them who obviously cared about her job a good deal. She was neatly but shabbily dressed, and her face was sensitive and intelligent.

She fell silent. Then she drew a deep breath and looked at us both intently, and then at the doctor.

'I can't believe that there is no money to help us,' she said quietly. 'Oporto is a rich city. Sometimes on Saturday afternoon I have to go down to the *baixa*. I see lots and lots of people in big cars, and women dressed in furs. Surely you know someone who would have money and heart enough to help us. They wouldn't even feel the price of a blanket or two. Please ask them.'

That night we too went downtown to the *baixa*, as the town centre is called in Portuguese, to have dinner in an expensive restaurant with a rich man. He was an agreeable, self-made man, an ardent Anglophil. We were told that as a boy he had gone barefooted and had not learned to read or write until he was grown up. Now he looked as distinguished as a career diplomatist would like to look. He did not interest himself in politics, they said. But once, long ago, in the days when the Liberal politicians were still plotting actively against Salazar, he had hidden one prominent republican ex-Minister in his attic for months.

We debated inwardly all evening. In our lofty English way, nurtured on the anti-charity sentiments prevalent in the Labour movement, we had always opposed individual benevolence. It diverts people from realizing that they must demand certain things from the State as of right – or so the argument ran.

Finally we related our day's adventures. We told him about our horror at conditions in the Misericórdia. We told him about the children's home and the sick child. We told him what the young woman had said to us. He looked serious and sympathetic as he sipped his Benedictine.

'Yes, yes, I know. It's all true. This government we have talks a lot but it does nothing for the people. What can one do . . . ?'

He raised his hands helplessly.

We hesitated.

At last one of us spoke.

'There is something you can do. It's not much. And it solves nothing in the long run. But at this moment just a little individual help can make life a bit better for a handful of children, and perhaps help one little boy to get better. You can do that, surely. If others felt like you, then a few more could be helped as well.'

We wondered if we had offended him.

But we had not. Perhaps it was because we were foreigners. Perhaps his social conscience was easily aroused. At any rate, he took out his cheque book and wrote out a cheque for a handsome sum. And he promised us that the following day he would have a supply of blankets sent from his textile factory.

It was the first time that either of us had ever begged for the poor. And we felt a little better afterwards.

In Oporto's slums

One day we spent several hours exploring the district behind the Sé, where tier after tier of ancient houses lead down to Oporto's narrow waterfront.

'It's just as well you haven't got cameras with you,' said the friend who took us there. 'Foreigners taking pictures in this part of town have been stopped from doing so by the police.'

Before he conducted us through the dark streets we went to see the Church of São Francisco. This extraordinary building, no longer in use, stands neglected by all except tourists, who have to rouse an attendant if they want to be taken round. As our eyes became accustomed to the gloom inside the great, dim structure we realized that we were in a hall of gold – gold everywhere, on walls, pillars and vaulted roof, and covering the figures and leaves that decorate the columns supporting the building. For an instant we imagined the place was built of gold; then we saw that of course it was not solid, for in part of the church, near the entrance, the gilt has been stripped off crudely and unlovingly, leaving the bare wood showing and breaking the carvings it once covered. The attendant said this had been done by Napoleon's soldiers when they pillaged the city during the Peninsular War.

Now the barbaric splendour of this six-centuries-old place of worship was dulled by the decades of dust and grime. It seemed strange that in this Catholic country no money had been provided to maintain so gorgeous a monument – a garish one, no doubt, but one that in its own way is magnificent, as well as historically interesting.

Yet it was just as well, perhaps, that São Francisco's church looked dreary and neglected. Otherwise the wretchedness of the sights we saw immediately afterwards would have seemed more grotesque than ever. For this quarter is a confusion of the narrowest alleys and steep stone steps you can discover anywhere in Portugal. These passages are filthy with the refuse of households without sewerage; on either side are doors, the top halves opening inwards like stable doors, through which you glimpse tiny rooms filled with beds, stoves, cooking utensils . . . It is clear that whole families live in these cramped hovels. It is also clear that in many there is no water supply, for now and then a woman or a child can be seen going in or out with a pitcher. Nor are there sinks. Dirty water, old cabbage leaves, potato peelings and fish bones are thrown into the gutters. Women sit on the doorsteps preparing food or sewing. Children cling about them, and skinny cats lurk against the walls or crouch apprehensively over pieces of rotting fish, ready to evade the inevitable kicks from passers-by.

As we pick our way carefully through the refuse, gasping at the foul smells that fill the air, a hand is stretched out here and there.

'Pãozinho, senhores, por amor de Deus. Dêem um tostãozinho para comprar leite para o bebé . . .' The piteous whine is familiar – but could anyone looking at the peaked faces of these women, and at their miserable dwellings, call them professional beggars? 'Bread, for the love of God, gentlefolk. A copper to buy milk for my baby.' We are the intruders here, not they.

Children follow us about. Little, nimble, brown-skinned boys and girls in rags, dirty and thin-faced. Some of them have sores around their mouths and on their hands. Great dark eyes gleam with merriment, and a shy smile breaks when we speak to them. But some are as fair as English children – blond hair, blue eyes and even freckles. It is said that the fair people you often see here in the north, especially in the mountains, are descendants of crusaders from northern Europe who got stranded here on the way to the Holy Land. Others say they are the descendants of the fifth-century German invaders.

From these fair faces the Latin cadences flow strangely; poverty sits on these people more strangely still. This is still Europe – not a 'backward', colonial country whose wretchedness the imperial-minded love to explain away. All these children, fair and dark, are children of a western nation. They creep up beside us begging for coppers, whispering and cajoling in the hoarse, sing-song voices of gutter children everywhere. Though it is the middle of the afternoon there are hordes of them, and we wonder why they are not at school.

This is nothing like Lisbon's Alfama, which seems clean and prosperous by comparison. It is sombre, dank and unutterably dreary. There is little colour here, and even the birds in cages are fewer and less noisy in these sunless alleys. The whole place is a maze. Now and then, at a break in the houses, you look straight into an upper room of a tall, narrow house on the level below. Like paths on a cliff face, the cobbles and steps drop to the quayside as we make our way to the river.

Yet once there were rich people living even here. For every now and again we come upon a house whose crumbling façade shows that once it was a dwelling of some importance. Above the dirty, broken-down doors you can still see the outlines of a coat of arms, recal ing times when *fidalgos* and rich merchants lived cheek by jowl with the poor who served them. Sometimes there are the remains of stabling, too, inhabited now by human beings; you wonder how horses, let alone coaches, ever manœuvred these narrow passages.

On the wharf, just up river from the first bridge, we looked upwards in amazement at the heights we had come from. Only now did we realize how deep and narrow is the Douro gorge. From here the Sé district seemed picturesque, and we recognized the picture postcard outlines that had seemed so fanciful a moment ago. But even here the tiny stores, taverns and barbers' shops were wretched and dismal when you looked into them, and you missed the cheerful bustle of the shops in the city centre.

*   *   *

As we walked along the quayside our guide told us that in 1809 the citizens of Oporto built a bridge of boats across the river to carry to the other side the terror-stricken populace fleeing from Marshal Soult's army. The bridge collapsed under the weight of its burden and most of the fugitives were drowned.

*   *   *

We passed a collection of fish-stalls presided over by brawny fishwives, and stopped to listen to the din. At last we understood how fishwives have become notorious. For the noise was not just that of venders crying their wares. The loudest shouts were those of abuse and insult. In all corners of the little quayside market fierce disputes were in progress. We stood in front of one stall where a sturdy young woman called on us to buy. Suddenly she turned to the woman at the stall beside her and broke into a torrent of vituperation in response to her rival's curses. The argument seemed to be conducted as much for the onlookers' benefit as in the interests of the women themselves. We gazed in fascination at the way ferocious rage was switched off for a customer and switched on again abruptly as soon as the deal was done.

In the prudish way the Portuguese upper classes have, our guide told us it was fortunate that we were not very familiar with demotic Portuguese. But his prudishness had its limitations, as we found when he took us by tram to Matosinhos.

This is the big sardine-canning suburb north of Oporto on the way to Leixões. Here we visited pottery markets where you can buy every kind of earthenware imaginable, rough and glazed, plain and decorated, large and small, pitchers and pipkins. The most you can pay for an article is about sixpence. Heaps of urns, bowls, jugs, plates, mugs, beakers, coffee-pots and braziers of all shapes are piled on the ground by the roadside. Many are chipped and cracked, so you must choose carefully. But when you do find a perfect specimen, you get, for a few coppers, a well-proportioned vessel that would cost you fifty times as much in a fashionable London furnishing store.

Here and there are stalls where ornaments and smaller items are laid out on shelves. Multicoloured cocks from Barcelos – the fertility symbol of peasants everywhere, but especially typical of the Minho – have flowers instead of feathers painted on their plaster breasts and wings. There are minute ones less than an inch high and huge ones three feet high. At these stalls you can buy small, crude figures of all sorts, especially musicians; you can, indeed, buy a whole brass band.

Everywhere are cribs with tiny figures of the Holy Family, shepherds, kings and devout beasts to complete the plaster Christmas scene.

Side by side with these pious images are others. Our friend pointed to them gleefully without a trace of the modesty he had displayed earlier about the fishwives' curses. They were tiny images of peasants, male and female, crouching over tiny chamber-pots. With crude realism the artist had reproduced in plaster, down to the most essential detail, the act of defecation. Our friend urged us to purchase some of these figures and was disappointed at our lack of enthusiasm.

A conversation with students

During our stay in Oporto we came to know this young man and his friends very well. In long conversations, in their homes and in the cafés, we began to understand something of the cramped and curiously antiquated social life of the north. One thing we learned was that the strict segregation of the sexes still general in Oporto is only superficially similar to the conventions we associate with Victorian England. It is something much older and more deep-rooted, smacking less of English nineteenth-century gentility than of the harem and the veil. For no one pretends, as our English great-grandfathers tried to, that sex does not exist, that nice women do not enjoy it, or that it is impolite to make any reference to natural functions. On the contrary, it is precisely because sex is so fascinating and dangerous and such a favourite topic of conversation that young people must not for one instant be exposed to the danger of each other's unguarded company.

The young people we were with were mostly students. They considered that they held advanced views; we gathered that nearly all of them were sympathetic to the Communist Party, though not unreservedly so.

'I am twenty-four years old,' one young man told us, 'and do you know that I have never gone out with a girl alone after dark in my life . . . .'

We stared at him. He was attractive and intelligent, and obviously very popular with the young women in his circle.

'It must be difficult for you to understand . . . And we are privileged because we are students and attend mixed classes. We talk to girls after lectures, and I may even take a girl for a walk through the town in the afternoon and perhaps go into a tea-shop with her, but she must always be home well before dinner-time or there would be endless trouble for us both.'

We asked the girls what they thought of this restriction. All of them disapproved, but they said it was very difficult to defy convention. Oporto was a provincial town. Every time you went out you met a dozen people who knew you. Everyone gossiped about everyone else, and tales were constantly carried home to parents by relations and friends and their servants.

We asked why they did not put their principles into practice and simply defy their parents and let the tongues wag.

'Ah, you don't understand how little freedom we have,' one of them replied. 'First of all, our families are very close knit. If you want to take any step, no matter how insignificant, everyone is interested and advice is offered from all sides. Grandparents, uncles, aunts, friends: they all come and tell you what you should do.'

'But the main thing,' another girl interrupted, 'is that although you may argue, and incur disapproval even for that, you can't really expect to get very far unless you're lucky enough to have either a very enlightened father or a very indulgent one.'

She looked round the group. There were ten of us sitting round the table.

'Everyone here is over twenty-one. Most of us are two or three years older than that. João is a doctor and Maria Júlia over there graduated last year. But all of us are still completely dependent on our families.'

She went on to explain that university courses lasted five years, that most young people did not enter university until they were at least eighteen, and that although you might be excused the relatively low tuition fees if your results in the annual examinations were good enough, there were practically no maintenance grants available.

'And there is no work we can do apart from a little coaching – there is too much unemployment for students to be able to get work here as your students can in Britain.'

One of the boys butted in, with some vehemence:

'Everything you see that is bad here in our country can be traced back to our general economic conditions. How can we defy our parents when we depend on them for our bread and our future until we are nearly thirty? It's this way with our private lives and with our political ideas too!'

He explained how the authorities tried to stop political activities by students.

'First, they ban our students' unions so that if we wish to debate political questions it can only be in small groups, in our homes. Then, when that does not work, they arrest us in the middle of the academic year, or just before exams. That is what happened in 1956 and 1957.'

He told us something of the unrest among students that had culminated in the mass trial of fifty-two young people in 1957.

'Even liberally-minded parents, as most of ours are, begin to object to their children taking part in politics when it means they are running the risk of missing a year or more at the university.'

João, one of the two graduates, agreed.

'Do you realize how long we have to wait before we get jobs?' he asked us.

'I graduated from the Faculty of Medicine two years ago – I'm still completely dependent on my father. Next year I shall get about 1,000 *escudos* a month for an assistantship in a hospital where I have at last been given a job. At the moment I am still an intern, and I don't get paid at all. But those 1,000 *escudos* will scarcely pay for my food alone.'

He told us how he had hoped to get a scholarship to go abroad and specialize, and how his professors had recommended him.

'But, you see, it's not a professor's recommendation that counts here – the political police is the first judge of academic merit.'

He explained that all candidates for scholarships, including those of some private organizations, had first of all to be passed by the *Instituto para a Alta Cultura*.

'That's supposed to be a learned institution,' we were told. 'In reality it's a branch of the political police, and its job is to clear you politically.'

Dinner-time was approaching, and the young women had to be back home. We walked slowly through the darkening streets and saw our friends on to their tram-cars. Then we walked back with our host to his house. He looked gloomy. Finally he spoke.

'Do you think it would be difficult for me to get a job in England?' he asked.

The Minho hills

Although we had found much to sadden us in Oporto the northern countryside enchanted us and raised our spirits. There is now a good motor road along the northern bank of the Douro for several miles, and it takes you through small villages and green, wooded country above the turbulent river.

If you turn off this road and climb the pine-clad hills you might at first suppose yourself in Scotland or north Wales. The lanes are lined with purple heather and yellow gorse, and the cottages are either granite or whitewashed. Then there comes into sight a lumbering ox-cart on great wooden wheels, with a barrel of wine on top, drawn by big, patient, sand-coloured cattle with liquid eyes and dark velvet muzzles. Or a flock of small, wiry, black goats driven by a ragged, barefoot boy straggles slowly round a bend in the road. But even when there is no sign at all of humanity you realize before long that this could not be part of the British Isles. The gorse is a different variety: it is not so thorny, and what thorns there are grow longer and are more pliable. The heather, though purple, is tall and lanky. And if you stumble over a stone a lizard gleams like a jewel and is gone in a flash. The air is fresh and enticing. Sometimes you catch the scent of eucalyptus, sometimes the delicious fumes of smouldering pine wood from where some charcoal burner is at his work in the forest.

As you come near dwellings there are the vineyards, large and small, acres and acres of them, dropping in terraces down the hillsides. This is the great wine-growing region of Portugal. We were sorry it was winter instead of summer or early autumn. Winter is the time of work in the countryside. There are no *festas* as there are throughout the summer months, when every village has its fair, and saints' feast-days are celebrated with music and fireworks, and peasants dance the old dances in their national costumes. Above all, we were sorry to miss the *vindima*, when the grapes are gathered in and pressed and another year's wine is celebrated in song and feasting. But although we missed the merriment that we might have witnessed at another season, it was difficult among these hills to believe that it was winter. The light was dazzling; and the few deciduous trees were scarcely to be noticed amid the exuberant conifers and the verdant fields.

*   *   *

Our road northwards struck inland, veered back to the coast, then swung inland again through Vila do Conde and Póvoa de Varzim. The latter is a fishing village which has grown into a resort frequented by people from Oporto. Though there are modern shops and smart

1. A southern village

2. A northern scene: the port wine harvest

3. On an Alentejo road

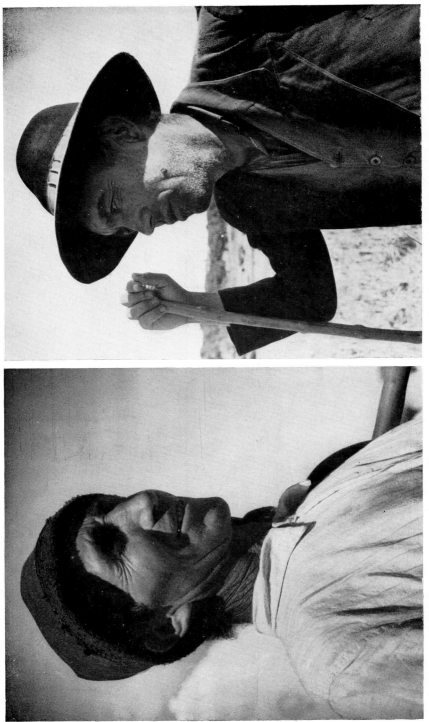

5.   A worker on one of the great estates of the Alentejo

4.   A landworker from Santarém

7. A peasant woman on pilgrimage

6. A peasant girl in the Douro vineyards

8. The Ritz Hotel, Lisbon

9 New housing in Lisbon

10. Some other Lisbon dwellings

11. A Lisbon street scene

cafés, down on the beach there is still a traditional Dutch auction of fish, held immediately the men come back with the catch. You can buy glistening silver sardines, halibut and sole practically straight out of the sea. As the men unload their cargoes the women take over, ranging themselves in a huge semi-circle in front of the piles of fish. A crowd has been gathering from the moment the boats began to return to shore. It has grown enormously. The whole town has come down to the sea to get a bargain. If you are simply on your way through Póvoa, or have only come for an afternoon out, you have to stop at the fish auction, for nowhere is fish fresher or cheaper. The women – nearly all of them blonde or auburn-haired – hold out their red, freckled arms, with their wares in their hands, and all shout together. The hubbub is deafening. Unless you are really close up, or very experienced, you cannot distinguish the words.

We pushed our way through the crowd to get to the front, determined to make out what was being said. Each woman is her own auctioneer. She stoops, picks up a fish from the piles and tubs behind, holds it out and cries for bids. On all sides her companions are doing the same. They are all shouting figures, rapidly, rhythmically, starting high and lowering the price until the first acceptance, which gets the fish. They invite you to examine it, tell you how plump and succulent it is, practically thrust it into your hands. You must keep still, for the merest nod means you have bought it. We were in grave danger of finding ourselves buyers of enough fish to feed a tribe. So we stepped back a little. Now we could no longer distinguish separate words. It was a cascade of sound, strident, sibilant, almost tangible, like a curtain between us and the sea.

*   *   *

From Póvoa we went on to Ofir and Viana do Castelo. Viana is very near the Spanish frontier, and from here gipsy smugglers go across to Vigo in Galicia, bringing back, with Romany guile, all those goods that are cheaper across the border and coveted on this side of it.

Viana lies white and low among the dunes that flank the River Lima, which the Romans called 'the river of forgetfulness'. It is a graceful, even stately town, with broad, tree-lined avenues. Behind it to the north is Monte Santa Luzia, high, majestic and covered with trees. From here you look down in wonder on Viana and towards the sea, where the dunes become whiter and the grass sparser and the trees fewer, till dunes merge with beach and meet the waves.

The mountain's benign watch over Viana has been spoiled by a church they built recently on the hillside, with a huge, ungainly dome. The only thing to be said for this building is that in front of it lies a terrace on which one can stand for hours looking westwards to the sea and eastwards to the far-off source of the Lima.

This is a strange coast, flat and cliffless but hauntingly beautiful. The pines wander down almost to the water's edge, and they lean like ballet dancers along the shore, in the direction the evening wind from the north has trained them. Their long, slender trunks are bare for yards; on top their green pompons are brushed forward by the wind. At their feet the silver sand is fine and soft under your toes – so soft that the slightest breeze whirls it in eddies until it settles back in rippled dunes for a while, awaiting the next gust.

But there is nothing bleak about the flatness and the sand and the whispering pines. You come down to them gently from the grandeur of the high hill, so that the sea steals upon you almost unawares.

A rural philanthropist

Some miles inland, among pine-scattered hills and vineyard-covered slopes, we visited the *quinta* of a man whom we shall call Dr Afonso Marques, though that is not his real name. Unlike many landowners. Dr Marques was not an absentee landlord but lived all the year round on his *quinta*, supervising the farming and attending to its administration himself.

He was a lawyer by training, although he had never practised, and anything he knew of farming he had taught himself. He lived in this remote country house because he had been born there and loved it too well to leave it for the city. And when we saw it we understood why he had preferred the small returns from his land to the more lucrative life of a city lawyer.

We approached the house down a long, winding mountain road, scarcely more than a cart-track, which bent in and out among the hills and trees. Suddenly the road sloped downwards and we came upon the house. With trees on either side and a flower garden before the front door, it stood at the head of a magnificent valley whose greenness stretched out into the distance between steep, wooded hills. From the front the house looked like a one-story bungalow, but soon we learned that the best of it was at the back. It was built on two levels. When we went inside we saw how well Dr Marques's grandparents had planned their home, for all the main rooms on both floors had a breath-taking view of the valley.

Dr Marques welcomed us with all the charm and hospitality the Portuguese lavish on visitors. He apologized for the simplicity and austerity of his house, explaining that he was a bachelor and had become too accustomed to living a solitary life. By the standards of an English country house of similar size there was certainly little luxury in evidence, but we found the simplicity of the place very appealing. It had been modernized – there was a bathroom, running water and electricity – but nothing superfluous was to be seen. The floors were of narrow, polished, blond pine board, bare of covering except for one or two rugs in the drawing-room. The walls were all half-panelled in wood, the rest being whitewashed. *Azulejos* covered the inside walls in the hall, stairway and corridors. It seemed that Dr Marques's only luxury was his library, a room on the upper floor that seemed all windows, books and sunlight.

After a lunch that was accompanied by wine from his own vineyards, he took us around the *quinta*. In comparison with many Portuguese landowners he was not a rich man. He had pigsties with half a dozen fine black pigs, leaner and more muscular than the kind we generally see in Britain. There were cattle-sheds for two or three teams of oxen and a small herd of cows. Everything was in perfect order, clean and well kept, and the livestock looked sleek and healthy. There were fruit trees everywhere, festive at this time of year with golden mandarins and oranges. The peasant girls working about the place were rosy-cheeked and jolly.

We asked Dr Marques how he managed. He told us that the land just paid for itself because he watched expenditure carefully and had tried to modernize methods as far as possible – simply by seeing that things were done sensibly and carefully and that there was no neglect. But his small capital, on whose income he relied for any luxuries, did not permit him to go in for any basic improvements or any great changes. There was no machinery. He did not own a car, and oxen were used for ploughing and for transporting produce.

Years before, he had tried to start a school in the village a few miles away, since none existed and it was too far for the children to go anywhere else. At his own expense he had procured premises for a schoolhouse and sent for a primary schoolteacher whom he employed. Then he had persuaded his own tenants to send their children there and had talked neighbouring property-owners into doing the same.

But soon he had run into a snag. He himself was not a believer, and never went to church. Furthermore, though he took no part in politics at all, his enlightened and scientific views on many social and cultural matters, and his contempt for humbug, had gained him a number of enemies, who spread it about that the purpose of the school was to indoctrinate the children in atheism. Before long he found that the local priest was up in arms against him, and the next thing he knew the Church had started a rival school under State auspices, with its own Catholic teacher, to which the children were soon transferred.

'However,' he said good-humouredly, 'I don't feel too bitter about that. At least it has made them start a school – and saved me the expense. But there isn't much to be said for the education it provides.'

Usually however he found that it was not so easy to provoke the authorities out of their inertia. And for one man alone, without much money, it was a heart-breaking task to challenge the old ways all at once.

'Only the most fundamental, wholesale attack by the State itself can really begin to change the backwardness of our rural life,' he said.

'Look at these cottages!' He pointed to a pair of tiny houses we were passing.

'You may already have learned that many of our peasants are used to living in houses with no chimneys or windows. Sometimes there is only one room, in which the whole family live – grandparents, parents and children, as well as chickens, a pig and other animals, that run in and out all the time. The filth is indescribable, and when there is no ventilation you can imagine that it is worse than a wild animal's lair.

'One of the first things I did when I came back to live here permanently was to have windows and chimneys built, and to have an extra room added when there was only one.

'Can you believe that the cottagers were not at all pleased, explain it how I might? Some of them even boarded up their windows.'

He led us towards one of the tiny dwellings and knocked on the door. A peasant woman opened it and invited us inside. It was very poor, but clean and neat, and the sunlight streamed in through the windows.

'Oh, I've won at last, on this point at any rate,' he said, 'but it's taken a long time, and sometimes I get disheartened.'

*   *   *

As he led us on down the road he told us what had happened only a few weeks before.

'There was an old woman living in that cottage over there. She was a widow, and her children had married and gone away. I could never persuade her to like the windows, and she kept them boarded up. She was seventy-two, and a few months ago she fell and hurt a leg as she was bringing water from the well. Neighbours carried her back to her house and sent to tell me. I took one look at her leg and realized that it was fractured, so I sent for a friend of mine who is a doctor living about ten miles away. He came at once and set the old woman's leg and put it in a splint. He also spoke to her and her relatives, who had all heard of the accident by this time, and warned them that a fracture was a serious matter at her age and she should follow his instructions about rest very carefully.

'I was present, of course, and I could see by their faces that they were not paying much attention to the doctor. As for the poor old woman, she was groaning and calling on the saints. But I did not expect what followed.

'Can you believe that about a week later, in response to their mother's pleas and complaints, two of her sons went off and fetched the *endireita*? This sort of person is to be found all over the country-side – I suppose in English you would call him a "bone-setter". He took off the splint, broke the leg again in two places and bound it up. And he charged them for it, too, of course. By morning the woman was in agony, but her children were afraid to let me know because they knew what I would say about the *endireita*.

'After a few hours her condition got still worse, and at last a neighbour came and told me. I sent for the doctor once more. He saw the woman and told her children that unless she was taken to hospital she would certainly die, since there was now a serious danger of gangrene. We got in touch with the hospital, which is about twenty miles away, and sent for an ambulance – not an easy thing to arrange in these remote places.

'But it was no use. The old woman screamed and cried and begged her family not to let her be taken away. She preferred to die at home sooner than go away to be cured. They gave in. I could not kidnap the woman. So the ambulance went away empty.

'A few days later she died.'

Dr Marques paused.

'I expect I sound like an old reactionary,' he said with a smile. 'But I am not telling you all this, as some people would, to show you that it is impossible to educate our peasants. On the contrary. I go on trying, because I am convinced that it can be done, and because no one else in this district is trying to do it. But I don't believe my way is either very economical or very effective. I am one man, a landlord, and I am fighting a whole way of life, which neither the Church nor the State nor the richer landlords around here are interested in changing. The peasants respect me, but they distrust me because I own the land, and because the priest preaches against me.'

He had spent a great deal of money on nitrates for fertilizer the previous year. This had been distributed among the peasants, and he had gone round explaining to them how to use it, and pointing to the success fertilizer had had on his own land.

'But some of them did not even bother to use it. No, what we need in this country is a revolution in agriculture and a campaign of education to turn these poor, ignorant people into human beings.'

*   *   *

We passed a woman sitting on her doorstep embroidering, and we stopped to admire her work. Three tiny children, who looked about the same age, played around her feet. Through the open door we glimpsed a baby.

'That woman,' said our friend as we walked on, 'is only twenty-five. She looks forty. She was one of the prettiest girls in the district when she was married eight years ago. She has had seven children, and six are living. I have tried to do something about this question, too, but it is very difficult.'

Whenever he had the opportunity he talked to the men about the need to limit the size of their families. They would look at him in embarrassment and finally say:

'But, *senhor doutor*, what is a man to do? It is only natural.'

And he would tell them that there were things that could be done. But it was impossible to convince them that the cost of contraceptives, dear though they were in Portugal, would be much less than that of the extra mouths they had to feed and would help their wives to be stronger and healthier.

Dr Marques smiled ruefully.

'I have seriously considered making the necessary investment myself and distributing contraceptives to the peasants. I have not done so, because I think it would be useless. The priest would learn of it and would not only intensify his campaign against me, but would make sure that the peasants destroyed them.'

He sighed. Dr Marques was faced with essentially the same problems that confronted Tolstoy in a not very different situation in old Russia; and, like him, he was finding that philanthropy, no matter how well intentioned, is a frail craft on the ocean of peasant ignorance and clerical superstition.

IV

How the Portuguese people live

We learn about housekeeping

We had not been long in our little house in the country before we acquired Joana. Since we were out most of the day and were living very simply it might be thought an incongruous luxury to have a woman in to do the housework. But in Portuguese houses things are not arranged for easy cleaning, washing or cooking. Anyone used to an English home, let alone an American one, is baffled by the contrast between the excellent structure of Portuguese houses and their primitive kitchen arrangements. Make some inquiries about such an elementary subject as rubbish disposal and a look of surprise comes over the face of your Portuguese friend.

'The rubbish? Well, I don't know what happens to it. The girl will attend to that.'

And so she does. You are left with the impression that if a middle-class house were servantless for a time the rubbish would mount up indefinitely. As one acquaintance put it: 'In Portugal a lady cannot take a rubbish pail downstairs and be seen emptying it.'

But we were in the countryside and there was no dustbin. Instead there was a rubbish dump down by the rivulet some fifty yards from the house, and there or in the fields the waste matter from the whole community was deposited. This we learned from Joana. Our friends could not tell us. As far as they were concerned rubbish disposal was a mysterious task accomplished automatically by the Joanas of this world.

In the countryside there are no amenities at all. Our chief preoccupation when we acquired Joana was the washing. This she took down to the communal *tanque*, a great cement water-container about twenty feet square. This is the women's centre of every village. All day long you could see the women rubbing and scrubbing in the cold water,

72

and a steady procession of them walking backwards and forwards
with baskets of washing on their heads. Farther on, through the woods
behind our house, there was an even poorer community, who washed
in a little river, rubbing the clothes against the stones. In these country
places the washing is often laid out on bushes or on grassy banks to
dry and whiten in the sunshine.

Joana's troubles were not ended with the washing. There was no
electric iron in the house. In any case, she said, she did not like them.
She used a large cast-iron affair whose top opened up like a grinning
mouth. Inside she put smouldering charcoal ignited in a brazier used
for roasting meat or fish, and fanned red hot with a round palm-leaf fan.
As she started passing the iron backwards and forwards over the kitchen
table we had visions of pieces of hot charcoal scorching nylon and
rayon. But we need not have worried. The result was a job you would
never get from an English laundry: a pile of snowy, beautifully ironed
garments, every button in place, every stain removed.

There was no sink in our kitchen. There was simply a cold water
tap, under which one put a large earthenware basin called an *alguidar*,
a name of Moorish origin, like the names of so many household
articles. The nearest drain for waste water was the maid's w.c. in a
tiny cupboard off the veranda. We were assured that the system of
separate w.c. and washing facilities for servants is on the way out;
that the girls will not use them. It may be so in Lisbon, but in the rest
of the country this form of segregation is still very much the rule.
When you ask about it the *senhora* shrugs her shoulders. Yes, of
course it may seem barbarous to visitors from a country where people
are educated in decent social habits. But here servants come from a
class totally devoid of any notions of hygiene or consideration for
others. We were not quite convinced. It seemed to us illogical to rely
on one of these allegedly ignorant, unhygienic persons to look after
one's children, and keep one's kitchen spotless, one's bathroom gleaming and one's table groaning with deliciously cooked food.

*   *   *

Joana was twenty-eight years old, pretty and young-looking, though
most women of her class age very rapidly. She had five children,
ranging from a girl of eight to a baby of twenty months. The eldest
lived with Joana's mother-in-law to avoid a long walk to school. But
primary school was for only half the day, from 9 a.m. to noon. There
were no school meals, and it was thanks to the generosity not of the

State but of a local rich woman that milk was provided for the children during school hours. Joana told us that children who were too poor to take a snack with them to school were also given a little bread. When we asked her who looked after her other children while she was at work she was surprised.

'Why, nobody. When it's fine they play out of doors. In the winter when it's raining I lock them up in a room so that they don't go out and get wet.'

We asked about the baby.

'The six-year-old is very good,' she replied proudly. 'He looks after the smaller ones.'

Joana's husband was a lorry-driver's mate. He earned 30 *escudos* a day – 7s 6d. He left the house at 7 a.m. and often got back as late as ten at night. He worked all day on Sundays when there was work, but often there was only half a day's work available. The same applied to public holidays. The only time off he took was at Christmas.

'He is lucky to have this job,' Joana told us, 'but it's very hard on his clothes because he has to unload dirty and difficult stuff like stones and cement.'

We asked whether he could not become a driver and earn more. She told us that if he were a driver he would get 50 *escudos* a day – if he had a licence. Why didn't he learn to drive then? we asked. She smiled apologetically.

'Oh, he can drive very well, and in fact he does when he's where there aren't likely to be any traffic police. But you see, a licence costs 1,000 *escudos*, and it's difficult for us to save.' This seemed an under-statement, with five children to keep on £2 12s 6d a week. But her husband had saved in the past.

'He did take the test,' Joana said, half-ashamed. 'But they failed him. You see, he can't read or write, and so, although his driving was good, he hadn't been able to study to answer the questions the examiner asked – but still he had to pay the money.'

We asked her why her husband had never learned to read and write. No, he had not been to school; but still, Joana said, he should have learned. His aunt lived in the house where he was brought up, and she was literate and had tried to teach him.

'I'm afraid he's a little dull,' said Joana shyly, 'but he's very good and the money I earn helps us make ends meet.'

We did some rapid mental arithmetic, and it was clear that even if she worked eight hours a day, seven days a week – an impossibility with the children – Joana's help could not bring their joint income beyond £4 7s 6d. We asked her what her rent was.

'We pay no rent. The house belongs to my mother – that's a great help.'

Even so, we were quite unable to imagine how Joana managed. Living is cheap in Portugal, especially in the countryside, if you have English money. But for our own part, living on the austere budget we had allowed ourselves, and with no rent to pay either, we were spending nearly 10s a day on food, bus fares, oil for the paraffin heater and sixpennyworth of wine. There were two of us and we were visitors, not needing to buy clothing or footwear. How could seven people manage on a total income of little more than the sum we were spending? We asked Joana if she or her husband ever went out or had any kind of entertainment. Was there a wireless set in the house?

No, they never went out together at all. With the children to see to she had no time. Her husband went out rarely. He was usually too tired when he got home at night. Occasionally, if he finished early, he would go to one of the little grocery shops in the village, where there were a few tables, and sit down to a game of cards. They had no wireless.

What about the cinema? There were films only in the summer, and it was too dear.

We found it hard to credit that anyone could tolerate such a life at all, let alone bear it with Joana's cheerfulness and good humour. Here was the happy, hard-working peasant beloved of the rich English traveller! She was reasonably happy, partly because she was strong and healthy and much better off than many others – a fact she emphasized with pride, pointing to the miserable collection of hovels up the hill. But partly, too, her very isolation – illiterate, never seeing newspapers, books or films, never listening to the wireless, living largely as her ancestors had lived through the centuries, enclosed in a tiny world with narrow horizons – surely this was the secret of her relative contentment.

But television has already reached the village. There was a set in the café adjoining one of the grocery shops. The horizons of the ancient way of life are slowly broadening. The Portuguese village is looking across from the eighteenth century to the twentieth.

And the upper classes are making the best of the short time that is left to them. For when they refer in florid speeches and editorials to what they call 'our traditional way of life' they do not mean the beguiling sight of soft-eyed oxen decked with flowers at a country *feira*. They do not mean the dazzling colours of some of the richest national costumes in Europe. What they really mean is the pomp and leisure of a way of life such as has not been seen in Britain since 1914, and which no longer exists anywhere on the Continent except in this south-western corner of it.

Maids and their mistresses

Opponents of Salazar condemn every sort of intellectual obscurantism. At the same time many of them take for granted practices that are downright feudal. The wife of one elderly and prominent Liberal, complaining of a servant's rudeness, told us as if it was the most natural thing in the world that when the girl became too impertinent she pinched her sharply on the arm a couple of times 'to make her know her place'. The husband heard this admission and nodded approvingly. We were told that the wife of one leading socialist is known to beat her maids, a practice that used to be widespread twenty or thirty years ago.

We hoped that this sort of thing was confined to the older generation, but a young man who had been in jail for his activities in the *MUD Juvenil* – a Left-wing youth movement[1] – astonished us when we visited him by punctuating the conversation with peremptory summonses to the maid. She was obviously busy in the kitchen preparing dinner, but he called for her for the most trivial things: to pick up a newspaper he had dropped on the floor and would not permit us to stoop for; to answer the telephone, which was at his elbow (the calls were invariably for him); to bring his cigarettes from the room he had left them in. And this boy was no *fidalgo*, or aristocrat, nor an heir to wealth. His family, through long and honourable resistance to Salazar, was in financial straits. There was only one maid. The boy, who was a student, frankly confessed that the only allowance he had from his father was for tram fares and tobacco. Nor was he the arrogant young prig one might expect from this kind of behaviour. On the contrary, he was gentle, unassuming and humorous, and not at all lacking in intelligence. It had clearly never occurred to him to treat servants otherwise, or that his behaviour would appear in any way improper to us.

At one lunch, with a family who prided themselves on their enlightened views, a revolutionary-minded young man treated us to a

[1] See pp. 217-18 below.

lengthy discourse on the appalling conditions of the poorer classes, especially maidservants. He spoke in a lively way and waved his arms about. He had already picked up the fork and spoon from the platter held at his side by the maid who stood patiently waiting for him to relieve her of some of its weight. But our young friend was too excited to think of food. The opportunity of airing his grievances to English people was too good to be missed. The face of the poor girl was a study as, arms aching, she was compelled to listen to an account of how sad her lot was. Finally we gently suggested that there were certain immediate measures that could be taken to better the conditions of one unfortunate. . . . The young man apologized with a smile and served himself. But his apologies were to us whom he had kept waiting for our lunch. . . .

On the whole however the men are a little more understanding on this subject than their womenfolk – in words, at any rate. They proclaim that the economic and social progress they want for their country depends on industrialization and a revolution in agriculture that will end chronic unemployment and low productivity. When pressed in discussion they admit that the corollary of full employment and high wages will be the disappearance of domestic servants and some radical changes in the Portuguese home. But whether they foresee the practical consequences for themselves of such changes is rather doubtful.

Even quite enlightened women are extraordinarily obtuse about this. Nowhere else, perhaps, does the married woman graduate have such freedom to exercise her profession and at the same time raise a family. In the last ten or fifteen years a growing number of young women have received university educations, and women doctors, lawyers and pharmacists are quite common. Women schoolteachers are perhaps more numerous than men. Women in these positions do not have the problem of career versus family that faces their English counterparts. Indeed, marrying an educated woman is regarded as a very sound proposition by Portuguese men. For the availability of servants guarantees the family an uninterrupted double income. Strangely enough the two incomes will often be equal, for the idea of paying professional women less than their male colleagues for the same work has never occurred to the otherwise anti-feminist Portuguese. No wonder these women dread the disappearance of servants.

Because 'treasures' are more abundant in Portugal than any other kind of wealth, the Portuguese home continues to have its primitive side, even in town among modern people who have money to spend on something more comfortable. Around Lisbon the average rate of pay for a maid or a daily woman is 2½ *escudos* an hour. Sevenpence halfpenny! In the Estoril district, in the summer season, it might be 3 *escudos*. And Portuguese *senhoras* complain of the prodigal foreigners who spoil their servants by giving them 4 *escudos* an hour.

A maid who lives in gets about 300 *escudos* (£3 15s) a month. For this sum she works seven days a week – and usually twelve hours or more a day. She will get a few hours off during the week at a time convenient to the family. Her day starts at about 6.30 a.m. She begins by waxing and polishing the floors, after which she takes her employers their breakfast in bed. Then she goes to the market and comes home laden with food for the day. That all the beds must be made by 10 a.m. is more than a rule: it is a fetish. The maid cooks two large meals during the day and washes up after them. Often it is nearly midnight before the washing-up is finished, for dinner is late in Portuguese houses, and if there are guests it is a prolonged affair.

The Portuguese maid is an artist at her work. Waxing, polishing, dusting are all done vigorously and thoroughly. On top of everything else she waits at table. She is ubiquitous; but her presence is totally ignored.

Room and board are, of course, provided for the maid who lives in. The room she sleeps in is often hardly more than a cupboard. If the family is better off, and two or more maids are kept, they will all share one room. It was once the rule, and it is still widespread, for servants to be provided with coarser food and wine than those of their employers. Larders are frequently kept locked, and sometimes a lock is fitted to the refrigerator. The mistress of the house takes food out before a meal is prepared, and afterwards things are locked up again. The explanation given for this is that otherwise food would be taken by the servants to give to their needy relatives.

We were assured on all sides that this sort of thing is disappearing. The 'servant problem' is discussed almost as it used to be in Britain in the thirties, when middle-class people still looked forward to getting a maid. Portuguese families who once had a cook and two maids now make do with one girl for all the work. But every family with any pretension to middle-class standards, from the bank clerk or primary schoolteacher upwards, still has ample household help.

Laundries do not exist. The latest modern house, tastefully and comfortably furnished with a refrigerator in the kitchen, and a shiny new car in the garage, will rarely boast a washing machine. Instead, in an open shed in the back garden, stands the small, domestic *tanque*. There the household laundering is done – not so dismal a task, perhaps, in Portugal's fine climate; but the chief cleanser is elbow-grease, not bleaches or detergents, which are reserved for dish-washing and woollens.

Imported mass-produced articles are dear in Portugal. Local labour of all kinds is cheap. And so you get that combination of luxury on the one hand and petty economies on the other which seems so curious to foreigners. With an abundance of Joanas, Júlias and Marias, whose labour power for an entire month costs less than the monthly hire-purchase instalment on a washing machine, no modernization in the kitchen is really needed. And no modernization in the kitchen means no social change – for the Portuguese kitchen is such an awkward and uncomfortable place that no one but a servant would consider working in it for long, let alone eating in it. Indeed the whole social pattern of Portuguese upper- and middle-class life is based on the existence of an army of women, young and old, who have practically no opportunities for other work and who provide an endless source of cheap labour.

Although customs are beginning to change in Lisbon, especially among younger people, it is still common in the rest of the country for two lavish meals to be served every day, one of which alone would keep an English family going for two days. The lunch break is long – two hours at least – and distances from home to work are short, so office workers and professional men almost invariably return home for lunch. The dining-room is the centre of the home, the largest and best-furnished room in the house, the place where all the family meet and important matters are discussed. Twice a day the table is laid with linen, glass and cutlery that even in a well-to-do English home would denote a very special occasion. The menu will almost always include soup, a fish course, a meat or poultry course, cheese, fruit and coffee. There will be red and white table wine, and port or a liqueur will be served after dinner. If there are guests or if it is a festive celebration there may well be a third main course of game or poultry, and a sweet in addition. It used to be common to have an egg course as well, and this is still sometimes served. When we lunched at the station restaurant at Vilar Formoso after crossing the frontier our introduction to Portuguese cooking was just such a meal – and the bill came to 30 *escudos* each, or 7s 6d!

It is hardly surprising that everybody talks about his health all the time. Practically all middle-class Portuguese seem to suffer from liver and digestive troubles. Before long we reached the conclusion that there are two kinds of Portuguese: those who do not have enough to eat and those who have too much.

But the lavish diet of the better-off is not necessarily an indication of great wealth. Many people who eat in this fashion do not own a motor-car and would not dream of taking a holiday farther afield than Spain. The women seldom possess fur coats. And in the brief winter the family sit around their lavish dinner-table with shawls and blankets thrown about their shoulders, shivering and sniffing with colds because efficient heating is regarded as a luxury.

As if two such meals a day were not enough, there is also afternoon tea. The English have persuaded the rest of the world that this was their invention; in fact it was Charles II's Portuguese queen, Catherine of Braganza, who introduced afternoon tea to England, and the habit still persists in Portugal. The tea is weaker and is usually taken without milk, but the idea is the same. There is buttered toast rather than bread and butter or sandwiches, and delicious little cakes of all kinds rather than one or two large ones. No wonder that Portuguese middle-class women past their twenties are generally on the stout side. So are their husbands – but the men at least have some exercise, even if it is only walking to and from the transport that takes them to their work and back. One wonders what the women find to do with their time. The *dona de casa* does no heavy housework. And, despite the teachings of the Catholic Church, middle-class couples nowadays have few children.

But listen to the conversation of these women for a while and you will soon realize that Parkinson's law is at work here too: the more servants, daily women, seamstresses, dressmakers, gardeners and chauffeurs that come to the house, the more indispensable are supervision, organization and discipline by the housewife. She must plan elaborate meals, tell the maids what to buy at the market, carefully scrutinize their purchases – deciding whether 4 *escudos* or 4½ was too much to pay for a dozen tangerines – and see that the meals are impeccably served, that her husband's clothes are immaculate and that she herself is always turned out with the elegance expected of the wife of a man in her husband's position. All this must be done despite the maids, not because of them, for a constant war goes on between the *dona de casa* and her servants, who are always on the look-out for some means of making just a little more than the miserable coppers they are paid, or of snatching a little more leisure than the few hours a week they are allowed.

'Ah, servants are not what they used to be,' the cultured and intelligent wife of a Liberal friend complained to us. 'Just imagine, I've caught one of my girls taking my cast-off nylons. She wanted to go out in nylon stockings! Really, the next thing, we shall see the servants wearing hats, just like us!'

This warfare seems to have intensified of late – to the point where the men too are complaining. But the reasons are not far to seek. For one thing, there is now beginning to be some alternative work in certain areas. More factories are opening and needing women workers – underpaid and overworked as they are, they are yet independent of the constant carping that reaches them even in their beds, when they are employed domestically. Again, the middle-class housewife has to make money stretch much farther than it used to. The complicated meals and formality must often come out of a salary as low as £50 a month, and this means watching every copper.

Rich and poor

For the well-to-do and very rich it is another matter. They do not have to pinch and scrape, and they continue to live on the same medieval scale as their predecessors did a century or even two centuries ago. Nowadays they have Cadillacs instead of horses and carriages, but the ritual is the same. Winter in town and summer in the country at the *quinta*, the country estate. Above all, leisure for everyone in the family. This is no stable, generations-old *bourgeoisie* with sturdy Protestant principles. Some of the richest men in the country today are the sons of poor, illiterate fathers. But they have taken over the Portuguese aristocratic tradition that the rich do not work for their money, and they want only one thing for their children: a university degree – the Portuguese badge of the gentleman, equivalent socially to a public school education in Britain. That achieved, if the family treasury is big enough the paterfamilias is quite happy to keep his children, their wives and husbands and his grandchildren in lordly idleness. He would be delighted if one of them decided to take a profession seriously and honour the family name with intellectual distinction. But, if not, it would be rather to the patriarch's credit than otherwise to let the world know that his children do not need to work. Because of succession laws, even where the father would rather see his children carving out a career for themselves they do not have much incentive to bother. They cannot be disinherited, and so they can simply sit around and wait for their father to die, knowing they are bound to get their share sooner or later. It is not so much a conscious idea. Rather is it a tradition in which people are reared, a centuries-old tradition which has no place for any sense of urgency, competition or industriousness. It is the legacy of almost a score of generations whose wealth sailed home from the fabulous gold-mines of the empire.

But often the atmosphere of ease is illusory. A fortune must be great indeed to survive years of living on capital and division among several children. This is one reason why the Portuguese countryside is dotted with broken-down estates and large shabby houses, a weather-beaten coat of arms over the main door that is kept shuttered and barred for most of the year, while the land is left untended and the oranges and apples, quinces and figs drop from the trees to lie rotting in the orchards.

The Portuguese family is a much larger unit than the English family. Family ties and family duty, making up a little for the State's deficiencies, extend to servants and tenants. This is the other side, the creditable side, of what would otherwise be unrelieved exploitation. For the Portuguese are a kindly and humane folk. If they seem to exploit their servants intolerably it is because they live in a society which is still in many respects semi-feudal. And because their notions are semi-feudal too they have preserved, amid the exploitation, much of the old, direct human contact which has disappeared from industrialized society. You will frequently find that a Portuguese household includes not merely parents, children and a mother-in-law, but also cousins, maiden aunts and other needy kinsfolk whom nobody would dream of leaving to fend for themselves. And often a bastard or two brought home by the head of the family and apparently accepted by the wife, who would not dare to thwart her husband's wishes. At mealtimes if you go into the kitchen you will often find that the servants of the house are not the only ones eating there. There may well be a servant's child or younger brother or sister; the relative of a tenant from the family's *quinta* who could not attend school in town unless someone were willing to provide meals and a bed; a poor neighbour; a peasant from near the *quinta* who has been brought to town at the family's expense for medical treatment. Charity of this sort is widespread. It reaches far beyond the narrow circles of the very rich. Beggars who go from door to door are seldom turned away empty-handed.

This is not conscience money, but rather a vestige of the humanity of the middle ages, the humanity of a hierarchical society where one's place was decided from birth and one's duties to those above and those below were fixed immutably, but where the cash nexus had not yet completely obliterated the warmth of direct human relationships. These values still found in an attenuated form in Portugal are much admired by foreign visitors who sense obscurely the dehumanization and alienation of life in Britain or the United States, and who therefore find agreeable this glimpse they get in Portugal of a world that in the rest of Europe has long passed away.

And when your memories of Britain include the jostling and squabbling in London tubes and buses at the rush hour; the rudeness of so many shop assistants; the difficulties in getting a restaurant meal outside the appointed hours; the refusal of taxi-drivers to take you where you want to go because it is not where they want to go; the heartlessness with which old folk are deposited in institutions by their children; and all the other examples of truculence and intolerance that make London life so grey and dreary – then the courtesy, kindness and helpfulness of the Portuguese are very attractive. No wonder our richer compatriots find the social structure in Portugal ideal. No wonder the retired British army officer or colonial official longs to end his days in Estoril or Sintra, where his pension will go so much farther and buy him so much kinder and more loyal service.

But what would an English working man think of it all?

A Portuguese friend told us of a young woman he knew who had worked as a servant for some English residents and who got the chance of going to England as a maid. She went off happily to earn £5 a week, live in a good room and work reasonable hours for grateful employers. She saved almost every penny of her wages and presently she married an English fireman, who was delighted to acquire a wife with so many old-fashioned housewifely virtues. But the girl was homesick. She longed for the sun and the wine and the friendliness of her own people. She was convinced that her husband, an ordinary worker in England, would do very well in Portugal – highly educated as he was by her standards. She finally persuaded him to return with her, and they sailed for Lisbon. But a fortnight was enough for him. He was horrified at the poverty and degradation of his own class in this foreign land, their abysmal wages and the total lack of those rights and amenities achieved long ago by a working class nearly two hundred years old. He packed his bags and went home.

And who could blame him? For the lives of the poor are really wretched. When the sun is shining and the servants in their starched white aprons are seen happily about their work in the houses of the well-to-do, things do not seem so bad. But go behind the scenes into their homes. It is not so much the inconvenience and squalor of these dwellings, the lack of running water, electricity and sanitation. The most pitiful thing is the ever-present, superstitious dread of illness or injury which haunts the working people. Once a working man can no longer labour, then unless he begs he can no longer live.

From a poor girl with whom we became friendly we learned how the scanty national assistance is administered. Her brother-in-law, who had been a door-keeper at one of the ministries, developed tuberculosis through long years of undernourishment. It was impossible for him to get a bed in a sanatorium, because beds for the poor are few. So he stayed at home, unable to work. This went on for three or four years. He was married, and fortunately there were no children – so his wife's earnings helped to eke out his meagre sickness benefit. But this allowance was not sent to him. Although considered too sick to work, he had to get up from his sick-bed every Saturday and go to the appropriate office to collect it. Then, two years ago, came the Asian 'flu epidemic. The weather was cold and rainy, and on the Friday the young man became feverish. But the next day was Saturday. The money was needed desperately. He got up and went down town to join the queue of sick people waiting for their benefit. They waited all day, but no one came. It turned out that the cashier too had caught Asian 'flu. So they all went home with empty pockets. That night the consumptive's fever developed into pneumonia. On the Sunday morning he died. He was thirty-six years old.

The charity of the rich, no matter how well-meaning they may be, is a drop in the ocean in a land where three-quarters of the people are abjectly poor.

Keeping their hands clean

Britons who go to the United States are usually favourably impressed by Americans' versatility. American youth are determined to get on and willing to turn their hands to any trade in order to do so. Lately we have begun to see the same thing in Britain. Most university students work in their vacations, and sometimes during term too, at any number of what were once considered menial jobs. They work as waiters, porters, farm labourers, shop assistants, post office sorters. And they are sometimes not quite clear themselves why these jobs no longer carry the old social stigma.

In Portugal nobody is in doubt. In a country where a working man cannot earn a living wage society despises him and insists on maintaining at all costs the distinction between manual and intellectual work. Although university fees are very low, and students from less wealthy families reaching a certain standard pay none at all, many young people pursue their studies with great difficulty because their families cannot afford to keep them. But working one's way through college is out of the question. When so many are out of work part-time jobs are hard to come by. In any case, the pay is so low and the hours so long that there would be no time for study. There is something to be ashamed of in soiling your hands. That is the deeply ingrained tradition. And so you get a whole host of curious social prejudices which no well-brought-up Portuguese would dream of questioning – until he goes abroad and finds out for the first time that he must help himself, for no one else will. Not even for money.

A Portuguese man thinks it quite unseemly to carry parcels in the street, and would not contemplate helping with the shopping even if the household were temporarily without servants. A middle-class woman regards it as really a sign of hard times if she has to go to the market and bring back the groceries herself. A conscientious housewife might well go there to supervise the purchases, but her servant would do the carrying. And the servants too have their prejudices. A self-respecting maid will not happily go out carrying a dilapidated shopping basket – it must be a basket of a certain kind, to mark her off from the poor women who are shopping for themselves and their families.

If you perform manual labour for your own entertainment you are looked on as an eccentric. The Portuguese middle class love gardens, but they would not dream of gardening. Designing the garden and supervising its development are the nearest they come to it. The do-it-yourself craze is regarded as a quaint foreign aberration by travelled Portuguese who do not understand that it is the only way to get interior decorating done quickly and cheaply in Britain today. Woodwork is not taught in secondary schools, and no respectable Portuguese man knows how to use a hammer, a saw or a screwdriver.

But since he is seldom in the house no one notices that he is not a handyman. The head of the family, devoted though he is to his family, is not often with them. He comes home to sleep, eat and entertain guests. Otherwise his wife and children rarely see him. And when they are big enough, his sons also go out as soon as they have eaten. All this is so taken for granted that most households have nowhere else for the family to meet but the dining-room. The family never gather round the living-room fire at the end of the day, as with us. The better-off will probably have a *sala de visitas*, a drawing-room, formal, uncomfortable and usually kept shuttered except on special occasions. It is not a living-room in any sense of the word. But even the most modest middle-class house may have an *escritório*, a study for the man of the house. On the rare occasions he does stay at home that is where he goes. But no one else in the house has anywhere to go except the bedrooms, unless the housewife is lucky enough to have a sewing-room, where she and her daughters will be found and where her women visitors will come to gossip with her. Here she will sit for hours on end, busy with embroidery, crochet or tatting, for, unlike her husband, she is nimble with her fingers. Although heavy housework is left to the servants most Portuguese women are skilled needlewomen and stay happily at home while their husbands sit in the cafés with their cronies or visit their mistresses.

Love and marriage

Like other Latin races the Portuguese think of themselves as romantic and passionate lovers. Probably every literate Portuguese of either sex has composed sentimental verses in praise of a beloved, at some time between the ages of twelve and twenty. The Portuguese enjoy their own picture of the phlegmatic Englishman who prefers to take a hot-water bottle to bed. Yet nothing in Portugal is quite so hedged about with dull rules and conventions as courtship and love-making.

The Englishman who goes to Portugal hoping for a holiday adventure with some dark-eyed southern beauty is in for a disappointment. So is the Englishwoman in search of a romantic, courteous Latin escort. The former will find his evenings filled with the chatter of elderly aunts, not his girl-friend's kisses; the latter will find that the Portuguese thinks that if she lets him take her out she will also let him sleep with her. In fact hunting foreign girls has become one of the

summer sports of Portuguese young men. And no wonder – their own
are so inaccessible.

Courting is called *namorar*, and from the age of twelve or so every
boy has his *namorada*, every girl her *namorado*. These words mean
sweetheart. Everyone is as aware of sex as in England, perhaps more
so – and without the artificial stimulation of lurid cinema posters.
But properly-brought-up young people are strictly segregated, and
their courtships take place in the true tradition of romantic love. Of
course in latter years things have begun to change under the influence
of the cinema. On beaches and in motor-cars young people are able to
mingle more easily. No doubt in Lisbon there is much greater freedom
in those circles where foreign influences are felt. But in Oporto, in
the provinces and in the capital's more old-fashioned households
things are still almost as they were fifty years or so ago, when *namorar
à janela*, 'courting at the window', was the rule. A young man would
woo his *namorada* from the street while she stayed indoors and talked
with him through the open window. Sometimes he would sing to her,
accompanying himself on a guitar. An enterprising youth might bring
his friends along to serenade the young woman in chorus. Today this
practice is confined to Coimbra, where students carry on the tradition
out of sentiment rather than from necessity.

But although *namorar* is now permitted at closer quarters than from
the public street, privacy is still not allowed. If a young man wants to
take a girl out he must be prepared for the outing to be chaperoned.
Perhaps her mother, aunt or sister will accompany the young couple;
the more modern practice is for the girl's brother to chaperon them.
Enlightened parents may let them go alone to a matinée at the cinema.
But there is no question of going unchaperoned to the cinema in
the evening, or out to dinner. The young man who wants to spend the
evening in his *namorada*'s company has to put up with the rest of the
family. An attractive girl, her mother, aunts and younger brothers
and sisters will sit stiffly round the dining-room table after dinner,
while the young man is forced to converse with them all in the hope of
a kind word from the girl.

Sometimes courtships go on for years like that. Even when the
namorados are promoted to the status of *noivos* and their engagement
is recognized – after a careful investigation of the financial prospects
of each party by the other's family – they are no freer. Among the
middle classes marriage is contracted early by women and late by men.
Very few middle-class men earn enough to get married on before they

are thirty or more, and then they look around for a bride well under the age of twenty-four. After that age a girl is really on the shelf. Marriages are frankly matters of convenience, often arranged by the young couple's families; nor do men consider it something to be ashamed of that they have married for money – rather is it something for their friends to congratulate them on and envy them for. It is usual among these classes for a romantic courtship to end miserably in the *namorada's* marriage to an older, more suitable partner chosen for her by her family, while her *namorado* is left heart-broken to wait until he has enough money to replace some other wretched young lover as the bridegroom of a girl several years his junior.

Namorar has little to do with sex. A young man seeks a *namorada* among girls of his own class – modest, well-brought-up virgins, who must stay chaste until the wedding night. His sex life, which often begins at a remarkably early age by English standards, is conducted elsewhere. It used to be fairly common in Portugal for a boy of fourteen to be given money by his father to go to a brothel. How far this is still done it is hard to say. But we have been assured by many Portuguese that most young men regard it as shameful if they are still virgins by the age of seventeen. The most usual way for a young man to have his first sexual experience is with maidservants. Working girls are often only too glad to have the chance of bettering their lot with the young men of the richer classes, who are denied the companionship of young women of their own class. So it is cheap and easy to arrange a mistress from among the thousands of servant girls, seamstresses and dressmakers who need a little comfort in their lives.

But woe betide the maid whose frailty is discovered by the *dona de casa*. Out she goes into the street. And it is often in the street that she remains – in a manner of speaking, that is, because you do not see prostitutes openly plying their trade in Portugal.

Prostitution is legal and is carried on in licensed houses. It is said that the State gets a lot of money from this source, and that this is one of the reasons why, despite protests, there seems little prospect of any change. In recent years however the government has to some extent bowed to public opinion by granting no new licences, while permitting renewals of old ones. Whether this has reduced prostitution or merely created monopolies in the trade it is impossible to judge.

One of the difficulties in establishing the facts about prostitution is the strict ban on any public, scientific discussion of it. A Portuguese friend who is a regular reader of the British Press commented on the contrast between British frankness on sexual matters and Portuguese official reticence.

'Do you realize,' he asked us, 'that articles such as those I have read recently in the *New Statesman* on the Wolfenden report and the Street Offences Act would, if published in Portugal, make their authors and publishers liable to heavy jail sentences for propagating pornography?'

Even scientific treatises on sexual matters are hard to come by. *A Vida Sexual* (Coimbra, 1901), by the great Portuguese neurologist Egas Moniz, is banned by the censor and may be obtained only by the medical profession. Under these circumstances it is not surprising that ignorance of elementary subjects, such as the recognition and treatment of venereal disease, is widespread. And knowledge about contraceptive techniques, as might be expected in a Catholic country, is both primitive and confined to educated people.

We were told that it was now a fairly common practice for young men, in order to economize and at the same time reduce the risk of disease, to club together in threes or fours to keep a mistress in common. The woman has the advantage of a regular income from a restricted clientele, and agrees not to accept others. Her clients have the advantage of knowing that she is not subject to infection from strangers.

We were also told that abortions, though illegal, are widespread among all classes and that more take place each year. This is said to be due to two main causes. First, town-dwellers are getting poorer. Secondly, abortions can be arranged more easily than they used to be. There are said to be innumerable abortionists, easily accessible, who started as half-trained male or female nurses or as medical auxiliaries of one kind or another. These persons, over whom the police apparently exercise little control, charge as little as 100 or 150 *escudos*. Women of all classes, mostly married women, go to them. One observant woman friend assured us that among her married women acquaintances she hardly knew one who had not been the customer, at least once, of such a 'nurse'.

The practice of married men keeping mistresses is such an accepted social custom that the dismay of many a rising business man's wife on learning that her husband is keeping another woman is tempered by a certain smugness. It proves to everyone that her husband has arrived, rather as her fur coat does. And if the mistress too were given a fur coat the wife's friends would tell her this news respectfully rather than indignantly, for who would not be proud of a husband who can afford to keep not merely one woman in luxury, but two?

There are probably as many jealous women in Portugal as in other parts of the world. But they are not expected to express their jealousy. And they do not do so to the same extent as an Englishwoman would in similar circumstances. There is ample evidence for this in the treatment of illegitimate children. Those Portuguese who get to know colloquial English are amazed that the word 'bastard' can be used as a term of abuse. They will sometimes cite this usage as one more example of English cold-bloodedness. For when the republic gave legal recognition to illegitimate children in Portugal it was merely giving legal force to the nation's traditional attitude. Natural sons and daughters, from those of the king and nobles downwards, had always been looked on as members of the family. And it is still so today. You will frequently hear a boy referring to another youngster in the family as his brother, whereas his mother calls the child her stepson. If you are inquisitive enough to ask whether her husband has been married before you may well be told that the child is *um filho natural*. Usually the natural child is the fruit of some pre-marital union of the husband's; and the wife would know before she married that the child existed and that she would be expected to mother it. Sometimes a natural child born long after marriage will be brought home by his father, and the rest of the family will be expected to treat him as they treat the legitimate children.

The only illegitimate children in Portugal who are made to feel shame are those who do not know who their father was, or who cannot prove their parentage – the children of women who have been seduced and abandoned, or, more likely, of women who have been undiscriminating. The former case is much less frequent than one would suppose. The Portuguese may not be ideal husbands, but they are usually devoted fathers. They love children in general and their own in particular, and the idea of abandoning their own flesh and blood goes very much against the grain.

English people in Portugal find these sentiments extremely baffling. They see little home life as we know it, and gross marital infidelity on the part of husbands. Yet in striking contrast are the devotion and respect for the family professed and practised by most Portuguese. The philandering husband profoundly reveres the institution of matrimony, and it is rare for such a man to abandon his wife and home and break up the marriage. Usually it is only infidelity by the wife that would provoke a man to do this. The wife must have altogether higher standards, and must reward her husband's infidelities with untainted chastity – although from the boasts of some young men it is fair to assume that a number of married women succumb to temptation.

The liberal divorce laws that the 1910 republic introduced were altered by Salazar. A civil ceremony is now unnecessary for those who are married in church; religious marriage has been given a superior status. The divorce courts are not accessible to those married in church – not simply because the Church forbids divorce, but because Salazar's laws reinforce the Vatican's and do not permit marriages solemnized in church to be dissolved in the civil courts. A married woman has very few rights. Even if a marriage contract is made before marriage, keeping her property in her own name, her husband is the one who administers it and she cannot alienate any of it without his consent. If a married woman wants to travel – even to join a husband already abroad – she must have his written authorization, legally signed and sealed, before the authorities will give her a passport. A married woman attains her legal majority only on her husband's death. He cannot disinherit her, and half his property will pass to her. For the first time she becomes her own mistress, the head of the household and entitled to vote. If her lack of educational qualifications did not permit this while she was a wife, bereavement now ensures her the rights of a citizen.

Parents dote on their offspring, spoil them outrageously, and in return are treated by their children with a veneration that often seems to verge on the oriental. Among old-fashioned people you may still see the children kissing their parents' hands when they greet them. Among modern people there is still kissing, but it is on the face. The frequency of this salutation is quite astonishing. In many households the entire family kiss one another on meeting for the first time after they get up, then again before they part for the morning. This performance is repeated before and after lunch, and again before and after dinner – and finally before going to bed at night. If you are a mere visitor you will be expected only to shake hands with everybody on all these occasions. So if you are staying with a family of six people you can fairly expect to shake hands a minimum of forty-two times a day.

What about the family life and courting habits of the common people? In general they are peasant habits – for even in town the Portuguese worker is still half a peasant – and much like peasant habits in the rest of Europe. Health, strength and above all a bit of land, especially if it adjoins the bridegroom's: these are the peasant girl's assets in the marriage market. In some poorer regions it is quite common for peasants not to bother to marry at all. They cannot afford the cost of the ceremony, and so they simply ignore it and hope that one day they may be able to save up enough to pay for a blessing on their union. This sometimes has the quaint result, where the family does prosper, that a pair of ancients will go to get married before an admiring audience of their children and grandchildren.

The clergy are supposed to be celibate. In Britain we usually associate scandalous tales about the private lives of Catholic priests with anti-Papist prejudices. But in Portugal it is hard to find anyone, even among the devout, who takes clerical chastity seriously. Jokes about the indiscretions of priests are as common as jokes about mothers-in-law. In the Portuguese colonies there is less pretence still. Some friends who had spent many years in Africa showed us an album filled with photographs of the plantation on which they had lived.

'And this,' they said, 'is the local priest, *padre* António.'

We looked at an insignificant little man in a biretta and cassock. There he was again on the next page, this time surrounded by a group of children of all shades and sizes.

'Are any of you among them?' we asked our hosts' daughter.

'Oh, no,' she answered, 'those are *padre* António's children.'

We wondered if we had understood, and we questioned her mother. But the girl was right. All of them – eight or nine – had been sired by the priest.

V

Food and drink

Pigs and barnacles

If you dislike onions, mistrust olive oil, loathe garlic and believe in putting the joint straight into the oven without seasoning it first, then you will not care for Portuguese cooking very much. But anyone who has already developed a taste for Mediterranean food is likely to be intrigued by what he gets to eat in Portugal.

In many ways Portuguese food is different from that of other south European countries. It is lighter than Greek, less farinaceous than Italian and not so spicy as some Spanish food. But the olive groves that stretch from one end of the Mediterranean to the other are to be found all over Portugal too; and here too olive oil is the traditional cooking fat, and olives – black and green, fresh, cooked and preserved – are eaten at almost every meal. Of course many of Europe's olive groves were destroyed in the war. Since it takes an olive tree about twenty years to reach maturity and produce any fruit, peasants prefer to plant crops that bring a quicker return; so in recent years there has been a world shortage of olive oil, and even in Portugal, which escaped the war, the price has rocketed. Consequently groundnut oil imported cheaply from the African colonies has largely replaced olive oil for cooking in all but Portugal's richest kitchens. But even the poorest people still try to find a little olive oil for making soup.

Hot summers mean the usual southern methods of making meat keep longer, and making old ox taste like young veal. Before cooking, you will marinade the meat for at least two hours – sometimes overnight. Or you will smoke meat of all kinds, either whole, or minced and chopped for sausages that will keep for years. So garlic, onions, bay leaves, peppercorns and wine vinegar (never malt vinegar) are all to be found in every Portuguese kitchen.

Onions, much milder and sweeter than the ones we grow in England,

93

hang in the kitchen in strings like those the Breton sellers bring across the Channel each year. Big heads of garlic, too, are hung on strings and are in constant use – though there are not as many Portuguese as there are Spaniards who will eat garlic raw on bread! Beside the onions and garlic there usually hangs a branch of bay leaves, dried and ready to crumble or put whole in the pot. A jar filled with peppercorns and another with fresh parsley in water, a bowl of coarse cooking salt, some pepper – black and white – a bowl of lemons, another of eggs, wine vinegar, white wine, a can of olive oil: all these are essential to the Portuguese cook. And a great many tomatoes, or tinned tomato paste for the more modern housewife.

The Portuguese love eating, and above all they love eating meat. Apart from pork, the meat is mostly dear and poor in quality, though a good cook works wonders with even the toughest cut. Since the pastures of the Alentejo have been converted to wheatlands, and afforestation schemes have reduced the flocks of sheep on the mountains, meat has become more of a luxury than ever. Most cattle have had a long working life before they come to the table; so veal rather than beef is the most prized and expensive of meats. For some reason sheep are esteemed more for their wool and the cheese made from their milk than for mutton or lamb chops, which the Portuguese do not care for. Kid is very popular, however. It tastes like rather sweet, lean lamb.

But without any doubt the pig is the king of meat-providers in Portugal. The succulence and versatility of its flesh are immediately appreciated when one tastes *bifes de porco* – every kind of steak is a *bife*, no matter what animal it comes from – *paio*, a wonderfully tasty sausage of smoked, pressed ham, or the countless different kinds of *chouriço*, the sausages that hang in profusion in every grocer's. The small black pigs of the Alentejo and elsewhere are nothing like so hefty as English porkers, nor is their flesh so fat. So pork is a lean, delicate meat, and Portuguese ham, smoked and served raw in fine, transparent slices, looks more like smoked salmon than like English ham and tastes delicious as an appetizer before a meal of sea food.

This brings us to the most typical aspect of Portuguese cooking: the abundance of wonderful things to eat that fishermen spend their lives winning from the wide Atlantic, even from as far away as Newfoundland. To glance at the fish stalls in the markets, or the little shops that specialize in sea food, or the weirdly decked windows of the beerhouses, you would think that the Portuguese eat pretty well everything that can be found in the sea. Most of the fish we get in England are all to be seen. But there are many more besides: sundry kinds of eel; lampreys; tuna fish; and sardines – not the little tinned ones that every Englishman knows as well as he knows roast beef, but fresh sardines almost the size of herrings, which are bought in dozens and grilled whole over a charcoal brazier to taste their most delectable. Then there are fish for which there are, it seems, no English names: *peixe-dourado*, 'golden fish', big and glowing; *peixe-espada*, 'sword-like fish', so named because the whole creature is the shape of a sword, and not to be confused with the sword-fish proper from tropical waters; *chicharro*, a small, plump and very cheap fish which is exceptionally savoury.

All these are recognizably fish and obviously edible. But many others are strange, or baffling, or even sinister, in their looks. Cockles, mussels, winkles, shrimps, prawns, lobsters: these are familiar. But there seem far too many varieties of crab, some moderately horrific, others much too much like great, pink, horny spiders, especially when they are suspended alive on strings and wriggle and wink at you through the beerhouse window. There is a nightmarish species of barnacle, long, black, scaly and ungual, looking for all the world like the grotesque, beckoning finger of some submarine monster. When these creatures are cooked and split open there is white flesh inside, and we were told that this is delightful to eat. But our imagination was too much for us, and we missed this treat.

Then there is the octopus family: squid, cuttle-fish and various small octopodes. These can be bought either fresh or dried. In the latter state they look like gorgons' hair. Fresh and raw straight from the sea they look scarcely less disgusting to the uninitiated. Cooked and dished up in a stew, however, or garnished with tomato sauce or a gravy of their own black ink, these sinister cephalopoda are extraordinarily delicate in flavour. Nowadays they are tinned and exported, and in Soho you can buy *lulas recheadas*, stuffed squid, in tins the size of sardine tins, straight from Portugal. Get a tin or two – there are about six small rolls of squid in each – and serve them to your friends on squares of toast as a *canapé* at a party without telling them what they are eating. They will clamour for more and will be quite at a loss to guess what this titbit is.

Traditionally the staple fish in Portugal is *bacalhau*, the humble cod. Not fresh cod, so well known in Britain, but dried, salt cod, which looks unappetizing and smells strongly as it hangs in huge plaster-grey fillets in the shops. This strange stuff is what lures hundreds of little Portuguese fishing boats out across the ocean every year to the Newfoundland banks, where they spend months catching, salting and drying the cod.

It is said that there are a hundred ways of cooking *bacalhau*. There are certainly at least twenty principal ways, all of which produce a mouth-watering meal remote in appearance and smell from the dehydrated stuff that arrives in the kitchen.

The Portuguese are so fond of chicken soup that they will rarely roast a fowl before it has been parboiled and a broth extracted. This makes Portuguese roast chicken rather a flabby affair; but the soup is excellent. Pigeon is a favourite dish, and so are even smaller birds. At one time sparrows and other tiny birds, plucked and roasted whole, could be seen all over Lisbon hanging in bunches in the shops or sold on sticks by little boys, a sight which outraged the soft-hearted British visitor. Turkeys are eaten all the year round. They are bought alive from men who drive their flocks along the roads and offer them for sale from door to door; it is customary for the housewife or servant to chaffer and drive a hard bargain. Before Christmas there are more of these flocks about than ever, and those who have the space – and even many who have not – buy a bird several weeks beforehand and fatten it for Christmas dinner.

Vegetables are varied and of excellent quality. Perhaps it is because they are fresh and unforced, or perhaps it is the sunshine, but tomatoes, lettuces, cabbages, and the ubiquitous watercress all seem to have more flavour than they do in Britain. Besides these and other familiar English vegetables like carrots and parsnips, there are aubergines, sweet potatoes, sweet peppers, an endless variety of beans large and small, and a special kind of Portuguese cabbage from which a sturdy soup is made.

Spaghetti and macaroni are not found in typical Portuguese cooking and are confined to dishes of Italian provenance, which the Portuguese enjoy but regard as definitely foreign. The chief carbohydrates in the national diet are rice, potatoes and beans. Rice is served almost as frequently as in oriental cooking, and is the base for many fish dishes. A favourite way of doing potatoes is called *batatas fritas à inglesa*. But they are nothing like English chips. Round, salted, wafer-thin slices are plunged for a few seconds in boiling oil and served hot and crisp with every kind of meat dish.

Fruit is so cheap and so good that a meal normally ends with a bowl of fresh fruit rather than a cooked sweet; the latter is usually served only on special occasions. Not that the fruit looks as good as it tastes – except for grapes, which both look and taste glorious. Nobody in Portugal seems to take the cultivation of any other kind of fruit really seriously. Orchards are left to themselves. As a result there is no grading, and oranges, apples and pears come in all shapes and sizes; and oranges often have black patches on their skins from a mild fungus disease. But none of this affects their flavour or their juiciness. Small, sweet bananas from Madeira are plentiful, and pineapples from the Azores are both cheap and good. In the winter tangerines and mandarins abound. In the summer melons are so cheap that you buy them by the score and keep them for months, well into the winter. No melon you get in England has the subtle, honeyed taste that these melons have. In the summer, too, water-melons are a great thirst-quencher; they are sold in pieces at the roadside and at railway stations to refresh the thirsty traveller.

Some easy recipes

We have selected a few typical dishes which we learned to prepare in Portugal, and which might easily be tried out in an English kitchen. All the ingredients can easily be obtained in this country.

First, soup, for this always starts a meal in Portugal, all the year round. No meat stock is needed, but the result is robust and nourishing. And if you own a modern electric mixer which shreds and pulps vegetables you are well equipped to make Portuguese soups very quickly.

Caldo Verde (Green Broth)

This is an easily made and very popular vegetable soup. It is made with the tall Portuguese cabbage, but it would be good with any green cabbage. For four persons you need 2 lb. of potatoes, two onions, two tablespoonfuls of olive oil, salt and pepper and a finely shredded cabbage. Boil the potatoes and onions with the olive oil in two pints of water until they are thoroughly cooked. Put it all through a sieve to reduce it to a *purée*. Return to the stove, season and put in the shredded cabbage. Boil for no more than five minutes and serve immediately.

*　　　　　*　　　　　*

A *purée* of the type described is the base for many soups. It can be varied in two ways: by using other root vegetables, such as parsnips, turnips or carrots, with the potatoes; or by using watercress or other green vegetables instead of the cabbage.

Other Soups

Onion soup, garlic soup or a mixture of the two are made very easily by lightly browning finely chopped onions and garlic in enough olive oil to cover the bottom of the pan. Add boiling water and continue to cook for ten minutes. Season and pour into dishes over a slice of toast. Bacon fat may be used with the olive oil for greater savouriness.

A good fish soup is made by boiling onions, potatoes and tomatoes with a little olive oil in the water in which fish has been cooked and then passing it through a sieve for *purée*.

Iscas à Portuguesa (Portuguese Enticements)

One of the most appetizing ways of preparing liver is to make *iscas* (literally, 'bait'). The liver should be sliced very finely and soaked in a marinade for at least two hours – overnight is better. For the marinade you need one glass of wine (red or white Algerian will do very well), a bay leaf, chopped garlic, salt and pepper. Pour it all over the liver. When you are ready to cook take the liver out of the marinade and fry it in lard. Heat the marinade and pour it over the liver when you have taken it out of the pan. This is excellent garnished with watercress and surrounded by

Batatas Fritas à Inglesa (English Fried Potatoes)

Medium-sized potatoes should be sliced whole to produce thin, round slices. Dry them in a cloth and season with salt and pepper. Cook quickly in a chip pan full of boiling oil till they are crisp and golden, and serve at once.

*   *   *

Fillets of pork or veal may be treated like *iscas*.

Açorda (Garlic Pudding)

This is an economical way of using up stale bread, but its appeal is strictly for the garlic-lover – and even he may find it a trifle on the soggy side till he is used to it. Portuguese children love it. Break brown or white bread by hand into a pan or bowl. Season with salt and pepper.

Add chopped garlic to taste and slowly pour hot water into the bowl until the bread is thoroughly soaked; but make sure the liquid is all absorbed or the result will be too soggy. Cover and leave for twenty minutes. Add a tablespoonful of olive oil and some chopped parsley and stir thoroughly. Put it all in a shallow, greased baking dish and bake in a hot oven until a golden crust begins to form. Make hollows in the surface and break an egg into each. Return to the oven and continue baking until the eggs are cooked. *Açorda* may also be made with sliced onions as well as the garlic.

*   *   *

If you want to try *bacalhau* you can get passable dried cod at any Greek or Italian grocery in Britain. Frozen, salt cod, only partly dried, which is processed by several Hull firms, is a good substitute and does not require such long soaking. Genuine *bacalhau* must always be soaked, not only to remove the excess salt but also to get it back into a moist enough state to be edible. Twelve hours is usually enough. The water should be changed occasionally. The cod is then skinned and boned, and for most dishes it is boiled. A very popular dish is

Bacalhau à Gomes de Sá (Gomes de Sá Cod)

For four persons you need about a pound of dried cod, double the weight of potatoes, a pound of onions, four cloves of garlic, four hard-boiled eggs, green or black olives, parsley, olive oil, lemon juice, salt and pepper. Boil the fish and potatoes together, and when they are cooked separate the fish into small flakes and slice the potatoes. Cover the bottom of a fireproof dish with olive oil and put in the fish, potatoes, finely sliced onions, olives, sliced garlic and chopped parsley. Pour the rest of the olive oil into the dish and squeeze half a lemon into it. Season with salt and pepper and stir gently until well mixed. Put in a hot oven, and when the onions are tender put the sliced eggs on top covered with a little chopped parsley. Leave in the oven for five minutes more and serve piping hot.

Another *bacalhau* dish, which goes very well as a snack with white wine, is

Bolinhos de Bacalhau (Cod-fish Cakes)

These keep for several days and are always better at least twenty-four hours after they are cooked, so they are a handy party dish which can be prepared ahead of time. You need a pound of boiled *bacalhau*, 2 lb.

of boiled potatoes, a pound of boiled onions, garlic, two teaspoonfuls
of chopped parsley, two eggs and the juice of half a lemon. Put everything except the eggs and the lemon juice through the mincer, making
sure the cod has been boned and skinned beforehand. Break the eggs
into the mixture and stir well. Add the lemon juice, and season with
salt and pepper to taste. Beat until light and creamy. Shape into balls
with two spoons on a pastry board and drop into rapidly boiling oil
in a chip pan; cook till golden.

Pasteis (Pasties)

The Portuguese make excellent fish and meat pasties. Minced meat,
chicken, fish in a white sauce and every sort of shellfish may be used
as a filling. But the pastry case is made of a special dough called *massa
tenra*, 'soft dough', and is not baked but fried. Served with fluffy white
rice, a dish of these pasties makes a meal. They are also a good party
or picnic dish. For a quarter of a pound of flour you need an ounce of
butter, an egg, salt and some water. Sieve the flour and salt, and work
in the butter in the usual way. Add the beaten egg and then the water to
make a fairly stiff dough. Roll out several times and leave for an hour or
so. Cut the dough into circles with a pastry cutter, place the filling to
one side of each circle and fold over, pinching the sides together. Fry
in very hot oil until golden.

We found these pasties, some *bolinhos de bacalhau* and a glass of dry
white wine made a most agreeable light lunch when we were in a hurry.
You can get them in *leitarias* – milk-bars! – as well as in restaurants;
a lavish quantity for two persons will cost less than 5s, including the
wine.

*   *   *

Most cookery books tell you that the term *à la portugaise* means 'with
tomato sauce'. But they do not often give a recipe for tomato sauce
as it is prepared in Portugal and used with many dishes: meat, fresh
fish and *bacalhau*. It is always served hot, and it bears little resemblance
to the well-known proprietary brands popular in Britain. This is how
we learned to make it:

Molho de Tomate (Tomato Sauce)

Finely chop two onions and as much garlic as you like. Fry
till pale golden in a pan generously filled with olive oil. Add half a
dozen large, chopped tomatoes, salt and pepper, finely chopped parsley

and a little cornflour mixed smoothly with water, and cook gently until the tomatoes are soft and the mixture thickens. Put it all through a sieve, and before serving return to the heat so that it does not cool.

* * *

Most typical Portuguese sweets are made with eggs and sugar as a base. The one other really characteristic sweet, eaten at breakfast or tea-time or after lunch or dinner, is made from fresh quince, or *marmelo*, normally unobtainable in England – though we are sure that Portuguese quince cheese, or *marmelada*, would appeal to every English palate. *Marmelada* is the exotic cousin of our own familiar orange marmalade, whose name comes from the Portuguese. But when you visit Portugal make sure that you get the real thing. There is a host of cheap substitutes; some made from apples, and good; others made from carrots, turnips and potatoes, and nasty.

Créme Queimado (Burnt Cream)

This makes an unusual variant of custard pudding. You need half a dozen egg yolks, one pint of milk, 9 oz. of sugar, a few drops of vanilla essence and a teaspoonful of cinnamon. Make a paste with the flour and two tablespoonfuls of milk. Bring the rest of the milk to the boil and add it to the paste. Add 8 oz. of sugar and a few drops of vanilla essence. Return to the pan and bring to the boil for two minutes. Beat the egg yolks lightly, and slowly add the mixture after it has cooled a little, stirring all the time. Return to a gentle heat until it has thickened. Pour into a shallow dish. Take the rest of the sugar and mix thoroughly with the cinnamon. Spread thickly over the top of the custard. Put under the grill – taking care that it does not catch fire – until the sugar and cinnamon have dissolved. This coating will become dark and crisp when it is removed from the heat, and gives a very special touch to the custard. In Portugal the burning is commonly done with a red-hot iron straight on to the custard, often in leaf or flower patterns which look very attractive. This dish may be served hot or cold.

* * *

A very rich sweet which is especially popular at Christmas bears a quaint name, and anyone with a sweet tooth will soon find out why:

Toucinho do Céu (Little Bacon from Heaven)

The recipe varies in different parts of the country. In some places ground almonds are added; we liked it better without them. You need half a glass of port wine, a pat of butter and some water, and one ounce of sugar for each egg yolk used. If your family likes sweet things allow one egg per person. Reduce the sugar to syrup by boiling in a pan with a small amount of water until it coats a spoon. Beat the egg yolks with the butter and port and add slowly to the cooled syrup, beating all the time. Pour the mixture into a shallow, buttered oven-proof dish and bake in a medium oven until it is set. Cut in squares and serve cold.

*　　　　*　　　　*

In England one of our favourite sponges is called Madeira cake. And an exceptionally light and sweet sponge-cake is a Portuguese speciality:

Pão-de-Ló (Sponge-cake)

It can be used for cream sandwiches, cup cakes called *fofos*, or eaten plain. Any way it is delicious, especially accompanied by a glass of port or Madeira. Beat six egg yolks with 12 oz. of sugar, and then beat in half a pound of flour and a pinch of baking powder (previously sifted). Beat the whites of the eggs till they are really stiff and fold them into the mixture. Turn into a greased baking tin, preferably the round, Continental kind with a hole through the middle, and immediately put in a hot oven for ten to fifteen minutes. As soon as the top is golden cover with greased paper.

Cheeses, wines and waters

Cheese, like wine, is served at every meal in Portugal. But there is not a great variety of cheeses produced, and they are little known outside the country. Yet the best Portuguese cheese, *queijo da Serra*, made from sheep's milk in the Serra da Estrêla, the Mountains of the Star, really deserves to be numbered among the great soft cheeses of Europe. Its subtle but insistent flavour is reminiscent of Italian *bel paese* though less bland. It is often eaten with *marmelada* – with knife and fork, for the Portuguese seldom put cheese on bread or biscuits. *Queijo da Serra* flows in viscid, piquant runnels when it is ripening. Autumn to midwinter is its season. There are many poor and poorish substitutes, but you will not buy real *Serra* cheese outside its home province, the Beira Alta, for less than 40 *escudos* a kilo.

Another soft cheese worth trying is Azeitão from Arrábida, south of Lisbon. There are some hard cheeses from the Azores, known as *queijo da ilha*, which are cheap and good. Most commonly served in restaurants, however, is *tipo flamengo*, a local imitation of Dutch cheese, which is acceptable but of no particular interest.

*   *   *

Portuguese wines are both varied and excellent. As we travelled round the country tasting the different local wines we regretted more and more that most English people know only port and Madeira – and then not port as it is drunk in Portugal, but a highly fortified wine designed for the upper-class English palate of a century or more ago. Portuguese table wines, though they do not boast a rival to the great wines of Burgundy and Bordeaux, are of a consistently high level. And the *vinho da casa*, which is how one asks for the *vin ordinaire*, is certain to be much better than its frequently adulterated French equivalent – and far cheaper too. By law no local wine may be sold outside the region where it was produced, which is an effective protection against the kind of practice that in France so often ekes out 'Beaujolais' with indifferent Algerian wine.

Of Portugal's major wines, some are now becoming deservedly celebrated in Britain. Many people who have not yet visited Portugal have discovered red and white Dão, from the lovely Dão valley north-east of Coimbra, at their wine merchant's. A satisfactory Dão can be bought in Portugal for 8 *escudos*, the equivalent of 2*s*. In Britain it costs almost four times as much. Red Dão is robust, with a delightful bouquet, and makes an excellent concomitant to meat or cheese. We did not find white Dão quite so outstanding; but that is a personal view. Colares, a delightful old village near Sintra, is the centre of an important wine-growing region and produces an exceedingly drinkable red table wine which many judges rank alongside Dão. Other favoured named wines, all of them to be found in good wine merchants' in Britain, are Grandjo, which resembles Sauternes; Bucelas, which resembles Graves; and our favourite among Portuguese white wines, Palmela, which until recently could be bought in Britain for as little as 5*s* a bottle.

But when you are in Portugal, unless you are celebrating and want to make certain your wine is first class, it is really more interesting to drink the ordinary local wine. Costing 3 or 4 *escudos* a litre – less than a shilling – it will almost always be good, and sometimes it will be first rate. It is produced so cheaply and abundantly that there is not enough space for it to be stored, so it is drunk new and is rarely adulterated with chemicals. In the countryside many an hotel or inn has its own vineyards or a private arrangement with a local farmer; if you ask for the wine of the house you will frequently be astonished at the excellence of a wine that is not to be found anywhere else.

Those in search of vinous novelties should try the sparkling *vinho verde*, 'green wine', which is very young wine, both red and white, from the north. There are many who prefer it to champagne. It makes a refreshing accompaniment to sea food. Its lightness can be deceptive, for it is rather potent; tired tourists who need to quench their thirst with a long, cool drink should not be tempted to try it if they want to do any more sightseeing that day. *Vinho verde* does not travel well and is rarely exported. In fact it is hardly amenable to transport inside Portugal itself, and that is why it is at its best in the north.

Portugal has no famous brandies or liqueurs, but what there are are agreeably cheap. Coffee and a glass of Macieira for two will cost less than half a crown.

*　　　*　　　*

Those visitors who do not care for wine – and those who are paying the price of caring for it too much – will find the wide variety of mineral waters both pleasant and salutary. Portugal is extraordinarily rich in thermal waters, and spas are as numerous as in Bohemia. *Pedras Salgadas*, one of the most popular of these waters, seems to be helpful in liver and digestive troubles.

The tourist will find that the *pastelaria*, 'pastry-shop', and *casa de chá*, 'tea-shop', provide a fascinating array of sweetmeats. There are many different kinds of rich, sweet cakes. But sweets as we know them hardly exist, although in Lisbon there is plenty of confectionery imported from Britain. The Portuguese go in more for crystallized fruits. Of the great variety of these, the most famous are the wonderful Elvas plums, which are exported all over the world.

Portuguese coffee, brought from the African colonies, is of splendid quality and very cheap. A small black coffee or *garoto* (literally, 'urchin') costs fourpence halfpenny, including tip! British visitors whose Continental holidays are marred because they can never get a decent cup of afternoon tea will find that it is available everywhere in

Portugal without any trouble at all. Simply ask for *chá forte e leite frio*, 'strong tea and cold milk', and instead of the usual weak brew, generally drunk without milk, you will be brought a pot of perfectly drinkable tea – which is more than one can say of central London in this Espresso age.

PART TWO

VI

Salazar and his régime

The week we arrived in Portugal 2,000 guests – said to have included the thousand richest men in the land – attended a banquet to mark the official opening of the Ritz Hotel in Lisbon. With 350 rooms on ten floors and a staff of 600, this hotel, built at a reputed cost of 200,000 *contos* (£2,500,000) and decorated by forty-one sculptors, painters and interior decorators, is the most modern and luxurious in Europe. The main speech at the banquet was made by a gentleman called Dr Manuel de Queirós Pereira, the chairman of the administrative council of the firm that built the hotel. Dr Pereira, who, needless to say, is a very rich man indeed, gave the guests his account of how the Ritz came to be and how he happened to be associated with it.

He had heard, he said, that none other than Portugal's Prime Minister, Dr Salazar, had asked a certain big banker if there did not exist 'a group of Portuguese capable of endowing the city with a large luxury hotel'. This banker had thereupon approached Dr Pereira and told him of these words that had fallen from the lips of the Portuguese dictator. Dr Pereira went on:

My devotion to his figure, and the gratitude which as a Portuguese I owe to his Work, obliged me to agree without hesitation . . . It was not in a commercial spirit that I entered upon this enterprise; it was to fulfil a duty, the duty to collaborate, as fully as I could, with the Public Man to whom we owe an era of thirty years of Peace, work and National growth. As far as the hotel is concerned, it was built because Salazar wished it.

And the headline that the *Diário de Notícias* gave these confessions was: 'The hotel was built because Salazar wished it.'

Now everyone in Portugal knows perfectly well that the building of Lisbon's Ritz Hotel was in fact a very profitable venture, and that the necessary capital was furnished by the biggest financiers in the country. There is no doubt that the hotel was built much more cheaply than any similar project would be in a country where workers are free to engage in collective bargaining. Not only was the manual labour cheap: the fees paid to the forty-one artists struck foreign architects visiting Portugal as shockingly low. Here for nine million Portuguese was one more demonstration of the way the rich among them provide themselves, at a much lower cost than they would have to meet anywhere else, with a standard of living unequalled in Europe.

But the high financiers of Portugal try to draw a veil over their profit-making. The veil is labelled 'Salazar'. The Public Man is famous for his iron rectitude, for his insistence on probity and on what a recent panegyric in *The Times* called 'such quiet virtues as thrift, temperance and assiduity'. While he preaches these quiet virtues, the rich men whose instrument he is practise with the utmost assiduity a few very quiet, and quietly lucrative, virtues of their own. And lest anyone suggest that the capital for such a non-productive enterprise as a lavish luxury hotel might have been better employed, dictator Salazar is neatly given a credit-line.

Who is Salazar? What does he stand for? And how has he managed to cling on to power for so long in a country with republican traditions, a country where the majority of the population is, to some degree or other, against him? To answer these questions we have to look at the history of Portugal before the Public Man came on the scene.

How Salazar came to power

Until 1910 Portugal was ruled, officially, by kings. In practice the kings had been handing over their power to various dictators, as did King Carlos to a dictator called João Franco (no relation to the present dictator of Spain). The father of Dom Carlos, Dom Luís, preferred to concentrate on a translation of Shakespeare that is said to be the best in the language; the son had a passion for oceanography, and went out in his yacht studying the habits of tuna fish while Franco suspended Parliament and governed by decree. Dom Carlos was assassinated in February 1908 together with his elder son Dom Luís Filipe.

All through the nineteenth century, under the influence of the French revolution, liberal ideas had been gaining ground among the middle class, and there was fierce strife between the Liberals, who wanted a constitutional monarchy on British lines, and the absolutists. From the seventies onwards there was also a steady growth of support for republicanism. A network of republican clubs sprang up throughout the country, at which men discussed how the future republic would work. Many of the more radical among them were influenced by the writings of Comte and Proudhon. In 1891 there was a republican uprising in Oporto, but it was suppressed. From then on the monarchy was propped up by force alone; and when on 5 October 1910, after some skirmishes in the Lisbon streets, King Manuel II was picked up by the royal yacht *Amélia* at the little port of Ericeira[1] and the green and red republican flag broke from the public buildings, this was but the formal proclamation of a republic that had long existed in men's minds. There had been no social revolution. Political power had passed, almost without bloodshed, into the hands of the professional classes and the intellectuals.

For the most part young, and possessing that romantic simple-mindedness that is the most endearing but least practical form of successful revolutionists' false consciousness of the world, the leaders of the new régime found themselves whirling in a maelstrom of problems. The crisis – economic, social and political – was not of their making. But they were not equipped to cope with it. 'Politically and economically,' writes one authority, the republic 'started with so severe a handicap that it never had a chance.'[2]

Portugal had never recovered from the Peninsular War, in which she was invaded three times and suffered large-scale destruction. The loss of Brazil in 1822 was a body-blow to her economy. She lacked the large armed forces necessary to keep a huge overseas empire together. She lacked so much as the rudiments of the home industry that might have compensated for the loss of her gold and coffee. Nor could the exploitation of Mozambique and Angola do very much very quickly to mend matters. By 1910 the national finances were in a disastrous state. The republic inherited a floating debt of 83,000 *contos* (at that time approximately £16 million) and a consolidated debt of 608,000 *contos* (about £120 million), 210,000 *contos* of which was foreign debt. Only twice were budget surpluses achieved under the republic, in 1912–13 and 1913–14.

---

[1] The king took refuge in Gibraltar, from where he was brought to England in the royal yacht of King George V. 'My departure must in no way be taken as an act of abdication,' he said in his parting message.

[2] J. B. Trend, *Portugal* (1957), p. 185.

Throughout the republic's sixteen years there was a constant succession of monarchist uprisings and counter-revolutionary plots, most of them led by Henrique Paiva Couceiro, a former governor of Angola, and other professional soldiers who had gained valuable experience in subduing the peoples of Mozambique and Angola with fire and sword, and who now ventured to practise in their own country the techniques of fire and conquest they had learned in Africa. Hardly a year passed without at least one such uprising, many of which were prepared in Spain with the full knowledge of the Spanish government. The republican leaders lacked the necessary firmness and resolution in dealing with these 'Africans' and their friends. They believed in not antagonizing their monarchist enemies, in being fair to them, converting them to better ways and disarming them by giving them jobs. On the other hand, they believed in governing not merely without the workers but against them. Though they recognized the right to strike, one of their first acts was to smash a strike in Lisbon in January 1912, which they did by declaring martial law, occupying the headquarters of the National Workers' Union and arresting over 1,000 workers. 'This is the bread the republic gives us to gnaw,' shouted a working-class woman holding up an apronful of stones, as the police dragged her away. The harsh treatment to which the sailors were subjected led to a naval mutiny in October 1919 which was put down without ceremony – though it was the ordinary sailors and soldiers on whom the republican leaders had relied in 1915 to turn out General Pimenta de Castro when he established a brief dictatorship. Altogether there were 158 general strikes under the republic.

Yet even at the same time as they refused to concede the demands of the poor the republican leaders did not hesitate to implement long-standing petty *bourgeois* democratic demands, often in a dramatic and demonstrative fashion, even when this meant challenging the Church and inflaming reactionary prejudices at home and abroad. In 1912 they expelled from the country the Archbishops of Portalegre and Braga. (Prime Minister Afonso Costa even declared that in two generations he would wipe out religion.) They secularized marriage, made divorce possible, provided help for unmarried mothers and gave illegitimate children the right to their father's name and a share in the inheritance. They abolished aristocratic titles, reformed the universities of Lisbon and Oporto and gave legal protection to tenants.

Portugal's entry into the first world war on the side of Britain, France and Russia, and her heavy losses on the western front and in east Africa, made the situation at home still worse.[1] Portuguese participation in the war was not very popular at home, and it became still less popular when food ran short, prices began to soar and speculators and profiteers started to line their pockets. The republicans had already split into a radical wing, known as the democrats, and a 'moderate' minority with support among the army officers. For a year the country was ruled by Major Sidónio Pais, leader of a successful *coup d'État* which arrested Afonso Costa, and which enjoyed the support of the 'moderate' republicans. There were democratic risings against Pais at Coimbra and Évora, and on 14 December 1918 he was assassinated. In 1919 there were four governments, and a monarchist uprising under Paiva Couceiro which for a time occupied Oporto, Braga, Viseu, Coimbra and Aveiro. In 1920 there were nine governments, one of which lasted for six days and another for twenty-four hours. In 1921 there were five. On 19 October 1921, in another unsuccessful *coup d'État*, five public men were assassinated, including Prime Minister António Granjo and Machado dos Santos, one of the leaders of the 1910 revolution. Between the March and the July of 1925 – a year in which there were five governments – military groups staged three more unsuccessful *coups*.[2]

In all, from 1910 to 1926, Portugal had eight presidents and forty-four ministries – the first government lasting less than ten weeks and the longest little more than a year – and witnessed twenty-four revolts and uprisings; while from 1920 to 1925, according to official police records, 325 bombs burst in the streets of Lisbon. Meanwhile the cost of living increased 25-fold and the currency fell to one thirty-third of its gold value. The *escudo* was worth 4s 5d in 1891, 3s 9½d in 1913, twopence halfpenny in 1922 and less than twopence in 1925. These are the statistics of a country in chaos.

There was in Portugal at that time not a single social class which was homogeneous and which knew with some degree of clarity what its needs were and how they could be fulfilled. In particular the two social forces which might have propounded their own specific solutions

---

[1] Before entering the war the Portuguese government lent the British 20,000 small arms and a destroyer. In February 1916 it complied with a British request that seventy-two German ships interned in Lisbon and other ports be seized; this act precipitated a German declaration of war the following month.

[2] When supporters of Salazar now point to the disorder that was prevalent under the republic they omit to add that most of the plots were organized by the very persons who were to bring Salazar to power: in other words, Salazar's régime is the fruit of the last of these plots – the successful one.

were too undeveloped, and lacked the cohesion and leadership necessary for the elaboration of political programmes and strategies. For there was no large-scale industry and, in consequence, neither a strong and stable big *bourgeoisie* nor a mature working class. Either, if organized, might have hoped to lead its country forward with some prospect of economic and social progress. Despite frequent strikes, the Portuguese workers had little real awareness of their class position, and the prevalence of anarchist tendencies among those who were militant showed that their Labour movement was far from ready to lead Portugal along a socialist road out of the crisis.

This was the scene when there shuffled on to the stage a naval commander, Joaquim Mendes Cabeçadas, and a general, Manuel de Oliveira Gomes da Costa, another veteran of the African campaigns and a former commander of the Portuguese expeditionary force in Flanders. In May 1926 – joined at the last moment by a second general, António Óscar de Fragoso Carmona, who was sponsored by the Church – these officers staged a march on Lisbon not unlike Mussolini's march on Rome four years before, forced the resignation of President Bernardino Machado, and established a military dictatorship which looked for support to those people who most desperately desired social peace: the traders of all kinds, from small shopkeepers to bankers; the small capitalists; the civil servants, who had grown tired of low salaries; and the Church – though the latter's support was at first cautious. The triumvirate soon became a diumvirate, for within a couple of weeks Cabeçadas had fallen out with his colleagues. Three weeks later Carmona quarrelled with Gomes da Costa, exiled him to the Azores – and promoted him to the rank of field marshal.

One of the factors leading to the *coup* was the dispute over the renewal of an agreement granting a monopoly in tobacco production to two large firms that between them accounted for the whole of this production throughout the Portuguese empire. This agreement was due to expire in the spring of 1926, and Parliament was debating its renewal. General Carmona had promised the tobacco interests a renewal of their monopoly.

The man Carmona asked to fill the post of Finance Minister was a little-known 'Professor of Economic and Financial Sciences' at Coimbra university; the curriculum shows that this subject corresponded rather to chartered accountancy than to what we understand by economics. António de Oliveira Salazar was thirty-seven. Displaying both arrogance and foresight, he played hard to get. Within a week of Carmona's offer he had rejected it because the post did not carry wide enough powers. He expressed his refusal in the lapidary phrase: 'I shall return to my university and wait', anticipating de Gaulle by almost a third of a century.

He did not have to wait long. The Carmona régime had its hands full. At home, it suppressed several attempts by the overthrown democrats to oust it. Abroad, it tried to get a loan of £12 million from the League of Nations. After sending a commission to Portugal the League said it would grant the loan only if Portugal's finances were submitted to some form of international control. This condition was indignantly rejected as an insult to the national pride. Then Salazar was again invited to become Finance Minister. This time the military clique accepted his terms, and he their offer. And his terms were nothing short of control of the entire machinery of government. He was to lay down what each government department was to spend, and could veto any proposed increases in expenditure.

On 27 April 1928, the day he assumed office, Salazar gave an interview consisting of a single sentence to the Catholic newspaper *Novidades*. 'Tell the Catholics,' he said, 'that the sacrifice I have made gives me the right to expect that they, of all Portuguese, will be the first to make the sacrifices I may ask of them, and the last to ask for favours which I cannot grant.' He made his intention of brooking no opposition to his plans still clearer when he ended his first official speech with the words: 'I know quite well what I want and where I am going . . . For the rest, let the country study, let it suggest, let it object, and let it discuss, but when the time comes for me to give orders I shall expect it to obey.'[1]

The sacrifices were soon imposed. Salazar used his powers to slash wages and government expenditure and raise taxes. In his first budget 200,000 *contos* of new taxes were levied. Within five years he had made himself Minister of Colonies and then Prime Minister and introduced sweeping constitutional changes, aimed at transforming Portugal into an '*Estado Novo*', a 'New State', along the lines of Mussolini's Italy. The new Constitution was railroaded through in a national plebiscite on 19 March 1933, by the devastatingly simple expedients of not letting more than a handful of people vote 'No' and counting all but

---

[1] 'Conditions of My Acceptance of the Ministry of Finance', Dr António de Oliveira Salazar, *Doctrine and Action: Internal and Foreign Policy of the New Portugal 1928–1939* (trans. Robert Edgar Broughton, 1939), p. 45.

a small number of abstentions as 'Yes' votes.[1] The main sacrifice
Salazar demanded of the Portuguese people was their liberty.

The man and his ideas

Fifty years ago four young students at Coimbra university dreamed
that one day they would be the rulers of Portugal. They were members
of the Right-wing *Centro Académico da Democracia Cristã*, and they
used to meet regularly at its Coimbra headquarters; they called the
room they met in '*Assalto a Portugal*', which might be translated as
'Operation Portugal'.

Half a century later the four are still firm friends. And, by and large,
their dream has come true. Manuel Gonçalves Cerejeira is Cardinal
Patriarch of Lisbon; Fernando dos Santos Costa was till August 1958
Minister of Defence; Mário de Figueiredo is Leader of the National
Assembly and president of the National Council of Education; and
Salazar is dictator of Portugal.

Salazar's father is variously described to various audiences as a
peasant, a poor country schoolteacher and an innkeeper in the village
of Vimieiro. Whatever his calling was, he wanted his son to become
a priest. But young António, though deeply religious, preferred the
atmosphere of the university to that of the Church. It was not a
question of choosing the rough and tumble of the real world in preference to the dedicated aloofness of the priesthood. For a man of
Salazar's temperament it was a choice between two different kinds of
cloistered calm.

For Salazar needs, not merely reasonable privacy, but seclusion.
Some say he lives quite alone in his house with its forbidding high
walls, just behind the Palace of the National Assembly; others that
he has a housekeeper who lives there too, and that she is none other
than the *tricana* – the Coimbra woman – who was his companion in
his student days. If this is true it shows how deep is his respect for
tradition, for most students at Coimbra university in his day used to
allow their *tricanas* a small pension after they graduated and went down.
Those who insist that Salazar is an ascetic say he neither drinks
alcohol nor smokes tobacco.

An unusual Portuguese? In his provincialism and essential small-
mindedness the dictator may share some of the characteristics of some

---

[1] The official figures were: for the Constitution, 580,379; against, 5,405; abstentions,
11,528.

of his countrymen of his own generation; but in his coldness and vanity he is far from being typical of them. This vanity, though he does his best to hide it under a show of modesty, is his most striking trait. His long and flowery speeches, with their pompous, rolling periods and laboured cadences that smell of the lamp, are obviously composed with an eye to re-publication in successive volumes. Salazar is a man who feels very keenly his place in history. His most poignant regret is that he cannot know the verdict that future historians will pass upon the Public Man and his Work. But he is fairly certain that they will share his own intense conviction that he alone has visualized all the problems clearly, knows the right solutions and possesses the ability, energy and will to put them into effect. He sees himself in fact as a national saviour – as a stern, wise father without whose admonitions and chastisements the family would get into debt, the children would be always quarrelling and all the food in the larder would be gobbled up in one meal.

But even more disagreeable than the paternalism which suffuses these speeches is the speaker's intense, egocentric pride. He is so proud that he shrinks from contact with people who might eclipse him. Except for occasional meetings with Franco at Corunna or Seville or Ciudad Rodrigo, none as much as a hundred miles across the Spanish frontier, he has never been out of Portugal since taking office. When the NATO Prime Ministers met in Paris in December 1957 Salazar was the only one who did not attend in person; he sent the Minister of the Presidency, Marcelo Caetano, to represent him. A Portuguese friend quoted to us the judgement of the French philosopher Maine de Biran in his *Journal intime*: 'If a man is distressed by his weakness, if he hates those who surpass him and seeks solitude only to avoid the humiliation of comparison, he is not humble but full of pride.'

'And that,' said our friend, 'sums up Salazar.'

The dictator has a very highly developed sense of how people should behave, and does not hesitate to intervene in the personal lives of his supporters, imposing decorum and formality whenever standards of behaviour seem to him to be slipping. It is said that a certain young man was offered a ministerial post and went to see Salazar, who, after the interview, conducted him to the door and handed him a hat.

'But this isn't mine,' said the young man. 'I don't wear a hat.'

'No, you don't,' replied the dictator. 'But from now on you are going to.'

And from then on he did.

On another occasion, so the story goes, Salazar intervened to prevent the wife of one of his Ministers from leaving her husband. The woman concerned was one of the most beautiful adornments of Portuguese High Society, and a member of a very rich and very influential family. Her husband was also rich – rich enough to enjoy the companionship of a number of mistresses, a form of recreation to which the wife objected, though it is far from uncommon among Portugal's upper classes. Salazar is said to have sent for her and instructed her to remain with her husband, since a separation would be injurious to the morale of the régime. And his instruction was obeyed.

Salazar has never made any secret of his profoundly reactionary views. He is a sworn enemy, not merely of communism, but of progress, of parliamentary government, of democracy, equality and universal suffrage. 'We do not want . . . to subordinate everything to material progress,' he says. 'We want to take the right steps in the right sequence.' A 'statesmanlike' sentiment; until you reflect that the majority of his countrymen live in grinding poverty, and that 'material progress' in the context of present-day Portugal means first and foremost alleviating an enormous amount of human distress.

For the masses of downtrodden Portuguese their Public Man has nothing but contempt mingled with hatred and fear. Asked to explain why he never made any appeal to the people, he replied: 'Our régime is popular, but it is not a government of the masses, being neither influenced nor directed by them. These good people who cheer me one day may rise in rebellion next day.' Elected to the National Assembly in 1921, he went to one meeting of it and never turned up again. He declares that democracy is an outworn creed. 'The truth is,' he says, 'that I *am* profoundly anti-parliamentary.' But he is realistic about it. As long as the majority of Portuguese feel sentimental, as he would put it, about their National Assembly, then he is prepared to tolerate it as a necessary evil; to try to abolish it would not be worth while. But universal suffrage? Equality? He told a French journalist in September 1958:

I do not believe in universal suffrage, because the individual vote does not take into account human differentiation. I do not believe in equality but in hierarchy. Men, in my opinion, should be equal before the law, but I believe it dangerous to attribute to all the same political rights.[1]

[1] These quotations come from *The Times*, 21 May 1959; *Observer*, 29 August 1954; António Ferro, *Salazar: Portugal and her Leader* (trans. H. de Barros Gomes and John Gibbons, 1939), p. 243; and *Figaro*, 3 September 1958.

The exact relationship, political and ideological, between Salazar and the fascist dictators of Italy, Germany and Spain is a vexed question, about which it is easier to be dogmatic than accurate. One perennial failing of the anti-Salazar opposition in Portugal is a tendency to spoil a good case by exaggerating it. Thus it is said that in the thirties Salazar kept a picture of Mussolini on his desk. Even if this is true we do not see that it is a significant criterion for judging his régime and its shortcomings.

Whatever Salazar's feelings for Mussolini and Hitler as individuals may have been, all three men shared essential features of the same ideology; and it is fairly clear that at the beginning of the second world war Salazar wanted the Axis powers to win and that he approved of the German attack on Russia. He permitted, and probably encouraged, Portuguese volunteers to join the Blue Division that Franco sent to fight alongside of Hitler's troops on the eastern front. But as it became evident that an Axis victory was not going to happen Salazar gradually and discreetly changed sides, at the same time toning down some of the more obviously near-Nazi aspects of his régime in preparation for passing it off as a good, clean-limbed, anti-communist 'western democracy' and candidate for membership of NATO. The turning-point was perhaps the granting of air and naval bases in the Azores to Britain in October 1943, in exchange for which a secret agreement is supposed to have been signed pledging Britain to support Portugal's claims to sovereignty in her overseas territories. Nevertheless on 3 May 1945 the Portuguese government decreed that all official flags would be flown at half-mast until noon on 4 May, in mourning for the death of Adolf Hitler.

Relations with Japan were somewhat different from relations with the other Axis powers. In November 1941 Salazar accepted a British offer of help in the event of a Japanese attack on Timor; yet he soon made a strong protest when the Dutch actually sent troops to Dili to prevent a Japanese landing. (It was stated in Sydney that the Portuguese forces on the island consisted of one company of 'native' troops armed with old rifles and four old machine-guns.) In January 1942 a thousand Portuguese troops set sail from Lourenço Marques to defend the colony. One of Salazar's main complaints when the Japanese landed was that whereas under Portuguese administration the 'natives' had lived happily and peacefully, under the Japanese there were risings. The only Portuguese resistance to the Japanese came from political deportees, who waged guerrilla warfare against them until Australian naval units took the deportees off the island.[1] Salazar's protests were feeble enough: diplomatic relations were never broken off, and a Japanese legation remained in Lisbon throughout the war. Compare Salazar's belligerent attitude towards India over the Goa case, though India has not invaded Goa.

As far as Salazar's part in the Spanish civil war is concerned the picture is quite clear. The conspiracy of the insurgent generals was hatched in Estoril, the fashionable and expensive seaside resort half an hour to the west of Lisbon. General José Sanjurjo, who was to have led the uprising, was killed in an aeroplane crash at nearby Cascais while taking off to join the fascist rebels. During the civil war Franco was allowed to operate a 'black embassy' in Lisbon's Aviz Hotel. German air force officers trained in Portugal for service under Franco. In the words of the Salazarist turned oppositionist Captain Fernando Queiroga:

> Portugal was the headquarters of Spanish reaction. Trains left daily loaded with war material for Franco's men. *Rádio Clube Português* relayed military messages sent from Burgos to Seville in the first phase of the civil war. An expeditionary force staffed with officers and sergeants of the army, the sadly celebrated *viriatos* [named after Viriatus, who led the Lusitanians' resistance to Rome in the second century B.C.], left for Spain, operating at the side of Italian divisions and the German expeditionary force.[2]

Hitler's chargé d'affaires in Portugal reported that when *matériel* for Franco arrived in Lisbon on the German steamships *Kamerun* and *Wigbert* it was 'sent on most smoothly', since 'Prime Minister Salazar removed all difficulties within a very short time by his personal initiative and *personal* handling of details'. Salazar, 'by his authoritarian influence . . . made the entire Portuguese Press serve the cause of propaganda for the Spanish nationalist revolution. . . . He even permitted a munitions shipment of the [Franco] revolutionaries *en route* from Seville to Burgos to pass through Portuguese territory . . . seeing to it that the shipment was expedited as much as possible.'

[1] This little-known episode of the second world war is fully described by Carlos Cal Brandão in his *Funo (Guerra em Timor)* (Oporto, 1953). The author is a lawyer who was in exile on Timor for twelve years and was rescued by the Australian navy. He served with the Australian army and returned to Portugal at the end of the war.

[2] Fernando Queiroga, *Portugal Oprimido (Subsídios para a História do Fascismo em Portugal)* (Rio de Janeiro, 1958), p. 208. Captain Queiroga goes on to make the claim that 'Portuguese casualties in Spain were greater than those we suffered when we fought on the side of the Allies in the first world war'. Portugal in fact lost 8,367 men in the first world war; about 6,000 of the *viriatos* were killed.

Nicolás Franco, the General's brother, was established in Lisbon under the cover-name of Aurélio Fernando Aguilar, to act as procurements supervisor for the Spanish fascists.[1]

As early as December 1937 the Portuguese government appointed an official Agent to represent it in Franco territory, and Franco appointed an Agent in Lisbon. Five months later Portugal formally recognized Franco's government in Burgos as the government of Spain. When the civil war was coming to an end Spanish republican refugees in Portugal were rounded up and sent back to Spain, to be drafted into forced labour camps or shot. 'The horrible slaughter at Badajoz is classic,' writes the then American ambassador in Madrid. 'When large numbers escaped to Portugal, they were driven back to their death.'[2] It is said in Portugal that these refugees included many Portuguese who had been fighting on the side of the Spanish republic. And when Franco's victory was sealed, Salazar lost no time in concluding a treaty of friendship and non-aggression with the victor, which was signed in Lisbon in March 1939. Two years later General Count Jordana, the Spanish Foreign Minister, visited Portugal, announced the formation of an 'Iberian Bloc', and was presented with the Order of the Tower and the Sword.

*   *   *

How has a man like Salazar managed to hold power for so long? The fundamental reason, we are convinced, is the weakness and disunity of his opponents, which we shall discuss later. But part of the answer certainly lies in his skill in manipulating people so that likely rivals or dissenters or enemies are gradually manœuvred into isolation. Only the lack of a clerical collar distinguishes him from the Jesuits who schooled him. He is subtle, wily and treacherous. He knows how to bide his time. He does not clash with the man he has marked down until he is quite ready to deal with him. And he has always been able to keep on his side that indispensable arm the secret police, plus part at least of the army, plus the Church – though latterly these last two props of Salazarism seem to have been proving rather shaky.

[1] *Germany and the Spanish Civil War 1936–1939* (Documents on German Foreign Policy 1918–1945, series D, vol. iii, HMSO, 1951), pp. 53, 55, 26. (Emphasis in the original.)
[2] Claude Bowers, *My Mission to Spain* (1954), p. 308. Trend comments: 'This, if correctly reported, is a blot on the new Portugal' (Trend, *op. cit.* p. 192).

The corporate State

On 20 March 1959, nine months after the septennial presidential election, President Américo Tomás sent a number of constitutional changes to the National Assembly. Some of these changes were quite unimportant. For instance the National Assembly itself would in future have 130 members, not 120. But since the government is responsible to the President, not to the National Assembly; since according to article 97 of the Constitution members of the National Assembly cannot initiate legislation affecting either revenue or expenditure; since the National Assembly sits for only three months in the year; since during the other nine months Salazar legislates by decree-laws that do not need to be confirmed by the National Assembly; and since the legality of any ordinance promulgated by the President cannot be challenged in any court – there was nothing in this change for anyone to become very excited about.

The one change in the Constitution that did show which way the wind was blowing provided that the election of the President of the Republic, hitherto by direct vote, would in future be carried out by a joint session of the National Assembly and a body called the Corporative Chamber (which consists of representatives of local authorities and of industrial, commercial, cultural and religious bodies, and which has no legislative power, though Bills are submitted to it for its opinion).

This alteration, already canvassed by Salazar in a speech in Lisbon on 1 July 1958, was a direct result of the presidential election, which had given the dictator and his supporters a rather disagreeable shock. Not merely had the opposition candidate secured a substantial minority vote, despite the disfranchisement of over half the population through illiteracy and poverty, the seizure of opposition voting slips and the arrest of opposition leaders during the campaign. The campaign itself had been marked by three weeks of tremendous public excitement, more intense than at any time since Salazar's accession to power. People came on to the streets to demonstrate; stones were thrown at the police; shots were fired, and a number of people, both demonstrators and police, were injured.

In typical Portuguese fashion everyone went back to work as usual after the period of unrest, despite the repressive measures that were taken and the lies that were told about the demonstrations. It was as if a safety valve had been opened and shut again.[1] Nevertheless Salazar was clearly shaken and angry. He made his state of mind quite evident in his 1 July speech. He was not prepared to risk any more public expressions of discontent. If that was where elections led, then clearly elections must stop. Too many people had shown themselves prepared to listen to and follow the first adventurer who came along. The office of President was so important that its occupant must be chosen by responsible and educated people – an electoral college of not more than 500 electors, instead of what had hitherto passed for universal suffrage (i.e., suffrage which in practice was restricted to about one tenth of the population).[2]

This was the first important change in the mechanism of the corporate State since its formal establishment in 1933 – and it was not a step towards liberalization but a step backwards, away from universal suffrage, away from democracy, towards Salazar's ideal 'catedratocracia', or aristocracy of dons.

The corporate State is based theoretically upon the ideas contained in the famous encyclical of Pope Leo XIII, 'Rerum Novarum' (1891), and its successor, Pius XI's 'Quadragesimo Anno' (1931). As it impinges on the daily life of the Portuguese people it is a curious blend of latter-day feudalism, paternalism, and public assistance doled out grudgingly and erratically to the sick and infirm. There are three main types of organization. The *sindicatos* (it is an error to translate this as 'trade unions' – trade unions as we understand them are illegal) are organizations of workers divided according to industries. The *grémios*, or 'guilds', are organizations of 'producers', by which term are meant the employers. And there are three *ordens*, or 'orders', of doctors, lawyers and engineers. Two categories are not covered by this structure: civil servants and self-employed persons, including peasants. But for everybody else membership of his appropriate *sindicato*, *grémio* or *ordem* is compulsory.

The government itself provides no medical or unemployment benefit. This comes through the corporative network. The unit which gives such help is called the *Caixa de Previdência*, roughly translatable as 'welfare fund'. Each *sindicato*, *grémio* and *ordem* has its own fund, separate from but associated with it. Those earning up to 1,000 *escudos*

---

[1] The 1958 presidential election is discussed in greater detail below, pp. 187–90.
[2] The official English translation of this speech appears in *Portugal: An Informative Review* (Lisbon: Secretariado Nacional da Informação), 2nd year, no. 4, pp. 189–200, July-August 1958.

a month pay two and half *escudos* to their organization and there are higher payments for those earning more. In addition everyone pays another five per cent of his earnings to the appropriate *Caixa de Previdência* as a form of health insurance, plus one-half of one per cent as a form of unemployment insurance. The employers also contribute to this fund. But the amounts paid out in sick pay and unemployment pay are very small indeed.

The *sindicatos* proper are supposed to protect the interests of their members against the employers. But in practice they do not do so. Nor could government-sponsored and government-run workers' organizations, whose officers are appointed from above, not elected, do more than make this empty claim, in a country where strikes are forbidden by law. At most, the activities of the *sindicatos* amount to no more than vocational training and courses in various cultural subjects for their members.

Civil servants and self-employed persons in the towns pay their contributions to an independent network of *Caixas de Previdência*. For the peasants – who constitute upwards of sixty per cent of the population and who yet fall wholly outside the corporative scheme! – there exist, on paper, bodies known as *casas do povo* ('houses of the people'), to which contributions are paid and from which benefits are drawn. But in practice these glorified benevolent societies do not work well. In most places, in fact, they hardly exist at all.

The official myth is that the *sindicatos*, *grémios* and *ordens* all arise spontaneously and naturally as a kind of social contract entered into by the people concerned. The government, it is claimed, has nothing to do with it. However, in case a particular *grémio* might have ideas about its industry which are not in line with the government's general policy, there exist in some industries councils for economic co-ordination, known as *juntas nacionais*, which are outside the corporative scheme of things, and whose existence is seen by some supporters of corporativism as evidence that the corporative system is not working properly.[1]

Quite apart from the civil service, the corporative system has created a vast bureaucracy in the officials of the various organizations, who have an interest in the maintenance of Salazarism, and who provide it with a substantial base.

All this is how the corporative State tries to gather into its fold

[1] In 1958 a clash between a *grémio* and a *junta* led to the disappearance of olive oil from the market for a time.

what is called the 'Portuguese family' – the poor relations being the peasants. But behind this creaky apparatus of social persuasion and pacification there looms an equally elaborate and rather more efficient apparatus of social coercion: the six armed forces which buttress the Salazar régime and stand in varying degrees of readiness to crush any attempt to overthrow it.

First there is the army, mainly composed of career officers and conscripts. The latter, many of whom are illiterate, serve for eighteen months at $4\frac{1}{2}d$ a day, are liable to immediate recall for twenty-five years thereafter and have to report for several weeks' training each year until the age of forty-five. No Portuguese between the ages of eighteen and forty-five may leave the country unless his military papers are in order.

University students, and others who have completed their secondary education, do their military service as officer cadets. This has led to a curious anomaly. Under a Salazar law coloured people, including *assimilados* (i.e., colonial-born coloured people with full citizenship rights), whether Indians or Africans, cannot serve as officers in the Portuguese army. And so coloured people who are university students or have completed their secondary education do not do any military service at all, since they would be entitled to serve automatically as officer cadets. It is no secret that this has not aroused many protests from the young men concerned.

Anyone whose education entitles him to be an officer, but who has been sentenced for a political offence, must serve in the ranks and often has to do so in a penal battalion. Since such service is very hard it is thought to deter students from engaging in oppositionist activity, as well as helping to keep opponents of Salazar out of commanding positions. But the régime has a more subtle device for promoting these ends. No officer may marry a woman who is not either a university graduate or the possessor of a dowry of at least 70 *contos* (£875). This rule was made by Salazar to tie the army more closely to the richer classes and to weaken its democratic traditions, which date back to the nineteenth century: even under the monarchy it was perfectly possible for the son of a sergeant of humble origins to go to a military academy, pass out as an officer and, despite his well-known republican views, become one of the king's adjutants.

There is another important restriction on the marriage of army officers. Though civil marriage is permitted to civilians, officers are allowed to marry only in the Catholic Church. Now Church marriages, according to a provision of the Concordat signed with the Pope in May 1940, are intangible even if the parties no longer wish to be Catholics (though the State does maintain the right to license divorce in certain conditions). So an officer can only marry a woman who is a Catholic, and it is practically impossible for them to be divorced. The intention presumably was to tie the higher echelons of the army more closely to the Church.

How far Salazar has been successful in altering the social composition and ideology of the officer corps is an open question.

Salazar's second armed force is the navy, which is run on more or less British lines, even down to the uniforms of officers and ratings. The navy has even more revolutionary traditions than the army, but it is not clear how far these traditions are alive. The fact that the President of the Republic is an admiral, while his opponent in the 1958 election was a general, might suggest that there may be less discontent among naval officers than among their opposite numbers in the army.

Thirdly, there are the civil police, who wear grey uniforms, carry pistols, and exercise the usual functions of civil police anywhere. They do not as a rule deal with political offences.

The fourth armed force at Salazar's disposal is the blue-uniformed National Republican Guard, whose title is a curious instance of the maintenance of republican nomenclature under the corporate State. The content has been destroyed, but the forms persist and, indeed, prove very useful to the régime. The National Republican Guard was formed under the republic as a special force to protect the republic's existence and interests against counter-revolutionary activities. Today it is an armed police force, not unlike the French *gendarmerie*, living in barracks and disposing of heavier weapons – tear-gas, for instance – than the civil police possess. It is called out to deal with strikes, demonstrations and civil disturbances.

Fifthly, there is the Portuguese Legion, Salazar's corps of green-shirts. This paramilitary organization was formed two months after the outbreak of the Spanish civil war, as a 'patriotic organization of Portuguese manhood' to protect the corporate State against communism, just as the National Republican Guard had been formed at an earlier period to defend the republic. Its members are volunteers between the ages of eighteen and fifty, fanatical supporters of the régime, who drill and parade and practise shooting in their spare time, under the command of retired army and naval officers. They might be described as a kind of Salazarist SA. It is interesting to note that the greenshirts used the fascist salute of Hitler and Mussolini until the latter part of the second world war – and that some of them still use a modified form of it. The Legion has a naval wing, the *Brigada Naval*.

Lastly, there is the notorious PIDE (*Polícia Internacional e de Defesa do Estado*), the ubiquitous and dreaded secret police, the Portuguese equivalent of the German Gestapo and the Hungarian AVH. Salazar's secret police deserves a section to itself.[1]

These six armed forces have been placed in what seems to us their ascending order of reliability and their descending order of suscepti-bility to popular influence. That is to say, the army is the least remote from the ordinary people, and thanks to this and its traditions and the apparent existence of some measure of dissatisfaction and some degree of monarchist sympathy among its officers, it must be accounted the least reliable of Salazar's military props. The PIDE, at the other end of the scale, is the most remote from the ordinary people; it exists, among other things, as a thought police, to prevent the dissemination of anti-Salazar sentiments; and it is clearly the most reliable instrument at Salazar's disposal.

To the social and military aspects of the corporate State must be added a third: the political aspect. There are two political organiza-tions which play some part, though of late perhaps a diminishing one, in educating, moulding and influencing its citizens. These are the National Union and the Portuguese Youth.

The National Union, founded in 1930, is the sole political party allowed to exist (leaving out of account the *Causa Monárquica*, which is scarcely a party as yet). Its official organ, the *Diário da Manhã*, is generally considered the most vulgar and yellow newspaper in Portu-gal. During the second world war there were people who wanted to demonstrate in favour of the Allies; the National Union thereupon staged what it termed 'anti-communist demonstrations'. These were not openly pro-Axis, but in the context they could be interpreted only in that way. Whenever there is an election to the National Assembly the National Union puts forward a list of candidates, and thanks to the peculiar electoral procedure this list is invariably elected. Between elections the National Union is not now very active.

Every Saturday and Wednesday afternoon all the boys and girls in Portugal between the ages of seven and fourteen attend meetings of

[1] See below, pp. 193-8.

the Portuguese Youth for two hours or so. Membership of the organization is compulsory between those ages. The children wear forage
caps and green shirts modelled on the uniforms of the pre-war German
and Italian fascist youth movements, and belts bearing a metal buckle
with the letter S on it. The S stands for Salazar.

The Portuguese Youth was formed in 1936. In the past it was very
much more belligerent in tone than it is today, and it drilled its members with wooden guns. Today, it tells them stories about Portugal's
past, present and future greatness and about the Public Man and his
Work, gives them religious instruction and provides them with sports
facilities and summer camps. Respect for the government is one of the
thirteen points in its disciplinary code.

Salazar's friends in Britain

Portuguese opponents of the Salazar régime are unanimous in regretting the official and semi-official support that the British government
and a section of British big business give to Salazar, and we think
British public opinion should also regret it and should protest about
it. There is not much one can do, of course, about the company
directors who in their annual reports praise Salazar and ignore his
victims in the PIDE's jails; nor about incidents like a British ambassador attending the funeral of a PIDE chief. But, remembering that
every royal visit to Portugal and every British trade fair in Lisbon is
seen by Portuguese democrats as the direct bolstering of a repressive
and reactionary administration, which discourages them very much,
there is a great deal that can be done by protests inside and outside the
House of Commons to dissuade those responsible for these ventures
from giving aid and comfort to the greenshirts and their boss.

Who are Salazar's friends in Britain? First of all, as might be expected,
there are the directors of firms with big Portuguese interests – men
like the late Sir Alexander Roger, president of the Anglo-Portuguese
Telephone Company Ltd (issued capital £6,910,000), of which he was
until 1960 chairman and managing director.[1] In his statement to the

---

[1] The present chairman of the Anglo-Portuguese Telephone Company is Mr A. F.
Roger, who is a director of Cable and Wireless (Holding) Ltd and of fourteen other
companies. Other British directors include: Lord Ritchie of Dundee, chairman of the
London Stock Exchange and of the English Association of American Bond and Share
Holdings Ltd; Mr Frank Hollyer, a director of Cape Electric Tramways (1949) Ltd,
which controls fifteen public transport concerns in South Africa; and Sir Norman
Hulbert, Conservative M.P. for North Stockport and House of Commons Temporary

company's seventy-first annual general meeting he told how during the previous year, as on frequent occasions during Dr Salazar's term of office, he had been privileged to meet him and discuss with him at considerable length national and international affairs and matters affecting the company. These conversations seem to have gone to Sir Alexander's head a little, for he said:

Undoubtedly the present strong and healthy condition of the Portuguese economy is greatly attributable to the wise guidance and counsel of H.E. Dr António Oliveira Salazar . . . The qualities of leadership and example which Dr Salazar has brought, and continues to bring, to the service of his country are recognized and appreciated not only throughout Portugal but also in many other countries.[1]

Sir Alexander was vice-president of the Federation of British Industries, honorary president of British Insulated Callender's Cables Ltd and a former deputy chairman of the Midland Bank. He held the Grand Cross of the Portuguese Order of Industrial Merit and was a Commander of the Military Order of Christ (the second highest decoration). And he was vice-president of the organized British friends of Salazar: the Anglo-Portuguese Society. At the Society's banquet in London in November 1957 a colour film of Queen Elizabeth II's visit to Portugal earlier that year was shown. Lord Selkirk, on behalf of the British government, praised Salazar as a champion of democracy. And the late Sir David Kelly, then chairman of the British Council, protested against what he called 'Leftist sniping' and the 'lie' of Portugal's oppression and misery. Her economy, he added, was 'one of the healthiest in Europe' and her people were 'happy'.[2]

Chairman and Chairman of Standing Committees. Another prominent Anglo-Portuguese firm is the Anglo-Portugu ese Bank Ltd (issued capital £1,250,000), a subsidiary of the *Banco Nacional Ultramarino*. Its chairman is Viscount Davidson, a Privy Councillor, who is president of the Engineering Industries Association and a director of Dorman, Long and Co. Ltd, the steel firm; and one of its directors is Mr W. C. Warwick, chairman of a large number of shipping companies. Sir Alexander Roger, who died on 4 April 1961, while this book was in the press, was also a director of Lisbon Electric Tramways Ltd (issued capital £1,376,592), whose chairman is Lord Rathcavan, a former Ulster Unionist M.P.

[1] *The Times*, 20 May 1958.

[2] Cf. Sir David Kelly's *The Ruling Few: or The Human Background to Democracy* (1952), pp. 142–3: 'My stay in Portugal coincided with the lowest point of the abyss into which the rotten parasitic republican régime dragged that pleasant country . . . At the rare official receptions senior officials and generals could be seen filling their coat-tail pockets with chickens or other eatables, and their wives shoved them into their corsages . . . Returning to Portugal eighteen years later . . . I was amazed by the transformation effected by Salazar.'

Harold Macmillan himself, in November 1959, chose the occasion of a visit to Britain by the defeated opposition candidate for the presidency, General Humberto Delgado, to make an exceptionally friendly reference to Salazar's Portugal in a message to the Anglo-Portuguese Society's twenty-first annual dinner. Lord Kilmuir, the Lord Chancellor, was guest of honour, and the then president of the Federation of British Industries, Sir William McFadzean, who is chairman and managing director of British Insulated Callender's Cables Ltd and a director of the Midland Bank, was present.

The Anglo-Portuguese Society is a somewhat shadowy organiza-tion. It was formed in 1938 as the result of a suggestion made at a dinner given in honour of the Portuguese ambassador. One of its aims was stated to be 'the dissemination of reliable information between the two countries'.[1] One of its two secretaries was Lieutenant-Colonel J. Cross Brown, who has been associated since 1905 with the Spanish and Portuguese copper-mining industries; he is a former chairman and managing director of Mason and Barry Ltd, which exploits sulphur and copper mines in Portugal, and he is a Commander of the Portuguese Order of Industrial Merit. In March 1960 the Portuguese ambassador presented him with a silver salver and other gifts to mark his association for twenty-one years with the Society, of which he is now chairman. Sir Charles Wingfield, British ambassador to Portugal, 1935–7, Mr R. T. D. Stoneham, a prominent City solicitor, the late Sir Francis Lindley, a former British diplomatist, and the late Sir Stephen Gaselee, the Foreign Office Librarian, were some of the Society's earliest supporters. Guests at its recent functions have been: Mr F. J. Erroll, Conservative M.P. for Altrincham and Sale and Minis-ter of State (Board of Trade); Mr William Deedes, Conservative M.P. for Ashford; Mr Robert Allan, Parliamentary Under-Secretary, Foreign Office; Lord Bossom, former Conservative M.P. for Maid-stone, who holds the Portuguese Order of Christ; Lord Grantchester, an official of the Liberal Party; Marshal of the Royal Air Force Lord Newall; Lord Norrie, a former governor general of New Zealand; Sir Nigel Roland, British ambassador to Lisbon, 1947–54; Sir Edward Wilshaw, governor of Cable and Wireless (Holding) Ltd; Sir Seymour Howard, Lord Mayor of London in 1954–5; Lord Dudley Gordon, a member of the executive committee of the British Iron and Steel

[1] *The Times*, 8 October 1938.

Federation; the Rev. M. F. Foxell, Domestic Chaplain to the Queen; and Sir Malcolm Sargent.

A fairly consistent apologist for the '*Estado Novo*' in Britain is the *Daily Telegraph*, and this is not surprising when one learns that its correspondent in Lisbon has close connexions with the National Secretariat of Information.

How does Salazar use official visits by British royal personages to bolster his régime? Very simply. During Princess Margaret's visit in 1959 – which came just after two months in which 1,050 people had been arrested on political grounds, including eight army officers, sixteen economists, seven priests and the president of a Catholic youth organization – Salazar staged a big military parade. He had 20,000 soldiers, equipped with seventy-ton Paton tanks supplied by NATO, march through Lisbon while heavy guns pounded out a salute in commemoration of the thirty-third anniversary of the 1926 *coup d'État*. The previous day, by some happy feat of timing in Whitehall, there had arrived in Portugal 410 British soldiers, and on the anniversary day itself, 28 May 1959, they were followed by an aircraft carrier, three destroyers and a frigate, together with some RAF planes. The latter staged an aerial display on 10 June; at the same time, by some remarkable coincidence, Salazar supporters were parading through the main streets of Lisbon.

Is there any wonder that the pro-Salazar Press hailed these coincidences as a demonstration of British confidence in the dictator, his greenshirts and his corporate State?

Officially of course the visit by British armed forces and regimental bands was part of the big publicity campaign for the British trade fair, in which over 500 British firms took part. No doubt Mr Geoffrey Stow, then First Secretary (Information) at Her Britannic Majesty's embassy in Lisbon – whose hand-out to the Portuguese Press on the British general election was so much to Salazar's liking that two Lisbon newspapers ran it as a serial – was pleased with the success of the campaign. One wonders whether he included in his reports to the Foreign Office the fact that Lisbon people called the trade fair 'the English circus'.[1]

[1] Here are some earlier examples of official and semi-official British support for the Salazar régime. In 1938 President Carmona was awarded the Order of the Bath, and in 1941 the University of Oxford made Salazar an honorary Doctor of Civil Law. In 1940 the Duke of Kent (closely followed by the Duke and Duchess of Windsor) was one of the first visitors to the 'Portuguese World' exhibition in Lisbon commemorating the eight-hundredth anniversary of Portuguese nationhood. In the same year – and only

After Salazar – what?

Every Portuguese who thinks about politics at all is constantly wondering and speculating about what will happen when Salazar dies. After all, the dictator is over seventy, and he is quite liable to die within the next decade. And the people who are at the top of the régime are wondering and speculating still more anxiously than are the oppositionists. For the really amazing thing about Salazar's rule is that he does not seem to be making any preparations for the situation that will follow his death. No one is being groomed for the succession. Salazar would hardly act differently if he fancied himself immortal.

But there is more to it than that. Not merely does Salazar make no preparations for the handling of affairs after he dies – he has been careful to dispose of any likely successor who has put in an appearance. This has happened too often to be anything but a considered policy.

There was the case of Armindo Monteiro, a professor of law who became Colonial Minister and later Foreign Minister. A man of great ability and culture, who knew the modern world better than many Portuguese of his generation, Monteiro was acquiring fame and prestige and seemed a likely successor. Salazar put an end to speculation by sending him as ambassador to the Court of St James's, where he served from 1936 to 1943. He died in 1955 without having returned to office.

There was the case of Teotónio Pereira, an immensely rich man who was the main architect of the corporative structure in the early thirties. When it looked as if people were tipping him as Salazar's successor the dictator got him out of the country by sending him to Washington, then London. He was a great success in Mayfair Society. Later however, during the crisis following the 1958 presidential election, Salazar was compelled to give Pereira the job of Minister of the Presidency – an office comparable, perhaps, to that of Lord Chancellor in Britain.

a few weeks after the fall of France – António Ferro, then Director of the National Secretariat of Propaganda, was made a CBE, and the British ambassador in Lisbon, Sir Walford Selby, declared: 'We all recognize the distinguished work of António Ferro as Director of National Propaganda' (*Portugal: Bulletin of Political, Economic and Cultural Information*. Lisbon: Secretariado da Propaganda Nacional, no. 28, p. 8, 31 July 1940). (Ferro first came to prominence when he published a series of eulogistic interviews with Mussolini. For an example of his 'distinguished work' see p. 198 n. Sir Walford Selby has described his term of office in Portugal in his *Diplomatic Twilight 1930–1940* (1953), pp. 83–129.)

And there was the case of Marcelo Caetano, another professor of law, the present Rector of Lisbon University, and an acknowledged authority on British and American constitutional law. In this role of expert on democratic constitutions he was useful to Salazar as giving a certain liberal colouring to the corporate State. So he was made Minister of the Presidency. Caetano's standing soon became very high, for three reasons. First, he is a very able man. Secondly, he is said to have had a large following among the Catholic youth at a time when they were beginning to be disillusioned in Salazar. And thirdly, he is popularly but no doubt erroneously supposed to have links with the opposition, being married to the daughter of an old democrat; Caetano himself is a former monarchist turned republican.

As soon as Caetano was widely spoken of as Salazar's successor the dictator dismissed him from his position as Minister of the Presidency.

Has Salazar, then, never considered what kind of situation will face Portugal when he dies? It appears that once, in the mid-fifties, he did begin to think about the best way of ensuring the smooth and stable continuity of the régime. But the solution he seems to have envisaged for a time was one which went completely against the grain of the majority of his supporters. Like Franco, he toyed with the idea of bringing back the monarchy, a step which would entail rescinding the laws which prohibit Portuguese kings from returning to Portugal.

So there arrived in Lisbon one day one of the two pretenders to the Portuguese throne, Dom Duarte Nuno.[1] This person had lived all his life in Austria and Switzerland and could not even speak Portuguese. But he began to learn, and the monarchist *Causa Monárquica* began to hold receptions for him in public buildings in Lisbon as soon as he could stammer a few phrases got off by heart.

The idea of the throne vacated by Dom Manuel II in 1910 being occupied once more, and by a foreigner at that, was profoundly shocking to the sentiments of many Portuguese. It was even shocking to some monarchists, for Dom Manuel's line is extinct and Duarte Nuno comes from a branch of the royal family, the Migueline line, which had been specially excluded from the throne in perpetuity way back in 1834. Not that there were any public protests. The Portuguese, generally speaking, grumble in the bosom of the family. It is safer that

[1] His full name is D. Duarte Nuno Fernando Maria Miguel Gabriel Rafael Francisco Xavier Raimundo António, duque de Bragança, de Guimarães e de Barcelos, marquês de Vila-Viçosa, etc., chefe da Sereníssima Casa de Bragança.

way. Some of the newspapers did venture sly digs at the pro-Duarte activity. Marcelo Caetano, himself an ex-monarchist, went so far as to come out openly and say it was not time to think of such a solution, since the Portuguese people were pretty solidly republican and a monarchy in Portugal was out of the question. It is known that there were protests inside the government and that the Catholic Church was not altogether happy about the proposal. So Salazar quietly dropped the idea, and the pro-Duarte section of the monarchists felt badly let down; which has had the piquant result of bringing one section of monarchist opinion, represented by the weekly journal *Debate*, into the anti-Salazar opposition, so that of all legally published journals *Debate* is now the one most outspokenly critical of Salazar.

The dictator was thus back where he had started. What is going to happen? We cannot forbear quoting the comment of one Portuguese friend that when Salazar dies 'all they will have to do is embalm him, and things will go on exactly the same as ever'.

Another, less cynical, friend believes that when the death is announced the army will act swiftly and take over, so as to forestall any popular rising. But even if this is what happens it is anybody's guess who will ultimately come out on top in the army. It may be monarchist officers, it may be a relatively Liberal section of the officers – or there may emerge a civilian who has the skill to do a deal with the generals as Salazar did in 1928. One guess we heard, for what it is worth, is that both Teotónio Pereira and Marcelo Caetano will re-emerge, and that Caetano's chances of attaining effective leadership are somewhat stronger than the other's, even though Pereira is a member of the government. How far either of these men would attempt or achieve any form of liberalization, and how long either could last before there was a successful democratic revolution, would depend on a complex balance of forces which has not yet even begun to take shape.

What is the Salazar régime?

Left-wing critics of Salazar usually describe Portugal under his rule as a fascist country. If by fascism we are to understand the open, terrorist dictatorship of the big capitalists, then this description of present-day Portugal is basically accurate. Yet the word 'fascist' has become so much a political swear-word for Right-wing régimes one specially disapproves of that it seems to us misleading merely to attach this pejorative label to the Salazar régime and leave it at that; particularly since this régime, both in its origins and the way it operates, is in many respects different from those of Hitler, Mussolini and Franco.

From the early days of the corporate State, Salazar and his supporters have imitated many of the outward features of Italian fascism and Hitlerism – of fascism as a movement, that is to say. They have imitated the salutes, the coloured shirts, the *Ballilas* and the Hitler Youth. They have paid fulsome tributes to their mentors. Until recently the official history books prescribed for use in Portuguese schools contained flattering photographs of Mussolini and Hitler and accounts of their lives that praised their deeds and concealed their crimes; history has now been rewritten. They have adopted fascist methods of dealing with dissent and dissenters. Newspapers are so strictly censored that they avoid white spaces by keeping a mass of 'overmatter' in reserve. And opponents of Salazar, especially the communists, are persecuted in very unpleasant ways.

But there are substantial differences too. Though Salazarism preaches Portuguese nationalism to the point of chauvinism, anti-Semitism is practically unknown in Portugal and has never been sponsored by the Salazar government; in fact there are scarcely a thousand Jews in the country, and those of them who are rich are notorious supporters of Salazar. Moreover, while stringent measures have been taken to preserve the system of exploitation and oppression in Angola and Mozambique, there is in metropolitan Portugal nothing that could be construed as an officially sponsored or officially supported colour bar – unless one counts the special case of legislation barring coloured people from becoming army officers, which is clearly designed to prevent the training of the *cadres* of future colonial liberation armies. Nor is there any social colour bar whatever. Finally, there seems to be little or no real cult of Salazar as there was of the Italian and German dictators. His portrait does not appear all over the place as theirs did when they were in power, and a picture of President Tomás hangs in the same sort of place as you would find a picture of the Queen in Britain.

In fact, of course, none of these criteria determines whether a country is fascist or not. The real peculiarity of Portuguese fascism lies in the gradual and relatively peaceful way it assumed control, in contrast to the seizures of power in Italy and Germany and the civil war in Spain. The Portuguese big capitalists achieved their dictatorship in a piecemeal fashion in the thirties, gradually replacing the dictatorship of the military clique that had seized power in 1926. Carmona's military dictatorship at first operated on behalf of the *bourgeoisie* as a whole, the reactionary strata of the middle class and the Church, against the Liberal strata of the middle class and the workers. The big capitalists were not yet powerful enough for the advance to a fully-fledged fascist State to be anything but gradual.[1]

When Salazar joined it the military-clerical dictatorship displayed many of the features of a Bonapartist régime. There was a delicate balance of classes in which an individual dictator found it possible to operate, as it were, along the resultant of a parallelogram of social forces. He could skilfully manipulate the different class interests; at the same time he himself came more and more to be manipulated by the most powerful class, which needed him as a façade since it was not yet strong enough openly to impose its will on society. Salazar himself is a petty *bourgeois* to the marrow of his bones. His original idea was that Portugal should be governed by the petty *bourgeoisie*, or at any rate their most responsible members, in the name of religion and the family. Everyone would be disciplined and enlightened and take his appropriate place in the corporative hierarchy. This was his vision – the Philistine, pedestrian vision of a plodding accountant who wants everyone to spend only ninety per cent of his income and save ten per cent of it, and who thinks that a country's budget is best balanced on the same lines. But Salazar never succeeded in moulding this enlightened petty *bourgeoisie* of his dreams, because the big capitalists stepped into the picture. They did not share his vision; they had aims of their own. But it suited them very well, and it suits them still, to keep at the head of the State a man who could mediate between them and the large and still quite powerful middle sections of society – sections that had confidence in Salazar and in corporativism.

When he took office Salazar based himself on the tremendous discontent among most of the middle class. The traders, the civil servants, the small business men, the Church: all, for their various reasons, saw in him their champion. He gave the traders social peace, the civil servants better pay, the small industrialists freedom from

---

[1] One who wanted it to be a good deal less gradual was the lawyer Dr Francisco Rolão Preto, who in August 1932 founded the blueshirted National-Syndicalist Movement. In June 1934 he addressed a letter to President Carmona strongly criticizing the government and urging freedom of the Press and full propaganda for all parties – no doubt so that the handicaps imposed on his own party might be removed. Publication of the letter was forbidden, and Rolão Preto and the general secretary of the blueshirts, Count Alberto de Monsarás, were arrested and deported to Spain for six months. In August 1934 the executive committee of the blueshirts resolved, in response to an appeal by Salazar, to enter the National Union. Rolão Preto is today an oppositionist.

strikes, and the Church an official underwriting and boosting of Catholic teaching about the home and the family. This social base he still retains, though today it is much less solid than it used to be. The big capitalists know he retains it, and from their point of view he and his ideology remain an indispensable façade – or, to change the metaphor, a buffer between them and the middle class. It is this that gives Salazar his own limited, but definite, power to tack and manœuvre. And it is the freezing of class relations in this pattern that is at bottom responsible for the curiously static and timeless nature of Portuguese political life.

But international events as well as the internal class structure have caused certain peculiarities in the development of fascism in Portugal. In the thirties, especially after the outbreak of the Spanish civil war, Salazar leaned heavily on Germany and Italy. During the second world war, thanks to Portugal's 'collaborative neutrality', as it was officially called, her big capitalists consolidated themselves still further by trading happily with both sides, selling them wolfram and tungsten,[1] and catching up economically to a small extent while the rest of Europe experienced widespread destruction. If the fascist powers had been victorious in the second world war the subsequent evolution of Salazar's Portugal can well be imagined. But the outcome of the war, and the failure of fascism on an international scale, made it politically expedient for Salazar and the class whose instrument he had become to lean on the British and Americans. To render the régime acceptable to its western allies, certain concessions had to be made to democracy. So much has already been said. In particular there were now opportunities, albeit limited ones, for electoral campaigns. Such opportunities had been unknown before 1945. Without doubt the relaxing of the censorship and certain other amenities provided at election times have been chiefly *para inglês ver*, 'for the benefit of the English', as is commonly said. Moreover these measures, in 1945 at any rate, have given the government an opportunity to size up its opponents' strength and find out who they were, so that the moment the campaign was over and discipline restored it could quietly go ahead and pick off the leaders and put them out of harm's way. But it can safely be said that during the years 1948–57 the authorities became less and less interested in any real persecution of the Liberal opposition and concentrated all their ferocity against the Communist Party and that party's

---

[1] In June 1944, under British pressure, Portugal stopped exporting wolfram to Germany, 'in order to shorten the war'.

supporters. They knew quite well that this would not offend Salazar's western allies in the least.

The 1958 presidential election was a turning-point in the history of the anti-Salazar opposition. For the first time this opposition, ranging from certain monarchists on the extreme Right to the communists on the extreme Left, eventually found itself united behind one candidate, and decided not to stage the customary last-minute boycott, despite the slender chance of beating the elaborate rigging of votes and other malpractices that it knew for certain would take place. The authorities were so alarmed that for a time after the election it looked as if they were returning to their old methods of wholesale repression. Venerable and distinguished Liberals went to jail once more, and people of all persuasions were arrested almost indiscriminately up and down the country. Did this in fact represent a new intensification of fascist methods? Some of those arrested were released after a very short time, and it seems clear that most of those who remain in prison and who from time to time are brought to trial are persons whom the government considers to be supporters of the Communist Party.

The Portuguese dictatorship, then, is a fascist régime with specific features arising from the way it came into existence, from Portugal's internal class structure and from her international relations. But the label is hardly the most important thing. In common with different régimes elsewhere in the world, Portuguese fascism practises censorship, the denial of free speech, arbitrary imprisonment and torture. Even if he were innocent of these crimes Salazar would stand condemned by this: that after a third of a century of power nearly half the population is still illiterate, there is widespread and crushing poverty and the figures for diseases of poverty and infant mortality are practically the highest in Europe. International High Society may be impressed by the luxury and elegance of Lisbon's new Ritz Hotel; but a similar amount of money spent on, say, new schools and hospitals would have enabled Portugal to improve a little on the truly wretched showing she makes in the social statistics compiled by the United Nations.[1]

[1]See Appendix, pp. 261–7.

VII

The wealth of a nation

'Portugal is a poor country!' This is how Salazar invariably answers those who criticize his economic policy. And many Portuguese tend to accept this view. But the Communist Party, the only section of the opposition to put forward anything like a systematic alternative programme, insists that Portugal is rich in natural resources.

Both views are partly true, of course. Like most countries, Portugal is rich in some things and deficient or totally lacking in others. Until recent years the absence of coal and iron made it impracticable to attempt any large-scale industrialization. But the development of hydro-electric power – not to mention atomic energy – and better means of transporting iron and other minerals could have made up for these deficiencies, and could still make up for them. Again, by British standards Portugal's soil is not very fertile for the production of cereals or as pasture land; it is tired and stony, and disforestation has caused the erosion of mountain slopes. But planned scientific measures could help to overcome these handicaps too.

At present, however, Portugal's productivity is extremely low; just how low is seen when one compares her national product per head of the population with those of other west European countries. In 1952–4 the average annual national product per head for seventeen west European countries was 625 US dollars. The figure for the United Kingdom was 780 dollars; for France 740; for Greece 220; and for Portugal 200.[1]

This low productivity is an essential strand in the general pattern of the Portuguese economy. According to the 1950 census nearly half the population was engaged in agriculture, less than a quarter in industry and the remainder in various services. Nevertheless agriculture

[1] *Per Capita National Product of Fifty-five Countries: 1952–1954* (New York: Statistical Office of the United Nations, Statistical Papers, series E, no. 4, 1957).

supplied only a little over a quarter of the gross national product, the balance being divided fairly equally between industry and services. What industry does exist is mainly devoted to the production of consumer goods and the processing of agricultural primary products. Comparatively few workers are engaged in mining, metal or the basic chemical industries; the great majority work in the food, textiles, clothing, building, woodwork and cork industries. Textiles and clothing in fact account for a third of all industrial workers.[1]

Like Britain, Portugal depends very much upon foreign trade, which accounts for almost a third of her national product. The proportion is even greater if her trade with her colonies is counted. But, unlike Britain, Portugal exports chiefly agricultural produce and foodstuffs. She exports cork and other raw materials for industry. She exports wine and sardines. Her imports, which come mainly from Britain, the USA and Belgium, consist largely of industrial equipment and luxury consumer goods. She has no serious balance of payments deficit, but only because of her colonies' foreign earnings.

All this – her low productivity, the structure of her economy and her dependence on trade with more advanced countries – is typical of an under-developed, economically backward country. But the acute poverty of three-quarters of her people cannot be attributed to under-development alone; it is also due to the unbalanced way in which her meagre wealth is distributed.

In the industrially advanced countries of North America and western Europe, where productivity is high, wages make up between 60 and 70 per cent of the national product, and interest, rent and profit between 30 and 40 per cent. In Portugal, though productivity is low, the opposite is the case. In 1950 wages accounted for 39 per cent of the national product, and interest, rent and profit accounted for 61 per cent of it.[2]

Average daily wages in industry were low enough then by any standard, and they have scarcely risen since. They varied from 42 escudos (10s 6d) in sugar production to 14 escudos (3s 6d) in the dairy industry. The average was 23.40 escudos, or just under 6s a day. But these figures refer only to days actually worked. Over the whole year the average income of industrial workers was £92 10s – less than £2 a week. Most workers' wives are therefore compelled to seek employment

[1] Anuário Estatístico, 1953 (Lisbon: Instituto Nacional de Estatística, 1954).

[2] Francisco Pereira de Moura, Luís Maria Teixeira Pinto, Manuel Jacinto Nunes, 'Estrutura da Economia Portuguesa', Revista (Lisbon: Instituto Nacional de Estatística, Centro de Estudos Económicos), no. 14, p. 116, 1954.

outside the home; and the abundant female labour is the worst paid of all. In agriculture the average daily wage is less than three-quarters of the industrial average. Moreover unemployment is widespread in the countryside, particularly in the south, and work is of a more seasonal character; and so the annual wages of landworkers are far lower than this comparison at first suggests.

It might be supposed that prices are correspondingly low, but this is not the case. To be sure, rents, wine, fruit, vegetables and some clothing are much cheaper than in Britain – but meat, butter, eggs, milk and fuel are almost as dear as they are here. The three government economists from whose study we have taken many of the foregoing facts came to the following conclusion:

                                                •

It is not therefore to be wondered at, in face of the *level of poverty* indicated by these figures, that we feel obliged seriously to reconsider the structure of industry, of the economy and of present-day Portuguese society, concerned as we are to uncover the fundamental causes of, and methods of transforming, a situation which offends against the dignity of man.[1]

Who owns Portugal?

When *senhora dona* Maria, the Portuguese Mrs Smith, buys a bar of the curiously mottled soap, not unlike marble to look at, with which she or her servant performs most everyday cleaning tasks, she is buying a product made by the *Companhia União Fabril*. When her husband *senhor* Silva orders a bottle of the pleasant, fizzy, lager-like beer with which he commonly washes down a plateful of shrimps in his local *cervejaria*, he is buying a product made by CUF. When she puts a pinch of salt in the soup, or he a handful of fertilizer on his bit of land, or either of them strikes a match – judging by our experience they will generally have to strike two or three before they get one that ignites – they are adding another infinitesimal to the gigantic wealth of CUF. Whenever the Silvas buy a new carpet, or a garden hose, or a sack, or a ball of twine, the chances are that it was produced in a factory owned by CUF. If they are lucky enough to have a passport – and they need a passport even if they only want to go to the Azores or Madeira, though these are parts of metropolitan Portugal – they will very likely book a passage on a ship ostensibly owned by the *Companhia Nacional de Navegação* or the *Sociedade Geral de Comércio, Indústria*

[1] *Ibid.* p. 137 (emphasis in the original).

e Transportes but in fact owned by CUF. The ship may even have been built by CUF. If they are rich enough to take a trip to Paris or London, and travel by air in a Portuguese aeroplane, it will belong to *Transportes Aéreos Portugueses*, another CUF subsidiary. If the Silvas have a banking account, and they deal with the *Banco de José Henriques Totta* in the Rua do Ouro, Lisbon's Lombard Street, a thoroughfare chock-a-block with money-changers, goldsmiths, jewellers and bankers, they are the customers of yet another branch of CUF.

CUF is Portugal's biggest, richest and most powerful combine, equivalent to Imperial Chemical Industries or Unilever in Britain. In 1957 it had a working capital of £51 million. As well as its Portuguese interests it has a finger in the colonial pie, notably in Angola, where it uses the exceedingly low-paid labour of Africans to extract the ore from the copper mines it owns. It is also involved in diamond mining in Angola, and in the diamond-cutting industry in Portugal. It owns the Pasteur Institute in Lisbon. And it owns practically the whole of the iron and steel town of Barreiro, on the south bank of the Tagus, the centre of the embryonic national steel industry. The letters CUF are to be seen almost everywhere in Portugal: on the sides of lorries and railway wagons, on factory walls, on neon signs, in prestige advertisements in the newspapers. Its tentacles reach into practically every branch of economic activity: medicinal drugs, tobacco, the cellulose industry, the electrical industries and hydro-electric development, cement, tin, plantations and cattle-raising at home and overseas, the cinema, real estate and insurance.

Another familiar combination of letters is SACOR, standing for *Sociedade Anónima Concessionária da Refinação de Petróleos em Portugal*. In 1938 a Rumanian oil magnate transferred his activities to Portugal, obtained a concession, built a refinery in Lisbon and founded SACOR. This is still the only refinery in the country; the company has concessions from the Portuguese government until 1976 to sell 50 per cent of all petroleum products consumed in the Portuguese mainland, Madeira and the Azores, a margin of profit being guaranteed to SACOR. The Portuguese government holds about a third of the capital, the rest being distributed among a French group represented by the founder, who has majority control, and Portuguese private shareholders.[1] SACOR's working capital in 1958 totalled £18 million;

[1] Cf. W. W. McVittie, *Portugal. Economic and Commercial Conditions in Portugal with Annexes on Madeira and the Azores* (HMSO, 1955), pp. 47–8.

in 1957 it made a net profit of £1,230,000. It is closely allied to the Anglo-Dutch firm of Royal Dutch Shell.

An important subsidiary of SACOR is the *Companhia Gás-Cidla*, which sells bottled butane gas for cooking and heating in the home. Its vans delivering two-foot-high steel-grey metal flasks and taking away the empties are seen every day in most residential areas, apart from Lisbon. A flask costing about £1 lasts an average household about a month. This service is very popular, since the only coal-gas works in the country is in Lisbon.

Another big monopoly is the M. Pinto de Azevedo group, which controls a large part of the textile industry. It has also large interests in cork, copper, insurance, colonial plantations and two leading Oporto newspapers, *O Primeiro de Janeiro* and the *Jornal de Notícias*.

A sociologist with whom we spent an evening told us that a photograph had recently appeared in a Portuguese newspaper showing the four richest men in Britain, whose fortunes were said to total less than £20 million. That Britain had so few multimillionaires, and that their aggregate wealth was so comparatively modest, rather surprised him; he told us that Portugal had far more exceedingly rich men, with far greater fortunes than their British counterparts – in a country with one-fifth the population of Britain and much lower productivity. When Alfredo da Silva, the founder of CUF, died in 1942 his personal fortune was reputed to be the sixth largest in the world. Our host was not claiming that the great Portuguese monopolies were richer than their British counterparts, but that the personal wealth of the individuals who controlled them far exceeded the personal wealth of Britain's millionaires. Figures to substantiate this claim are not easy to come by; but the small proportion of the national product paid out in wages, and the extremely low level of taxation on profits, are evidence strongly suggesting that it is true. 'Millions of *contos* here and the people are starving,' said a whitewashed slogan we saw on the wall surrounding a huge mansion a mile or two west of Cascais. We should not care to dismiss this as mere propaganda.

But the question 'Who owns Portugal?' cannot be fully answered without a glance at foreign investment in the Portuguese economy. The national monopolies already mentioned, and others, are linked in varying degrees with foreign capital. But, in addition, American, British, west German, French, Dutch and Belgian financial interests are each individually entrenched in the Portuguese economy, and especially in the economies of her colonies. The latters' raw materials

– oil, manganese, bauxite, iron, diamonds, gold, uranium – are all being exploited by foreign corporations, mainly American and British ones. These foreign firms often enjoy direct concessions.

There is in Portugal a feeling, dating back to the nineteenth century and even earlier, against foreign concessionaries and foreign capital. Much of it may stem from the British ultimatum of 1890, which 'demanded and exacted' the recall of a Portuguese expedition led by Serpa Pinto from territory which is now Rhodesia but was then claimed by Portugal – claimed with a certain legal and historical justification, though there was no effective occupation to back the claim. Even under the monarchy, when an administration granted a concession to a foreign firm it was common for people to say it was in the pocket of that firm's government. When General Norton de Matos became governor general of Angola in 1912 one of his ideas was that he would attract foreign capital to the colony; he was promptly attacked for 'selling Angola to the foreigners'.

The Salazar régime has always been very sensitive to this widespread sentiment and has been careful to pay lip-service to it in numerous public statements. It has also laid it down that in new industries of national importance a majority of the capital should be held by Portuguese shareholders. But behind the scenes foreign investment has continued on an increasing scale. Whereas in the 1953–8 State development plan only £5,175,000 came from abroad – and this was almost entirely devoted to the construction of the Limpopo railway in Mozambique – 'for the next plan it is admitted that it will not be possible to avoid having greater recourse to foreign capital'.[1]

The obvious, everyday example of penetration by foreign capital is the Anglo-Portuguese Telephone Company, which in 1958 paid dividends totalling £288,593. Thanks to Britain's being first in the field with a telephone service, Portugal's public telephone boxes are in size, shape and colour almost identical with those in Britain, a circumstance which lends an odd familiarity to the Lisbon street scene. Compared with the British telephone service, that of Portugal is extremely efficient; it is also, like Hull's municipal service, a good deal cheaper.

Portugal's biggest producer of wolfram is a British company operating mines near Fundão in the Beira Baixa. The Borralha wolfram mines in the north are owned by a French firm. British and Belgian companies mine pyrites; electric light bulbs are made by

[1] *The Times*, 26 August 1958.

subsidiaries of French and Dutch firms; Portugal's chief tyre factory is an offshoot of the General Tyre and Rubber Company of Akron, Ohio, and its management and technicians are Americans; the Firestone Tyre and Rubber Company is said to be going to invest in the MABOR tyre firm. There is a British interest in the largest sugar refinery, situated in Lisbon. The new motor-car industry is to have investment from Fiat, though the majority of the capital will be kept in Portuguese hands. Belgian and German concerns have interests in Portuguese explosives manufacture. In April 1958 the Standard Oil Company of New Jersey signed an agreement with the Portuguese government to spend a minimum of seven million dollars over five years for oil exploration and development in Portuguese Guinea. An affiliated company will explore a concession of eleven million acres; the income tax paid to the government on the oil produced will not exceed 50 per cent. In Angola the new Cabinda oil wells are being operated by the Gulf Oil Company, the drilling being done by the Santa Fé Drilling Company.

There can be no doubt that any expansion of the Portuguese economy requires the investment of capital from abroad. What is objected to by opponents of Salazar is that the foreign firms at present operating in Portugal are among the first beneficiaries of a cheap labour system which there is no hope of changing as long as the present régime continues. Some of these firms are very powerful. It is their voices that are speaking when one hears praise for Salazar from eminent foreigners.

The crisis in agriculture

If you were to take an outline map of Portugal and mark on it a small black dot for each individual landowner, irrespective of the size of his holding, you would obtain a result that might surprise you. In the north your dots would cluster thickly. In the north-west the over-populated coastal province of the Minho would be fairly peppered with dots. They would probably run together into a solid, dark mass, unless the scale of your map were very large indeed. For in this province there are over 20,000 separate holdings not even entered in the tax register, so minute is the revenue they yield to the tax collector. Farther south, in the Beira Baixa and still more in the Alentejo, the dots would suddenly become few and far between. The change would be a dramatic one, the white on the map suggesting the open spaces of the great central plain, the region's enormous estates and far horizons. Farther south still, in the Algarve, the dots would become rather more frequent again. But the extraordinary lack of balance in the structure of Portuguese agriculture, the vivid contrast between north and south, would be inescapable. In the north the family units have been sub-divided over and over again till, atomized, they can scarcely support their owners. In the south the smallest holdings are of the order of 7,000 acres. And the four greatest landowners in the country – Posser de Andrade, Santos Jorge, the Duke of Cadaval and the Duke of Palmela – between them own 95,000 hectares (235,000 acres); the same amount of land is held by 50,400 small farmers.[1]

Not only is each of these two forms of land ownership in its own way an expression of Portugal's backwardness, as is their coexistence within one national State; each is an obstacle to overcoming this backwardness and bringing prosperity to the country's hard-working but hungry peasants and farm labourers. In the north it is uneconomical to make use of modern farm implements. The smallholder cannot afford to invest in a tractor – especially when it would be working on fields that are often little bigger than an English back garden. In the Alentejo the big landowners have introduced tractors since the end of the war, concentrating them on the more fertile land, leaving the less fertile land uncultivated, and aggravating the region's grave problem of seasonal unemployment. Most of the farmworkers of the Alentejo work only two, three or four months of the year – at seed-time and harvest. To these landless labourers mechanization merely means there is less hope of work as they stand around their villages and towns waiting for someone to hire them.

So far Salazar's government has come up with only one solution to the problems of both north and south. Its panacea is public works. It has built some new roads, some public buildings and some impressive dams, like the 147-foot high Ponsul dam at Idanha–a–Nova, near Castelo Branco, which has a capacity of sixty million cubic metres. The object of these dams is to provide both hydro-electric power and water to the villages and farm communities. Unfortunately one essential ingredient has been omitted. Nothing has been done, it seems, to educate the peasants who are supposed to use the water. Wedded to their age-old methods, they have no notion of pumps and conduits and scientific agriculture. Nobody has ever explained the twentieth century to them

[1] This comparison is based on data in the archives of the *Registo Predial*, the Portuguese equivalent to the Land Registry.

in terms they can grasp. And so you have the tragic paradox of modern dams making available copious supplies of life-giving water – and peasants who do not know how to use it to refresh their parched and scanty soil. The water goes to waste, and the face of peasant farming remains unchanged.

The building of these dams is only one example of the completely haphazard, empirical approach to problems that is characteristic of Portugal's present rulers. There is rarely any serious preliminary study of a problem, any real investigation of social and economic conditions, before some grandiose scheme is announced from the roof-tops. In Britain we frequently criticize the slowness of royal commissions in arriving at their conclusions. In Portugal, until 1959 at any rate, there were no investigating commissions to complain about. For one thing, trained people who could sit on them are exceedingly rare; for another, Portugal's rulers evidently have an imperfect understanding of the far-reaching implications of certain administrative measures. In no sphere is this lack of knowledge and lack of imagination more glaring than in agriculture. And what the Portuguese call the 'wheat question' and the 'afforestation question' afford good illustrations of this.

The wheat question came to the fore some thirty years ago. Portugal did not have enough wheat, so the government decided to buy wheat from the producers at fixed prices, which were kept high in order to encourage the highest possible production of this crop. Today wheat is a very attractive cash crop, and is grown all over the country – a good deal of it, even in the north, on land that is better suited to other crops. Where land that would make excellent pasture is being used for wheat-growing instead of cattle-raising, a curious and sad contradiction results: peasants have more money in their pockets, or under their beds, than they had before – yet they are living more poorly than they did before. There is less land for growing vegetables, so vegetables are scarcer and therefore dearer. There is less land for raising cattle, so cattle are fewer and meat is dearer. Peasants are paid extra for growing bumper wheat crops – yet they are not eating so well as they did before their pasture lands were put under the plough. This is the outcome of one of Salazar's short-sighted expedients.

The other example of his lack of vision when introducing revolutionary-sounding measures comes from the north. The afforestation question there has been widely discussed in the last few years. In the hilly north, as we have already seen, every possible scrap of land has been cultivated, even the tops of the mountains, in order that the dense population may be supported. In bringing the mountain tops under the plough, the peasants cut down the forests that had hitherto covered them. Denuded of trees, and tilled year in and year out by the most primitive methods, the soil of these mountains was steadily eroded, until in many places there were at last neither trees nor crops. Suddenly the government decided to solve this problem by launching a vast reafforestation scheme. All over the place saplings were planted and tended by government foresters. But for this scheme to be successful it was necessary to ban people from entering the new forests, and this was done. The peasants' 'small cattle' were banned, too: their precious sheep and goats, which had up to then roamed those slopes undisturbed. Where once the north was swarming with flocks of sheep and goats, today, with few exceptions, these flocks no longer exist. The English peasant once cried, through Sir Thomas More, that sheep were devouring men; today the peasant of north Portugal cries that trees are killing sheep. The planting of trees is the planting of hunger in communities that find themselves deprived of their meat supply by decree. And in parts of the Trás-os-Montes province this has led to open fighting between the angry peasants and the government foresters.[1]

But the government's lack of an agricultural policy has been too glaring, its mistakes too grave, the tragedies that have resulted too appalling, the danger of alienating Salazar's foreign friends too great, for the situation to remain completely unchanged. In the last year or two the government has been compelled by fear of home and foreign opinion to modify its attitude, and to test public opinion to a limited extent before further new measures are put into effect. A study is to be made of Lisbon and its social and economic problems, and a commission of seventy-five members has been appointed to do this. There is a plan to make a similar study of the problems of Trás-os-Montes. There is a plan for an inquiry into the possibility of juridical measures to overcome the constant subdivision of smallholdings that afflicts the north. And there is a plan for a study to be made of the large estates in the south, with a view to establishing the maximum economic size for such estates and ensuring that they do not exceed it.

These projects seem to indicate that the government is beginning to realize that, in its own interests, it must work more systematically

---

[1] It was Aquilino Ribeiro's discussion of this question in his novel *Quando os Lobos Uivam* (*When the Wolves Howl*) that led to the banning of the book and the prosecution of its author. See pp. 186–7 below.

and more seriously on problems that for an entire generation have been left to the portentous decisions of an all-wise dictator.

A planned economy?

The most grandiose of recent projects is the six-year development plan initiated on 1 January 1959. It is the central plank of all government propaganda. And it must be admitted that at first sight the provisions of this plan are quite impressive. Its purpose is stated to be to improve the national standard of living and to rectify the present lack of balance between imports and exports. The total investment required under the 1959–64 plan is £375 million, which means an annual investment equal to about half the ordinary budget of under £120 million a year. About two-thirds of this special investment is earmarked for metropolitan Portugal; the rest will be devoted to projects in the country's overseas territories, which in addition have their own development plans.

The most spectacular single provision of the plan is a bridge over the Tagus to the west of Lisbon; it will probably be followed by a railway tunnel. Lisbon is to be given a shipbuilding yard; the railways are to be improved and modernized; fifteen liners, ten cod-fishing vessels and fifty-seven trawlers are to be built. There is to be more electrification. There is to be an increase in Portugal's oil refinery capacity. And new airports are to be constructed in Madeira and at Horta in the Azores. Great importance is attached to the successful fulfilment of these aims. *The Times* was no doubt echoing the views of high officials of the Salazar government when it wrote:

The stability of Portugal must depend largely on the success of the plan in achieving its ends. What is needed above all is the creation of new wealth. An old-fashioned bureaucracy must be overhauled, fresh housing provided for the poor, agriculture brought up to date, the resources of the empire exploited: in brief, both government and people have to roll up their sleeves in order to press forward the work of the last thirty years.[1]

Now the first development plan (1953–8) was not fulfilled. Supposing that the present plan is fulfilled, what effect will it really have on Portugal's economic backwardness in relation to the rest of Europe? It has been calculated that *if* the rhythm of progress could be accelerated

[1] *The Times*, 22 May 1959.

to an annual increase of five per cent in the national product per head, then Portugal could reach the present level of western Europe by – 1980.[1] In fact, however, the 1959–64 development plan provides for a gross annual increase of only 4.2 per cent, a net annual increase of only 3.5 per cent. This is a derisory coefficient of expansion. And in fact, in the opinion of many Portuguese, the plan, like its predecessor, is not an example of genuine economic planning at all. Rather is it an effort to persuade people that something pretty drastic and far-reaching is being done to alleviate their poverty and catch up with the twentieth century. It is true enough that for many years the Salazar régime did nothing to solve Portugal's fundamental economic problems, and that it is now seeking to foster the idea that big strides forward are being made, or are about to be made. Critics call this idea an illusion, and the propaganda for it a mystique.[2] The plans, they say, are the result not of scientific thinking about Portugal's backwardness and her people's plight and how to end these things, but of a political decision that criticism of the régime can be stifled only if a hullabaloo is made about 'economic planning' and its benefits.

Where is the evidence for this assertion? The critics point, first of all, to the way the plans were prepared. In neither case was there any scientific research along modern lines. The necessary careful, serious study was not made of the country's total needs and total resources, the way her people live, their specific problems and aspirations in each of the various regions. There was not one conference of economists, geographers, industrialists, statisticians, technicians or social workers, to pool their knowledge and chart the way forward. There was no public discussion whatever. There was not even the pretence of consulting the people. The plans were drawn up by men sitting at desks in the Ministry of Economics and the Ministry of Corporations

---

[1] Pereira de Moura and Teixeira Pinto, *Problemas do Crescimento Económico Português* (Lisbon: Associação Industrial Portuguesa, 1958), p. 45. Cf. *Economic Bulletin for Europe* (Geneva: Secretariat of the Economic Commission for Europe), vol. xii, no. 3, p. 24, November 1960: 'Even if the scheduled optimum rise of gross national product over the whole period of the plan by 32 per cent (or at an annual compound rate of 5.7 per cent) is actually attained, the achievement would be still quite modest in the light both of the urgent need to raise income per head to levels comparable with those prevailing in western European countries and of the possibilities for more rapid progress provided by a strong external position.'

[2] It is significant that the critics of Salazar's economic policy are not confined to the ranks of the opposition. Several critical speeches were made during the discussion of the second development plan in the National Assembly, and during the subsequent budget debate, and fourteen deputies voted against the proposal to levy more taxes.

– men whose work was a belated, shoddy and stopgap response to the general uneasiness about the government's incompetence.

This criticism of Salazar's 'planning' does not seek to evade the fact that even an unscientific plan only partly fulfilled may yet succeed in doing something to bring modern technique to Portugal.

A second criticism, no less fundamental, is commonly heard. It is that the tremendous emphasis placed on industrialization in both the earlier plan and the current one leaves almost entirely out of account the great problems confronting agriculture. There are irrigation schemes to bring into use the bare lands south of the Tagus, and an extension of the national grid system to bring cheap electricity into some rural areas. But this is merely scratching the surface. As long as the countryside remains backward, as long as the rural population's standard of living and cultural and educational level remain low, industrialization will be on the shakiest of foundations. There is scarcely any market yet in the villages for the things modern industry produces. First and foremost, there is scarcely any market yet for modern agricultural equipment. Any real improvement in the standard of living of those two-thirds of the Portuguese people who live and work outside the towns is wholly dependent on radical improvements in agriculture, and on educational work on a mass scale in the villages. Otherwise there will be no effective demand for the products of the new industries that the present plan aims to create. In general the peasants and agricultural labourers do not yet realize the benefits of substituting tractors and combine harvesters for their oxen, mules and horses and their primitive ploughs and hoes. Nor indeed would they ever realize this unless mechanization were accompanied by a redistribution of the land.

This second criticism of Salazar's 'planning' likewise does not evade the fact that even a modicum of industrialization is to be welcomed – if only because industrialization, on even a fairly modest scale, will create one further exceedingly difficult problem for the dictatorship, quite apart from the problem of the market for the new industries' products. There is no doubt that the multiplication of large-scale enterprises employing skilled workers will undermine the ideology of corporativism, relax labour discipline and make it progressively less easy to suppress the development of genuine trade unions. Admittedly these effects will be resisted, and resisted hard. But they cannot be prevented if industrialization is to be carried through.

It should be added that the publicity for the current development plan is not intended merely for domestic consumption, but also to impress Portugal's foreign allies. Salazar badly needs to convince these allies, and also to convince such organizations as UNESCO and OEEC, that Portugal, though backward, is capable of governing herself and her colonies and is making substantial and courageous efforts to go forward. And the fact that all this talk of planning and economic development occupies a large place in official propaganda may give some people abroad the idea that Portugal under Salazar enjoys some form of planned or even socialized economy. This idea is quite false, and was specifically denied in a paper read before the May 1956 congress of Salazar's fascist party, the National Union: 'Corporativism has not created a special type of economy but rather an economic bureaucracy, organized, well or badly, by the State.'[1]

The six-year development plan, then, is in no sense comparable to the five-year economic plans of communist countries, nor, for that matter, to the kind of economic planning advocated by the British Labour Party. It is merely an investment plan. Despite constant State interference in every sphere of economic activity – the operations of the 'economic bureaucracy' – Portugal's economy remains a capitalist one, whose every sector is firmly in the hands of private enterprise; even in the railways the State holds only 45 per cent of the shares. What is more, it is a capitalist economy functioning under exceptionally favourable conditions for the capitalists, from three points of view. First, practically all the leading men in the government are either big bankers, industrialists or landowners, or else are closely linked with such people. Secondly, these men owe their riches to the abnormally favourable share of the nation's wealth taken by profit. Thirdly, they have behind them a State apparatus which effectively prevents the operation of that aspect of free enterprise that business men find least agreeable: the right of workers to strike for higher wages and better conditions.

Portuguese business men are given to complaining bitterly about State interference in economic activity through the *grémios* and all the other organisms of the corporate régime. But the only ones who really suffer are the small men, who have not enough money or influence to

---

[1] *IV Congresso da União Nacional, Resumo das Comunicações,* segunda secção, 'Vida Económica', pp. 122–4; quoted, António Sérgio, *Antologia Sociológica. Trechos Portugueses e Estrangeiros Seleccionados, Comentados e Prefaciados,* 1.° caderno (Lisbon: Edição do Autor, 1956), p. 21.

cut through the mass of red tape. Even these are grateful that they do not have to meet wage demands.

The six-year development plan is claimed to be an attempt on the part of the State to encourage, and to back with State funds, private investment in such economic activity as Portugal's rulers think desirable. This is true as far as it goes, especially as regards some of the more sensational provisions. But there is no doubt whatever that the plan is also a useful device on the part of Portugal's rich men to raise the necessary capital from public revenue for ventures from which they hope to extract even bigger profits. And this is the heart of the matter.

The £375 million the government will spend during these six years has to come from somewhere. In the final analysis it will come out of the pockets – and out of the mouths – of the overwhelming majority of the population. They, of course, have never been consulted about it.

Portugal and her neighbours

Salazar's foreign policy was always an isolationist one. He always believed, and still believes, that his country can enjoy political and economic autarky; and to a great extent he has succeeded in achieving this. Here is one of the reasons why the rest of the world knows little, and often cares little, about Portugal. But when the second world war ended it was no longer possible to keep up this isolation in the old way. For one thing, having supported Germany and Italy till it became clear that they were going to lose the war, Salazar needed to appear respectable in the eyes of the western victors. What better argument against the Liberal opposition could he produce than the admission of Portugal to the community of 'democratic' nations? Again, membership of NATO would give him unlimited security of tenure, virtually guaranteeing that any revolution sponsored by the Communist Party would call down on itself the wrath of Portugal's new military allies. Moreover, Salazar needed military aid from the United States to strengthen and re-equip his army. For these reasons he took Portugal into NATO and into the United Nations – once he could be certain that the United States would have a majority, and that his representative would be in the company of representatives of fellow democrats like Chiang Kai-shek and Syngman Rhee. He evidently reckoned that the *cachet* which membership of NATO and the United Nations would give his régime outweighed the attendant dangers: external interference with Portuguese sovereignty; and the introduction into Portugal of ideas that were modern, foreign and – from his point of view – subversive.

The plan for the creation of a European Common Market, however, placed the Portuguese government in a dilemma. For the countries concerned were major consumers of many of Portugal's basic products, especially colonial products like coffee and cocoa. Naturally the government did not want to run the risk of losing these markets. On the other hand, if Portugal did enter the Common Market, she would do so as an unequal partner. The others had heavy industries; Portugal had only the rudiments of one, and was herself a market for foreign motor-cars, commercial vehicles, tractors and other manufactured articles, an increasing proportion of which she obtained from west Germany. Membership of the Common Market might well conflict with plans for Portugal's industrialization.

Fortunately for the Portuguese government Britain hesitated for a very long time before defining her attitude towards the Common Market; and while Britain hesitated the dilemma could remain unresolved. When Britain's negotiations for a counter-market got under way Portugal found herself able to enter the European Free Trade Association, the Common Market's rival, on favourable terms. And so the Portuguese economy is tied, formally at any rate, to that of Britain instead of those of France and west Germany.

Whatever forms the European Free Trade Association and the European Common Market may take in the future, liberalization of trade and the breaking down of national barriers in western Europe can only augur ill for Portugal's survival as a nation unless, fairly quickly, there are some very far-reaching changes in her economy. Portugal still has one great source of wealth: her people's labour power. Under certain circumstances a great part of this could be lost for ever; and then it would be too late to talk about altering the economic structure.

The rate of emigration from Portugal is already one of the highest of any European country. Almost 37,000 persons leave Portugal permanently each year – nearly a third of the natural increase in her population. Now about 25,000 people leave Britain each year to seek work overseas. If Britain, with over five times Portugal's population, were losing her people at the same rate that Portugal is, then our annual emigration figure would be, not 25,000, but over 200,000. Let us put it another way: if emigration from Portugal continues at the present rate, then in twenty years' time she will have lost almost a million people. And, most serious of all, this loss of manpower is not spread evenly over the population as a whole but is accounted for chiefly by men in the prime of life, the most productive section of the population.[1]

If the ideal of a united western European economy, with freedom of movement across frontiers, is realized within the next decade or so, while Portugal remains poor and backward, the present rate of emigration will in all probability increase in a spectacular manner. Under such circumstances Portugal might well become a second Ireland, inhabited by old men and young children. Already this is the fate of many of her mountain villages.

Flight from hunger

Those who emigrate are mainly very poor people, many of them from rural areas such as Trás-os-Montes and the overcrowded Minho, or from the Algarve coast. Quite a number of migrant workers go to France for several months at a time and then return home. None who goes to France expects to make a fortune. The countries where Portuguese workers go to make money quickly are Brazil and Venezuela, though of latter years Brazil has made entry more difficult because of her own unemployment problem.

Emigration is both open and clandestine. In Portugal it is much more difficult to obtain a passport than it is in Britain. There are different types of passport, and a tourist passport is not given to a poor man. Nowadays everyone under thirty who applies for one must have sponsors to testify to his character and the purpose for which he wants one. This is directed against young people who want to go to world youth festivals in eastern Europe. A worker – that is to say, a man whose occupation is shown on his identity card as *operário* – may have a passport for only two purposes: either to travel on behalf of his employer, who must attest to this fact, or to emigrate. An emigrant's passport is granted only for a specific country, which the applicant has been assured he will get a visa for, and only on presentation to the authorities of a contract to work for an employer in that country or a formal letter of summons from a close relative there. In practice this means that the poor, uneducated Portuguese

[1] Cf. *Demographic Trends in Western Europe 1951–1971. A Report by the Manpower Committee* (Paris: OEEC, 1956).

who wants to find a better life in a more prosperous land is able to do so only if someone else, who knows the ropes, can arrange these formalities for him. For many the problem is solved if they have kinsfolk who have blazed the trail. But the man who has no connexions of this sort is easy prey for the racketeers who carry on a flourishing business obtaining passports, the necessary labour contracts and other documents – often spurious – on the payment of fantastic sums of money.

Here is one such case we encountered. A countryman, the father of five children, who was fortunate enough to own several acres of good land in a tiny village south of Oporto, wanted to see his children grow up with better opportunities than he could give them. He had done some work as a forester, and had heard that lumberjacks in Canada could earn high wages. But he had no idea of how to get there, until one day a man came to his village ostensibly looking for prospective emigrants. He told the peasant that he could arrange a job for him in Canada, could get the necessary documents and would organize the journey. It would of course have to be illegal, added the stranger. Neither the peasant nor any of his fellow villagers knew that Canada has encouraged the immigration of many thousands of Portuguese in recent years, and that the whole matter could have been arranged quite legally through the Canadian legation in Lisbon, and would then have cost him very little more than his fare. The stranger demanded 30 *contos* (£375), and the peasant mortgaged his only possessions – his fields – for that sum.

He went with the stranger, first to Oporto, where a tourist passport for France and Britain was procured for him; and then by train to Paris. He had almost no money in his pocket – he had handed it over to the stranger. They spent a month in Paris, the peasant staying indoors all day, waiting for his companion to come back from the mysterious errands he said he had to make to arrange a passage to Canada. At last they crossed the Channel to Britain, where the man landed as a tourist. Once again he found himself in a strange country, waiting for the promised boat ticket to Canada. One night his companion failed to return, and the peasant was left penniless and desperate in London. Fortunately, in this case, chance brought him in touch with an honest compatriot, who was able to help him get work in Britain.

We visited his village to take some money to his wife, who was overcome with emotion at having first-hand news of her husband. She could not read or write, and his few, painfully written letters had to be read to her. England, France and Canada were all one to her;

her village was reached from the main road by a cart-track over the hills, and she had never been farther from it than the little town of Oliveira de Azeméis. She had not liked the look of the '*vigarista*', the bandit; but her husband would not hear anything against him, since he desperately wanted to have enough money to educate his children. But when she heard how long he was having to stay in France she began to fear that something had gone wrong. So had the village priest, who told her that the stranger must certainly have been a communist. This was the kind of thing that communists did to people . . .

Officially the Portuguese government encourages emigration. In fact one of the major criticisms that oppositionists level at the régime is that one of its main solutions for unemployment is to sponsor the transportation of Portugal's rural poor to the African colonies. The idea being that if white emigration to Angola and Mozambique is encouraged there will be a greater chance of these territories remaining Portuguese. It seems strange that a government which welcomes emigration is not interested in preventing the heart-rending exploitation of simple country people by unscrupulous confidence tricksters. Rather do the complicated regulations provide an opening for the latter.

On our return journey through Spain and France we saw something of the hazards of this kind of clandestine emigration. The train was filled with Portuguese workers, one or two of them accompanied by their wives and families. Until we reached the frontier they were all circumspect about their plans. At the frontier we waited for two hours as officials interrogated our travelling companions. Soon a rumour spread along the train: someone was being taken off and sent back to Lisbon. We saw a young man who had been sitting in the next compartment bundled on to the platform with his luggage. He was marched away by officials of the PIDE, one of whose functions is the scrutiny of passports. We gathered that the young man had a tourist passport. The PIDE officials had taken one look at his hands and at the awkward way he wore his smart new suit, and had begun to question him closely about his journey. The young man was hesitant. The PIDE officials made him open his suitcase. Inside were heavy boots, a boiler suit, a tool kit and a few old clothes. So they made him get off.

Our fellow passengers were indignant. The young man must have paid between £15 and £25 for these tourist papers, not to mention the £10 for his fare. In all, more than a month's wages had gone on this abortive trip. The more seasoned among them, who had witnessed similar scenes many times before, and who proudly peppered their

Portuguese with the gallicisms they had learned in French factories and on French building sites, were contemptuous of the youngster's lack of skill in carrying off his pretence and of his ingenuousness in imagining that the PIDE would be anything but suspicious and hostile.

Once we pulled out of Vilar Formoso and were beyond Salazar's jurisdiction the train fairly hummed with complaints and criticisms. It was as if a bandage had been taken off each one's mouth. They were oblivious of the fact that we were now in a country where terror is even more widespread. What mattered to them was that Portugal had been left behind, and that soon we should be in France, where, they said, a man is treated as a human being. Before the PIDE officials their faces had been expressionless, and their voices had held no rancour as they had politely answered questions put to them with an arrogance amounting at times to brutality. As we had watched the performance – noting the officials' change of tone when it came to our turn – we had wondered what these poor people really felt about it. Now we knew. Out it poured.

Those who had been to France before pointed their criticisms of life in Portugal with accounts of French provisions for social security, the right of French workers to organize, the provisions that French trade unions made for them as foreign workers to join and to share the benefits won by their French brothers. They did not know much about French politics. De Gaulle, the Algerian war, the whittling away of civil liberties in France: none of these things came into their conversation. All they knew was that in France a working man could speak up, everyone was 'monsieur' or 'madame', and a poor man was not automatically treated as an animal by anyone with a mite of authority. Those who were making their first trip were round-eyed, almost unbelieving.

They began to tell us of the misery that had driven them to leave their homes, and the hopes they had of the new life ahead. But not one of them thought of going away for good. After all, they were the lucky ones. They knew that in France they could earn the fare home in one week. We thought of the others, who leave their wives and children behind to cross the Atlantic, with very little hope of returning. We felt it was sad that all these workers were going into voluntary exile, whether temporarily or for ever. We too regretted leaving a country whose beauty, hospitality and endearing traditions are marred only by the appalling indifference of her rulers to the well-being of the great majority of her people.

VIII

First and last empire

Portugal's was the first of the great European overseas empires, and
it looks as if it may well be the last, for its rulers say they will never give
it up. They no longer call it an empire, but refer to their colonies as
Portugal's overseas provinces. More than eleven million people live
in these colonies, which are dotted half-way round the globe. There
has been growing interest in them during the past two or three years,
so that a good many people are less interested in Portugal than in her
colonies; one reason for this is that the most important of the latter are
in Africa.

The largest is Angola, on the west coast of Africa, bigger than the
Rhodesias and Nyasaland put together. This huge land mass lies to
the north of Verwoerd's South Africa, with which it is linked by strong
economic ties. Mozambique on the east coast provides an outlet to the
sea for the Rhodesias and the Transvaal. It is a little smaller than
Angola, but even so is still one quarter the size of India. Mozambique
too is closely connected with South Africa, with which it marches for
over 300 miles.

In fact these two colonies of Angola and Mozambique, territorially
the largest in the Portuguese empire and with a total population bigger
than Portugal's own, are flanked by regions that represent the two main
opposing forces in Africa today. To the north lies the independent and
restless Congo, to the south the land of *apartheid* and potential
revolution. And between Angola and Mozambique is the tense Central
African Federation.

These two colonies once seemed quiet backwaters remote from the
twentieth century. Now they have become important, politically,
economically and strategically, to all the interests that are struggling
for supremacy in an awakening continent. And inside Portugal itself
the question of the colonies is rapidly coming to dominate political
life.

Portugal has also some smaller possessions in Africa. The Cape Verde islands are in the Atlantic Ocean just off Senegal. The coffee and cocoa islands of São Tomé and Príncipe lie off the mainland in the Gulf of Guinea. Portuguese Guinea, on the mainland, is next-door neighbour to the newly independent republic of Guinea, an avowed enemy of European colonialism.

On the Malabar coast of India, Portugal still rules about 700,000 people in the tiny territories of Goa, Damão and Diu. The authorities claim that about a third of these people are Catholics, and it is a fact that many, particularly among the educated classes, bear Portuguese names. But beyond their troubled borders, in the Republic of India, refugees and immigrants from Goa say that a free plebiscite would yield an overwhelming vote for integration with India.

In China, Portugal still rules Macao, a port just west of Hong Kong that was first rented to the Portuguese traders in the sixteenth century. Its fluctuating population is almost entirely Chinese. In 1950 Macao had 187,000 inhabitants, but it is said that when there has been a large influx of refugees from China this figure has at times reached 800,000.

Most remote of all Portuguese possessions is Portugal's half of the island of Timor in the East Indian archipelago. This colony is inhabited by some half a million people whom the authorities describe as Malays. Before the last war Timor was used as a place of exile for Salazar's opponents, who were transported there, often without trial.

These are the remnants of Portugal's once huge empire. None of her territories in Africa or the east was lost to her through nationalist revolution. It was either by capture, or by outright sale for money by her improvident monarchs, that cities and lands in Africa, India, Malaya and the East Indies passed into Dutch, British and French hands.

Not even remnants are now left of Portugal's colonies in the New World. Instead there is perhaps the best heritage a colonial empire can hope for: a vigorous new country tied to its motherland by language and by a thousand historical links, and now a giant beside her. But Brazil, once the most treasured of all Portugal's prizes, was not like her present colonies; and what happened to Brazil is no pointer to the future of Angola or Mozambique. Brazil's position was analogous to that of Britain's thirteen American colonies, or to that of the so-called white dominions. The movement for independence came, not from an oppressed native population, but from the dissatisfaction of

Portuguese plantation owners and settlers, who resented government from Lisbon. The formal separation itself took place in a curious way. During the Napoleonic invasion the prince regent who was later the Portuguese king João VI went with the royal family to Brazil. He stayed there for twelve years, during which time his mother died and he succeeded to the throne. In 1821 he returned to Portugal, leaving his son Dom Pedro as regent of Brazil. And in 1825 Dom João signed a treaty with his son recognizing Brazil as a separate State and Dom Pedro as its emperor.

Today Portugal's rulers are not so tractable. Alone among Europe's colonial powers – with the exception of France in her relationship with Algeria – Salazar's government insists that its colonies form an integral part of the metropolis. The provinces of Angola, Mozambique and the 'State of India' (i.e. Goa, Damão and Diu!), are, it says, as Portuguese as the Minho or the Algarve. And it gave this notion legal force in good time for Portugal's entry into the United Nations in 1955. Before the *Acto Colonial* promulgated by Salazar in July 1930 the overseas possessions were called provinces; from 1930 until the new Constitution of 11 June 1951 they were colonies in law as well as fact; since the new Constitution they have again been provinces of Portugal, and in 1951 the Ministry of Colonies was renamed the Overseas Ministry. So the United Nations Charter, with all its inconvenient provisions about the responsibilities and duties of member States to their dependent territories, does not apply to Portugal. Or so it was hoped. On 11 November 1960 the General Assembly's trusteeship committee, by 45 votes to six with 24 abstentions, asked Portugal to give an account of her stewardship 'without delay'; this request was later endorsed by the General Assembly, by 68 votes to six.[1]

[1] The six countries voting against the resolution were Belgium, Brazil, France, Portugal, Spain and the Union of South Africa. On 15 March 1961 the Security Council adjourned consideration of the question of Angola after failing to adopt a proposal that a subcommittee be appointed to examine and report on the situation there. The proposal would also have called on the Portuguese government 'to consider urgently the introduction of measures and reforms in Angola' to implement the anti-colonialism resolution passed by the General Assembly on 14 December 1960. Ceylon, Liberia, the United Arab Republic, the USA and the USSR voted for the proposal. The United Kingdom abstained, as did Chile, Ecuador, France, Turkey and the representative of Chiang Kai-shek; and the proposal therefore failed to get the seven votes needed for adoption by the Council. The United States vote was one of the first confirmations of a new State Department policy towards Portuguese colonialism. This new policy had been foreshadowed in a confidential report submitted to President Kennedy by his advisers on African affairs, which recommended concerted Anglo-American pressure on the Portuguese government to liberalize its colonial régime, and which described Portuguese rule

Official statements on colonial policy, as well as the streams of speeches and articles which daily fill the newspapers, contain a fantastic mixture of mysticism, sentimentality and obscurantism. History, religion, psychology and even anthropology are all laid under contribution to justify Portugal's inalienable right to rule for ever her possessions across the seas.

The Portuguese mission

The argument runs something like this:

Each nation has a destiny. Portugal's destiny became clear in that fateful century when her mariners went forth to discover the world. Bad luck, misgovernment and conflicts with the destinies of other nations have lost her many of her possessions. But the fact that a good deal still remains after more than 400 years does prove that Portugal has a special mission. This mission is to carry Christianity and civilization to remote parts of the world – Catholic Christianity and Portuguese civilization. Neither of these necessarily entails technical development or a better standard of living or better education. Civilization is brought to savage lands by 'Lusitanianizing' them.

This process is inevitably a slow one, but it can and will be carried through. That this is possible has already been shown by the fact that in Portuguese Africa, unlike other parts of the continent, life is peaceful, there is no movement for independence, the Africans regard themselves as Portuguese and they everywhere respect and admire the European Portuguese above all other white men. Many tales are told, and are repeated in official publications, of the way in which African labourers from Mozambique who have migrated to the South African mines, or have been sent there, treat Portuguese whites with special reverence when they meet them in South Africa.

There is no such thing as racial discrimination in the overseas provinces – the argument goes on – because the Portuguese have always had a special knack of dealing with coloured peoples, of treating them humanely and with affection. The Portuguese have never been ashamed of loving coloured women and acknowledging their children by them. A professor at the *Instituto Superior de Estudos Ultramarinos*, the place where colonial administrators are trained, suggests that this

in Africa as 'intolerable'. Cf. *Foreign Report* (published by *The Economist*), 23 February 1961.

is part of a special role assigned to Portugal for the unification of mankind. The monogenetical theory of man's origin, he says, is now accepted by all scientists ('Unanimous is perhaps an exaggeration', he glosses in a footnote). By this he means that at some time in the descent of the human species there appeared on the earth one man and one woman from whom the whole human race is descended. Unfortunately historical events caused their progeny to split up; human beings divided off into races and nations. It now falls to the Portuguese, with their marvellous genius for trouble-free miscegenation, to correct matters and eventually bring together coloured and white, thus contributing to the goal of universal Christian brotherhood. He goes on:

Starting out from a monogenetic point, human expansion had attained the maximum dispersion, pulverization and differentiation, and now, moved by a monotheist ideal, it endeavours to return to its supreme unity. The so-called Portuguese overseas expansion has, therefore, a meaning of high transcendence in the history of mankind. The action of the Portuguese cannot be confused with the movements of the capitalist colonizing nations, which introduced a type of human relations based on racial segregation, in which the superior dominating race is contrasted with the inferior dominated race. By this I do not wish to convey that we were always exemplary – far from it, because we are also human beings – but to show the fundamental difference of procedure . . .

For the Portuguese the heart has always been the measure of all things; and it would be better if throughout all transformations he remained faithful to that form of measurement which is the only one capable of allowing him to accomplish fully the universalist mission that for centuries he has been carrying on, and which can never be mistaken with colonization put in terms of mere material interest and racial segregation.[1]

Nor are these the personal views of one eccentric academic. They are embodied, more succinctly, in article 133 of the Portuguese Constitution, which says:

It is of the organic essence of the Portuguese Nation to carry out the historic function of colonizing the lands of the Discoveries under its sovereignty, and to communicate and spread among the populations existing there the benefits of its civilization . . .

[1] Jorge Dias, 'The Expansion of the Portuguese . . . Overseas in the Light of Modern Anthropology', *Inquiry on Anti-Colonialism, Estudos de Ciências Políticas e Sociais*, ii (Lisbon: Ministério do Ultramar, Junta de Investigações do Ultramar, Centro de Estudos Políticos e Sociais), pp. 241–2, 245, 250. 1957. (In English in the original.)

There are glaring discrepancies between this official mystique and what really happens in the colonies. The laws defining the status of 'natives' and governing the system of forced labour; the official statistics; the available economic data; numerous official declarations not designed for foreign consumption: all these show why the Salazar régime has good reason to dread any independent inquiry into how it governs the Portuguese empire.

In the eyes of the law

Take first the legal position of Portugal's colonial subjects. Although the lands in which an Angolan or Mozambique African were born are said to be as Portuguese as the Minho or the Algarve, this legal fiction by no means extends to all who live in these lands. In Angola, Mozambique, Portuguese Guinea and Timor there are two kinds of subject. There are the citizens, who may be of any colour, and who enjoy all the rights – few though these are – of citizens of metropolitan Portugal. And there are the *indígenas* ('natives'), i.e., 'those of black race, or descended therefrom, who by their attainments [*ilustração*] and customs do not distinguish themselves from the community of their race'.[1]

This distinction is said to protect the 'natives'. It is referred to in the Constitution; but its definition and full implications are to be found in the *indigenato*, the body of laws governing every aspect of 'native' life. These laws apply to more than 95 per cent of the populations of those colonies where the distinction holds good: Timor and all the African colonies except São Tomé and Príncipe. Portugal's Indian and Chinese subjects are all considered 'civilized'.

The provisions of the main laws which make up the *indigenato* are lengthy and complicated.[2] Their chief meaning is that all but a minute fraction of the peoples of these colonies are deprived of even the scanty civil and property rights accorded to full citizens. This is done on the pretext of protecting their interests. They are dependent for every social need on the whims of a poorly paid administrator who may have as many as 50,000 or even 100,000 'natives' in his area. The normal

[1] Marcelo Caetano, *Tradições, Princípios e Métodos da Colonização Portuguesa* (Lisbon: Agência Geral do Ultramar, 1951), p. 30.

[2] The main laws are: *Lei Orgânica do Ultramar Português* (Law no. 2,066, *Diário do Governo*, 1st series, no. 135, pp. 877–92, 27 June 1953); *Estatuto dos Indígenas Portugueses das Províncias da Guiné, Angola e Moçambique* (Decree-law no. 39,666, *ibid.* no. 110, pp. 560–5, 20 May 1954).

courts are not open to them – the administrator is judge, jury, prose-
cutor and defence counsel, and he supervises the execution of his
sentence, which he pronounces as peremptorily and casually as a father
chastising his children. 'Natives' may be ordered corporal punishment
for the slightest misdemeanour: disobedience, rudeness and imperti-
nence are all offences for which men can be beaten. These beatings,
which are a commonplace in the administrators' headquarters, are
inflicted on the upturned palms with an instrument called the *palmatória* or *baramatola*, a wooden object like a table tennis bat with holes
in it which raise painful blisters. A mere complaint is enough to subject an African to this punishment. No judicial investigation or witnesses are necessary. Africans are likely to incur this treatment at any
time so long as they are on Portuguese territory, whether they are
working for themselves, working under contract or living in the city.

Africans may not travel without permission. They cannot so much
as go from one administrator's area to another without the formal
consent of both officials. Travel outside the colony is even more difficult. While we were in Portugal we were told a story which illustrates
the helplessness of Africans under Portuguese law. A family we knew
had some relatives home on leave from Africa. They had brought with
them an elderly Negro woman who had served them and nursed their
children for many years. The time came for them to return to Africa.
But the Negro woman's mistress had fallen out with her old servant
and told her that as soon as they got back home to the plantation she
would have to go to work in the fields. The servant was desperate.
She had been a domestic worker from her youth and was devoted to
her employers' family. Moreover she liked living in Portugal, which
to her meant a life of freedom such as she had never before known.
In the streets and the markets poor people treated her as one of themselves; white people were not simply rich plantation owners and
officials. So she went to one of the children she had reared, now a
grown up man, and begged him to let her stay behind and work for
him and his family for nothing. If he would not help her she would
kill herself rather than go back.

Without his help she could not stay. The authorities had only
allowed her to travel under the tutelage of a 'responsible' person, i.e.,
someone with property or education. Unless another 'responsible'
person would take her over she could not stay in Portugal and find a
job.

The story had a happy ending, because the man – it was he who told us about it – persuaded his relatives to hand their servant over to him and managed to satisfy the authorities. But he assured us that things often turned out differently; that many an African brought to Portugal has tried to run away and find a job on equal terms with Portuguese workers. Without papers they soon fall into the hands of the police and are shipped ignominiously back to a homeland they never want to see again.

On top of the lack of rights, on top of the constant threat of the *palmatória*, there is the indentured labour system. Of all aspects of life in Portugal's colonies which give the lie to official propaganda about the 'unity of the Portuguese family', none is more inhuman than this. 'Indentured labour' and 'contract labour' are euphemisms for forced labour – forced labour under the most onerous conditions. It is legitimized by the Constitution, which in two contradictory paragraphs – and this is characteristic of Salazarist laws – sanctions it and frames fair-sounding rules for its use:

Article 146. The State may only compel the natives to work on public works of general interest to the community, on tasks of which the finished product will belong to them, in the execution of judicial sentences of a penal character or for the discharge of fiscal liabilities.

Article 147. The system of native contract labour shall be based on individual liberty and on the right to a fair wage and assistance, the public authorities intervening only for the purpose of regulation.

The forced labour system

One commonly hears forced labour justified on the ground that the African is by nature a lazy fellow who will not work and who lives off the labour of his womenfolk. In fact the Africans in the Portuguese colonies form what must be nearly the cheapest source of labour in the world. The Portuguese and other interests that benefit from this state of affairs are determined that it shall continue.

It is in the province of Mozambique that the forced labour system is most perfected and affects most people. There are four types of forced labour there. Three of them are done for wages, under contract: first, work for the government and public authorities on road making, port works and public sanitation; second, work for private employers within the province; third, work in the mines of South Africa and Southern Rhodesia, for which Africans are recruited under international agreements. The fourth type is compulsory agricultural labour, the Africans being compelled to sow, cultivate and harvest a particular type of crop.

Far from being something new which came in with the Salazar régime, the forced labour system is nearly a century old. Under Salazar it has simply been intensified and given legal cover. Nor is forced labour in Mozambique something which affects only a small minority, bad enough though that would be. It is not incidental. It is the system on which the colony's entire economy depends – and on which depends also a good deal of the economic life of neighbouring territories.

Before the great mining regions in the Boer territory of the Rand were opened up during the second half of the nineteenth century. Portuguese economic life in Mozambique was largely confined to small-scale slave trading and trade in diamonds and precious metals. In 1878 slavery was abolished and a reasonably liberal labour code introduced which guaranteed a man's right to work or not, as he wished. But this did not last long. With the discovery of gold in the Transvaal was born a need, which has continued to this day, for an unlimited and easily available source of cheap labour for the mines. It is not generally realized that without the incredible cheapness of African labour these mines would long ago have been abandoned. Nearly four and a half tons of ore must be dug, from great depths, to extract one ounce of gold. In the early days, of course, when seams were richer and nearer the surface, the yield was much higher than the present 425 tons of gold a year. But in those early days mining techniques were crude, and life was as cheap as labour power. It has been estimated that since 1902 a total of 81,166 Mozambique recruits have died working on the Rand.[1] This does not include those who have returned home maimed by disease or injury contracted while working in the mines.

As soon as the gold was discovered the Portuguese authorities realized the advantage that lay within their grasp: Lourenço Marques, with its natural harbour, was the mining region's nearest outlet to the sea. They set to work building port installations and railways. Meanwhile the mining companies were freely raiding Portuguese territory

[1] Marvin Harris, *Portugal's African 'Wards'. A First-Hand Report on Labor and Education in Moçambique* (New York: American Committee on Africa, Inc., 1958), p. 27, citing *Anuário de Moçambique*, 1917 and 1940, and *Anuário Estatístico*, 1940–54. Throughout this section we are greatly indebted to Professor Harris's booklet.

and carrying off all the able-bodied African labour they could find.

This foreign impressment of the Africans was simply a continuation of a system known as *shibalo*-hunting, which was carried on widely by the Portuguese themselves. *Shibalo* is a Bantu word for tributary workers. Now the *shibalo* system has always been illegal. There are numerous laws forbidding it. So when the Portuguese authorities say that forced labour is illegal and quote these laws they are telling part of the truth; but about the numerous provisions in the opposite sense, embodied in the Constitution and in other laws, they are always reticent.

These provisions confirm that the principle laid down in the labour code of 1899, introduced when the gold-mines were beginning to need workers on a large scale, is still in full force. This principle is that the 'native' is under moral obligation to work, and that although he is free to choose the type of work he will do, failure to work will result in his being compulsorily drafted. This applies to all able-bodied male Africans between eighteen and fifty-five years of age. The various qualifications that exempt men from being stigmatized as idle are laid down. In practice, except for a handful who may have learned a trade, the chief exceptions to the obligation to wage-labour are Africans who are officially registered as 'African farmers' or who possess a minimum of fifty head of cattle. These categories together embrace only a few thousand persons. The rest, probably some 95 per cent of all able-bodied men, must work for wages or be conscribed.

The authorities make regular demands in the various areas for specified numbers of labourers to work on public projects. The district officer (*chefe de posto*) then rounds up the required number among those who are 'idle' and obliges them to enter into contracts of up to eighteen months' duration. Working conditions are onerous. Wages are wretched, varying according to the regional legal minimum from less than 15s a month to about £1 15s plus board and necessary clothing. Africans faced with this prospect are only too ready to accept a little more from a private employer. The government's use of forced labour thus acts as a bulldozer to impel the Africans into what amounts to forced labour for the private companies. When it becomes known that there is to be a round-up of 'natives' in a particular area, agents of private employers at once appear and have no difficulty in signing on labour at once. Several writers have observed that the Portuguese district officers' low salaries conduce in such circumstances to fairly widespread venality.[1] In many cases conscription drives are timed by prior agreement with private concerns in the district officer's area. Most of the men employed on private plantations are said to have been engaged in this way. In 1953 there were 90,000 of them; their average daily wage was less than 1s 3d.

This indictment of Portuguese rule is not the whole story, however. And in the most tragic and shameful part of the story the blame cannot be laid wholly at the door of the Portuguese. For the majority of the Mozambique Africans who find themselves torn from their little plots of land and forced into wage-labour are not destined to work in their own province, but for the mining companies that operate in Southern Rhodesia and the Union of South Africa. There are stern British critics of the Portuguese forced labour system who do not seem to have realized that its main beneficiaries are the great international interests that have reaped huge profits from it, and that help to maintain it by their connivance.

The transportation of large numbers of Africans far from home, and far from their ancestral farms, is not some illegal traffic carried on by desperadoes. It is an established system pursued in the full light of day and with the full weight of international treaties behind it. These treaties operate to the mutual benefit of the Portuguese and the British, American, South African, Southern Rhodesian and Dutch mine-owners – at the Africans' expense. The first of them was the Transvaal-Mozambique convention of 1909. This was followed by the Portuguese-South African convention of 1928, which was revised in 1934, 1936 and 1940. The latest version gives permission to the Transvaal Chamber of Mines to maintain at the mines an average yearly maximum of 100,000 contracted 'native' workers from Mozambique. In return for this human labour the South African government guarantees that 47·5 per cent of all imports by sea to the Johannesburg area will pass through Lourenço Marques. In addition to this valuable economic guarantee – which is sometimes varied, when more labour is needed, to provide additional traffic through Portuguese ports – the Portuguese are paid a fee of about £1 16s for each recruit. The Portuguese authorities are allowed to maintain in the Union tax collection stations, called curadorias. Finally, the South Africans pay half the African conscripts' wages to the Portuguese authorities, who are supposed to hand it over to them when they return home. The contracts are limited to eighteen

[1] See, e.g., John Gunther, *Inside Africa* (1955), p. 574.

months at a time, and the South Africans undertake to repatriate the Mozambique labourers at the end of that period.

Portuguese apologists for the system say that wages are good in the mines and that the Africans are glad to go there. It is hardly surprising that the Africans, when faced with the alternatives of forced labour for the Portuguese government, forced labour for Portuguese private employers or being drafted to the mines, may prefer the latter. But it is not to make money that they choose the third of these three evils. Wages in the mines are said to be lower today in real terms than they were in 1896. (Despite this, and despite the more evident signs of *apartheid* in South Africa than in Mozambique, these wages are a little higher than they would receive at home.) The real motive for migration is that for a short time the migrant workers escape the arbitrary rule of the Portuguese administrators. From the dread of Portuguese rule the Witwatersrand Native Labour Association benefits. This body has been given the monopoly of recruiting for the mines in southern Mozambique. And when in a given area the 'natives' learn that the administrator is looking for 'idle' Africans because workers are needed by the government, the Association is inundated with applications.

On the basis of official figures the number of Mozambique Africans working outside the province, in the Union of South Africa and the Rhodesias, is estimated at about 350,000. There are probably about another 50,000 clandestine emigrants, who are mainly from southern Mozambique.

The consequence for African life in this area has been disastrous. Two-thirds of the able-bodied men are employed beyond the frontier; many more are away from home, in other parts of the colony, under contract to the Portuguese. Still others have fled to the cities to escape this fate. This state of affairs has prevented the development of modern farming and made most of the African farms dependent entirely on female and child labour for their survival. In consequence, the productivity of African farms has steeply declined.

As a result of their labour policy, the Portuguese have achieved something of a demographic miracle. They have succeeded in converting the male half and only the male half of a farming people into permanent wage labourers. By making it impossible for the African male to live in his own home, they have not only prevented the development of modern homestead farming, but they have reduced the productivity of homestead agriculture below its level in primitive times. It need scarcely be added that the absence of practically all mature, able-bodied males has had profound effects upon the social organization and general well-being of African society.[1]

In the north of Mozambique the fourth type of compulsory labour has affected agriculture even more directly. The Portuguese authorities are determined to have cheap raw cotton for Portugal's textile mills. Neither Mozambique's soil nor its climate is very good for cotton growing. The yield per acre is exceptionally low. But this is of minor importance. Portuguese laws specify that the 'native' farmers may be assigned land and ordered what to plant, cultivate and harvest. Of late, in the north, they have been ordered to plant cotton and give up food production. Failure to do so brings the *palmatória*. If the yield is not high the authorities are not very worried. Their only expense is the seed. No wages are paid, and the Africans' only remuneration is the price they get when they sell their cotton harvest; this price is officially fixed. Counting women and children, nearly a million Africans are engaged in this form of agriculture. In 1956 they earned less than £4 a year each.

Describing what compulsory cotton planting has done in one part of his diocese, the Catholic Bishop of Beira wrote:

After the cotton campaign was begun there, the fertile fields ceased to supply food for the neighbouring populations and the people of the region itself also commenced to feel hunger. There belongs to my diocese a region in which for six months the black spectre of hunger reaped the lives of the inhabitants . . . I know of districts in which the native . . . received as payment for his harvest from 50 to 90 *escudos* [12s 6d to £1 2s 6d]. And in the same region, and in the same locality, if the native worked at planting other crops, he could grow in an equal area of land, and perhaps with less effort, from 2,000 to 4,000 *escudos* [£25 to £50] worth of products.[2]

In Angola, according to official figures, not so many Africans are victims of forced labour as in Mozambique. In 1958 there were 130,141 *contratados* – indentured workers – in Angola; their earnings came to 216,039,000 *escudos*, or just over £20 a year each.[3] Angolan nationalists say the figures for Angola are falsified, and that it is not so easy to fake the Mozambique figures because of the immigration into Rhodesia

[1] Harris, *op. cit.* p. 30.
[2] Sebastião Soares de Resende, *Ordem Anticomunista* (Lourenço Marques, 1950), quoted, Harris, *op. cit.* p. 34.
[3] *Anuário Estatístico de Angola*, 1958 (Luanda: Repartição de Estatística Geral, 1959).

and South Africa, which is shown in those countries' official returns.[1]

Life in Angola

Angola is regarded as more advanced than Mozambique. It is seen as the land of large-scale white settlement, as a future Brazil in the Old World. How do the Africans benefit from this?

According to the 1950 census the population of Angola was 4,145,266. Of these, 135,000 – to the nearest thousand – were 'civilized' and the remaining 4,009,000 'uncivilized'. The 'civilized' minority was made up of 79,000 whites (the entire white population), 26,000 mulattos (all but 3,000 of the total mulatto population) and 30,000 Negroes (a mere 0·75 per cent of the total Negro population). In other words, after 400 years of Portuguese rule, over 99 per cent of the Negro population of Angola is classed as 'uncivilized'. At this rate, Portugal's 'civilizing mission' will take another 50,000 years to accomplish.

The official figures about the educational level of the tiny 'civilized' minority raise serious doubts about the qualifications of the Portuguese civilizers. Over 23 per cent of the white population in 1950 were unable to read or write. Another 28 per cent could read and write, but had not completed primary school. A further 34 per cent had primary schooling only. The other 14 per cent had been to secondary school.

Of the Negroes in Angola only 0·36 per cent could read and write in 1950 – i.e., 14,751 out of a total Negro population of 4,036,792. There may be more Negroes able to read and write than this figure

[1] On forced labour in the Portuguese colonies, see *Report of the Ad Hoc Committee on Forced Labour* (Geneva: International Labour Office, 1953), pp. 64–5: 'The Committee finds—(a) that forced or compulsory labour is prohibited in principle by Portuguese legislation, but that there are certain restrictions and exceptions in this legislation which permit the exaction of forced or compulsory labour; (b) that the provisions protecting indigenous workers against unfair methods of recruitment do not, however, exclude a certain amount of compulsion, and it is possible that in practice certain pressure is brought to bear upon workers by responsible officials to induce them to conclude contracts of employment offered by recruiting agents; (c) that, with regard to the recruitment of indigenous workers in Mozambique for the mines in the Union of South Africa, conditions of forced labour might be created by the combined application of pressure at the recruiting stage and of the South African legislation governing breaches of labour contracts; (d) that the labour of workers in São Tomé is of considerable economic importance to the territory, and their situation appears to be similar to that of workers under a system of forced labour for economic purposes.'

suggests – former mission school pupils, for instance. But the official statistics give details of literacy and illiteracy only among 'civilized' Negroes; in any case, most 'uncivilized' ones who learn to read and write soon change their status.

Of the total non-white population only 1,148 – or 0·028 per cent – had a secondary education. And 781 of these were mulattos.[1]

Angola has no university. (In fact the only institute of higher education overseas is the medical school of Goa.) As Colonel Sá Viana Rebelo, a former governor general of Angola, put it:

For various reasons it has been thought preferable that our Negro *élites* should be educated in Lisbon. The universities which are provided for Angola in the future will not have more than the early years of courses. The final phase of studies will always be undertaken in Lisbon, so that our African students will be well impregnated with the notion that Portugal and Angola form a whole . . . The native's access to higher levels of society can be granted only with prudence.[2]

From the information available it is difficult to assess how far the Portuguese have successfully tackled the problem of combating disease in Angola – the one sphere in which it can be argued that European colonization of Africa has certain achievements to its credit. The official publications themselves warn that figures for births and deaths are incomplete and depend on voluntary registration and records of a religious nature, such as baptisms. Nor are comprehensive figures given for infant mortality, death in childbirth or the incidence of specific diseases. Of the 30,995 deaths reported to the civil administration in 1958, 24,750 came under the all-embracing heading of 'senility and badly defined causes'. It is significant that all but 100 of these were among black 'uncivilized' persons. So although the Portuguese 'civilizers' contrast the humaneness of their role in Africa with the actions of other powers, they still do not know how many of their black subjects die in Angola each year, nor what the causes are of most of those deaths which do come to their notice.

There is no doubt that the reason for the dearth of information is

[1] It is quite likely that the 1960 census will show an appreciable relative increase in the total number of 'civilized' and literate persons in Angola, owing to increased immigration from Portugal. Between 1950 and 1955 there was a 37 per cent increase in the white population; since 1955 the government has encouraged immigration still further.
[2] In an interview given to *L'Avenir* (Leopoldville) on the position of the 'native' in Portuguese society, reprinted in *A Voz de Angola* (Luanda: Direcção dos Serviços de Economia), no. 192, pp. 3–6, March 1958.

the poverty and lack of equipment of the State medical service. In 1957 there was one doctor for every 22,400 of the population and one medical auxiliary (either nurse, orderly or midwife) for every 9,576.[1] (In Portugal, poor as its health services are, there is one doctor for every 1,500 and one medical auxiliary for every 1,659.)

Supporters of Portuguese rule have objected that these figures embrace only medical personnel in the State service and that there are in fact dozens more doctors in Angola, either practising privately or else employed as medical officers in big enterprises. But private medical practitioners in the Portuguese colonies are concentrated in the few large towns; their presence necessarily mainly benefits the white population, for the Africans are much too poor to pay for private treatment.

The Africans' poverty and their position on the free labour market, as opposed to the forced labour system, may be judged from the fact that the wages of European craftsmen are on average almost three times as much as the wages of Africans doing the same work. For instance, in Luanda, the capital, where wages are higher than elsewhere, a European carpenter earns £39 a month, while an African carpenter earns £21 2s 6d. An electrician earns £38 10s a month if he is a European, £12 15s 6d if he is an African. A white cook earns £41 7s 6d, an African cook £6 5s a month. A European stoker earns £50, an African stoker £5 3s 6d a month. A European driver of light vehicles earns £31 10s, an African driver £15 a month.[2]

In recent years there has been considerable inflation in Angola; the cost of living is generally higher than in Portugal itself. So these wretched wages have in fact almost as low a purchasing power as their sterling equivalent suggests.

All this points to the most open and ruthless economic discrimination against Africans. Apologists for the régime claim that those Africans who have ceased to be 'natives' and have become *assimilados* ('assimilated persons') enjoy complete social equality with Europeans. In the first place it is clear that few Africans ever do attain this status. This is not surprising, for the sole judge of a man's qualifications is the local administrator; the inadequate educational facilities and the general nature of the régime greatly limit the number of Africans who can hope to qualify.

[1] Figures based on *Anuário Estatístico do Ultramar, 1958* (Lisbon: Instituto Nacional de Estatística, 1959). We have estimated the 1957 population at 4,549,000.
[2] *Anuário Estatístico de Angola, 1958.*

Moreover, it is doubtful whether there is in fact social equality for those who do assume the full rights of citizens. Take one criterion: marriage. In Angola in 1957 there was a total of 218 marriages between 'civilized' persons; of these, 150 were between whites, 19 between white men and mulatto women, one between a mulatto man and a white woman. In 27 of the marriages both parties were mulattos; in 18, Negroes. There was one marriage between a mulatto man and a Negro woman, and two between Negro men and mulatto women.[1] No mention whatever is made of any marriage between whites and Negroes. (Nor is any mention made of such marriages in the statistics relating to any of the other African colonies.) It must therefore be assumed that such marriages do not take place. In fact throughout the African colonies there were in 1957 only 73 marriages between white and coloured persons.

This is the pattern of a society that is racially divided, socially if not legally. It is not the pattern of a society where assimilation is taking place. And accounts of life nowadays in Angola and Mozambique confirm this. We were told by several Portuguese who had recently visited Africa that in towns like Luanda things are now very different from what they were a generation ago. White residential areas and the business centre are now virtually all-white. Menial jobs, once performed by Africans, are now done by white people. There are white waiters in cafés and restaurants, white servants in private houses, white drivers and conductors on the buses, white shoeblacks on the streets. It is the increased immigration from Portugal of poor and illiterate people that has displaced Africans from these occupations.

This change seems to fit in with the desires of the white settlers. One informant told us he had the impression that the settlers wanted to put as great a distance as possible between themselves and the African population, to confine them to 'native' areas of the city, to restrict them to work on plantations, in the mines and on public works. The old patriarchal life typical of the Brazilian 'big house' – where white children were brought up by coloured servants and every young white man had a Negro mistress – is fast disappearing in Angola.[2] There is little doubt that in spite of Lisbon's official condemnation of racialism the white settlers in Portuguese Africa today share the attitude

[1] *Anuário Estatístico do Ultramar, 1958.*
[2] There are today far fewer mulattos in relation to the number of whites than was the case sixty years ago. In 1900 there were 9,000 whites and 7,000 mulattos, in 1930, 30,000 whites and 13,500 mulattos, in 1955, 109,600 whites and 30,400 mulattos. (*Anuário Estatístico de Angola, 1958.*)

of all other white settlers in African countries, and are far more influenced by the South African example than by pious references to a tradition that is now practically dead. In Mozambique the influence of South Africa is particularly strong. It has become fashionable there for Europeans to send their children to school in South Africa, so that they return home speaking not only English but also the language of *apartheid*. This is beginning to happen in Angola too.

There may be no signs saying 'White only' anywhere in the Portuguese African colonies; but effective segregation takes place without such signs. When a tram-car journey costs a quarter of an African's daily wage, few Africans will ride in tram-cars. While Africans are too poor to go into restaurants, cinemas or other places of entertainment, this economic barrier is no less effective than signs are.

Repression and revolt

The first of the Portuguese colonies to come into the news after the end of the war was Goa. Its anomalous position on a sub-continent that had achieved independence was bound to lead to unrest sooner or later. A great many Goans engaged in passive resistance; but this was more than the Portuguese police State was prepared to tolerate. Between 1946 and 1957 over 2,000 Goan nationalists were arrested; thirteen leaders were deported to the Cape Verde islands, Angola or Portugal; about 300 received sentences ranging up to 28 years' imprisonment; and 87 were either shot or tortured to death.[1] On 17 February 1957, in Ponda, some Goan nationalists were tied to a jeep, dragged for about two miles, soaked in petrol and set alight.[2]

In the last three or four years there have been numerous reports of widespread arrests in Angola, deportations of political offenders, and a mass political trial which the leading counsel for the defence, Dr Palma Carlos, was not allowed to attend. An appeal by Angolan nationalists to the United Nations declares that Portuguese military installations in Angola are being strengthened, and that military forces

[1] Information supplied by the Goa League. Some further details are given in *Goa News* (London, 1957–9).

[2] In letters to the *Guardian* (25 November and 8 December, 1960) this incident was denied by an employee of the Portuguese embassy in London. On 12 January 1961 Mr Peter D'Costa of Bombay wrote in the *Guardian*: 'I was in Ponda at the time and saw the incident myself, and I am surprised at this denial by the Portuguese embassy in London of an incident which was noticed by hundreds of people . . . Why are the Portuguese so afraid to allow independent international jurists to make their own investigations in Goa?'

there will soon number 60,000 men. The appeal accuses the military authorities of organizing brutal raids into African communities and adds that the Salazar government aims at creating in Angola another Algeria.[1]

The *Movimento Popular de Libertação de Angola* (MPLA), some of whose leaders visited London in December 1960, accuse the Portuguese authorities of doubling head taxes on Africans to pay for military expenditure; seizing over £12,500 from African savings banks; compelling some Africans who have motor-cars to pay taxes on a daily basis so as to control their movements more closely; executing Africans without trial; and dropping the bodies of African political prisoners into the Atlantic from aeroplanes, so that there shall be no evidence of their murder.

The Portuguese authorities make it impossible for these allegations to be investigated. A representative appointed by the International Commission of Jurists to attend the mass political trial referred to above was refused permission to do so on the ground that the Commission's request was an insult to Portuguese justice. When the *Guardian* published the allegation by a leader of the MPLA about the use of aeroplanes to dispose of political prisoners' bodies an indignant denial came from the Portuguese embassy in London. The *Guardian's* Commonwealth correspondent replied that the MPLA leader 'was in fact only repeating information that had already come to me, from a source I regard as trustworthy, when I was travelling in African territories adjoining Angola'.[2]

Not all the victims in Angola are Africans. White people too have proved themselves vigorous opponents of Salazarism and colonialism. Some have been arrested and held without trial; others have been transported to Portugal; and on 11 August 1960, the Luanda military court passed sentence on seven Europeans. Three of them were sent to prison for three years, two for two years, one – a woman doctor – for one year, and one for three months. The first six will also be subjected to 'security measures' for anything up to three years after their sentences expire, which means that they can be detained for this further period at the discretion of the political police.[3]

[1] *Appeal to the Member States of the UN* (Conakry and London: Executive Committee of the Movimento Popular de Libertação de Angola, 1960).
[2] *Guardian*, 8 December 1960. The embassy official's remark about 'vile, unfounded accusations', added the Commonwealth correspondent, 'would come better from a government which allowed outside observers to go and see fair play for themselves.'
[3] The result of the trial was reported in *República* (Lisbon), 12 August 1960.

That opposition to Salazar among white Angolans has been widespread for some time was evident from the results of the 1958 presidential elections. Although only 0·7 per cent of the population of Angola voted, and access to the polls was made as difficult there as it was in Portugal, 10,300 of the 32,600 votes cast in the colony were for the opposition candidate Humberto Delgado.[1]

Yet it cannot be assumed that a vote for Delgado automatically meant a vote against colonialism. Recent travellers to Angola whom we met in Portugal told us that there was admittedly a good deal of feeling among the white population against Portugal's present rulers – but that much of this feeling arose from dissatisfaction with the régime's inefficiency and bureaucracy, and with its lack of vigour in expanding white settlement and providing capital for the exploitation of Angola's wealth. One informant said many white settlers were talking of a Brazil in Africa: not the old colonial Brazil that Portugal's rulers would like to see transported to twentieth-century Angola, but an independent, white-dominated Angola along the lines of the Union of South Africa.

This kind of dream is not very realistic. All Salazar's attempts at white settlement cannot increase the tiny white population to significant proportions very quickly. The struggle in Angola is clear-cut. On one side there are the millions of Africans, on the other the repressive forces of Salazar's police State. In such a struggle the views of a handful of whites, many of whom are illiterate and all of whom are themselves deprived of democratic rights, are nugatory.

Angola is not like Goa. It is a vast territory; more important, it has never been thoroughly subdued. Until the twentieth century effective Portuguese occupation hardly went deeper than the coastal strip. In the past sixty years there has been constant unrest, with African uprisings in 1922 and 1939. Young Angolan Africans remember how their fathers and grandfathers fought against the Portuguese. So it is not surprising that today, when other African territories – some only just across their frontier – have become independent, the people of Angola are not willing to tolerate Portuguese rule.

There are at present in Angola four movements of resistance to Portuguese occupation. The MPLA we have already referred to. The

[1] These figures were given by the governor general of Angola in a broadcast reported in *A Voz de Angola*, no. 195, pp. 4–6, June 1958. He drew this extraordinary conclusion: 'Thus more than two-thirds of the population of the province voted for the candidate of the National Union . . .' (p. 4)!

others are: the *Alliance des Ressortissants de Zombo* (ALIAZO), an organization of the Zombo people, in the north of the colony; the *União das Populações de Angola* (UPA), an inter-tribal organization; and the *União Nacional dos Trabalhadores de Angola* (UNTA), a trade union organization.[1]

During his visit to London at the end of 1960 we spent an evening with Viriato Cruz, the young poet who is one of the leaders of the MPLA in Angola, and he told us something about the origins of the Angolan nationalist movement. Viriato Cruz is thirty-two; he has been interested in politics since he was fifteen and still at secondary school. But his activity was not at first directly political. Along with other young Africans in Angola who were lucky enough to have some education, he became interested in the literature, art and music of his own people. In the first few years after the war conditions in Angola were more liberal than in Portugal, and the colony was flooded with Brazilian literature, much of it Left wing. Many of the Brazilian writers were interested in the African contribution to Brazilian culture. And their young Angolan readers became critical of the fact that the only 'African' literature being created in Angola was really a Portuguese literature peppered with a few African words and other exoticisms, and set in Angola. It was much the same with sculpture and painting, which were produced for tourists rather than as a natural development of a native tradition.

Working in legal African organizations such as the *Associação dos Naturais de Angola*,[2] these young Africans launched the slogan: 'We are going to discover Angola.' They began to realize that they were virtually foreigners in their own country, educated in the Portuguese language, Portuguese history and the geography of Portugal, brought up in European traditions. They discovered that the peoples of Angola had a long history of their own: one of their languages, Kisi-kongo, was committed to print as early as 1624, in a Portuguese missionary's treatise on Christian doctrine, and a grammar of it was published in Rome in 1659; another, Kimbundu, was illustrated by Italian

---

[1] In Mozambique there is the Mozambique African National Union. In Portuguese Guinea there is an organization called the *Partido Africano da Independência* (PAI); immigrants from that colony have formed two bodies, one in Senegal and the other in the Republic of Guinea, each called *Movimento de Libertação da Guiné e Cabo Verde* (MLGV).

[2] A similar organization in Mozambique, the *Associação dos Naturais de Moçambique*, was the only organization in that colony in which some form of representation of the Africans was allowed. On 12 December 1960 the *Diário de Lisboa* reported that its leading committees in Lourenço Marques and Beira had been dismissed and replaced by government nominees.

missionaries in religious pamphlets and catechisms in 1622–3 and 1661–4, and its grammar was published in Lisbon in 1697.[1]

Viriato Cruz and his friends decided to fight against the rootlessness that the Portuguese policy of 'assimilation' had foisted on them; they set themselves the task of developing a genuinely African culture: a literature that would interpret the daily life of their peoples, not as the Portuguese colonizers thought it was – or should be – lived, but as the ordinary Africans in fact lived it.

As their ideas became clearer so did the authorities become more and more hostile. In 1952 a journal, *A Mensagem*, appeared; it was banned after its second issue. An attempt was made to organize a congress on Angolan literature, and UNESCO was asked to help. PIDE agents in the African organizations began to interfere. After his first two-year term in government service Viriato Cruz's employment came up for review, and he was dismissed; the same thing happened to many others.

These experiences convinced the young nationalists that cultural efforts alone would not solve their people's problems. The government itself, which hoped to prevent the rise of a nationalist movement, compelled them to take a clearer and clearer political stand. And the nationalists realized that it was no longer possible to work openly in the legal organizations – that their work, if it was to be effective, must now be done underground.

So was born a movement of resistance to Portuguese colonialism, forced labour, national degradation, the imposition of an alien culture, ruthless economic exploitation and the denial of elementary human rights. This movement has received a tremendous impetus from the emergence of new, independent African States. Its programme calls for a struggle, by every means, to end Portuguese colonial domination

---

[1] An English translation of the Kisi-kongo grammar (H. Grattan Guinness, ed., *Grammar of the Congo Language as Spoken Two Hundred Years Ago, Translated from the Latin of Brusciotto*) appeared in 1882; the Kimbundu grammar is Pedro Diaz, *Arte da Língua de Angola*. Sir Harry H. Johnston wrote in his *Comparative Study of the Bantu and Semi-Bantu Languages*, vol. ii (Oxford, 1922), pp. 106, 104: 'Both Kisi-kongo and Kakongo . . . had been elaborately developed by the natives themselves without the influence of the white man, and Kisi-kongo especially may be looked on as one of the Bantu classical tongues, so flexible, so nicely ordered that, like Kimbundu, it could easily become the speech of a completely civilized people.' 'During the nineteenth century [Kimbundu] became quite a literary language under the impulse of Portuguese half-castes.' Forty years later, in a speech to the National Assembly, Salazar was claiming that 'to those who were dispersed and could not understand one another's dialects' Portuguese colonization 'brought within their grasp a higher form of expression – the [Portuguese] language' (*Novidades*, Lisbon, 1 December 1960).

in Angola and establish the immediate and complete independence of the Angolan homeland; looking farther ahead, it envisages the election by universal suffrage of an assembly of the people of Angola, which will appoint a coalition government. An agrarian reform and the planned development of the economy are also provided for.[1]

Far from giving the Portuguese government pause, these developments have only made Salazar more obstinate still. The trusteeship committee resolution asking Portugal to give information on her colonies drove the régime into a chauvinistic frenzy. Mass demonstrations were organized in the streets of Lisbon and other cities – in a country where football matches are the only open-air gatherings normally permitted – and on 30 November 1960 Salazar himself spoke. Calling on the nation to unite against the cruel attacks from abroad, he declared before the National Assembly:

We have been in Africa for 400 years, which is something more than having arrived yesterday. We took there a doctrine, which is not the same as being carried away by self-interest. We are there with a policy which authority is carrying out and defending, and this is distinct from abandoning human destinies to the so-called 'winds of history' . . . We are not disposed to accept the abusive intervention of third parties in our internal life . . . It is impossible for us to accept for our overseas provinces, which make up part of the Nation, a position equivalent to territories under United Nations trusteeship and destined for eventual independence, or to render accounts [in the United Nations] of how the Portuguese see fit to govern themselves in their own house. It is illegitimate on the part of the United Nations to pass a discriminative resolution against Portugal; the General Assembly has no competence to declare the territories of any power non-autonomous. This is the juridically correct interpretation, and the one which has always been given to the principles of the Charter. On these terms we were admitted, and had there been another interpretation of the texts it is certain that we should not have applied for membership of the organization . . . I do not see that there can be any pause in our work, nor any other preoccupation than that of gripping the plough with one hand and the sword with the other, as did our forbears throughout centuries. This new task, whose weight we can scarcely measure, is a challenge flung down to the present generation, and it will be one of the greatest trials of our history. It is necessary to prepare our minds for it; it will demand from us great sacrifices, the most absolute dedication, and, if necessary, the blood from our veins also, as has already

[1] Movimento Popular de Libertação de Angola (MPLA), *Programa* ([London], n.d. [1960]). An English summary appeared in the *Portuguese and Colonial Bulletin* (London), vol. i, no. 2, pp. 9, 16, March 1961.

happened in Goa and elsewhere. That is our destiny; that is the mission of our life, which is not to be cursed but to be blessed for its loftiness and nobility.[1]

Through the sabre-rattling, this much is evident: that Salazar knows his régime cannot survive without the colonies. But if France, after seven years of total war, has not been able to defeat the Algerians, it is hardly likely that 100,000 Europeans backed only by the Portuguese army will be able to suppress over four million people for long, if those four million are determined to win their independence. Yet what alternative has Salazar but to try? However astute he has been through three decades, however many storms he has weathered, his 'Estado Novo' now faces shipwreck on the rock of colonialism.

As we shall see, however, Salazar's opponents in Portugal are by no means all of one mind about the significance of the African awakening. The storm that threatens to engulf Salazar also threatens to drive the opposition off its course.[2]

---

[1] *Novidades*, 1 December 1960. The official English translation of this speech appears in *Portugal: An Informative Review*, 4th year, no. 6, pp. 353–66, Nov.-Dec. 1960.

[2] Since this chapter was written full-scale colonial warfare has started in Angola. One British journalist in Luanda has estimated that between 30,000 and 50,000 persons, all but 1,000 of them Africans, were killed in the first three months of the fighting (*Observer*, 21 May 1961). To augment Portugal's tiny armed forces, private firms in Angola have been authorized to form their own private armies, and Europeans may now import arms freely into Angola. White civilians, including women and children, are being trained in the use of weapons. The Portuguese authorities say they are facing an attempt at genocide; but all the evidence shows that if anyone is bent on genocide it is the Portuguese government. It is hardly surprising that spontaneous tribal revenge has been taken upon Portuguese; the reply has been the razing of entire villages and the use of napalm (apparently made in Britain and supplied through NATO). The 'civilizing mission' has gone by the board. Here are the words addressed to 3,000 young soldiers about to embark for Angola at the beginning of May: 'We are going to fight savages. We are going to fight wild beasts – wild beasts who are not Portuguese, because they obey orders from international communism. We are face to face with terrorists who have to be fought as wild beasts are fought' (*Jornal de Notícias*, Oporto, 6 May 1961). These words were spoken by Brigadier Mário Silva, the new Minister for the Army.

IX

Portrait of a police State

A Portuguese who opposes the dictatorship of Dr Salazar renders himself liable to one or more of the following sanctions:

(1) Imprisonment for a long period without trial;
(2) Improper methods of interrogation by the political police, including torture;
(3) A secret trial;
(4) Interference with the rights of his defence lawyers;
(5) A sentence of excessive length – or even of indefinite duration.

All these penalties are being suffered by democrats in Portugal, not in the infancy of a new régime, but today, a whole generation after that régime first imposed itself on the Portuguese people.

Freedom of association

In theory, the Portuguese Constitution guarantees freedom of association. In practice, if you live in Portugal you cannot form or belong to any overt organization unless the government approves of its existence. And the government does not permit any organization to exist which does not approve of *its* existence, ideology, policies and methods. Soon after the 1926 *coup d'État* the leaders of the political parties were imprisoned and prevented from engaging in political activity; many of them were exiled to the Portuguese islands or to the colonies. Today the pro-Salazar National Union is the only party that functions legally. There is, to be sure, the *Causa Monárquica*; its existence is assured by its support for Salazar. There are a number of religious organizations, which have always sought to gain mass support for the régime; where Catholic opposition to Salazar has manifested itself it has always been repressed immediately, and its leaders imprisoned or exiled. Salazar's intolerance is by no means confined to bodies that might propagate Marxist ideas. In June 1956 a number of persons who wanted to form a Portuguese United Nations Association applied for permission to do so. The application was considered for ten months and then turned down. Despite Portugal's membership of the United Nations, propaganda for the principles of the United Nations Charter was evidently too dangerous to be allowed.

Till recently there was one apparent exception to this blanket denial of freedom of association: the existence of a Portuguese League for the Rights of Man, a lawyers' association which was founded in 1922 and which has been affiliated to UNESCO. It was small, weak and semi-dormant; police shorthand writers were present at its infrequent meetings; and in November 1960 its offices were raided by the political police and its files were seized.

The law which governs 'associations and organizations carrying out their activities in Portuguese territory' makes curious and enlightening reading. They are obliged to provide the civil authorities of the districts in which they have their headquarters, branches or committees with copies of their constitutions and rules and lists of their offices and the persons who fill them. They must give any other supplementary information about their activities which may be requested from them 'for reasons of order and public security'. Failure to comply with these requirements is punishable by fines, imprisonment and loss of pension. Ordinary members of organizations 'carrying out their activities, in whole or in part, in a clandestine or secret manner' may be imprisoned for varying terms; there are stiffer sentences for persons in leading positions.

Particular attention is devoted to controlling the thoughts of civil servants, who appear to have few civil rights:

> No individual may be appointed to a public position, civil or military, in the State or in the administrative organizations or corporations, without presenting a document authenticated or executed by the chief of the service concerned, with a sworn declaration to the effect that he does not belong, and will never belong, to any of the associations and organizations referred to . . .[1]

Civil servants who show, or have shown, 'a spirit of opposition to the fundamental principles of the Political Constitution, or who do not guarantee to co-operate in achieving the higher aims of the State,

[1] Law no. 1,901, articles 1, 2, 3, *Diário do Governo*, 1st series, no. 115, p. 699, 21 May 1935.

will be suspended or retired, if they have the right to that, or, if not, will be dismissed'.[1]

Links with organizations of any kind abroad are specifically forbidden unless government approval is obtained.[2]

Such laws bear very heavily on two sections of the community who in most other western countries practise a freedom of association that has largely been won piecemeal in struggle and is therefore cherished: the industrial workers and the students.

In Portugal it is a criminal offence to form a trade union. But all workers *must* belong to their appropriate *sindicato*. The *sindicatos* bear as little resemblance to genuine trade unions as do the State-controlled 'trade unions' in communist countries. Strikes and lock-outs are illegal. A worker who goes on strike is liable to be sent to prison for anything from two to eight years.

The activities of students are circumscribed by a decree-law promulgated under the stimulus of the 1956 mass trial of fifty-two young oppositionists in Oporto. Students' unions may co-ordinate their activities only for special purposes, for which the Ministry of National Education gives its authority in each case. Relations with foreign national or international students' organizations may be maintained only through the intermediary of the Ministry. Members elected to executive committees or finance committees of students' unions, or as chairmen or secretaries of students' general assemblies, may take up their posts only after the Ministry has approved their election or nomination. Each students' union functions under the direct surveillance of a permanent delegate of the principal of the college, nominated by him from among the teaching staff; this delegate's task is 'to maintain respect for the established social order and for discipline'. Students' unions which engage in any form of activity 'contrary to the established social order or to discipline' may be suspended or banned by the Ministry, which may also appoint a new administrative committee if after two successive elections the majority

[1] Decree-law no. 25,317, article 1, *Diário do Governo*, 1st series, no. 108, pp. 649–50, 13 May 1935. Thirty-three university professors have been dismissed from their posts under this decree-law. Another decree-law seems designed to encourage spying on and denunciation of one's colleagues; it threatens heads of departments with suspension, retirement or dismissal 'if any of their respective officials or employees subscribe to subversive doctrines and it is ascertained that they did not use their authority or did not inform their superiors' (Decree-law no. 27,003, quoted, *Bulletin of the International Commission of Jurists*, The Hague, no. 7, p. 39, October 1957).

[2] Decree-law no. 37,447, quoted, *Bulletin of the International Commission of Jurists*, no. 7, p. 37, October 1957.

of the members elected are not to its liking. The students' organizations were given sixty days to apply to the Ministry for approval of the new rules which had to be drawn up in accordance with the new law: 'associations and organizations failing to apply within this period shall cease to exist'.[1]

Censorship

There is as little freedom of speech in Portugal as there is freedom of association. Publications of all kinds are subjected to a rigorous censorship, and scarcely any criticism whatever of the government is allowed. The imprint 'Passed by the censorship committee' appears on all newspapers. No periodical may be launched without government approval. The seizure of books is a commonplace. The censors can intervene against any publication which in their view might 'induce the public to error concerning the social or political doctrines therein habitually defended'. Nor may any foreign publication be imported, distributed or sold if it contains 'matter whose disclosure would not be permitted in Portuguese publications'[2] – and while we were in Lisbon two issues of the *New Statesman* containing outspoken accounts of life under Salazar were not available at the bookshops which normally stock that periodical. The practice with the *New Statesman*, the *Observer* and a number of other British journals that might from time to time have a harsh word to say about Salazar is that they are kept at the bookshops, but out of sight, while one copy is read by the censors. If nothing objectionable is found, then that issue may go on display.

A recent instance of how the censorship operates was the banning of the novel *Quando os Lobos Uivam* (*When the Wolves Howl*) by the distinguished writer Aquilino Ribeiro, founder and first chairman of the Union of Portuguese Writers and a member of the Portuguese Academy and of the Academy of Bahia. This book dealt openly with one disastrous consequence of Salazar's policies: the afforestation question in the north, to which we made reference in Chapter VII. Accused of bringing the State into disrepute, Portugal's greatest living writer – as many regard him – had to put up a bail of 60,000 *escudos*

[1] Decree-law no. 40,900, articles 6, 7, 12, 13, 14, 15, *Diário do Governo*, 1st series, no. 269, p. 1,896, 12 December 1956. The students' union of the Lisbon university Faculty of Medicine has been banned since 1956.
[2] Decree-law no. 26,589, articles 2, 5, 7, *Diário do Governo*, 1st series, no. 112, p. 520, 14 May 1936.

(£750), and his book was impounded by the censor. It was feared that he would be imprisoned, but the prosecution pending against him was dropped under an amnesty. He had written a dignified letter to all Portuguese newspapers, but the censors had forbidden its publication. We were shown a copy. In it he wrote that the authorities accused him of making injurious or offensive statements against the Portuguese Bench and other authorities under cover of literary fiction. He went on:

> My ethics as a writer, which are proved to all, authorize no one to affirm that I use fiction to attack anyone – institutions or men. When I do that I do it openly and directly. The official statement could well have limited itself to prosecuting me, without saying this.

The Aquilino affair has not attracted a fraction of the attention, either among British writers or the public at large in Britain, that the Pasternak affair attracted. It seems to us imperative that Aquilino's stand for freedom as a writer, and for the lifting of the ban on his novel, should be supported with equal energy and ardour by all who, rightly, oppose political interference with the artist in communist countries.[1]

Elections

Until 1958 no presidential election had ever been contested under Salazar. In 1949 General Norton de Matos, the candidate of a united opposition, withdrew from the contest on the ground that no free or fair election was possible. In 1951 there were at first two opponents of the government candidate. Professor Rui Luís Gomes, the mathematician, did not receive governmental approval and was disqualified. Admiral Quintão Meireles, a former Minister of Foreign Affairs, withdrew from the election on the ground that the conditions in which it was held did not permit a true expression of the people's will.

The main obstacle to a genuinely democratic election appears to be a law which provides that literate adults or persons paying a certain minimum in taxes are eligible to be on the electoral roll.[2] Since almost half the population is illiterate, and poverty is widespread, well over half the population is effectively disfranchised. Moreover, to have your

[1] The full text of the indictment and of Aquilino's defence are given in *Quando os Lobos Julgam a Justiça Uiva* (São Paulo, n.d. [1960]), in which it is shown that the economic reality is far worse than he had suggested in his banned novel.
[2] Law no. 2,015, quoted, *Bulletin of the International Commission of Jurists*, no. 7, p. 35, October 1957. The restrictions described in this section apply to both presidential and National Assembly elections.

name entered on the roll you must make a personal application and submit proofs of your educational attainments or of the taxes you pay. It may well require considerable courage to insist that your name go on the roll. Even then there are provisions for disqualifying people, according to criteria so flexible that the meshes of this net that the government has woven to protect itself from the effects of 'universal' suffrage can be adjusted as desired. If you are thought unsuitable to have a vote there are always ways of preventing you from having one. There are many university graduates – we met some of them – who have never been allowed to vote in their lives. When it comes to the casting of votes, the electors may put into the ballot-boxes either the official list of government candidates (distributed by the police) or, if there is one, the opposition list (distributed by opposition canvassers); but the government never permits any representative of the opposition to be present at the count as a scrutineer. During the 1958 presidential election 90,000 of the opposition candidate's voting slips were seized while on their way to Santarém. And during and after the election several hundred opposition supporters were arrested.

To sum up, Salazar has no fewer than seven distinct devices for preventing really free elections: (1) opposition candidates must be approved by the government; (2) poor or illiterate persons may not vote; (3) the onus is on the individual citizen to get his name on the electoral roll; (4) electors may be disqualified at the government's discretion; (5) opposition representatives may not attend the count; (6) opposition voting slips, essential for the casting of anti-Salazar votes, may be seized by the police; (7) opposition supporters may be arrested.

In the light of all these handicaps, the vote of 236,528 that the opposition candidate Humberto Delgado gained in 1958, against 758,998 for the government candidate Américo Tomás, was a victory for the opposition.

During the 1958 election campaign the Portuguese government, despite its manifold precautions, was in a state of fear. After the Liberal opposition had scratched its candidate Meireles, and the communist-supported candidate Arlindo Vicente had asked all his adherents to vote for Delgado, the resulting straight fight aroused great public excitement. The events that followed were described to us by a Portuguese friend in these words:

'There was an air of great expectation, but at the same time great calm and discipline. People wanted to know what was going on.

Above all they wanted to know what attitude the army would take. It was thanks to Santos Costa, then Minister of Defence but afterwards dismissed by Salazar, that the army remained faithful to the régime. Santos Costa, though a very unpopular figure, managed to keep his finger on the pulse of events. There had been meetings of officers all over the place, but he kept a firm hand on things. One day, to show people where the army stood, he filled the whole of the Praça do Comércio with tanks, and every now and then they would go up and down the Avenida. In the middle of all this Delgado came back from the north, where he had been received with acclamation. He was to have made a tour of Lisbon on his return, and thousands went to the Santa Apolónia station to wait for him and welcome him. But his car was diverted by the police and he was not allowed to go through the city. At certain points the police opened fire with machine-guns, and the people began to pick up stones from the pavements and fight back.[1] The police say they fired into the air, but many people were hit and five were seriously wounded. A lot were taken to prison. A few days later there was a big meeting at the Camões high school. The police sealed off the part of the city where the meeting was held and told those who had no invitation that they could not pass the barrier. This led to further clashes, and many more people were hurt and three were killed.'

This was in May 1958. In the first clash, according to official figures which are certainly an understatement, nineteen people were injured, and in the second about eighty, including twelve policemen. There were similar incidents in Oporto, where tanks patrolled the streets and twenty-seven people were injured, and in the industrial town of Braga. A National Union *communiqué* declared that these riots followed 'the communist pattern' and that they had been caused by 'the imprudence of unwise words'.[2]

That a quarter of a million votes should have been cast for Delgado despite all the precautions was so unpalatable to Salazar that his speech

[1] Almost all pavements in Lisbon are constructed of stones small enough to be ripped up and thrown with ease.

[2] *Diário da Manhã*, 19 May 1958. The *Manchester Guardian* commented (20 May 1958): 'Such paternal language should not deceive anyone. The régime has fearful punishment in store for unwise words, discreetly administered in secret proceedings by special courts created to deal with political offences . . . Convinced opponents of the régime are punished rigorously. But those who can be frightened into conformity – "transformed into inoffensiveness" is the official term – may be shown some mercy. That also seems to be the principle for conducting the presidential election campaign. Its result . . . therefore seems tolerably certain.'

of 1 July 1958, to district leaders of the National Union, was widely spoken of, even among his followers, as the speech of an angry and vindictive man. We have already seen that he mentioned the possibility of abolishing presidential elections by direct suffrage – a step that was later taken. He also warned that any strikes of political protest, such as those into which some workers and industrialists had, he alleged, been led by agitators, would be dealt with by the government with the greatest severity.

Delgado was soon punished for his success. He was dismissed from his post as director-general of civil aviation and relieved of his army commission. The official *communiqué* announcing his 'separation from the service' contained a threat of criminal proceedings against him. Since he was being watched all the time by agents of the political police, and was told by his friends in government circles that he stood in danger of imminent arrest, he took refuge in the Brazilian embassy in Lisbon. After several weeks the insistence of the Brazilian ambassador finally gained a guarantee from the Portuguese authorities of safe conduct to Lisbon airport, where Delgado boarded an aeroplane which took him to Brazil and freedom.

The pendant to this story illustrates Salazar's vindictiveness. Álvaro Lins, the Brazilian ambassador who refused to hand over Delgado, and who secured his safe conduct to the airport, was later removed from his post as a result of Portuguese government pressure. His reply was the dignified gesture of handing back the Order of Christ that government had awarded him for his services to Luso-Brazilian relations.[1]

The Bevan case

In November 1958 the Portuguese government refused to allow an unofficial visit to the country by the late Aneurin Bevan, who was to have given two lectures on democracy in the modern world. The group that invited him included Delgado, Rear-Admiral José Mendes Cabeçadas, Admiral Quintão Meireles, Dr Francisco Pinto da Cunha Leal, a former Prime Minister, and Dr Jaime Cortesão, the historian. This was how the government explained its refusal:

The position of the promoters of the invitation, the political complexion of the person invited, the programme itself, the obvious disproportion between

1 Álvaro Lins has described his term of office in Lisbon in *Missão em Portugal*, vol. i (Rio de Janeiro, 1960).

the capacity of the halls chosen and the small number of people capable of understanding the orator in his own language – all indicate a continuation of the process of agitation in which it has been sought to maintain the country since the presidential election. However great the consideration that Mr Bevan may deserve, the intervention of foreigners in Portuguese internal politics is considered inadmissible by us. Mr Bevan's talks have not been authorized.[1]

To this the opposition replied that during the war many Germans had been invited by the government to come and indoctrinate Portuguese youth, and that many Italians had been invited during *and since* the war to lecture on the corporate State.

Four of those who had invited Bevan were then arrested and kept in jail for a week: Cortesão, Dr Azevedo Gomes (one of Delgado's nominators), Vieira de Almeida and António Sérgio. All were over seventy years old. The government said their arrest was not due to the invitation, but to their alleged responsibility for the distribution of subversive leaflets issued under their names.

On trial

In Lisbon and in Oporto special courts for hearing political cases, with special judges, are sitting continuously. These courts are called *plenários*. They are empowered to apply to those convicted of crimes against the security of the State the 'security measure' of internment for up to three years – a measure which, as we shall see, may be extended indefinitely at the discretion of the political police.

Three trials in the past few years have excited interest outside Portugal: the trial of Professor Rui Luís Gomes and four others, which opened before the Oporto political court on 18 June 1957; the trial of fifty-two young people before the same court between December 1956 and June 1957; and the trial of Captain Henrique Galvão in Lisbon in March 1958.

Rui Luís Gomes and his companions were prosecuted because they had sent an article to the newspapers appealing for the restoration of free elections, the right of free speech, the right to form political parties, the annulment of the PIDE's powers to keep people in prison indefinitely, and negotiations with the Indian government over the dispute that had arisen about the Portuguese colony of Goa. The

[1] Quoted, *The Times*, 11 November 1958.

article had not even been published, because of the censorship. But its authors were arrested and convicted. They appealed, and a new trial was ordered; but they were kept in jail for over a year until it took place. When it began the defence lawyers asked for an adjournment on the ground that they had not been able to talk with their clients for over a year. The court granted them an adjournment of one hour. According to Gerald Gardiner, Q.C., who attended this trial, the prosecuting lawyer sat on the bench next to the judges, there was no shorthand note or other record of the evidence, and the defence lawyers themselves were not allowed to take shorthand notes. On 31 July 1957, four of the accused were sentenced to two years' imprisonment and the fifth to ten months'.

Of the fifty-two young people charged with forming conspiratorial organizations and engaging in activity against the security of the State, two-thirds were students. Their crime seems to have been that they denounced the imprisonment of Rui Luís Gomes. Only three of them were over thirty; their average age was twenty-two; the youngest was seventeen when he was arrested. Seven of them were young women. They were sentenced to varying periods of imprisonment.

Henrique Galvão, who was to leap into prominence in January 1961 when he led the rebel group that seized the liner *Santa Maria*, had taken part in the 1926 *coup d'État* and later held a number of offices under Salazar, including that of director of the national radio. In 1947, as chief inspector of colonial administration, and deputy for Angola in the National Assembly, he wrote a report on conditions in Angola, revealing the existence of maladministration, corruption and forced labour there. Under pressure from Angolan business and plantation interests, the government pigeon-holed the report, but copies were circulated among the opposition. There are some who say that it was not so much the result of a sensitive conscience as of personal spite against his political colleagues. Be that as it may, Galvão is unquestionably a man of immense personal courage and resource. And from that time onwards he has never wavered in his hostility to Salazar.

In 1948 he made a speech in the National Assembly repeating his allegations and criticizing the government for ignoring them. When new elections to the National Assembly came along he was not included in the National Union's list of candidates; he resigned the post of chief inspector of colonial administration. He was arrested in 1951 and, after months in prison, tried on a charge of attempting a *coup d'État* and sentenced to three years' imprisonment. A new trial was staged in

12. One of Captain Galvão's officers addressing the crew of the *Santa Maria* after her seizure. DRIL stands for Revolutionary Centre for Iberian Liberation

13. Some of Captain Galvão's men on board the *Santa Maria*

14. General Humberto Delgado

15. Captain Henrique
Galvão

16. Professor Mário Azevedo Gomes, a Liberal elder statesman

17. The novelist Aquilino Ribeiro

18. Álvaro Cunhal, leader of the Portuguese Communist Party

19. Salazar, dictator of Portugal

20. Four pillars of the 'Estado Novo' in their student days. Standing: Santos Costa (L.) and Manuel Gonçalves Cerejeira (R.); seated: Salazar (L.) and Mário de Figueiredo (R.). (See p. 116.)

21. Two rivals for the succession to Salazar. Above, Teotónio Pereira, former ambassador in London; right, Marcelo Caetano, professor of law

22. A member of the greenshirted Portuguese Youth gives the Hitler salute as members of the government, among them the Minister of Education, arrive at one of the movement's celebrations. This picture was taken in 1959

23. Part of the crowd waiting to greet General Delgado when he visited Oporto during his 1958 election campaign.

24. One response to the government's anti-American campaign, which followed the U.S. vote against Portugal in the Security Council on the Angola question. The demonstrators are attacking the library of the American embassy in Lisbon

25. Viriato Cruz, a leader of the Angola liberation movement

1958, which Galvão refused to attend on the ground that it was a farce. Found guilty of publishing anti-government pamphlets allegedly written in prison and smuggled out, he was sentenced to sixteen years' imprisonment.

In January 1959, while guarded by secret police in hospital, he escaped by the time-honoured device of putting a bolster in the bed, and took refuge in the Argentine embassy in Lisbon. Four months later he went to South America, where he set to work preparing the dramatic *coup* that at the beginning of 1961 suddenly brought Portugal into the world headlines.

Among Liberals the Galvão case has been something of a *cause célèbre*, since it illustrates the government's cat and mouse methods with opponents whom it wishes to remove from public life. The communists have tended to suggest that the Liberals have campaigned with disproportionate energy on Galvão's behalf, in contrast with their silence about Álvaro Cunhal, one of the secretaries of the illegal Communist Party, who escaped from prison in January 1960, after ten years, and about the many other communists who have been in prison for a very long time.

In Portugal in 1959 there were 3,811 trials leading to convictions for crimes against religion or against the security of the State, or for other political offences; 1,586 of these trials were initiated by the secret police.[1] Between March and July 1960 a total of 103 people were tried on political charges; they were sentenced to a total of 138 years in prison, loss of political rights for a total of 725 years, and 'security measures' – prolongation of sentence after its expiry – totalling 123 years. In October 1960 alone there were six political trials before the Lisbon *plenário*, involving twenty-three persons. Five of them were students, five labourers, four printers at the State printing house and one a woman schoolteacher. The prison sentences imposed totalled forty-four years, the schoolteacher and another accused each being sent to prison for eight years.

The secret police

The PIDE, or International and State Defence Police, is the chain which binds Salazar's dictatorship to the living body of the Portuguese nation. Without its unceasing work of domestic espionage Portugal would soon be free, and Salazar would go the way of the Mussolini and

[1] *Anuário Estatístico, 1959* (Lisbon: Instituto Nacional de Estatística, 1960).

the Hitler whom at one time he so much admired. The PIDE's record of brutality towards its prisoners is the most glaring index of the dictator's lack of confidence. He dare not allow any public discussion of his policies, or of the plight of the people he rules. The only way to prevent such discussion is to wage constant war against those Portuguese brave enough to open their mouths. In this war PIDE is his weapon. Its enemies and victims are the anti-fascists who pass on crudely printed leaflets and illegal newspapers in the factories and universities, produced on extremely thin paper so that they can be folded and refolded and slipped from palm to palm in a handshake; or who endure indefinite imprisonment and degrading tortures. Salazar has managed to recruit one Portuguese in ninety to wage this war against his fellow countrymen; and this minority who are prepared to spy on their own people and persecute them are held in almost universal contempt.

In every village in the country there is someone who is working unofficially for the PIDE. Sometimes the methods employed are so crude and clumsy that the agent and his activities become well known. In one small town we stayed in we were told to be especially careful of what we said if a certain man who lived just down the road was anywhere in the vicinity. This individual had no obvious means of support, yet he lived quite comfortably. Every day after lunch he took the train into Lisbon. But he did not go to work in an office or a factory. His destination was a café, but he did not go there to take coffee with his friends. He was a paid informer, and his duties consisted in sitting in Lisbon cafés and listening to conversations.

In this work of internal espionage the PIDE has always found a powerful ally in the Church. It is extremely common for parish priests to question servants closely about their employers' views and activities, and to ask for reports of the conversations they overhear and of the visitors who come to the house. Whether or not the information is passed on to the PIDE in a formal way it certainly reaches them sooner or later. We were told that the betrayal of confessional secrets has been the cause of many imprisonments.

The powers of the PIDE were legally defined in decree-law no. 35,042.[1] Whereas before the advent of Salazar the police could not arrest and detain anyone without bringing him before a court on some charge, this law enables them to arrest anyone and imprison him without charge for three months. With the permission of the

[1] *Diário do Governo*, 1st series, no. 233, pp. 839–50, 20 October 1945.

Ministry of the Interior this period can be extended by two additional periods of forty-five days, making six months in all.[1] In case these powers should prove insufficient a later decree-law gave the political police power to prolong prison terms for an indefinite period – power in fact to transform any prison term into a life sentence. The imprisonment 'may be extended by successive periods of three years as long as they continue to show themselves dangerous'. 'They' here are 'those who found associations, movements or groups of a communist nature, or who carry out activities of a subversive nature', 'those who belong to such associations, movements or groups, collaborate with them or follow their instructions, with or without prior agreement' and 'those who knowingly make possible the aforesaid subversive activities, supplying a place for their meetings, subsidizing them or promoting their propaganda'. In practice this is applied not only to communists but to all who oppose the government in a serious fashion. In the memorable words of this decree-law: 'The indefinite nature of the imprisonment permits it to be said to the prisoner that it is in his hands to be free, which can be an effective means of stimulating salutary reactions in his mind.'[2]

There is one further decree-law from which the PIDE derives its powers. This one established a Council of Public Security consisting of the commander-in-chief of the National Republican Guard, the commander-in-chief of the civil police and the head of the PIDE. It created various classes of people subject to police supervision. It gave the PIDE extensive powers to ban meetings, close public performances, 'search the residences of the individuals supervised' and close 'places which serve as headquarters or may be used by their owners to facilitate subversive activities'. It provided imprisonment for those 'who print publications, manifestoes, pamphlets or other literature of a subversive nature'. And it provided that employers who engage men in districts away from their homes must report their engagement to the police.[3] It is notorious that no professional person may obtain a job, or a licence to teach, without the approval of the PIDE.

[1] 'One young man I talked to,' reported Gerald Gardiner after his visit to Portugal in 1957, 'had spent most of the last two years in the prisons of the political police without ever having been convicted of any offence, having been three times arrested, imprisoned for some months, and then released' (*Manchester Guardian*, 19 October 1957).
[2] Decree-law no. 40,550, *Diário do Governo*, 1st series, no. 52, pp. 321–4, 12 March 1956.
[3] Decree-law no. 37,447, quoted, *Bulletin of the International Commission of Jurists*, no. 7, p. 39, October 1957.

The rank and file of the PIDE are fully aware of their powers, and they take their duties seriously. At the trial of the fifty-two a PIDE witness was asked what he would do if someone wrote on a wall: 'Peace on earth to men of good will.' He replied: 'I should arrest him.' And people are arrested and imprisoned in just this arbitrary way.

From the mass of recent cases we were told about we have selected a few typical ones. Rogério Rodrigues de Carvalho was an insurance worker in the wine town of Anadia, not far from Coimbra. During the 1958 presidential election campaign he went canvassing for Delgado. To the PIDE this was 'subversive activity' and 'organizing secret and illegal action'. They arrested him, poured hot and cold water alternately in his ears until he lost his hearing, and shone a bright light continuously in his eyes. He was sentenced to five years' hard labour; 'security measures' for an indefinite period of six months to three years after the completion of his sentence; loss of political rights for fifteen years; and a fine of 1,000 escudos (£12 10s). José Lívio Pinto Veiga, an Algarve corkworker and the former president of his sindicato branch, was arrested with two companions and imprisoned for the kind of electioneering activities that in Britain are the most normal thing in the world. Leandro Darromba, a woodworker, was sentenced in May 1959 to fourteen months' corrective detention and a fine of 1,000 escudos for incitement to strike and the distribution of illegal publications in Olhão and Santiago do Cacém. Joaquim Vicente, a labourer, was sentenced to six months' imprisonment and a fine of 1,000 escudos for similar crimes. In the Alhos Vedros district, on the Setúbal peninsula, about a hundred corkworkers were arrested and put in jail simply for holding a meeting . . .

In 1957 Gerald Gardiner met a jurist who had been arrested in the middle of the night and deported without trial to Timor. 'The fortunate ones', he wrote later, 'are tried.'[1] The deportation camps in Timor and Portuguese Africa, and the concentration camp of Tarrafal on the island of Santiago in the Cape Verde archipelago, have been closed because of the government's fear of contact between political prisoners transported there from Portugal and the various national liberation movements.[2] Transportation from Portugal is no longer practised.

---

[1] *Manchester Guardian*, 19 October 1957. The lawyer referred to was Carlos Cal Brandão, who was once more arrested in November 1960 and released after a week. (Cf. p. 120, n.1.)

[2] This decision may have been influenced by the rising against the imposition of forced labour in São Tomé in February 1953, in which over 1,000 Africans out of a total population of 40,000 were killed by Portuguese troops and civilians.

But prisoners are still tortured, some till their bodies can no longer stand the pain and they die. The first thing you are told when you arrive in Oporto is that the back door of the local PIDE headquarters, whose address is 329 Rua de Heroísmo, connects with a cemetery. The street is well named. The young men whose bodies have been carried out through the back door were among the flower of Portuguese youth. Their murderers, the *esbirros* – the word signifies hangmen or butchers, and one's informant spits it out with hatred – were trained by the Gestapo. It is said that the former PIDE chief Neves Graça[1] was trained by Kramer, who went to Portugal for the purpose, and who was later in charge of the Belsen concentration camp. And it is said that during the Spanish civil war Mussolini sent a number of Italian instructors to give the PIDE the benefit of their experience, and that on the eve of their return, at a special party given in their honour, President Carmona pinned on their tunics the insignia of the Order of Christ, Portugal's second highest decoration.

And the PIDE learned well. The names of its victims, and the abominable things done to them, are known outside the prison walls within days or even hours of each fresh atrocity. The names of those responsible are known, too, and it is certain that one of the first acts of the democratic Portugal of the future will be to try these men for their crimes.

We heard how Óscar Reis and Francisco Pinto were forced to stand on their feet for days on end, and had their genitals nailed to the wall. We heard how Pedro dos Santos Soares, a grammar school teacher, was imprisoned in 1934, sent to Tarrafal for four years, whipped, deprived of his glasses though he is very short-sighted, put in solitary confinement in a notorious cell known as the 'refrigerator' till he nearly died; how he was sent back to Tarrafal in 1942 for another three and a half years; how he was again imprisoned in 1954 and again deprived of his glasses till he went on hunger strike to get them back; how he was yet again imprisoned on 5 December 1958, and prevented from sleeping for twelve successive days and nights. We heard how the worker Raul Alves had his hands burned before he was thrown to his death from the third-floor window of a PIDE head-quarters. How Joaquim Carreira was for ten days made to lean against a wall with only his fingertips touching it – the torture known as 'the statue' – and was brutally beaten. How Adélia Terruta, a young woman

[1] He was dismissed soon after the escape of a number of political prisoners from the fortress of Peniche in January 1960.

in the last stage of pregnancy, was savagely beaten on the belly. How the labourer António Farrica is a cripple after being in the hands of the PIDE. How the miner Manuel da Égua was made to do the 'statue', and had his head beaten against the wall, over and over again, till he went mad. How Joaquim Lopes de Oliveira, described by the Liberal newspaper *República* as 'a truly good man', died on 15 February 1957, after fifteen days at PIDE headquarters. How Manuel da Silva, who distributed leaflets about Lopes de Oliveira's death, was himself arrested and beaten to death on 2 March 1957. How Hernâni Silva, one of the fifty-two tried in Oporto, was made to do the 'statue' for seven consecutive days and nights, with short intervals for food . . .

It is common knowledge in Portugal that these things take place there. Prominent lawyers have made outspoken and, under the circumstances, exceedingly courageous statements asking for an independent inquiry into the conduct of the PIDE. On 23 March 1957, seventy-two Lisbon and Oporto lawyers issued such a statement. They wrote that they had been informed repeatedly that the PIDE normally used as methods of investigation reprehensible forms of torture, both physical and moral, including the well-known 'statue', other physical punishments and insistent interrogations, sometimes at all hours of the night. Referring to the deaths of Lopes de Oliveira and Manuel da Silva, the statement declared: 'The signatories, for moral, humane and professional motives inherent in their duties, are unable to associate themselves with acts of such gravity or to identify themselves with them by their silence or indifference.' Many of the signatories declared themselves ready to produce proof of the illegal actions which had been committed.

A similar request was made to the government by thirty-three Coimbra lawyers of varying political views, 'some supporters of the present political régime and others not, but all fraternally bound by the same concern for the dignity of the juridical and allied professions'. They included Martim Afonso de Castro, deputy civil governor of Coimbra, and João Faria, president of the Condeixa town council.

The inquiry that 105 leading Portuguese lawyers have demanded has not been carried out.

But one day it will be.[1]

---

[1] Salazar's own attitude to the use of torture has been made clear by his hagiographer, António Ferro, who quotes him as saying: 'We arrived at the conclusion that the prisoners who really had been ill-treated were always or almost always of the class of terrorist extremists, people who manufactured bombs, and who, in spite of all the police questions,

X

Resistance movement

Disunited family

The public statements by lawyers quoted at the end of the last chapter opened a season of unrest and manifestoes. The official legend that the Portuguese people is one united family was wearing fairly thin. The disturbances that accompanied the 1958 presidential election showed how discontented people were becoming, and how uneasy the government was getting about its dwindling support. Six months after the election, in one of the most massive proclamations of non-confidence in the Salazar administration, 142 business men, doctors, lawyers and army officers in the north issued a manifesto which declared: 'The election results . . . show that obstacles, difficulties, intimidation, imprisonment and even shooting could not quell the determined and avowed opposition of the nation to a government which has finally disillusioned and wearied everyone, including former supporters of the régime.'[1]

And Salazar knew this, the signatories added, quoting from a recent speech of his to the executive committee of the National Union, in which he had made some extraordinary admissions after three decades of power. 'I cannot say', he had warned, 'that times are favourable or that [your] burdens will be light. Quite the contrary: they will be very heavy, at least until we are able to awaken the sleepers, encourage the hesitant and rekindle faith everywhere.' Recognizing that the 'united front' of which he used to boast was no longer so united, the aging dictator had added: 'The passions released during

---

refused to reveal where they had hidden their criminal and murderous weapons. It was only after the employment of violent methods that they decided to speak the truth. I ask myself even while I suppress such abuses of the police whether the lives of a defenceless crowd, the lives of little children, do not broadly justify half a dozen timely beatings [*safanões*] of such sinister creatures' (Ferro, *Salazar*, p. 184. The translation has been checked with the original and slightly amended).

[1] *Aos Portugueses* (Braga, 14 January 1959).

the last election campaign threatened to split this front, from which we lost some companions who had been with us from the outset.'[1]

Three months after this speech an open letter to Salazar signed by one hundred prominent citizens of Lisbon declared that 'the obsessed intransigence which guides Your Excellency's policy hinders the reconciliation of the Portuguese family' and suggested that 'the occasion of Your Excellency's last lecture at Coimbra be also the end of Your Excellency's political life'.[2]

In 1958 and the early part of 1959 there were many important changes inside the government. Immediately before the election Salazar dismissed his old friend of student days, Colonel Santos Costa, a man who was almost universally hated for his brutality and his Nazi past. General Craveiro Lopes, the outgoing President, was not nominated for re-election. It was rumoured that his feud with Santos Costa and his disgust with the régime he was nominally the head of had driven him into silent opposition. In November 1958 the Minister of the Interior, Professor Pires Cardoso, who was said to have opposed the ban on Aneurin Bevan's lecture tour, asked to be relieved of his post; he was replaced by Lieutenant-Colonel Arnaldo Schultz. And practically the entire executive committee of the fascist National Union was replaced.

But the most noteworthy single fact of that whole election year was this: that it was a man from the ranks of the régime, a man schooled in the 'Estado Novo', behind whom the entire opposition eventually united. For General Humberto Delgado was neither an old-fashioned Liberal nor a Left-winger; and until he decided to run for the presidency no one knew that he was even a critic of the government.

Liberals without a party

There are, broadly speaking, two main streams in the opposition movement. There are the old republicans, os velhos Republicanos – elderly men who were young, vigorous and active in public life long before Salazar came to power. They have been persecuted, exiled, imprisoned and often deprived of their means of livelihood; yet they

---

[1] The official English translation of this speech, which was delivered on 6 December 1958, appears in Portugal: An Informative Review, 2nd year, no. 6, pp. 319–25, Nov.-Dec. 1958.

[2] This document was sent to Salazar on 18 March 1959. A photostat of the printed leaflet that was made of it is in the authors' possession.

have kept faith with the ideals of their youth. And there is the Left, whose most prominent and only organized representative is the Communist Party. For the most part its adherents are a generation or more younger than the old republicans; few of them can remember life before Salazar, for no one in Portugal under the age of fifty has any experience of living, as an adult, in a democracy.

Many of the old republicans have a large personal following, especially in the republican strongholds of the north. They enjoy nation-wide prestige; they are venerated by many as living reminders of freer times; their steadfastness and refusal to be bought over are widely respected – but they have no party. They embody a good deal of republican tradition – but they have no adequate programme.

In the early years of the dictatorship they engaged in numerous conspiracies to overthrow the government. All their attempts failed, the conspirators were either arrested or fled abroad, and what could have been their most productive years have been spent in exile on Timor, the Azores or Tarrafal. It was Salazar who remained in Lisbon . . .

Many of the old republicans are distinguished men of letters, and in latter years their activities have been largely literary – but their ideas are very old-fashioned. They know little about the modern world, still less about present-day political and social science. For the most part they are romantics, still steeped in the liberal ideas of the nine-teenth century. The acute problems facing Portugal – the organizing of an expanding economy; industrialization; the colonial question – bewilder them; they have no answer except to blame Salazar and clamour for liberty. Not in all the three and a half decades they have been outside official life have any of them succeeded in drawing up a comprehensive plan that would show their countrymen how the liberty they clamour for might fruitfully be used.

They speak always with emotion of 'the people' – but with few exceptions they are totally uninterested in the political organization of workers and peasants. The masses of the people are merely crowds to be manipulated by leaders. The only large groups whose support the old republicans would value are, first, the army, because it would have the force to back them up; secondly, the students, because they are the future intellectuals and administrators.

Once or twice a year, when there is a diplomatic set-back for Salazar, renewed repression or some important national occasion such as the anniversary of the 1910 revolution, the old republicans will join together to sign a manifesto or an open letter to the President. Otherwise any political activity they engage in is carried on as individuals, in a small circle of old friends confined to the region a particular individual lives in. It is often hard to get unity even for manifestoes and open letters. Dr X in Coimbra is only prepared to sign if he knows that Professor Y in Lisbon is in agreement – and neither of them will sign if Colonel Z's name is to be included.

Since they are a collection of individuals the old republicans are unrepresentative; their committees, like the recently formed *Directório Republicano*, are *ad hoc* committees elected by nobody. And as they have had no chance to govern for thirty-five years, nobody really knows whether they could govern. For all that, and apart from their personal following as individuals in a given area, the old republicans as a school have supporters, mainly middle-aged ones, all over the country – though many of these are tired and disillusioned, continuing to give allegiance to the old republicans, but blaming their fellow countrymen for Salazar's survival.

'A people gets the government it deserves,' they will say. 'The régime is bad, but the fault lies with us. We are not capable of the sustained effort and sacrifice necessary to prepare and carry through a successful revolution.' One friend remarked to us gloomily: 'A revolution here could only take place between Monday and Friday. Nobody is willing to have his weekend interrupted for unpleasant activity.'

But not everyone is pessimistic. At the other extreme, an educated and informed acquaintance assured us soon after we arrived that the régime was on its last legs. 'You may think things are peaceful,' he said. 'They seem like that on the surface, but underneath everything is seething. The people are at the end of their patience. Salazar is senile; he will be finished within six months.'

This was said in December 1959.

The romantic optimists rarely adduce any facts to show that the opposition has progressed towards unity, or stronger organization, or the formulation of a political programme. They base their hopes on symptoms of real or alleged weakness within the régime itself. The pessimists, for their part, listen to rumours of strife among the Salazarists with mounting despondency.

'If Salazar goes,' they ask, 'what are we to replace him with? Where is the alternative? The worst thing that could happen would be for the régime to end, not by revolution, but by Salazar's death.

There would be chaos for a month, and afterwards the same people who are in power now would be back stronger than ever.'

Pioneers of Labour

The common people of Portugal have a long tradition of what we should call friendly societies. In the second half of the sixteenth century there were formed in various parts of the country communal granaries (*celeiros comuns*) from which, in famine years, small farmers and landworkers could obtain at a low price the grain, vegetables and seed they needed. Providence societies, known as *montepios*, began to operate at the same period; their members paid a monthly instalment and could claim benefit in case of sickness or death. Such *montepios* flourished among schoolteachers and industrial workers in the nineteenth century. The public employees of Lisbon formed one in 1840. Men like the army officer Sousa Brandão, strongly influenced by the ideas of Fourier, helped to organize loan associations, consumers' and producers' co-operatives and people's banks. In April 1850 they launched the first workers' paper, *O Eco dos Operários*, which soon became the organ of the Workers' Association, the first attempt at a purely working-class organization. The next twenty years saw many more such attempts.

The socialist movement was launched in Portugal under the direct influence of the Paris Commune. The year 1871 was one of exceptional intellectual ferment in Portugal. A group of young writers, among them the great poet Antero de Quental, arranged a series of 'Democratic Lectures' in Lisbon. Before long the Prime Minister, the Marquis of Ávila, forbade them to continue with the series. Into a country whose educated youth was seething with new ideas there came in June 1871 three emissaries from the General Council of the International Working Men's Association. These three Spaniards met with Antero, José Fontana and Jaime Batalha Reis on board a little boat on the Tagus: this was a favourite way of holding clandestine meetings out of earshot of the police. In January 1872 the Workers' Brotherhood Association was founded, and a month later a journal (*O Pensamento Social*) – the first of a quite incredible number of Left-wing journals – was started, its expenses being met by Antero's pamphlet *O que É a Internacional*.

But it was another three years before the Portuguese Socialist Party was formed, and a further two before it held its first congress.

Almost from the beginning it was riven by factional differences between Right and Left. The Marxists had the upper hand: the programme adopted at the first national conference in 1882 – setting the aim of 'seizing political power, the point of departure for a social organization in which each worker will enjoy the entire product of his labour' – was unequivocally Marxist.[1]

The Socialist Party contested elections, supported strikes, had one of its writers, Magalhães Lima, jailed for two months for having numbered the King of Portugal among the world's 'celebrated bandits', and died away almost to nothing under the joint blows of repression and doctrinal differences. In the 1892 elections the two factions, 'possibilists' and Marxists, put up separate lists of candidates. A national conference in 1895 adopted a new Marxist programme written by Azedo Gneco, the printer who led the revolutionary wing. Almost immediately there were differences within the ranks of the Marxists themselves over the degree to which socialists should support the republicans' propaganda campaign.

Meanwhile both trade unionism and anarcho-syndicalism were gaining strength among the industrial workers, and bitterly fought strikes in the first decade of the new century showed that the anarchists could command considerable support among Lisbon printers, transport workers and arsenal workers.

After the 1910 revolution the Socialist Party did moderately well in elections. Though party congresses kept reaffirming their opposition to participation in republican governments, three socialists did in fact hold the portfolios of Labour and Finance for short periods in 1919–21.

The *coup d'État* of 1926 and the transition towards fascism gradually made Left-wing politics more and more difficult and hazardous. The working-class parties were not so much outlawed at one stroke as forced gradually into illegality. Premises were closed down; party leaders were arrested and exiled. The Socialist Party quickly dwindled in size and influence. In 1928 its membership was estimated at 2,500; its last two flickers of life were a banquet in 1931 to celebrate its fifty-sixth anniversary, and a fourth – and last – national conference, held in Coimbra in 1933, which adopted with unconscious irony a new party programme. The anarchist-led General Confederation of Labour, which in the twenties claimed a membership of 100,000, advanced the disastrous slogan of 'proletarian neutrality' towards the

---

[1] The programme was written by José Ribeiro, a printer. A French translation can be found in Benoît Malon, *Histoire du socialisme*, t. iv (Paris, 1885), pp. 1,498–1,503.

1926 *coup*; within seven years its membership had dropped to 15,000. The Communist Party, formed in 1921, had shrunk by 1928 to a tiny, isolated sect with no more than fifty members in Lisbon and twenty in Oporto;[1] after a drastic reorganization in 1929 it began to gain ground at the expense of the anarchists.[2] By the end of the thirties the communists, their ranks strengthened by the adherence of a number of old anarcho-syndicalists, had become the undisputed party of the Portuguese working class. But the long night that had fallen had already dimmed, if it had not destroyed, most of the traditions the Portuguese communists, as the sole survivors, inherited from the pioneers.

The underground

A Portuguese Liberal can today voice his views fairly loudly, and so long as he never does anything about them he runs little risk. But if someone openly utters Left-wing opinions, or opinions that might be construed as Left wing, his liberty is seriously imperilled. So it is harder for a foreign inquirer to find communists and socialists. And until they know you well they will only talk in generalities. Yet supporters of the Communist Party are numerous among intellectuals and students – especially in literature and the fine arts – though its main strength is among industrial workers and landless farmworkers.

If the old republicans can be divided into the too pessimistic and the too optimistic, most Portuguese Left-wingers are in their own way at once more optimistic, yet less romantic, than other critics of Salazar. They are optimistic because they can take comfort from communist successes elsewhere and persuade themselves that they are on the winning side; eventually Salazar too will be defeated, and Portugal will join the growing number of people's democracies or national independent democracies. At the same time they are less prone to romantic illusions about an imminent democratic revolution in Portugal, because they hold that Salazar is only a tiny pawn in the world strategy of imperialism and the cold war. The fight for peaceful coexistence and the ending of NATO must be won on an international level before Salazar and his *bourgeois* backers lose the Anglo-American support which keeps him in power. Meanwhile at home the

[1] *The Communist International between the Fifth and Sixth Congresses* (London: CPGB, 1928), p. 280.
[2] The communist newspaper *O Proletário* was published legally until 1931; the party then launched *Avante!*, which was banned in 1934 and has since been published clandestinely.

Communist Party works underground to organize the masses in the factories and the countryside; and one day, when the time is ripe, the masses of the people will rise. This is an article of faith. The actual extent of communist influence among the people is something that in the nature of things cannot be measured in a Right-wing dictatorship. The party's successes and failures alike are secrets; probably the party itself does not know the size of its support with any degree of accuracy. Barreiro, the new steel centre; the government arsenal; the docks; the fishing fleets of the north; the Alentejo villages: these are said to be communist strongholds. But communist activity among working people is not conducted in the light of day. If a poor person falls into the hands of the PIDE and is accused of such activity he can expect no mercy at all; he has no influential friends or relatives to protest on his behalf; there is no one to make known the fact that he has been seized; he is quite defenceless.

In fact, and partly because of its members' bravery, the significance of the Communist Party in the Portuguese opposition is considerable. It has neither confined itself to issuing manifestoes nor engaged in insurrectionary plots. It has conducted a constant and extremely arduous struggle against Salazar among many strata of the population. It has become the main object of PIDE persecution. Alone among opponents of Salazar, its militants endure the dangers and hardships of underground activity – and endure them for years on end. The communists run the risk of savage police reprisals all the time; other oppositionists only when there are open demonstrations.

Although nobody ever openly says he is a communist, everyone knew that Left-wing students, supporters of the Communist Party, were active in the students' unions until the latter were virtually banned by the government in 1956. And if you take a list of Portugal's leading intellectuals, the majority will be found to be either communists or communist supporters; for obvious reasons we cannot give the names of any of them. At the same time, the party has lost the support it had just after the war in the sciences. Scientific work is not possible on a free-lance basis, and the Left-wing scientists have been witch-hunted, dismissed from their posts in universities and research establishments and driven abroad or into industry, where they are no longer so influential as they were in academic circles. Though writers and artists often have a struggle to make ends meet, they are more independent and less vulnerable to economic sanctions. That the Left remains so strong among them embarrasses the government very much, because they are able to influence students, and because government propaganda is hampered by a serious shortage of court poets, writers and painters. In 1956 there was an exhibition in Lisbon dedicated to Portuguese cultural achievements during Salazar's rule; more than half the exhibits were the work of men who had been jailed, or dismissed from their jobs, or both, because of their opposition to Salazar. Outdoing Franco, who claims Federico García Lorca for his own – now that the murdered poet is no longer here to bear witness against fascism – Portugal's rulers are cynical enough to claim credit for their victims' art while they are still alive.[1]

Till 1961 the Communist Party was alone in having a programme.[2] Approved by the party's fifth congress in 1957, it is much like the recent programmes of other west European communist parties, with appropriate adaptations to Portugal's police State conditions and backward economy. It is not, properly speaking, a Marxist analysis of the country's problems but rather a series of suggestions around which the opposition might be united; few members of the British Labour Party would find these suggestions exceptionable. The programme has something in it for practically everyone except the big landlords, monopolists and members of the PIDE; the emphasis throughout is on unity of all anti-Salazarists to eliminate the dictatorship by peaceful means and avoid civil war. The most urgent demands, not surprisingly, are for political amnesty, the dissolution of the PIDE and the punishment of all responsible for its crimes. Unlike any other section of the opposition, the Communist Party firmly declares its support for self-determination for the Portuguese colonies.

The 'North American imperialists', to whom Salazar and the big monopolists and landowners have sold out, are said to be the country's real masters and finally responsible for low wages, repression and preparation for war; the programme calls for Portuguese neutrality in the cold war and the ending of American economic penetration, war bases and controls over the Portuguese armed forces. A sort of demonology is exhibited which substitutes for economic analysis the

---

[1] Salazarists too have done their share of claiming the dead. A place of honour in the 1956 exhibition was given to the physician, writer and artist Dr Abel Salazar (no relation to the dictator). His laboratory in Oporto had been wrecked by the PIDE fascists, and he had been dismissed from his hospital post and from the Chair of Histology at Oporto university, and hounded to death.

[2] *Programa do Partido Comunista Português Aprovada no V Congresso* (Editorial *Avante!*, October 1957. Published clandestinely),

vision of malevolent Yankee millionaires issuing orders to the Portuguese monopolists, who in turn transmit instructions to Salazar and the PIDE. If this were an accurate picture, and the real enemy were in Washington, incomparably stronger than anything even a united Portugal could muster, what would be the point of organizing a united movement for Salazar's downfall?

Though it goes back as far as the *bourgeois* revolution of 1383-5 for examples to prove the 'Portuguese people's love for a free and independent life', the programme nowhere tries to examine why reaction has been so persistent, and democracy so recurrently defeated, throughout Portuguese history. But its major weakness is that it makes no real effort to come to grips with the problems that a Portugal divested of colonies will face.

Since its 1957 programme was issued two further statements by the underground Communist Party have shown that it considers the possibility of a peaceful overthrow of the Salazar régime is diminishing.[1]

Not only is the Portuguese Communist Party the only organized force opposing Salazar. In the absence of a socialist party (though there are some small socialist groups) it probably commands the support of a high proportion of the industrial workers – and other opposition elements seem to recognize both this fact and its significance when they seek communist support for their activities, and when they regularly ask the communists what their attitude would be to this or that projected move. It is possible that the Communist Party will have a big say, not only in the overthrow of Salazar, but also in the shaping of the new Portugal.

Revolt in the Church

At the top of Lisbon's Avenida da Liberdade stands a huge white marble statue of the Marquis of Pombal, its base flanked by decorative beasts and symbols honouring the eighteenth-century statesman who tried to rebuild Portugal on modern lines. Pombal is famous for three fights he waged: against foreign economic interests, against the

[1] An appeal issued in the autumn of 1959 said: 'The fascist resistance may compel our people . . . to use force' ('People of Portugal Step up the Struggle', *World Marxist Review*, vol. ii, no. 11, pp. 54-6, November 1959); a year later, in the party's message to the Russian communists on the anniversary of the 1917 revolution, it held that 'only the further development of political events will show whether it will be possible to put an end to fascism without resort to violence' (*Pravda*, 10 November 1960. We are indebted to Mr Victor Zorza for this reference).

aristocracy and against the Church. Like Henry VIII of England two hundred years before, he disbanded monasteries and convents; and he expelled the Jesuits from Portugal. During the nineteenth century his work was largely undone, and the Jesuits crept back; but Pombal's ideas lived on and took a new lease of life with the 1910 revolution.

One of the first acts of the Salazar régime was to make peace with the Church and restore favourable conditions to it. Now the Jesuits were back openly. Except for the very pious, the new friendship between Church and State found little favour among the Portuguese. One morning, not long after Salazar had effected this reconciliation, people passing the Pombal statue were delighted to read, in enormous letters of black pitch – all shiny on the white marble – the following inscription:

> *Vem cá baixo, marquês,*
> *Porque eles estão cá outra vez!*

> 'Come down, Marquis,
> Because they are back again!'

In vain did the police try quickly to remove the sticky tar. The painters had done their work well. Finally, a fence was put up round the base of the statue for a few days while the police worked and Lisbon laughed.

Although Portugal has always been a Catholic country, anti-clericalism has been widespread for nearly two centuries. Older people will tell you that fifty years ago, even under the monarchy, no self-respecting young townsman would dream of going to church. Religion was a matter for women, and even for them an excess of it was frowned on. Priests were generally rude and ignorant men, mostly the sons of peasants who sought to restrict the division of their land – at the same time as placating God and increasing their social prestige – by sending as many sons as possible into the seminary.

Today far more people go to church, and the clergy are often better educated and lead more pious lives than used to be the case. Though Salazar has never tried to end formally the separation of Church and State brought about by the 1910 revolution, it has become progressively more difficult to propagate anti-clerical or anti-religious ideas. It has also become very difficult to succeed in many walks of life if one does not go to church. Old Portuguese anti-clericals, in whom the sight of a priest or a nun arouses the deepest antipathy, point with scorn at the young men going to mass on Sunday, missals and rosaries in hand. In their day, they say, the young men would hang around outside the church on a Sunday to eye the pretty girls as they came out from mass in their best clothes. Nevertheless, despite the government-sponsored religious revival, and the traditional Iberian persecution of freemasonry – often quaintly confused with communism – there are in Portugal no traces of that persecution of Protestantism which is so flagrant in Spain. Indeed, freedom of religious practice seems to be one of the few constitutional guarantees that the Salazar government does respect. The small number of Portuguese Protestants and Jews seem to encounter no difficulties, though less orthodox cults, such as spiritualists and Jehovah's Witnesses, are discouraged.

More important, in recent years the Salazar régime has made enemies inside the Catholic Church; so that one of the most significant developments in the anti-Salazar movement has been the growth of Catholic opposition. One might now almost speak of a third opposition current in addition to the two main streams, the old republicans and the Left. In July 1958 the Bishop of Oporto, Dom António Ferreira Gomes, in a private letter to Salazar unexpectedly released to the public, came out briefly but trenchantly as a critic of the government's social policy. The letter criticized the régimes of both Spain and Portugal. It said that even in rural areas of northern Portugal, supposed to be staunch in their support of Salazar, the men walked out of the church in indignation when the priests referred in their sermons to the elections. The Bishop declared that 'the cause of the Church is being lost in the soul of the people, of the workers and the youth' as a result of its support for Salazar. Contrasting Portuguese standards with what he had seen abroad, he wrote:

I cannot say how grieved I am by the now exclusively Portuguese privilege of the beggar, the barefooted, the man in rags and tatters; and indeed by our melancholy distinction of having the highest levels of malnutrition, defiled [enxovalhadas] and anaemic children, and pale faces – from hunger? from vice?

And he revealed the tremendous change there has been in Catholic opinion: 'I even think that the greatest necessity for Catholics is to go beyond the mentality of the [pro-Salazar] *Centro Católico*, which daily becomes more and more the mentality of the catacomb or even of the ghetto, and from which the Church can expect only the kiss of death.'[1]

Some observers go so far as to suggest that the Vatican has broken with Salazar, fearing that continued support for so discredited a régime will favour the growth of communism. Salazar himself, they say, now recognizes that the Church prefers Christian democracy, and that is why the régime is now hostile to certain Catholic activities. And they point to a series of facts: that, unlike the situation in other Catholic countries, Catholic Action has no legal standing in Portugal; that it is almost impossible for a priest to have any connexion with the *sindicatos*; that the last national congress of worker-leaders of Catholic Action was not allowed to publish its proceedings, and there was PIDE intervention to compel the alteration of the congress programmes and the banning of certain subjects for discussion; that there was similar interference with the national congress of the Catholic men's organization and that of the Catholic University Youth; that the Catholic weekly *O Trabalhador* was suspended and leaders of Catholic Action were forced to resign; that some priests have been dismissed and others sent out of the country; and that efforts to found a Catholic university have been blocked.

In his speech of 6 December 1958, to the executive of the National Union, Salazar gave his views on the break by some Catholics from the 'National Front'. He as good as warned the Vatican that if the rebels were not called to order the relations of Church and State, and even the Concordat itself, might be imperilled.[2] Not very long ago it would have seemed hardly conceivable that Salazar would be issuing such threats to an institution which has always been regarded as a pillar of his régime.

In a sense it has been the ideological battle against anti-clericalism and communism which has brought about this state of affairs. To combat materialist and Left-wing ideas in a country whose intelligentsia was traditionally sceptical, the Church's youth and student organizations were compelled to adopt a serious platform on social questions. The papal encyclicals on these questions, and the theory of

[1] António, Bispo do Porto, *Ao Exmo Senhor Presidente do Conselho* (Oporto, 1958. Mimeographed). Salazar's indignation at the Bishop's letter was so great that he did his best to persuade the Vatican to dismiss him. The Vatican refused to do this directly, but it later transferred the Bishop to a position abroad.

[2] *Portugal: An Informative Review*, 2nd year, no. 6, p. 320, Nov.-Dec. 1958.

the corporate State, were expounded to earnest young people so that they would use these ideas to combat the Left-wing students prominent in the students' unions. To a great extent this plan misfired; many young Catholics found themselves in agreement with Left-wing social criticism and unable to square their theories with the corruption and poverty to be seen all around them. And so a situation gradually developed where, in many students' unions, members of the Catholic University Youth were actively co-operating with communist-led students.

Parallel with this development in the universities there has been considerable pressure on parish priests from their flocks. One Catholic leader told us that this, not any high-level decisions in Rome, was the fundamental reason for the changes beginning in the Church. The poor village priest, he said, was very close to the people. He might not agree with them, but he had to listen to what they said. And nowadays the people had only complaints about the régime; the priests could not ignore this widespread discontent; in turn they passed it on to the bishops.

This particular Catholic spokesman was bitterly opposed to Salazar; but he was hardly less sharp in his criticism of the old-fashioned opposition.

'In Portugal,' he said, 'we have always had a rotten ruling class and a rotten middle class. But our simple people are good and hard-working. I don't see any future for this country unless we have a Left-wing government with broadly socialist ideas. You will never get such a government in Portugal without the communists on the one hand—or without the Catholics on the other.'

He and a number of other Catholics, including priests, were working for unity with the communists, a thing he thought was possible in Portugal's special circumstances because of the isolation of the Portuguese Communist Party and its relative lack of the kind of experience, and outside influence, which had discredited many other communist parties.

A spokesman of the *Centro de Informação Católica* has referred in these terms to the communist bogy that is used by the government to frighten Catholics and justify the dictatorship:

Neither the international political situation nor the level of development of the Portuguese economy and people suggests that a communist type of régime is likely to be set up in Portugal in the near future. Moreover the strength, great or small, of communism among us flows not from the integral adoption of the principles of international communism, but above all from an aspiration of a part of the idealistic youth of Portugal for decent and honest justice. And this strength will increase to the degree that oppression and injustice continue to exist. However, even were these statements inaccurate, if there are to be violence and persecution of any kind at all it seems preferable that Christians, on principle, should be on the side of the persecuted, not the persecutors.[1]

Why has Salazar survived?

During our stay in Portugal we met no one at all who was a whole-hearted supporter of the Salazar administration. Even among persons of conservative outlook, who two years earlier would still have considered themselves loyal adherents of the dictatorship, there was harsh criticism. In the privacy of their homes these people repeat with relish the steady stream of jokes and anecdotes about Salazar and his Ministers. Bitterly they recount to each other example after example of corruption and inefficiency. Often they are ardent Catholics with monarchist sympathies – the sort of people who for years have been the backbone of the 'Estado Novo', the sort of people who used to tell you that democracy was not suited to the Portuguese temperament and that Salazar's aim was to purify the country of all the old corruption and disorder. Now they tell you with disgust of the excesses of High Society, of the profits made by this or that newly enriched business man.

'Salazar,' they say, 'did much for the country at the beginning; but he has been in power too long . . .'

How then, with practically the whole country against him, does Salazar continue to hold power? And moreover how has a fascist dictatorship that has never enjoyed the kind of mass support mustered by German and Italian fascism survived, nevertheless, for over thirty years? To blame the disunity of the opposition and to say no more is to tell only half the story; to appreciate the whole truth we have to look once again at the beginnings of the régime.

Until the corporative Constitution came into force in March 1933

[1] Engº Francisco Lino Netto, *Considerações dum Católico sobre o Período Eleitoral* (Lisbon, June 1958. Mimeographed). Lino Netto and sixteen other Catholics were later accused of the crime of defaming Portugal in the foreign Press because certain French newspapers had reproduced a statement by them; they have since been amnestied.

the fascist nature of Salazar's policy was not clearly apparent. In the early days of the dictatorship the chief victims were men who had been prominent in public life before the 1926 *coup d'État*. The new régime had to prevent the old parties from making a come-back; it did so by decapitating, not outlawing, them; by administrative measures, not legislation. It was only with the rise to power of German fascism and the call, heard all over Europe, for a crusade against communism, that Salazar began to pay really serious attention to the working-class movement. In September 1933 he promulgated a National Statute of Labour prohibiting strikes and substituting fascist 'syndicates' for the workers' trade unions. More than 60,000 workers took part in the movement against this measure – the first time in Portuguese Labour history that a united front of anarchist, communist and reformist workers was achieved. The movement erupted in a general strike on 18 January 1934, and only mass arrests and the use of troops prevented a revolutionary upsurge. The central electric power station in Coimbra was dynamited, and the workers were for a time masters of the glass manufacturing centre of Marinha Grande, disarming the police and occupying the town's administrative buildings.

During this first decade of the dictatorship none of Salazar's opponents dreamed that he would remain in power for as long as he has. By 1931 Spain had become a democratic republic; it was quite easy for Portuguese to cross the frontier and meet with Spanish Liberals and socialists; it was easy to get to France and confer with the French Left. And this is what the Portuguese *bourgeois* democrats, with their representatives in Madrid and Paris, depended on. They raised money at home and took it to France to buy arms; in the tradition of Portuguese politics they believed the only way to dispose of the government was by an armed rising. The arms were sent to Spain and – except for some that were discovered by the Spanish police in 1934 – were stockpiled there against the day they would be needed. But history could not wait; the Spanish civil war, hatched on Portuguese soil, brought a pressing need for these weapons . . . Thus Franco's rebellion not only succeeded in defeating Spanish democracy; it also effectively vanquished Portuguese democracy. Within a month Franco held Galicia[1] and other regions adjoining the Portuguese frontier. Portugal was sealed off from democratic Europe. Portuguese

---

[1] But Galicia, whose language and culture resemble those of Portugal, was not subdued without ferocious terror. See *Lo que han hecho en Galicia. Episodios del terror blanco en las provincias gallegas contados por quienes los han vivido* (Paris, n.d. [1938]).

volunteers fought with the Spanish People's Army and the International Brigade. In September 1936 the crews of the Portuguese warships *Afonso de Albuquerque*, *Dão* and *Bartolomeu Dias* mutinied in the Tagus and tried to take their ships to join the Spanish republic's fleet, but they were shelled by shore batteries west of Lisbon and forced to surrender; six of the sailors were later reported to have 'committed suicide'. And the arms bought with Portuguese funds to fight a Portuguese fascist dictator were used by anti-fascists in the long defence of Madrid.

The part played by the British and French governments in the Spanish civil war has often been described. What is never realized is that the shameful policy of non-intervention sounded the knell for Portuguese democracy too. The nine years following the outbreak of the civil war in Spain were the blackest years of the Salazar dictatorship, when a mood of utter hopelessness prevailed and every section of the opposition was made to realize that it was powerless against a régime supported actively by two of Europe's great powers, passively by two others.

Only towards the end of the second world war was a new mood apparent. The fascist losses, the Atlantic Charter, the public statements of Churchill and Roosevelt: these began to put new life into the old republicans, who thought that a United Nations victory would mean defeat for the Iberian dictators. And the young men and women who had known nothing but dictatorship, and who tended to be cynical about the democracy of their fathers and of the British and Americans – their imaginations were fired by Russia's blows against Germany. They too believed that a United Nations victory would bring about Salazar's downfall, and a socialist Portugal into the bargain.

Lisbon during the second world war is generally thought of as a haunt of spies, a centre of international intrigue. No doubt it was. But it was also a place of fierce, secret hopes, of ordinary people listening behind closed doors, as anxiously as ever people did in occupied Europe, to Allied broadcasts. When things went well for the troops of the Allies people smiled at each other and began to look forward to tomorrow.

So there was born, at first underground, then in a semi-legal twilight, the *Movimento de Unidade Democrática* (MUD), which embraced the entire opposition from old republicans on the Right to communist supporters on the Left. Soon after the war ended, when

Salazar and his government were wondering how the post-war world would treat them, the first elections to the National Assembly were announced. For three weeks there was a political thaw. For forty-eight hours all censorship ended. The country was in an uproar; people who had been gagged for nearly twenty years shouted their protests. The MUD was to contest the elections. But, as suddenly as it had been lifted, the censorship was reimposed. People who during the brief spell of liberty had revealed their opposition were seized and put in jail, and it became clear that the elections were to be a trick – a trick with a double edge. On the one hand, carefully misrepresented abroad by government propaganda, they would prove that Portugal was no dictatorship but an 'organic democracy', as Salazar had taken to calling it; on the other hand, as we saw in Chapter VI, the elections gave the authorities a chance to appraise the opposition's strength and to strike at it where the blows would be felt most keenly. The MUD therefore decided to boycott the elections, declaring them a farce and calling on the government to allow proper conditions for free elections; this became the pattern of subsequent elections up to the summer of 1958.

In 1945 those who supported the MUD were still hopeful. They did not believe that fascism could fall in Berlin and Rome, yet remain entrenched in Madrid and Lisbon. But before long whispers began to reach them from abroad. The policy of the USA and Britain in North Africa had already hinted at it; soon Churchill's Fulton speech confirmed it: the United Nations were not so united. The post-war world was going to be a hard place for anti-fascists to live in. For a time, despite the lack of support from abroad, and despite the great deal of attention given in the Portuguese Press to the anti-communist campaign now in full blast throughout the western world, the opposition remained united. Cut off from the outside world, accustomed to disbelieving everything that appeared in a censored Press, Liberals and communists alike were scarcely aware how deep was the rift between east and west.

And so in 1948, when presidential elections were announced, the MUD chose as its candidate General Norton de Matos, an old republican of immense prestige, a former ambassador to the Court of St James's and former governor general of Angola.[1] If the election

[1] When Norton de Matos died in 1955 at the age of eighty-seven, *The Times*, despite his distinguished career, found room for only an eight-line report of his death, and carried no obituary.

campaign had been a really free one Norton de Matos would almost certainly have been elected. Popular enthusiasm was so great that in Oporto a crowd of half a million gathered to hear him. This was more than the total population of the city; people had come from all over the north to give their support.

But this was to be the last united demonstration for a decade. Government repression persuaded a section of the MUD that it would be foolish to proceed with the candidature unless certain minimum guarantees could be wrested from the government. It is said that Norton de Matos himself was prepared to proceed whether guarantees were given or not. In any event, serious disagreements arose within the MUD; and at the last moment the General stood down. A breach between Left and Right had been opened which was to wreck the MUD, and which the authorities took full advantage of. The breach has persisted ever since.

How far each side is to be blamed for the disunity it is difficult to say. By 1948 the Communist Party was no doubt co-ordinating its line with that of the Cominform; and 1948 was the year of the hardening of international communist policy. At the same time the old republicans were also becoming aware of the international atmosphere. Russia had not lifted a finger to help the Portuguese opposition. Towards the end of the war the latter had pinned its faith on the victorious United Nations' removing Franco from power and so paving the way for the Portuguese revolution; but the Soviet Union had not insisted that Franco be declared an enemy, despite the participation of his Blue Division in Hitler's attack on Russia. Britain and the United States seemed to be more predictable and more congenial allies for the old republicans; and these two States clearly would not favour oppositionists who maintained links with communists, no matter how opportunist those oppositionists' motives might be. And so, for the most part, the old republicans dropped their collaboration with the communists as if it might burn their fingers. They have never resumed it.

Among young people it was a different story. They had their own opposition movement, the *MUD Juvenil*, which took its name, but its name alone, from the adult organization. Among the youth there were no old republicans and precious few young ones; it was the communists who commanded the respect of young people, and so the whole trend of the *MUD Juvenil* was towards the extreme Left. The organization was active in the universities and high schools; it remained united and strong long after the **MUD** had dissolved; and it attracted to its ranks a large part of the country's rebellious and idealistic youth.

When the Left wing of the **MUD** re-formed into the *Movimento Nacional Democrático* (MND) in 1953 the *MUD Juvenil* gave the new organization its full support. But the MND never managed to rally the sympathy the MUD had enjoyed. Its leading members publicly associated themselves with the communist-sponsored world peace campaign and thus became an easy target for the authorities. Perhaps its most sensational activity was its call for democracy in Goa to enable the Goan people to decide their future for themselves. It was the activity in support of this MND appeal that led to wide-spread arrests of students and other young people and the trial of the fifty-two in Oporto in 1956.

We have taken the story of public political opposition up to the appearance of Delgado on the scene in 1958. Before bringing it up to date we should add that out of the public eye there have also been numerous conspiracies, even in recent years. The nature of these activities makes it hard to learn much about them. Just after the end of the war there were several plots that came to nothing. On 10 October 1946 there was the better-known but equally abortive *revolução da Mealhada*, a pathetic attempt by no more than fifty junior army officers and men to seize power.[1]

Since the 1958 election there have been at least two more plots involving army officers, students and other young people. In neither was a single shot fired against the régime, because on both occasions the officers informed the students at the last minute that they were not proceeding with the jointly agreed plans – and this on the second occasion (March 1960) despite a number of Ministers, warned of the preparations to arrest them, having taken refuge in the barracks of the Portuguese Legion on the Cais do Sodré. A leader of the Catholic Working Youth, Manuel Serra, was convicted of being the main leader of the second conspiracy; he escaped from the prison hospital, took refuge in the Cuban embassy and was later granted asylum in the Brazilian embassy. The second plot had an ignominious sequel: one of the young conspirators killed a comrade with whom he was in hiding after the plot had misfired.

Whenever there is a conversation about the future of the opposition

[1] The story is told by Captain Fernando Queiroga, who led the troops that did revolt, in his *Portugal Oprimido*.

and its chances of success someone always raises the question of the army. The ordinary soldiers, who are peasants and fishermen in uniform, and the NCOs and junior officers are said to be bitterly resentful of Salazar's generals. From time to time mimeographed broadsheets appear purporting to come from groups of dissident officers. How far they reflect real unrest in the army it is hard to say. But force is what counts in a police State; so everyone is anxious about the army's position.

This is probably what caused so much hope to be aroused when Delgado decided to stand as an opposition candidate in 1958. Here was a serving officer – an air force general – not a former soldier who had long ago lost contact with the service. Moreover he was not discredited in the eyes of any section of the opposition, unless his past services on behalf of the régime could be held against him. On the whole however, apart from some repugnance at first among veteran anti-fascists, it was the very fact that he was new to the opposition that made Delgado so effective. To be sure, the communists at first denounced him. His candidature, they said in clandestine leaflets, had been planned in the British and American embassies. But as support for Delgado grew, this charge was dropped. And it may well be that this initial communist antagonism helped Delgado by making it difficult for the government to pin on him their favourite label.

And yet, though support for Delgado was massive, so massive that he would undoubtedly have won if the elections had been free, the army made no move on his behalf. On the contrary, when tanks were ordered on to the Lisbon streets to threaten the rebellious people there was no hint of disobedience.

The Portuguese armed forces, formerly ragged, half-starved and ill-equipped, have benefited greatly from the NATO alliance. Not only have they now got modern weapons; both officers and men are probably a good deal more comfortable than they used to be. They now wear woollen tunics in place of their old ones of thin cotton; they look healthy, smart and well fed. If dissent does exist in the army, it can hardly be encouraged by close collaboration with the American and British armed forces and the constant exchange of military missions. And the recent choice of Lisbon as NATO's official naval headquarters may help to ensure that the Portuguese navy will do nothing to oppose Salazar as long as he remains a member of the Atlantic alliance.

Living without an empire

In the last few weeks of 1960 the Salazar government made a determined effort to rally its crumbling support. Though it had been unable to give an effective answer to any of the criticisms levelled against it on domestic questions, international developments now enabled it to postpone a reckoning by appealing to patriotic sentiment.

One of the major obstacles the opposition has always had to face has been indifference or hostility abroad. There can scarcely be any other anti-fascist movement in the world which has been accorded so little international solidarity. Take Britain alone. Search through questions in Parliament about repressive régimes in other lands, or through foreign affairs resolutions at the Trades Union Congress and the Labour Party conference – not to mention the proceedings of all the various organizations existing to give practical solidarity to victims of fascism. Search as hard as you can, but you will scarcely ever find the name of Portugal. No wonder the Portuguese opposition has felt isolated and abandoned and cut off from a heedless world by Franco Spain on one side and the Atlantic on the other.

This isolation has not merely handicapped the opposition by sapping its self-confidence. It has also had a crippling effect on its ideological evolution.

Inside Portugal – the position is obviously different among the growing number of Portuguese democrats outside the country – you are struck by a certain provincialism, by a clinging to outdated methods, among the opposition's Right and Left wings alike. You will, for instance, find Liberals who believe neither in colonial freedom nor in the emancipation of women; and you will find supporters of the Communist Party who think that the speech of Khrushchev denouncing Stalin's crimes was concocted by Salazar's propagandists. During the whole lifetime of the majority of the population there has been no intelligent public discussion of the kind of problems the British people are used to seeing mentioned every day in their newspapers. The entire intellectual life of the country is stifled under a censorship that is arbitrary, moronic and narcotic.

In consequence, although Salazar has never won the intellectuals, the marks of a totalitarian upbringing are to be found even on some of the best of them. The lively intellectual life of pre-Salazar days has been crushed; there is no longer a tradition of speculative discussion. And one question that has not been discussed for many years is what is going to happen to Portugal when she loses her colonial empire.

Accordingly, to show the nation that no friendship from abroad can be expected, Salazar has been able to point to the sudden foreign interest in Portugal, the articles on Angola in the British and French Press, the United Nations General Assembly decision that Portugal's overseas possessions are in fact colonies, the condemnation of Portuguese colonialism by United Nations delegates from the newly independent African States, the criticism within NATO, and the American vote against Portugal in the Security Council.

In appealing to their patriotism, Salazar hopes to unite people behind him in the same way as the republicans rallied the people to their cause seventy years ago when they protested against the British ultimatum. But the republicans expressed the people's democratic aspirations at that time; the nationalist upsurge was directed against threats from hostile imperialist nations. Only the naïve or the cynical could compare the two periods.

Nevertheless, though many understand how little there is of principle and how much of opportunism in Salazar's calls for national unity against foreign attacks, the attacks themselves have touched many Portuguese on a very raw nerve. And of course Salazar knows this. However demagogic his call for national unity may have been, he must have been certain that there would be disunity within the opposition on this question. To promote this disunity he declared an amnesty towards the end of 1960; a number of people not associated directly with the Left had charges against them dropped or penalties imposed on them removed. They included Aquilino Ribeiro and a group of Catholics who had been charged with defaming Portugal in the foreign Press. But Manuel Serra and persons accused of communist activity were not affected.

How far will Salazar succeed in rallying support, or at any rate paralysing the opposition with sharper disunity than ever? This is a question that many enlightened Portuguese are asking. The colonial question is far and away the most dangerous of all political topics in Portugal today. Opponents of Salazar will only discuss it behind closed doors.[1] Some of them admit that colonialism is a thing of the past and

---

[1] At an early stage of the diplomatic conflict with India over Goa, Professor Rui Luís Gomes and other leaders of the MND were arrested for saying – among other things – that the peoples of the colonies were, like the Portuguese people, victims of a dictatorship, that only in a democratic system would the colonial peoples be free to choose their government, and that there should be a referendum in Goa. (See pp. 191-2 above.) Apart

that Salazar's policy is a disastrous one. But there are many others, particularly among the old republicans, who, sincere as their opposition to the dictatorship may be, are horrified at the prospect of losing the colonies. If this happens, they say, the blame must lie with Salazar. Losing Portugal's empire will go down in history as his greatest crime; a democratic Portugal would never have committed the excesses which have led to unrest among the colonial peoples. They do not seem to have noticed that fierce anti-colonialism can exist – and triumph – in colonies of countries with democratic systems of government. Then there are oppositionists who pay lip-service to the right of colonial peoples to their freedom, but say that the question should not be mentioned in any political platform. They say this, not out of fear of government repression, but because they believe that frank espousal of the colonial peoples' cause will discredit the opposition among the ordinary people, who, it is insisted, are not able to understand the problem and would be driven to support Salazar for patriotic motives. There are still other oppositionists who believe that if the dictatorship can be overthrown there may be time to come to an understanding with the nationalists in the colonies. Concessions may then be made which will stem the tide of revolt and keep the ramshackle empire together in some kind of commonwealth, on the British model.

None of these points of view seems to us well founded; each seems to arise from inadequate information about the modern world. Whatever system of government Portugal has in the future, her colonial empire is bound to disintegrate, as the British, Dutch, French and Belgian empires are disintegrating. National consciousness in Portugal's colonies is not primarily a result of Salazarist excesses; it is part of a world-wide awakening. If anything, Salazarist repression until recently put a brake on this development in the Portuguese colonies, whose backwardness and isolation under Salazar account for the relative weakness and lateness of the nationalist movements there. But in the last few years these movements have found powerful new allies in the recently independent States of Africa and Asia, whose support is enabling Angolans and others to fight back effectively for the first time.

In conversations with representatives of these movements we have found that, while they understand and sympathize with the sufferings

---

from the communists, no one has gone farther than this in public statements. In November 1960, 300 prominent individuals of all opposition trends signed a letter to President Tomás asking for permission to hold a congress of democrats and publish an opposition newspaper, so that the colonial problem might be fully discussed and an alternative to Salazar's colonial policy might be worked out.

of the Portuguese people under Salazar, and express friendly feelings towards the Portuguese people as distinct from their rulers, they are not looking to the Portuguese opposition for guidance in the anti-colonial struggle. Nor, they say, can there be talk of united action on a merely anti-Salazarist platform. Of course, Salazar is the common enemy; but the aim of nationalists in the Portuguese colonies is not merely the overthrow of Salazar, but the overthrow of the colonial system. Unity with Portuguese opponents of Salazar can only be on this basis.

Now, whether the Portuguese like this point of view or not, it seems to be based on a sound assessment of the way things are moving in the world. Moreover it is a point of view that is likely to win support, not only in the Afro-Asian countries, but also in America and western Europe. For it is not only Left opinion in the west that is beginning to feel concerned about the Portuguese colonies, as the criticism of Portugal inside NATO has shown. For the first time for many years the curtain of silence around the 'Estado Novo' is being lifted. Now that open conflict has broken out in the Portuguese African colonies, Portugal and her affairs are being spotlighted in the world as never before. And the various trends in the Portuguese opposition are facing a crucial test.

What the opposition needed, one friend said to us, was not an alternative colonial policy, but a programme, based on careful analysis, that would show how Portugal could survive in the world without colonies. If no such programme was worked out very soon, he emphasized, the loss of the colonies would bring about a national tragedy that not even the disappearance of Salazarism would mitigate. The tragedy, he said, was already in the making. Backwardness of industry, the crisis in agriculture and the dangerously high level of emigration would not automatically end with a change of régime. In fact a mere change of government, unless accompanied by a fundamental change in every aspect of economic policy, would result in chaos. This did not mean that Salazar was the lesser evil. Inevitably Salazar would go – but his three and a half decades of misrule would leave a terrible legacy behind. Yet so far no one in the opposition, however well intentioned and self-sacrificing, had produced a thought-out programme that grappled with these problems.[1]

We asked whether the masses of the people were so affected by

[1] At long last, on 11 May 1961, the old republicans issued their *Programa para a Democratização da República*, a 20,000-word document signed by sixty-one prominent

official propaganda that they would be unlikely to support such a programme. He thought not. The masses were against the present system; they lived in abject poverty, for which they held their rulers responsible. They would support anyone who came forward firmly against Salazar. That – and not because of his policies or his personal qualities – was why they had supported General Delgado. But it was important for the future that something better than Delgado and his minimal demands should be put forward. If it was to enjoy their support for long, the government that replaced Salazar would have to feed the people. Freedom, said our friend, might sustain the people for a few days or weeks – but unless it also filled their bellies they would soon become disillusioned.

If bread, not national glory, was the chief concern of the poor, matters stood differently among the middle classes and the intellectuals. Here it was the lack of a clear, straightforward alternative to colonialism that permitted Salazar's spurious patriotism to find some echo. So long as this vacuum persisted the opposition would be paralysed. If people were shown how a free Portugal could become prosperous on the labour of her own population alone, then not only would Salazar's jingoism have little effect, but his days would be numbered.

In the elaboration of an opposition programme, our friend concluded, there was one idea, once the common property of advanced thinkers in Portugal but now scarcely ever alluded to, which might profitably be re-examined: this was the idea of some closer form of

oppositionists. (There was some delay in making it public: it is dated 31 January 1961 in honour of the anniversary of the 1891 rising.) The programme lists a great number of social, economic, fiscal and political reforms, paying particular attention to improvements in education and scientific research. On the colonial question – a postscript (p. 39) points out that this section was written before the uprising in Angola – it calls for administrative 'decentralization' for the colonies on the same lines as in local government in Portugal itself. This is to be accompanied by economic integration of the 'overseas territories' with the mother country. Racial discrimination of any kind will be severely punished; the overseas possessions will benefit from similar basic reforms as Portugal (p. 10). While repudiating 'colonial imperialism' (p. 10), the programme repeats the traditional notion of 'the historic role of Portuguese civilization' (p. 38). In foreign policy the main emphasis is laid on Portugal's membership of the United Nations, the strengthening of the British alliance and friendship with Brazil; diplomatic relations will be established with all countries (p. 38). There is no specific mention of relations with either Franco Spain or a future democratic Spain. The programme makes no attack on existing property relations. It is essentially a list of desirable reforms, some of them very costly; nothing is said about how these measures are to be paid for; the economic expansion envisaged is all predicated on the continuance of Portuguese sovereignty overseas. The reforms outlined for the colonies would cost more than those for Portugal itself, because of the lower starting-point. But what if the colonial peoples do not want to wait till Portugal can afford such reforms? On this the old republicans are silent.

association between the Portuguese people and the other peoples of an Iberian peninsula liberated from the twin despotisms of Franco and Salazar. If history would not tolerate Portugal's rule in Africa much longer, might not prosperity be found in the progress along a common road of the Portuguese and the Castilians, together with Catalans, Basques and Galicians freed from Castilian hegemony?[1]

[1] One of the most encouraging aspects of the *Santa Maria* affair was Galvão's message to the Portuguese people afterwards. He declared that the coming Portuguese revolution 'will also open the doors of the overseas colonies to freedom, progress and independence'. He raised the question of social reconstruction in Portugal: 'We want a revolution [that] will have as its starting-point the destruction of an iniquitous social order, and . . . will be based on agrarian reform and urban reform . . . We shall implacably destroy the privileges of the Portuguese plutocracy which divide men from birth into rich and poor.' Not least, he linked the cause of democracy in Portugal with the struggle against Franco: 'We are . . . at war with the Portuguese and Spanish dictatorships . . . We are the nucleus of the future liberation army of Portugal and Spain.' (The message, dated 2 February 1961, was not reported in the British Press. It was translated in full in the *Portuguese and Colonial Bulletin*, vol. i, no. 2, p. 11, March 1961.) General Delgado has concluded an agreement with General Emilio Herrera, head of the Spanish republican government in exile in Paris, proposing the abolition of passports between Portugal and Spain when they are freed, a general relaxation of travel restrictions, mutual consular services, common postal and telegraphic charges, a Customs and currency agreement, and economic co-ordination. A supreme Spanish-Portuguese Council is to carry out opposition activity in foreign countries. The signatories accepted each other as the 'legitimate democratic oppositions' to Salazar and Franco.

PART THREE

XI

Language and culture

Latter-day Latin

The Portuguese language is a modern form of rural Latin, for the most part more archaic than the other Romance languages because of Portugal's historical isolation.[1] Though an Englishman needs a glossary to read Chaucer, a literate Portuguese can read what his ancestors wrote and sang in the twelfth and thirteenth centuries: the love songs and satirical verses composed by troubadours, kings and commoners. This antiquity of many aspects of the language makes it at once so appealing and so baffling to foreigners. It is far more difficult than Castilian, and an Englishman cannot hope to 'pick it up', even on a long visit. But knowing something about everyday speech will make his visit more interesting, even if it does not help him much in practical matters. Of course, Portuguese does have much in common with Castilian, which is a younger language; every educated Portuguese understands Spaniards when they speak, and frequently reads Spanish books, though with poor people the less literate they are the less they understand of Castilian, especially when it is spoken rapidly. An English person with a smattering of Castilian will find it helps him to get by in Portugal, in the same way as Italian is of use in Spain and German in Holland.

But the first sound of Portuguese, especially when several people are speaking it together, as not infrequently happens, is not what you expected. The cadences are not very much like those of other Romance languages, and if you have been in eastern Europe or have heard much Russian you fancy at first that you are among Slavs. And when you hear a Portuguese speaking English you recall those skilled Russian interpreters who, even the most fluent of them, cannot quite master the English *l* or *e* in a word like 'lend'. What adds to this Slavonic

[1] Recent linguistic research makes this a controversial statement. Cf. Serafim da Silva Neto, *História da Língua Portuguêsa* (Rio de Janeiro, 1952), pp. 114 ff.

impression is the Portuguese pronunciation of *s* at the ends of words –
s forms the plural and occurs in a great many verb-endings – and in the
middle of words where *s* is followed by a consonant. In these cases *s* is
pronounced as the English pronounce it in the word 'usual'. When a
group of such words is spoken quickly, as in *os homens estão na estala-
gem*, 'the men are in the inn', you get almost the same soft hissing that
occurs in the name of the Soviet Prime Minister when it is correctly
pronounced.

Another unexpected sound that is difficult for foreigners to master is
the nasal diphthong in words like *mãe*, 'mother'; *pão*, 'bread'; and
põe, 'he puts'. This is pronounced rather like the *ng* in 'sing' – but that
is only an approximation. This nasal sound comes in many verb-
endings.

All this gives Portuguese a curiously soft and blurred colour, in
striking contrast with the crispness of French, the fluidity of Italian and
the roughness and clarity of Castilian.

Apart from the difficulties of pronunciation, two major obstacles
for the beginner are the complicated grammar, especially that of the
verbs, and the old-fashioned, almost oriental formality of address.
The first thing you want to do with a language is talk to people. But in
Portugal you are quite liable to be addressed in four, or even five,
different ways, each having a distinct degree of intimacy or respect and
firmly fixing your relationship with the person addressing you. Nothing
so simple as the French choice between *vous* and *tu*. The second person
plural *vós* is rarely used in Portuguese, being reserved for addressing
the Deity or large audiences. The second person singular *tu* is used by
adults to children (but among old-fashioned people not by children to
their parents), between brothers and sisters, lovers, husbands and
wives, close friends and schoolmates, even long after they are grown
up. *Tu* is the most intimate form possible. It is also used to indicate
condescension: servants are addressed in the second person singular
but must address their employers in a respectful way.

Less close friends, and acquaintances of the same social rank with
whom one wishes to be a little warmer than mere civility demands, are
addressed as *você* with the verb in the third person. This word, now
used as a pronoun, is a corruption of the archaic *vossa mercê*, 'your
Honour'. No one remembers the origin of *você* when using it, although
among country people *vossa mercê* may still sometimes be heard.[1]

---

[1] In Brazil *você* is the common word for 'you' among all classes and is now replacing *tu*
even between intimates.

If a person is of the same rank as you but a stranger, or not so close as to be addressed as *você*, he will use *o senhor* or *a senhora*, 'the gentleman' or 'the lady', *o menino* or *a menina*, 'the boy' or 'the girl' (the ordinary words for 'boy' and 'girl', *rapaz* and *rapariga*, are never used in addressing young people). Here again the verb takes the third person.

But if someone wishes to be especially deferential, for example a shopkeeper or a particularly old-fashioned person who wants to please you, then you will be *vossa excelência*, 'your Excellency', or, more briefly, *vossência*. The verb is in the third person.

Now this is a complex and perilous system, full of dangers for the uninitiated. Mistakes and carelessness can bring retribution – though not to the foreigner, who is excused everything – because the Portuguese among themselves are touchy about these matters, and an absent-minded use of the wrong form, or a change to a more distant form, may well be interpreted as a rebuff. And if you wish to be deliberately chilling, or even offensive, to someone there is ample scope for many a subtle slight.

There is, however, an escape clause. In conversation you commonly drop the pronoun and rely on the verb-ending for your meaning, as in Latin; pronouns are more for emphasis than for clarification. If you are in doubt as to the precise way you should address someone the simplest thing to do is not to breathe those dangerous expressions *você*, *o senhor* and *vossa excelência*, but keep to the plain verb. Possessive pronouns are always the same, and so with a little skill you can bide your time until you have found out more about the person in question and what form of address he merits.

To this list must be added the numerous titles in common use in Portugal. Titles of nobility were abolished after the revolution of 1910, but there are plenty of others. All university graduates other than engineers are *doutores*, 'doctors'. They are addressed as *senhor doutor*. Graduate engineers are *senhor engenheiro*. Army officers are *senhor major*, *senhor coronel* and so on. But often an actual occupation becomes a mode of address. Thus a primary schoolteacher is *senhor professor*. The chairman of a company will be *senhor director*, a Minister of the government *senhor ministro* and a policeman *senhor guarda*.

There does not seem to be any move to simplify forms of address in Portugal as there has been in Brazil, and even the most liberal cling to the old tradition. We were told what happens when high councils of the old republican opposition are held. Needless to say, these are not public gatherings. The participants have been intimates from boyhood. Some of them have been in jail or exile together. Privately they address one another as *tu*; but when they are discussing ways and means of bringing democracy back to Portugal they invariably address one another as *vossa excelência*.

In Portugal there are two classes of the female sex, as once there were in England. There are *senhoras*, 'ladies', and *mulheres*, 'women'. Having established that the female person you are addressing is a *senhora*, an assumption that should certainly be made if she is not in peasant dress, you will call her *minha senhora*, 'my lady'. This is done by all men, even if they themselves are *senhores*, by children, by younger *senhoras* addressing older ones, and by women who are simply *mulheres*.

Women are not known by their surnames, as men are. A young girl called Maria Teresa, of the class that grows up to become *senhoras*, is known as *a menina* Maria Teresa. If she marries a man called, say, Carlos Silva, she becomes *a senhora dona* Maria Teresa, never '*senhora* Silva', as many foreigners persist in thinking even after they have lived in Portugal a long time. And so, to address a *senhora* correctly, you have to know her Christian names. After marriage a female person who is not a *senhora* will be simply *dona* Maria.

This is the usage among the middle and upper classes – and the kind of address they expect from their inferiors. Working people among themselves are more casual. The story is told of a country doctor who was sitting in his surgery one night when a peasant arrived outside on horseback. The man was tired and hungry after a journey of twenty kilometres from his remote village. He came in to the doctor, took off his cap and said:

'*Ó senhor doutor*, my woman has died. It is too late for you to help her now, but will you please issue a death certificate so that she can be buried?'

Unless the circumstances are suspicious it is common in these outlying places for doctors to issue a death certificate without seeing the body when to do so would mean a long trip.

'Certainly,' replied the physician, taking out a form. 'What was your wife's name?'

'Her name, *ó senhor doutor*?' asked the man, looking puzzled.

'Of course, her name. Come, come, I can't issue a certificate without a name on it.'

The man scratched his head.

'*Ó senhor doutor*, I can't remember ... I always called her "*mulher*".'

So the man had to ride back twenty kilometres to his village without the death certificate, in order to find out from her kinsfolk the name of the woman with whom he had been living for more than thirty years.

It is unlikely that there are many working people quite like that couple. But it is certainly usual for poor people to be known only by their Christian names. The cobbler will be known as *senhor* António and the milkman as *senhor* João to both their superiors and their equals. When they talk to each other they will use *você*.

In the incident recounted above the peasant is quoted as saying '*ó senhor doutor*'. The *ó* here is not the masculine definite article, which bears no accent; it is an interjection standing before the noun in the vocative relation, as 'O' used to do in Latin and English.

Another of the charms of the language is the frequent use of the diminutive: the addition to a noun or adjective of the suffixes -*inho* in the masculine and -*inha* in the feminine (often, in practice, -*zinho* and -*zinha*) – or, less commonly, -*ito* and -*ita*. At first it seems as if almost any noun can be used in the diminutive form. But you can only do this safely when you know the language well, because the diminutive bears a variety of subtle meanings besides that of physical smallness. The particular meaning can be understood only in the context. Most commonly the diminutive is used to indicate affection: *minha mãezinha*, 'my little mother'; Teresinha, 'little Theresa'; Joãozinho, 'Johnny'. And this affection can be extended to things as well as people. If you hear someone referring to a possession in the diminutive you should not assume that the object in question is a small one. The delighted owner of a new American motor-car may well refer to it as *o meu carrinho* or *o meu automòvelzinho*, the -*inho* indicating the large place it has in his affections rather than its small size. An old man six feet tall may often be referred to as *o velhinho*, 'the little old one', by those who are fond of him.

In other contexts the diminutive may imply pity or sympathy. The largest woman when ill will be called *pobrezinha*, 'poor little thing'. Or more often *coitadinha*, which means the same. The word *coitado* or *coitada* is one of the most commonly used in the language. It is the word you murmur softly, often in the diminutive, when you wish to express sympathy with anyone who needs it. It has the same emotional content as 'dear, dear, I *am* sorry'.

If somebody has been unwell you will ask him if he is *melhorzinho*, *melhor* meaning 'better'. When you want to be particularly sympathetic

you extend your affection to his ailment as well: *O senhor está melhorzinho do seu reumatismozinho?* 'Is your rheumatism a bit better?' If
someone tells you that *um homenzinho está à porta* you must not assume
that a dwarf is at the door. The 'little man' may well be huge; he will
certainly be poor or otherwise an object of compassion.

The diminutive is also used to diminish the importance of some
event or thing; this may be either from modesty or from contempt.
The Portuguese has a habit of mock humility and may invite you to a
banquet by calling it *um jantarzinho* or *uma festazinha*. This is self-
depreciatory. But the diminutive also comes in handy if one wants to
be spiteful. Speaking of an artist whose work one considers trivial, one
might say: *Tem feito umas pinturazinhas*, 'He has done some bits of
paintings'.

And so the diminutive can express a wealth of meaning: all the
emotional content of smallness, from gentleness to pettiness. To know
exactly when and where to use it to most effect you must know the
language well. But the foreigner who wants to create an impression
will go far if instead of simply thanking people by saying *obrigado* he
says instead *obrigadinho*, the quite untranslatable diminutive of 'thanks',
which conveys more rather than less gratitude.

Portuguese experience shows how hazardous spelling reforms may
be. Over the last fifty years there have been several such reforms, the
most recent being the subject of an official agreement between Portugal
and Brazil.[1] In theory this has simplified spelling; but it has not
made for consistency. And those whose business is the printed word
do not seem to have taken the matter very seriously, as a glance at any
newspaper will show. In the same article you may well find two
different spellings of the same word – and a third variant in the headline. A man will cheerfully spell his name 'Marcelo' or 'Marcello', as
the mood takes him. It seems that your ideas about spelling, if you are a
Portuguese, depend entirely on your age and on which particular
reform was in force when you were at school: there have been too
many reforms to keep up with. The professional writer or journalist
spells in the way he was taught and leaves the rest to the printers; the
printers, alas, do not seem to be of one mind. Officially, then, there are
now no *k*, *w* or *y* in Portuguese. *Ph* has been replaced by *f*; no double
letters are permitted except for *rr* and *ss*, which have different sounds
from *r* and *s* respectively; *z* has been replaced in many instances by *s*;
and the use of accents has been altered more than once.

[1] There are still minor differences between the orthographies of the two countries.

But there is a more serious objection than the danger of inconsistency. After all, that could be overcome with a little care. What happens with a too zealous reform of spelling is that the etymology of various words becomes obscured and it is often hard to see at a glance what a word's origin is. During our early days in Lisbon we were intrigued by a word we saw all about us, sometimes in neon lighting. The word was *quiosque*. Nothing, it seemed, could be more Latin. But what could it possibly mean? Suddenly we got it. Kiosk! What else? The *k* having been eliminated, how else could this word be spelled?

Literature and learning

Though architecture is one of the glories of Portugal, there is not room to discuss it here; in any case, it is described in many other books.[1] Nor shall we write about Portuguese painting, except to say that the great double triptych of the fifteenth-century painter Nuno Gonçalves, when it was shown for the first time outside Portugal at the exhibition of Portuguese art in London in 1955–6, came as a revelation to British critics, who acknowledged it as one of the great paintings of Europe. Here again, there are books of reproductions and criticism available, notably the *L'Art portugais* (Paris, 1953) and *Nuno Gonçalves* (London, 1955) of Professor Reinaldo dos Santos.

Up to now the Portuguese have contributed surprisingly little to serious music; their composers have mostly imitated Italian, French and German models. Yet the country's folk music extends far beyond the now stereotyped and monotonous *fado*, commercialized to death in the tourist haunts. It is puzzling to know why so little significant music is composed, for most educated Portuguese are keen music-lovers, and concerts and opera performances are well attended.

In literature, however, Portugal is exceedingly rich, though unfortunately her classical writers are better known on the Continent than in Britain. The great nineteenth-century novelist, Eça de Queirós, whose works, full of dry humour, are a biting commentary on every aspect of Portuguese social life, has suffered at the hands of some of his English translators. This is a pity, for while his works are very Portuguese their quality makes him a writer of undeniably European stature. Three of his novels have appeared in English in the past decade. *The*

---

[1] For instance, Sacheverell Sitwell's *Portugal and Madeira* (1954). See also J. B. Bury, 'Architecture, with Special Reference to the Sixteenth Century', in H. V. Livermore (ed.), *Portugal and Brazil: an Introduction* (Oxford, 1953), pp. 146–65.

Relic (1954) is a reissue of a lively translation by the scholar Aubrey Fitz Gerald Bell; *Cousin Baxilio* (1953), a kind of Portuguese *Madame Bovary*, is cut by a third without any indication that this has been done, and is full of elementary errors of translation. *The City and the Mountains* (1955) is poorly translated, too.[1]

Long before Eça – as he is affectionately known in his own country – there was a fertile literary tradition, dating back to the improvised poems of the twelfth century, and described in Bell's *Portuguese Literature* (Oxford, 1922).[2] The twelfth or so English translation of *Os Lusíadas*, the great epic of Luís de Camões glorifying the Portuguese mariners who discovered the world, came out as a Penguin Classic in 1952.[3] Eça and Camões are virtually the only Portuguese writers known in Britain.

On top of this ignorance of the great writers of the past, there is scarcely an inkling anywhere outside Portugal of modern developments in Portuguese writing. Yet these developments reveal, both in what the writers say and in what they do not say, a very great deal about the peculiar nature of present-day Portuguese political and social life. To anyone who is interested in the role of the writer in society and the controversy about 'commitment', the character, quality and sheer volume of literary creation, the vigour of literary criticism and the diversity of literary trends are startling and exciting. They would be so under any circumstances, in a country with a population of nine million. But Portugal suffers from a poor educational system and mass illiteracy; there is little money to spare for the buying of books; there are no public lending libraries to speak of; there are only about three writers who are able to live by writing. The literary ferment that exists despite these handicaps is astonishing. Though fascist régimes have been notorious for their cultural poverty, Portugal is an exception. All Salazar's censorship and repression have not succeeded in silencing the writers; all his propaganda has not succeeded in producing a single writer of merit who is friendly to the régime.

It was in fact during the first years of the '*Estado Novo*' that the foundation of modern Portuguese literature was laid. But it had

---

[1] Other English versions of works by Eça de Queirós are: *Our Lady of the Pillar* (trans. Edgar Prestage, 1906); *The Sweet Miracle* (trans. Prestage, ed. 4, Oxford 1914); *Perfection* (trans. Charles Marriott, 1923); *José Mathias* and *A Man of Talent* (trans. Luís Marques, 1947).
[2] See also his 'Perspectives of Portuguese Literature', in Livermore, *op. cit.* pp. 107–29.
[3] The best modern translation (in verse) is Leonard Bacon's *The Lusiads* (New York: Hispanic Society of America, 1950).

nothing at all to do with the ideology of corporativism. Neo-realism came to Portugal through the influence of French writers, the American generation of the thirties – Hemingway, Steinbeck and Dos Passos – and Brazilian writers like José Lins do Rego and Jorge Amado. At first these influences found expression chiefly in magazines[1] which held that literature in the twenties had been too abstract and too preoccupied with metaphysical questions. Writers began to be concerned with social reality – Portuguese social reality, but not merely the kind of realistic portrayal of the social life of the middle and upper classes that Eça de Queirós had done so well fifty years before. For the first time Portuguese literature began to reflect the life of the masses of the poor, especially the life of the peasants. Strangely enough, the new school was welcomed by the critics, and the neo-realists were at first pampered.

The earliest of them was Ferreira de Castro, who has some claim to be considered the greatest living Portuguese novelist; his first work, *A Selva* (1930), has been translated into fourteen languages, including English.[2] The new trend was more clearly developed in novels by Alves Redol (*Avieiros*, 1942, and *Fanga*, 1943) portraying the struggle of the *alentejanos* against the big landowners of their province. The Alentejo became the conscience of the Portuguese writers, and they returned to it again and again. Manuel da Fonseca, in *Cerromaior* (1944), described the imprisonment of villagers after their land had been seized. Virgílio Ferreira's *Vagão J.* (1946) told of the migrant workers who travel round the country in cattle wagons looking for jobs; this novel was soon banned. Even Gaspar Simões, earlier a psychological novelist – he was the critic who introduced Proust, Joyce and Lawrence to the Portuguese public – ventured into neo-realism with *Uma História de Província* (2 vols., 1934–36), which portrayed the tedium of rural life and the social customs of the rural middle class.

Other neo-realists discovered industry. Manuel do Nascimento wrote about life in the mines (*Mineiros*, 1944); Carlos de Oliveira, about the effects of modern machinery and monopolization on the fortunes of the owner of a small tilery and his family (*Casa na Duna*, 1943).

Apart from those of Ferreira de Castro, all these books were very

---

[1] *O Diabo* (1934–41) and *Sol Nascente* (Oporto, 1937–40), which were suppressed, and *Vértice* (founded 1939), which still exists.
[2] *Jungle* (trans. Charles Duff, 1934).

much concerned with economic questions, and they came under fire from critics who eventually began to find a succession of semi-political tracts somewhat wearying. Works less militant but more mature began to appear: Alves Redol's trilogy *Ciclo Port-Wine* (1949–53); Carlos de Oliveira's anarchistic *Alcateia* (1944), banned by the authorities; Fernando Namora's *Casa de Malta* (1945) and *Retalhos da Vida dum Médico* (1949), the first a book of short stories about homeless casual labourers, the second a collection of sketches about the life of a poor country doctor; *Esteiros* (1946) by Pereira Gomes, a story about child labourers by a writer who died, while still a young man, in the prison where he was being detained on a political charge.

Virgílio Ferreira passed from neo-realism to a kind of Catholic existentialism in *Aparição* (1959), a complex and skilfully written attempt, but an unsuccessful one, at a philosophical novel.

Manuel da Fonseca has stayed faithful to the Alentejo, and his sensitively written *Seara do Vento* (1959) is a great advance on some of its predecessors. It is the story of a peasant with a tiny plot of land who comes into conflict with those who own his village. He is an individualist; his daughter, who typifies the new Portuguese peasant, brings into the house revolutionary leaflets advising the peasants to organize; but she fails to persuade him to co-operate in the struggle. The old man avenges himself in the traditional way – by shooting the estate owner. His family are against this way out. The home is broken up, and the peasant fights a lonely and doomed battle with the police until he is shot dead.

Other more or less political novels that should be mentioned if we are to convey any idea of the immense fertility of modern Portuguese writers are Alves Redol's *A Barca dos Sete Lemes* (1958), the story of a spiv, and *Uma Fenda na Muralha* (1960), a study of the life of Nazaré fishermen, divested of false, tourist-brochure glamour; Ferreira de Castro's *A Curva da Estrada* (1950), set in Spain just before the civil war; and José Cardoso Pires's *O Anjo Ancorado* (1958), whose theme is the conflict between the old republicans, now tired and disillusioned, and the new generation of oppositionists.

In the fifties there emerged a number of women novelists, among them Ester de Lemos, a product of the Portuguese Youth who nevertheless displayed in *Companheiros* (1960) the smarting conscience of a middle-class Portuguese Catholic, and Graça Pina de Morais, whose *Origem* (1958) shows how a young and sensitive woman is shocked by the indifference of the rich to social injustice.

A promising newcomer on the literary scene is Augusto Abelaira. His *A Cidade das Flores* (1959) is set in Florence at the time of Mussolini; but this is simply a device to avoid the censorship. The central figure is a young painter of democratic views. There is a poignant scene where the painter, looking down on the street, sees an English tourist passing by, and wonders what it is like to be a man from a free country . . .

These are only a few of the modern Portuguese writers whose works are widely discussed. Outside this main stream of writing that is more or less politically aware there are other writers who are in no sense 'committed'; for all that, none of their work can be construed, even remotely, as pro-Establishment. We mean writers like the poet and novelist José Régio, whose autobiographical novel *Os Avisos do Destino* (1953) rages against middle-class hypocrisy, and Almada Negreiros, who is also a talented painter. Negreiros's books are lively and filled with irony; one of the best-known, *Nome de Guerra* (1938), recounts the behaviour of rich men from the countryside when they come to Lisbon to enjoy the company of prostitutes in the cabarets and night-clubs.

Also outside the main stream, but dominating the literary scene, is Aquilino Ribeiro. The critics have always said that his regionalism – which includes an insistent use of the dialect of his home province of Beira, so that few Portuguese who were not born there can understand him fully – has diminished his claim to be considered a truly front-rank national writer. But for fifty years, despite the critics, Aquilino has been one of the very few Portuguese who earn their living solely by the pen. Though politics have never come into his work before, he is today, towards the end of his life, and with all his immense prestige, taking his stand openly on the side of the peasants of his country in his defence of his banned novel *Quando os Lobos Uivam* (1959).

Poets are as abundant and as dissident as novelists – a fact that is hardly surprising in a land where practically everyone writes verse. Before the second world war there were influential modern movements associated with the journal *Presença* (1927–40); and the series of anthologies called *Novo Cancioneiro*, which began publication in Coimbra in 1940, was devoted to 'committed' poetry. A typical poet in this genre is Alexandre O'Neill, one of whose books is characteristically called *No Reino da Dinamarka* (*In the State of Denmark*) (1958). Jorge de Sena – also a sharp-penned critic, and a translator of Edith Sitwell, T. S. Eliot, Graham Greene and William Faulkner –

cares little for the prejudices of the average Portuguese reader, and his verse (*Coroa da Terra*, 1946, is one of his best books) has caused great controversy. Like many of Portugal's writers, Sena is now in Brazil. The surrealist poet Mário Cesariney de Vasconcelos sets out in *Pena Capital* (1957) to show the absurdity of an intellectual's existence in Portugal, and parodies religious ideas in a way that has not been done there for a generation.

There is also a school of philosophical poets, led by Sofia de Mello Breyner Andresen: these are Catholics who, finding the dictatorship intolerable, have gradually come to take a stand against Salazarism.

Literary critics are more influential in Portugal than their counterparts in Britain. Among the most prominent are Óscar Lopes and António José Saraiva; their monumental *História da Literatura Portuguesa* (ed. 2, Oporto, 1957) is a model of its kind.

The Portuguese themselves seem largely unaware of the extraordinary impact that modern Portuguese literary achievement makes upon a foreigner. Like the Russians under tsarism, Portuguese intellectuals are given to national self-depreciation. This is to be discounted, especially when one compares the number of outstanding writers under the Liberal monarchy, and again under the republic – two periods when there was no censorship – with the number that exist today. In those days there were not more than five or six at any given time. Today there are at least twenty. This is not to say that all of them, or even a majority, produce international masterpieces, nor even that they can all be counted among the best European writers of their time. But what they set out to do – to describe Portuguese life with skill, integrity, compassion and courage – they achieve, almost always with credit, and often with distinction.

But if imaginative writing has prospered in spite of Salazar, in philosophy and the sciences the picture is very different. Polemics are not allowed; there are few reliable sources of information; above all, there is no official encouragement for independent work. Talk to any research worker in Portugal, whatever his field, and he will reel off an endless list of complaints; especially will he show bitter resentment of the fact that philosophical or sociological or scientific works with a humanist or materialist or anti-religious bias are sedulously kept out of the country. And so there are not many Portuguese scholars who can keep in close enough touch with what is being done in their own fields abroad to be able to produce anything of real value, or with real relevance to new and controversial ideas.

The great exception is António Sérgio. But his well-stocked mind was already trained before Salazar came to power. He has never faltered in his incredibly voluminous output of philosophical, sociological and historical writings. And he has defended consistently his own individual variety of rationalism. Magalhães Vilhena, a young Portuguese philosopher now at the Sorbonne – whose own thesis on Socrates is further proof that, given the right conditions, the Portuguese can do valuable original work in the realm of ideas – believes that António Sérgio is a thinker of the same stature as, say, Ernst Cassirer, and that this would have been recognized long ago had Salazarism not prevented Sérgio from fulfilling himself.

It has been as a direct reaction against Sérgio's influence that the government-supported school of philosophers, headed by Álvaro Ribeiro, has revived scholasticism under the slogan: 'We can do without modern philosophy.'[1]

In historiography the best work is being done outside Portugal. For instance, a group of young historians in Paris, led by Magalhães Godinho, are re-examining the history of the Discoveries, the economic basis of which has never been thoroughly studied. Scientific work of this kind, which may well clash with the official myth of Portugal's unique past and civilizing mission, would not be possible at home.[2]

Portuguese natural science is terribly handicapped by the lack of subsidies, the shortage of laboratories and equipment, and the low level of industrial development. Yet Portugal has produced several notable scientists, whose work has won recognition abroad. The neurologist Egas Moniz, who died in 1955, was awarded the Nobel prize in 1949 for his discovery of pre-frontal leucotomy as a method of treating certain psychoses. The Portuguese school of mathematics was founded by Rui Luís Gomes, who is now a political exile in Argentina. Manuel Valadares, a distinguished physicist who was dismissed from his university post by Salazar, is now director of France's leading nuclear research establishment.

[1] One of this school's periodicals, *Tempo Presente* (founded in 1959), takes its title from the first line of Eliot's *Burnt Norton*.
[2] Magalhães Godinho and his colleagues are following the path blazed by the late Veiga Simões, a republican diplomatist. Veiga Simões published little; but one of his historical studies, on Henrique 'the Navigator', dealt a shattering blow to official propaganda myths. When he died in 1954 Veiga Simões left a mass of notes and a number of unfinished books. It is said that his widow, on the advice of her confessor, has refused to let her husband's literary remains be examined or published, and it is feared that they may have been destroyed.

'Salazar has built a concentration camp in the human soul,' one scientist said to us, as he listed the talented colleagues of his who had been banned from teaching posts and research work in the universities, or who are in exile and would face imprisonment if they returned home. Here and there serious men of learning can be found who do not openly oppose the government; but, whatever the dictator's propagandists may say about the number of dons in the government, there is practically no one of any consequence in science or letters who holds an official position – and in Portugal university posts are official appointments. The dictator who boasts of his country's past, present and future greatness has stifled independent thinking as far as it lies in his power to do so, and has handed the direction of intellectual life over to tenth-raters, time-servers, obscurantists and hacks.

XII

The spirit of Portugal

The uniqueness of Portugal

In the year 1940 a great exhibition was organized in Lisbon to celebrate the eight-hundredth anniversary of Portuguese nationhood. One of the organizers was Henrique Galvão, the man who became world famous twenty years later when he led the seizure of the *Santa Maria*. It was the most ambitious yet of Salazar's propaganda efforts to unite the people and arouse passionate nationalism, with himself as patriot-in-chief. But, unlike Galvão's later exploits, the exhibition created little stir. The outbreak of war in Europe and the halt in international tourism prevented it from having the intended impact on the world; and so Portugal's eight-hundredth birthday passed virtually unnoticed beyond her borders.

Portugal formally became a nation on 25 July 1139, when Dom Afonso Henriques defeated the Arab occupants of the south-western part of the peninsula at the battle of Ourique. The victor was Count of Portucale, a former vassal of the King of León, one of the peninsula's four Christian kingdoms. Now, to León, Castile, Navarre and Aragon, there was added a fifth, for Dom Afonso Henriques celebrated his victory by assuming the title of King of Portugal, and four years later swore allegiance to Pope Innocent II as his sole spiritual and temporal lord. But it was not until 1250 and the final expulsion of the Arabs from the Algarve by Dom Afonso III that Portugal assumed its present shape on the map. From 1268 on, the Portuguese monarch called himself King of Portugal and of the Algarve. From that day to this Portugal's frontiers have remained almost unchanged. Portugal is the oldest nation State in Europe.

She is also the most homogeneous. Apart from a few gipsies she has no national minorities. The Jews were expelled or forcibly converted; the Arabs were assimilated. Over the centuries there have been welded together the original inhabitants and the successive waves of peoples that came to settle along Europe's most westerly coast: Phoenicians and Greeks, Celts and Carthaginians, Romans, Swabians, Visigoths and Arabs. Later, as a result of Portugal's overseas conquests, Africans too came, first as slaves and then to be assimilated in their turn.

If the persistence of a single nationality and a single language is striking, the survival of Portugal as an independent political unit is more remarkable still. There are in the peninsula other nations as ardent in their nationalism, as distinct, or more so, in their language. But the Catalans, Basques and Galicians all fell under the hegemony of Castile. And Spain – from which the Arabs were not finally ousted until three centuries after the Portuguese *Reconquista* was completed – is a State made up of several restless peoples, chafing under Castilian domination, traditionally hostile to centralized government.

Why then has Portugal never been absorbed into this Spanish State? And, occupied by Spain from 1580 to 1640, how was she able to free herself from the Spanish yoke?

To answer these questions fully would require a whole book. The answer lies partly in geographical factors;[1] partly in the comparatively early successes against the Arabs, which gave the Portuguese a sense of unity not found on the other side of the frontier; partly in the national pride, and economic links with the east, created by the century of the Discoveries. But there is still another factor. The maintenance of Portuguese independence through centuries of decadence, economic stagnation and incompetent government is in great measure due to the alliance with England. This alliance was signed at Guimarães in 1373, after John of Gaunt had fought against Castile alongside Dom Fernando I.[2] Spain was to be one of England's most powerful enemies for many centuries. And for England the preservation of Portuguese independence from Spain was a major strategic need.

Not that there have not always been strong forces pulling the other way. Portuguese history is full of plot and counterplot for union with Spain. Royal marriages were contracted, or cancelled, with this always in mind. The Castilian ruling house always hoped to win Portugal, if not by force of arms then by dynastic means, and thus unite not only the peninsula but also the two overseas empires; Portuguese national

[1] Discussed at length in Dan Stanislawski, *The Individuality of Portugal: a Study in Historical-Political Geography* (Austin and Edinburgh, 1959).
[2] The alliance was sealed in the Treaty of Windsor, a treaty of perpetual peace and friendship, signed in 1386.

pride was England's best instrument in frustrating this hope. Terrible crimes have been committed to prevent such marriages, or to prevent the children of a Spanish mother from succeeding to the throne. The murder of Inês de Castro, Spanish mistress of Dom Pedro I and mother of his children, and the fearful revenge that followed, make one of the darkest and most tragic love stories of all time. An ancient adage says:

> *Nem bons ventos*
> *Nem bons casamentos*
> *De Espanha vêm.*

Neither good winds nor good marriages come from Spain.

After the ruin of Spain in the Napoleonic wars and the loss of her American possessions in the years that followed, dynastic union ceased to be a threat. The emergence of Liberal and, later, socialist ideas in both countries caused Portuguese and Spanish thinkers alike to look at the question of peninsular unity in a new light. A time came when republicans and progressives on either side of the frontier saw Iberian federation as an answer to the problems that beset both peoples, and a way forward out of poverty and stagnation.

In latter years Iberianism has been largely forgotten. To many Portuguese anti-Salazarists the very mention of it is an affront. The reason for this dimming of what was once the brightest hope for peninsular advance is the rule of General Francisco Franco in Madrid. In the early days of his dictatorship there was a good deal of talk about pan-Hispanism; during the war Portuguese Liberals feared that Franco might do a deal with Hitler by which Portugal would come under the former's rule. Although this did not happen, Franco's power has long been regarded as the main obstacle to a successful democratic revolution in Portugal. And there is little doubt that, unless strong international pressure prevented it, Salazar would try to save his dictatorship by invoking the mutual assistance treaty between him and Franco.

Thus *iberismo* has become something of a dirty word. What is no longer remembered is that Iberianism as it was understood in the nineteenth century was fundamentally hostile to reaction and dictatorship. During the great ferment of ideas that was taking place as the Portuguese monarchy became more and more unpopular, Iberianism was the recognized banner of the Left. One of the greatest champions of republican ideas declared that he could not acknowledge as a republican anyone who was not at once an Iberian federalist, a socialist and a free-thinker.[1] As early as 1868 Antero de Quental, the great poet and socialist pioneer, attributed Portugal's ills to what he called her 'unnecessary amputation . . . from the great body of the Iberian peninsula'. Portugal was a sick nation, and her recovery could only be assured by means of a close association with the peoples of Spain.[2] Teófilo Braga, later to become the first President of the Republic, was a fierce opponent of the idea of union with Spain through the monarchy. But he was a passionate Iberian federalist. He regarded federation as 'part of the natural order of things'.

But for this to be brought about organically, it is necessary that a democratic Spain, paying regard to the ethnic elements of that people, should transform itself politically in accordance with federal principles. Only thus may Portugal, together with the Spanish free States, form a confederation of united peninsular States.

There could be no final victory over reaction in Portugal so long as it found support across the frontier. 'The republic cannot be established in Portugal while a democratic régime is not triumphant in Spain.'[3] He did not fear Castilian hegemony in an Iberian federation; on the contrary, federation would end for ever this danger that has haunted the Portuguese ever since they became a nation.

When the republic divides Spain into the autonomous States of Galicia, Asturias, Biscay, Navarre, Catalonia, Aragon, Valencia, Murcia, Granada, Andalusia, Extremadura, New Castile, Old Castile and León, then will Portugal, having safeguarded for ever her autonomy from Iberian incorporation or unification, be able to join without hesitation and with dignity in the constitution of the Federal Pact of the Peninsular or Iberian Free States.[4]

---

[1] Magalhães Lima, *La Fédération ibérique* (Paris and Lisbon, 1895), quoted, Archer de Lima, *Magalhães Lima e a Sua Obra* (1911), p. 223. In the same work he wrote: 'A republic proclaimed in Portugal or in Spain which has not got federalism as its ideal and objective will be a narrow republic, devoid of revolutionary meaning and destined to disappear inside a more or less brief space of time. Iberian federation not only represents an ideal of justice; it also represents a great material interest for the two peoples' (quoted, J. Casas-Carbó, *El Problema Peninsular, 1924–1932. Història d'una campanya epistolar a favor de l'autonomia de Catalunya i de la unió d'Espanya amb Portugal*, Barcelona, 1933, p. 264).

[2] Anthero de Quental, *Portugal perante a Revolução de Hespanha: Considerações sobre o Futuro da Política Portugueza no Ponto de Vista da Democracia Ibérica* (1868). He returned to this theme in his *Causas da Decadência dos Povos Peninsulares* (Oporto, 1871), the text of one of the series of 'Democratic Lectures', soon suppressed by the government.

[3] Theóphilo Braga, *História das Ideias Republicanas em Portugal* (1880), pp. 352–3, 381.

[4] Theóphilo Braga, *As Modernas Ideias na Litteratura Portugueza* (Oporto, 1892), vol. ii, pp. 472–3.

In Spain, too, the idea was popular among republicans. In 1854, for example, some of them drafted a Constitution of a Federal Iberian Republic, which managed to deal with many of the grievances that are still current in the peninsula by providing for universal suffrage, trial by jury, a consolidated tax, freedom of Press, association and religion, a national militia in place of standing armies and the renunciation of wars of conquest. 'There are no longer to be any colonies,' said this Constitution. 'They will be changed into provinces and administered on provincial principles. Slavery shall be abolished.'[1]

To be sure, not all the Iberian federalists had entirely selfless motives. Magalhães Lima saw federation as a way out of the British alliance that would enable Portugal to keep her colonies. And he saw in the division of Spain into a large number of tiny provinces a road to Portuguese hegemony in the peninsula, with Portugal emerging as the strongest single unit and Lisbon as the most suitable federal capital.

Nevertheless, many of the federalists' arguments are still valid today; and some have been strengthened by the course of events. The prediction that while reaction still ruled in one of the two countries a republic in the other would not be viable has been fulfilled. The first Spanish republic only lasted from February 1873 to December 1874. During the sixteen years' existence of the Portuguese republic those who constantly plotted its overthrow and finally introduced the Salazar régime got arms and support from Spain. Franco's plot was largely prepared on Portuguese soil. Like water finding its own level, reaction has always burst through the feeble dam that is all democracy in a single one of these two countries has been able to construct.

Is this pattern to be repeated? As long as Franco rules Spain, can the Portuguese people overthrow Salazar and put in his place a democratic régime that has any chance of consolidating itself?

A growing number of Portuguese – at least among the anti-fascists in exile – think it is high time to reopen discussion of the Iberian question. For now this question is no longer, or even primarily, a political one; it is also an economic question, of the gravest kind. Whatever arrangements Salazar's successors may make for the colonies, the world-wide colonial awakening makes it inevitable that these arrangements will be quite temporary. On the other hand, the cream of Portuguese manhood is leaving the country, year by year. Can Portugal be industrialized and can her agriculture be modernized at the necessary *tempo*

---

[1] A partial translation appeared in the *New York Daily Tribune* on 16 September 1854; see Karl Marx and Frederick Engels, *Revolution in Spain* (New York, 1939), pp. 131–3.

before she has been reduced to the status of Ireland, whose population today is half what it was a century ago?

Yet another question arises. Is a national heavy industry economic at all in a country which has such a small home market, and which has come on the scene too late to hope to compete seriously with established foreign manufacturers? Salazar's industrialization is aimed mainly at colonial markets. What happens when these disappear? Will not Portugal's shortage of iron and lack of coal add a crippling cost to native heavy industry?

It is hard to see how the Portuguese can begin to answer these questions until they stop gazing across the ocean as they have been doing for centuries. There may at present be few who would say, as one of our Portuguese acquaintances did: 'For my part, I would welcome an end to the empire. The colonies have never done any good to the majority of our people. Now it is time for us to discover our European character, and to look to the peninsula for our future.' But this may well be the way more and more Portuguese will be thinking as time goes on, and as stubborn facts compel them to see where their true interests lie.

Things are very different today from what they were in the days of Antero and Teófilo Braga. Spain, though poor, has a heavy industry. The coal-miners of the Asturias and the metal-workers of Barcelona have a history of working-class struggle second to none. Their labour is the basis for Spain's well-established locomotive and motor-car industries. They feel the oppression of Madrid. So do the barefooted Basque fishermen and the gaunt villagers of Galicia. So do the poverty-ridden peasants of the arid, infertile Castilian plateau, who benefit in no respect from Castilian oppression of the other peoples of Spain. Like the Portuguese poor, these others too leave the peninsula in their thousands every year to emigrate to South America. Surely an economic union of all of them, on a basis of equality, could bring more benefit than the grandiose fantasies, in both countries, of nationalist revival?

The expansion and modernization of industrial northern Spain could provide Portugal with the goods she needs, thus eliminating her dependence on Britain or west Germany. It could provide Spanish workers with jobs and better wages. Spanish-made tractors and combine harvesters, and fertilizers from Spain's chemical plants, could help in the modernization of Portuguese agriculture, which in turn would not only feed the hungry Portuguese but also help to feed the hungry people of Spain. Lisbon, long coveted by the Spanish merchants, would at last become the great Atlantic seaport for the whole of South America; the additional traffic would at the same time aid Spanish trade and increase Lisbon's prosperity.

Would all this reduce Portugal to the level of an agricultural appendage of Spain? In the light of the manifold advantages that economic integration would bring to Portugal, this objection seems hard to sustain. Without some drastic economic reorientation a Portugal bereft of colonies is certain to become an appendage of some kind; there are those who maintain that she already is an appendage of Britain and the USA. But Portugal has special natural riches of her own which only need coherent organization and exploitation to make the expression 'the garden of Europe' a living reality instead of a guide-book cliché. She has the most equable climate in Europe, whose sunshine and rainfall enable her to produce, in abundance, excellent wine and the highest-quality olive oil and cork. With a little attention to her orchards Portuguese oranges could be as famous as those of Jaffa or Seville. The sea that laps her coasts teems with countless species of edible fish. Ancient and celebrated crafts that have been extinguished in northern Europe still flourish in her towns and villages; nor have they yet been perverted by industrialization. Portugal's stone-masons and iron-workers, jewellers and lace-makers, potters and weavers, basket-makers and boat-builders could beautify the lives of people far away. Could not Portugal, with the application of modern methods, safeguard her uniqueness, enrich her citizens and preserve their birthright, as the people of Denmark have prospered by specializing in what they do best?

The uniqueness of the Portuguese

When the news broke of Henrique Galvão's spectacular seizure of the *Santa Maria* a columnist in one British weekly remarked how fascinated Eça de Queirós would have been with the affair, which was so contrary to 'the accepted Portuguese tradition of *saudade* or wistful melancholy'. Several years ago a French writer was surprised that there should be a saying in France: '*Les Portugais sont toujours gais.*' She had found in Portugal nothing but sadness. And an Irishwoman we know, who has lived in Portugal for ten years, was astonished when she was shown a film, made about forty years ago, of a demonstration in the streets. 'How different they look!' she exclaimed. 'They are happy and lively. Nowadays the Portuguese always look so sad.'

Are the Portuguese really a melancholy, passive race, and was Galvão's extraordinary action out of keeping with their national character?

In fact the extraordinary thing about the seizure of the *Santa Maria* is how very Portuguese it was.

'Thirty-five years of dictatorship,' a friend had told us, 'have altered the character of our people. We have grown dull, apathetic and intellectually blunted.' If Galvão has done nothing else, he has at least proved that this, however true it may seem on the surface, does not go to the heart of the matter. Along with wistfulness, which certainly plays a part in the Portuguese temperament, there is also a long tradition of courage, imagination and almost lunatic daring. There is a streak of fantastic merriment and mischief, too – a trait that has come to full flowering among the Brazilians, who are perhaps the gayest and most irreverent people in the world.

This side of the Portuguese character seemed to have evaporated. But only seemed. In fact it has been bubbling away under the mountain of Salazarism all these years, till the glorious prank of the *Santa Maria* (for, as well as other things, it was also a prank) brought it back into the light of day. When we forgathered with Portuguese friends in London on the day the news became known, it was this aspect – the audacity, irreverence and comic spectacle of a Portuguese merchant vessel defying the navies of the world – that kept effervescing through all the more serious political considerations. Even the harshest critics of Galvão, suspicious of his motives and his plans, would suddenly abandon caution and burst out laughing at the sheer incredibility of the feat. Everyone felt that something had been restored to the Portuguese – that they had been given back their sense of high adventure.

This will to dare the unknown has been seen again and again throughout Portuguese history. But it has not always brought good fortune to Portugal, many of whose ills have arisen from her people's yearning for impractical exploits.

When Dom Sebastião, the twenty-four-year-old king, sailed out of the Tagus in June 1578 to conquer Morocco from Mulei Abde Almélique, he carried with him not only 23,000 men but also his country's hopes. It was an insane enterprise undertaken against all his older counsellors' advice; but the half-mad youth, burning to emulate his forbears and egged on by his youthful supporters, had refused to heed any warning. When the brief but terrible battle of Alcácer-Quibir in North Africa was over, only fifty soldiers managed to escape. Over eight thousand lay dead. The rest were taken captive. Dom

Sebastião himself was last seen fighting, sword in hand, among the ranks of the infidel; his body was never recovered. Thus arose the belief, which persisted for decades, that he was still alive and would return one day to save his country.

In fact he had led Portugal to disaster and to sixty years of Spanish rule. But throughout the Spanish occupation there kept appearing one false Dom Sebastião after another, each to gain a following and to keep alive the hope of eventual liberation.

Sebastianismo became a cult in Portugal, one which still lingers on. It embodies not only all the yearning summed up in the word *saudade*, but also a leaning towards insane exploits based on the fantastic hope that by some miracle they might succeed. *Sebastianismo* also involves a kind of Messianic belief that one day there will appear a liberator from oppression.

Other fascist régimes have been able to put on the mantle of heroism and rally their populations – or considerable sections of them – for wars of conquest. Such mock heroics could not be convincingly staged under the deadly rule of a dull accountant. And one of the grievances against Salazar is that he has turned Portugal into a country where nothing happens. Perhaps this is why present-day tourists come away with the impression that melancholy is uppermost in the Portuguese character. There are many sad stories to hear, and many sad sights to see. Heroism in public affairs has had to be confined to underground activity. But now and again the daredevil streak has shown itself in non-political matters. A few years ago a young Portuguese stowaway went to Brazil as an illegal emigrant. He chose an aeroplane instead of a ship. And he chose the outside of the aeroplane. That he survived was a miracle – but he landed in Brazil. People recalled that a more orthodox but equally daring crossing had been made in the early twenties by two Portuguese airmen who were the first to take an aeroplane across the South Atlantic.

*   *   *

To the centuries of frustration and backwardness the Portuguese owe their tendency to carry every one of their excellences beyond its limit, so that it turns into its opposite. With some, patriotism is transformed into chauvinism; with others, a feeling for history degenerates into morbid nostalgia. Adventurousness may lead to recklessness; politeness may congeal into formality; seriousness may turn into melancholy;

humour may acquire a cruel or cynical edge. Joy in the handling of words may engender an oratorical style inflated and florid beyond belief. Paradoxically, though, there are some Portuguese whose national pride does not prevent their fawning on foreigners, especially when those foreigners carry British passports. Paradoxically, the apathy born of three decades of fascism tends to cancel out recklessness; upper-class arrogance often nullifies genteelisms and ceremony; *saudade* rarely interferes with the rich man's enjoyment of two six-course meals a day. And the habit of everyone talking at once makes of conversation a piquant counterpoint rather than an exchange of the pompous soliloquies that Portuguese statesmen utter on formal occasions.

Not that there is anything specifically Portuguese in any of these traits; most of them may be found wherever there are insularity and a sense of national disappointment. What is important is that among young people there is a healthy revolt against their parents' provincialism – a determination that they are going to share in, and contribute to, the shrinking of the world, the cross-fertilization of cultures, the ferment of ideas, the spread of humanism, the rebellion against the mess the older generation have made of things. So there are young people who love the Portugal of Pombal, Eça and Egas Moniz – but not the Portugal of Dom Sebastião, Paiva Couceiro and Salazar. There are young people who are beginning to look at their history with new, clear eyes, untroubled by vain regrets for past glories; who recall that Pombal, forty years before the French revolution, was the first European statesman to declare war on clerical reaction and obscurantism; who believe that the best pages in their country's history are yet to be written – and that they will be written, not by a nation which oppresses others, but by a nation which has great new discoveries to make in the conquest of disease and great new contributions to art and architecture and literature to offer the world.

This generation feels ashamed when it hears one of Salazar's tame professors comment on the first sputnik that it is clearly a Russian hoax; or one of his tame diplomatists at the United Nations object to world disarmament on the ground that it would leave mankind defenceless before an invasion from Mars . . . It feels hatred of a dictator and a social system which have not only made their country a laughing-stock, but which try to cloak poverty, hunger and repression in the national flag.

This book has been written with similar feelings: with admiration for a people so talented and hard-working, so impulsive and generous, so noble and at the same time so simple, that it is impossible to live among them and not love them, not merely for what they are now in their degradation, but for what they will be when they are free; and with anger against a régime that impoverishes them, prostitutes their patriotism, regiments them and impairs their spiritual life.

We had it in mind to introduce Portugal to those who wanted to know what our 'oldest ally' was really like. As we were coming to the end of our work, our hope of interesting British readers in the Portuguese travail received a tremendous fillip. Suddenly the newspapers were ablaze with Portuguese affairs; and personalities hitherto relegated to brief, down-column items on inside pages blossomed forth overnight across the top of the front page and had profiles written about them. We were very glad of this, because Salazar's curtain of discreet silence, now it has been torn aside, can never be wholly replaced. This means that our Portuguese friends have a better chance of settling accounts with their dictator, which they will do in their own way. There is an awakening. Forgotten Portugal, neglected Portugal, is now, it seems, to be famous Portugal. What is more to the point, it may soon be free Portugal. If this book makes a small contribution to such a long-awaited transformation, then its authors will have done the job they set out to do.

Lisbon-London,
January 1960–January 1961

A note on books

The best historical introduction is the late J. B. Trend's *Portugal* (London, 1957), compact and unobtrusively scholarly. Charles E. Nowell's *A History of Portugal* (New York, London and Toronto, 1952) is a highly readable book of similar scope by an American enthusiast for Portuguese history. Among longer works, H. V. Livermore's *A History of Portugal* (Cambridge, 1947) is very detailed and informative, especially for earlier periods, but suffers from emphasis on dynastic, diplomatic and military history at the expense of social and economic factors. The recent Pelican by William C. Atkinson, *A History of Spain and Portugal* (Harmondsworth, 1959), cannot be recommended. *They Went to Portugal* (London, 1946), by Rose Macaulay, is a fascinating study of the experiences and writings of English people who have visited Portugal since relations between the two countries began.

On the Discoveries, there is much of interest in Professor C. R. Boxer's contribution to H. V. Livermore (ed.), *Portugal and Brazil: an Introduction* (Oxford, 1953). A very useful biography of the Marquis of Pombal is Marcus Cheke's *Dictator of Portugal: a Life of the Marquis of Pombal, 1699–1782* (London, 1938). No satisfactory account exists in English of the civil wars of the nineteenth century, the 1910 revolution, the history of the republic or the events of the last thirty years; nor has any work been done on the history of the Labour movement. A great many panegyrics of Salazar appeared in the thirties and again in the fifties; almost the only book hostile to Salazar was Ralph Fox's brief sketch, *Portugal Now* (London, 1937). The only travel book critical of the régime was bought up by agents of the Portuguese government; a British supporter of Salazar then wrote a travel book with the same title.

Periodical literature is for the most part of ephemeral interest, exceptions being Norman J. Lamb, 'Notes on Some Portuguese *Emigrado* Journals Published in England', *Bulletin of Hispanic Studies* (School of Hispanic Studies, University of Liverpool), vol. xxx .no. 119, pp. 152–60, July-September 1953; and Benjamin de Mott,

'Glossing a Portuguese Diary', *Hudson Review* (New York), vol. xiii, no. 2, pp. 261–9, Summer 1960.

The indispensable study of Angola and Mozambique under Portuguese rule is James Duffy's *Portuguese Africa* (Cambridge, Mass. and London, 1959).

Turning from history and politics, there are two recent books, each in its own way quite remarkable, that convey much of the spirit of Portugal. One is Huldine V. Beamish's *The Hills of Alentejo* (London, 1958), by a woman who has farmed livestock, dairy, arable, fruit and vegetables in the Alentejo since the end of the war; the other is *South of Lisbon* (London, 1960), by Frank E. Huggett, a writer who spent several months in a poor town in the Algarve, and who has controversial things to say about the Portuguese character.

Works of lasting value on special subjects are Dan Stanislawski's *The Individuality of Portugal: a Study in Historical-Political Geography* (Austin, Texas, and Edinburgh, 1959); Aubrey F. G. Bell's *Portuguese Literature* (Oxford, 1922); and Rodney Gallop's enchanting *Portugal: a Book of Folk-Ways* (Cambridge, 1936).

Chronology

1891	January 31	Republican rising in Oporto.
1906–08		Dictatorship of João Franco.
1908	February 1	Assassination of D. Carlos and Crown Prince.
1910	October 4–5	Republican revolution.
1915	January 23–	
	May 14	Dictatorship of Pimenta de Castro.
1916	March 9	Portugal enters first world war.
1917	December 5	*Coup d'État* of Sidónio Pais.
1918	December 14	Assassination of Sidónio Pais.
1926	May 28	Military *coup d'État*.
1928	April 27	Salazar becomes Finance Minister.
1930	July 8	*Acto Colonial.*
	July 30	National Union formed.
1932	July 5	Salazar becomes Prime Minister.
1933	March 19	Corporative Constitution adopted.
	September 23	National Statute of Labour.
1934	January 18	General strike.
1936	July 18	Spanish civil war begins.
	September 30	Portuguese Legion formed.
	October	Portuguese Youth formed.
1939	March 18	Treaty of friendship signed with Franco.
1945	May 4	Half-day of mourning for Hitler.
	October 12–14	Censorship of the Press lifted for forty-eight hours.
	November 18	National Assembly elections boycotted by MUD.
1946	October 10	Abortive *revolução da Mealhada.*
1947	April	Unsuccessful revolt by army officers.
1948	August 12	Trial of 107 persons accused of 'subversive propaganda'.
1949	February 13	Presidential election. Norton de Matos withdraws; Carmona re-elected unopposed.
	April 4	Portugal signs North Atlantic Treaty.
	November 13	National Assembly elections boycotted by opposition
1950	May 11	Communist leader Álvaro Cunhal sentenced.
1951	April 18	Death of President Carmona.
	July 22	Presidential election. Rui Luís Gomes disqualified; Quintão Meireles withdraws; Craveiro Lopes elected unopposed.

1952	December	
	11–12	Court martial of supporters of Quintão Meireles.
1953	November 8	National Assembly elections largely boycotted by opposition.
1954–56		Dispute with India over Goa.
1955	July 25	India breaks off diplomatic relations with Portugal.
	October	President Craveiro Lopes visits Britain.
	December 15	Portugal admitted to United Nations.
1957	February	Visit by Queen Elizabeth II of England.
	June	Fifty-two young people sentenced to imprisonment at Oporto.
	July	Rui Luís Gomes sentenced to two years' imprisonment.
	November 3	National Assembly elections largely boycotted by opposition.
1958	March 18	Captain Henrique Galvão sentenced to sixteen years' imprisonment.
	June 8	Presidential election. Humberto Delgado, according to official figures, receives 22·5 per cent of the vote; Américo Tomás declared elected.
1959	January 15	Galvão escapes from prison hospital.
	May	Mass arrests.
	June	Visit by Princess Margaret.
1960	January 4	Cunhal and others escape from fortress of Peniche.
	November 30	Salazar's 'plough and sword' speech.
1961	January 22	Seizure of *Santa Maria*.
	February	Rebellion breaks out in Angola.
	April 13	Government reshuffle. Salazar takes over Ministry of Defence.

APPENDIX

APPENDIX

Portugal's social statistics compared with those of other European countries

Table I

INFANT MORTALITY RATE, 1958

This table gives the number of deaths of infants under one year of age per 1,000 live births in seventeen European countries. Fœtal deaths are not included.

Austria	40.7	Netherlands	17.2*
Belgium	30.3*	Poland	72.8*
Bulgaria	52.2	Portugal	84.0
Czechoslovakia	29.5*	Spain	47.4
Finland	24.5	Sweden	15.8*
France	31.5	Switzerland	22.2
W. Germany	36.0	UK	23.3
Hungary	58.1	Yugoslavia	86.2
Italy	48.2		

*Provisional

Source: *Demographic Yearbook, 1959* (New York: Statistical Office of the United Nations, Department of Economic and Social Affairs, 1959).

Table II

LATE FŒTAL DEATH RATIO, 1958

Number of fœtal deaths (of at least 28 weeks' gestation) per 1,000 live births. The data for Portugal are stated to be 'unreliable or of unknown completeness'.

Austria	16.5	Hungary	14.1
Bulgaria	11.9	Netherlands	17.0
Czechoslovakia	11.1*	Portugal	38.7
England and Wales	22.0	Scotland	23.4
France	17.3	Switzerland	12.6

*Provisional.

Source: *Demographic Yearbook, 1959.*

Table III

DEATHS OF CHILDREN UNDER FIVE, 1958

A comparison is made of three European countries the size of whose estimated populations is similar: Greece (8,173,000), Hungary (9,917,000) and Portugal (9,052,000). The figures show the number of children under five who died in each of these three countries in 1958.

		Greece*	Hungary	Portugal
	Male	3,192	5,350	9,930
Under 1	Female	2,871	3,854	7,917
	Total	6,063	9,204	17,847
	Male	702	735	3,431
1 to 4	Female	626	658	3,220
	Total	1,328	1,393	6,651
Total under 5		7,364	10,597	24,498

*Data 'unreliable or of unknown completeness'.

Source: *Demographic Yearbook, 1959.*

Table IV

MORTALITY RATE FROM TUBERCULOSIS, 1957–58

Deaths per 100,000 of the population caused by tuberculosis.

		Tuberculosis of the respiratory system	*Other forms of tuberculosis*	*Total*
Austria	1958	22·4	2·7	25·1
Belgium	1957*	18.9	2·0	20·9
Czechoslovakia	1957*	33·6	2·8	36·4
England and Wales	1958	8·9	1.1	10·0
France	1958	21·7	2.6	24·3
W. Germany	1957*	17·1	1·7	18·8
Hungary	1958	28·7	2·6	31·3
Italy	1957*	18·2	2·6	20·8
Netherlands	1958*	3·4	0·9	4·3
Portugal	1958	44·5	6·5	51·0
Spain	1957*	27·2	5.1	32·3
Sweden	1957*	7·8	0·8	8·6

*Provisional

Source: *Demographic Yearbook, 1959.*

Table V

DEATHS CAUSED BY TUBERCULOSIS, 1958

Again a comparison is made with two other European countries whose populations are comparable in size to that of Portugal.

	*Greece**	*Hungary*	*Portugal*
Tuberculosis of respiratory system	1,381	2,829	3,996
Other forms of tuberculosis	149	260	584
Total	1,530	3,089	4,580

*Data 'unreliable or of unknown completeness'.

Source: *Demographic Yearbook, 1959.*

I*—O A

Table VI

EXPECTATION OF LIFE AT BIRTH

		Male	*Female*
Austria	1949–51	61·91	66·97
Czechoslovakia	1956	66·65	71·63
Denmark	1951–5	69·87	72·60
England and Wales	1958	67·95	73·69
France	1952–6	65·04	71·15
Hungary	1955	64·96	68·87
Italy	1954–7	65·75	70·02
Netherlands	1953–5	71·0	73·9
Norway	1951–5	71·11	74·70
Poland	1955–6	61·6	67·1
Portugal	1957–8	59·8	65·0
Scotland	1958	66·22	71·35
Spain	1950	58·76	63·50
Sweden	1951–5	70·49	73·43
USSR	1955–6	63	69
Yugoslavia	1952–4	56·92	55·98

Source: *Demographic Yearbook, 1959.*

Table VII

PERCENTAGE OF DWELLINGS WITH PIPED WATER AND ELECTRICITY

		Piped water inside			Electricity		
		Urban	Rural	Total	Urban	Rural	Total
Austria	1951	44·9	21·2	34·2	97·2	82.7	90·7
Belgium	1947	—	—	48·5	—	—	95·4
Czechoslovakia	1950	—	—	—	94·7	79·1	85·2
Denmark	1955	100·0	63·5	—	99·5	96·3	98·4
France	1954	75·4	34·3	58·4	95·4	89·5	93·0
Greece	1951	23·0	0·6	18·1	53·2	2·9	28·7
Hungary	1949	—	—	—	75·1	27·2	46·1
Italy	1951	—	—	35·9	—	—	82·7
Portugal	1950	42·5	3·1	14·5	46·9	8·5	19·5
Spain	1950	58·9	13·2	34·2	86·4	73·8	80·5
Switzerland	1950	88·5	39·3	67·0	100·0	95·1	—
UK	1951	97·9	79·9	94·5	—	—	—

Source: *Statistical Yearbook, 1959* (New York: Statistical Office of the United Nations, Department of Economic and Social Affairs, 1959).

Table VIII

FOOD SUPPLIES AT THE RETAIL LEVEL

Kilograms per head per year

	Cereals	Potatoes and other starchy foods	Sugar	Pulses and nuts	Meat	Eggs	Fish	Fat	Milk	Protein	Fats and oils (fat content)
Austria											
1957–8	116	94	34	2	49	10	3		7	8	19
Denmark											
1957–8	83	120	48	5	72	8	16		8	8	28
France											
1957–8	110	112	29	6	69	10	5		5	6	17
W. Germany											
1957–8	91	151	28	4	53	12	7		6	7	25
Greece											
1957*	151	41	11	16	19	5	7	4		4	16
Italy											
1957–8	142	44	18	13	24	8	5	4		4	15
Netherlands											
1957–8	87	88	39	4	43	11	5	7		9	24
Portugal											
1957	110	110	16	10	16	3	20	1		1	15
Sweden											
1957–8	75	101	41	4	52	10	18	10		9	20
Turkey											
1957–8	216	41	10	13	15	2	2	2		2	3
UK											
1957–8	85	97	49	6	71	14	13	8		7	22
Yugoslavia											
1953–4	185	60	8	9	21	3	1	3		4	9

*Provisional

Source: *Year Book of Labour Statistics, 1959* (Geneva: International Labour Office, 1959).

Table IX

CALORIES FROM FOOD SUPPLIES AT THE RETAIL LEVEL

		Calories per head per day
Austria	1957–8	2,940
Denmark	1957–8	3,420
France	1957–8	2,910
W. Germany	1957–8	2,960
Greece	1957*	2,650
Italy	1957–8	2,600
Netherlands	1957–8	2,900
Norway	1957–8	3,070
Portugal	1957	2,470
Sweden	1957–8	2,910
Turkey	1957–8	2,890
UK	1957–8	3,300
Yugoslavia	1953–4	2,710

*Provisional

Source: *Year Book of Labour Statistics, 1959.*

INDEX

INDEX

Note: figures in bold type refer to illustrations.

A

Abde Almélique, emperor of Morocco, 250
Abelaira, Augusto, 239
abortion, 89
Acto Colonial, **161**, 257
address, forms of, 230
afforestation question, 94, 147–8, 186
Afonso III, king of Portugal, 243
Afonso Henriques, king of Portugal, 243
agriculture, 14, 21–2, 37, 64, 66–7, 70, 94, 139–40, 247, 248; crisis in, 145–9; in Mozambique, 170–1; mechanization of, 146; 'planning' of, 149, 151; unbalanced structure of, 145–6, 148
Alcácer-Quibir, battle of, 250–1
Alcoforado, Mariana, 46
Alentejo, 37–9, 45–8, 94, 145–6, 206, 237, **238**, 256; **3, 5**
Alfama, 24, 32–4, 59
Algarve, 36, 37, 39–45, 48, 146, 155, 161, 164, 196, 243, 256
Algeria, 161, 177, 182
Allan, Robert Alexander, 130
alliance, Anglo-Portuguese, 14, 244–5
Almada Negreiros, José Sobral de, 239
Almeida, Francisco Lopes Vieira de, 191
Alves, Raul, 197
Amado, Jorge, 237
anarchists, 114, 204–5, 214
Andrade, Posser de, 146
Andresen [de Sousa Tavares], Sofia de Mello Breyner, 240
Anglo-Portuguese Bank Ltd, 129 n.
Anglo-Portuguese Society, 129–31
Anglo-Portuguese Telephone Company Ltd, 128, 128–9 n., 144
Angola, 13, 111, 135, 144, 157, 159–82 *passim,* 216, 221; **24, 25**; African culture in, 179–80; American economic penetration of, 143–4, 145; assimilation not taking place in, 175; CUF's interests in, 142; diamond mining in, 142, 144; disease in, 173; education in, 172–3; election results in (1958), 178; forced labour in, 171–2, 192; Galvão report on

conditions in, 192; illiteracy in, 172–3; immigration to, 173 n., 178; influence of South Africa in, 176; languages of, 179–80, 180 n.; marriages in, 175; medical services in, 173–4; nationalist movements in, 176–82, 223; opposition to Salazar among white inhabitants of, 177–8; political trials in, 176–7; racial composition of population of, 172–3, 175 n.; racial discrimination in, 174–6; United Nations debates on, 161, 161–2 n., 221; uprising in (1961), 182 n., 222, 224 n., 258; vital statistics of, 173; wages in, 174
anti-clericalism, 209–10
apartheid, 159, 170, 176
Arabs, *see* Moors and Moorish influence
architecture, 23, 24, 235; Manueline style of, 30–1
army, 153, 219; and Salazar régime, 121, 125–6; democratic traditions in, 125; in 1958 presidential election, 189; monarchists in, 127, 134; oppositionists in, 134, 218–19, **257**; under republic, 113
assimilados, 125, 174
assistance, public, 123–4
Associacões dos Naturais (Angola and Mozambique), 179, 179 n.
Atkinson, William Christopher, 255
Australia, 119–20, 120 n.
Avante!, 205 n.
AVH, 127
Ávila and Bolama, António José de Ávila, 1st Marquis of, 203
Azevedo, Manuel Pinto de, 143
Azevedo Gomes, Mário de, 191; **16**
Azores, 29, 97, 103, 119, 141, 142, 149, 201
azulejos, 22, 50, 67

B

Bacon, Leonard, 236 n.
Ballilas, 128, 135

271

Cracking Your Church's Culture Code

To my wife, Brenda; my daughters, Rachel and Deborah; and my granddaughter, Adeline Joy—they all give up so much to make my dreams a reality. Because of them, I never lack for constant and consistent encouragement.

Acknowledgments

I acknowledge the thousands of senior leaders who have allowed me to learn from them and their organizations. This book is possible because of their honesty and vulnerability. The contents of this book are a collage of the personal pain and frustration leaders face as they create healthy cultures to fulfill their visions. I also want to thank my friend Pat Springle for working with me to shape the contents of this book.

of disciplines, with individual titles providing perspective on one or more of five primary areas:

- Enabling effective leadership
- Encouraging life-changing service
- Building authentic community
- Creating Kingdom-centered impact
- Engaging cultural and demographic realities

For additional information on the mission or activities of Leadership Network, please contact:

Leadership Network
2626 Cole Avenue, Suite 900
Dallas, Texas 75204
800-765-5323
www.leadnet.org
client.care@leadnet.org

About Leadership Network

Leadership Network, an initiative of OneHundredX, exists to honor God and serve others by investing in innovative church leaders who impact the Kingdom immeasurably.

Since 1984, Leadership Network has brought together exceptional leaders, who are focused on similar ministry initiatives, to accelerate their impact. The ensuing collaboration—often across denominational lines—provides a strong base from which individual leaders can better analyze and refine their individual strategies. Creating an environment for collaborative discovery, dialogue, and sharing encourages leaders to extend their own innovations and ideas. Leadership Network further enhances this process through the development and distribution of highly targeted ministry tools and resources—including video, podcasts, concept papers, special research reports, e-publications, and books like this one.

With Leadership Network's assistance, today's Christian leaders are energized, equipped, inspired—and better able to multiply their own dynamic Kingdom-building initiatives.

In 1996 Leadership Network partnered with Jossey-Bass, a Wiley Imprint, to develop a series of creative books that would provide thought leadership to innovators in church ministry. Leadership Network Publications present thoroughly researched and innovative concepts from leading thinkers, practitioners, and pioneering churches. The series collectively draws from a wide range

W9-BKJ-955

To Order, contact:

Info-Tec
1005 Abbe Road North
Elyria, OH 44035
1(800)995-5222 x4632
FAX: 1(440)366-4113

First printing: May, 2001

© *2001 Info-Tec*

Library of Congress Data
Library of Congress Control Number: 2001131927

ISBN: 0-940017-28-8 (paperback)
ISBN: 0-940017-29-6 (hardcover)

Jacket Design: Brian Sooy & Co.

Printed in the United States of America

Table of Contents

CHAPTER 6—*TEACHING AND LEARNING WITH TECHNOLOGY*

Table of Figures

Acknowledgments

A major revision of a publication such as this depends upon the contributions and support of many individuals. Although it is not possible to recognize all, some are of such importance as to deserve special mention.

First and foremost, I am indebted to Catherine Worden who stepped forward to assume the role of editor and publisher in bringing the book not only to its proper structure but also in carrying out the many details necessary for its successful printing and publication. Her contributions were essential to "making it happen". We are indebted to Peggy Nesbit for editing and proofreading, as well as for the page-layout, and to Brian Sooy & Co. for the cover design.

We are especially appreciative of the contributions of those professionals who use the *Handbook* for their completion of the surveys and their suggestions. Those suggestions contributed greatly to the changes in content to enhance and improve the book.

Of special note is the contribution of Gary Wheeler, whose knowledge and ability to put into words the impact of technology is a major contribution. Finally, and of equal importance, are the contributions of Janet Greive for her efforts in preparing the manuscript. To these individuals and all others whose suggestions were incorporated, I am forever grateful.

Don Greive

Preface to the Fourth Edition

It has been over a decade since *A Handbook for Adjunct/Part-time Faculty and Teachers of Adults* was first published with the intention of supporting adjunct faculty in their teaching role. In that time the book has reached hundreds of colleges and universities and thousands of adjunct faculty throughout the U.S. and Canada. In recent years, however, the mission of higher education instruction has shifted to a greater emphasis upon student-centered learning and the utilization of technology. This revision of the *Handbook* attempts to recognize that shift and provide adjunct and part-time faculty with the contemporary tools necessary for successful classroom instruction.

I believe that we have accomplished that goal in this revision without sacrificing the fundamental strengths of the original publication, i.e. emphasizing instructor-proven techniques and strategies for teaching. The use of adjuncts continues to increase, however, and the fundamental problems remain… most adjunct faculty still maintain full-time jobs outside the institution and have limited time available for extensive reading and research concerning teaching. This publication is designed to accommodate that situation by providing faculty with brief and enlightening information, available at their fingertips for easy reference, presented in a practical informative format.

Don Greive

How To Get the Most Out of This Book...

One of the major changes in the new edition of this handbook is the use of icons to highlight important information for the reader.

Keys to Success: Whenever you see this icon, you'll want to take special note because these are tried and true tips to improve your classroom performance.

Caution Light: Whenever you see this icon, you'll know that other successful adjunct and part-time instructors have discovered what NOT to do while teaching.

In addition to the icons, an index has been compiled for ease of use. As with the previous edition, the table of contents has remained very detailed to get you to the topic that most interests you at the moment.

So you can read this handbook from front to back or keep it handy as a quick reference on many of the most important areas of concern for new and experienced adjunct and part-time faculty.

This is your quick reference for good teaching. You may use this book as a manual, a guide, or for professional reading. It contains practical and informative tips to assist you with your instructional tasks. It is written in a user-friendly manner for your convenience. Enjoy it and GOOD TEACHING.

TEACHING: WHAT'S IT ALL ABOUT

Orientation to College and Adult Teaching

In the coming decades, teachers of college and adult students will be faced with many challenges that did not previously exist. Compared to the classroom of former years, the evolution to the modern classroom has caused significant changes. The influx of multicultural and multilingual students, the impact of technology, and the admission of students with differing academic preparation have demanded the attention of educators everywhere. In addition, changing economic and political pressures throughout the world have impacted education and, you, the instructor.

You will feel the impact whether you teach in a continuing education program for business/industry or the military; in a liberal arts college with time-honored traditions and values; in a community college with an open door policy; in a public research university with postgraduate programs; or in an adult education center. The students of today will be more highly motivated, more challenging, and in many ways, more enjoyable to teach.

With the concern for accountability and the realization that there are established strategies and techniques for instruction, there is greater emphasis upon quality instruction. Adult students employed in business and industry expect a planned and organized classroom. It is no longer a question of whether there are going to be instructional objectives and strategies for teaching; it is a question of how skilled instructors are in developing and delivering them.

One of the most important factors, however, remains the human element of teaching. If you enjoy being a teacher, there is nothing wrong with telling the students that you are there because you

enjoy teaching. Being cheerful, open, and understanding is always an asset to good teaching. Students will like to hear your experiential anecdotes — share them. Look upon the class as a project. Adult students expect planning and preparation and will not rebel if it is required. Be aware of your cultural and intellectual environment. Strive to be a good and successful instructor and your teaching experiences will be exciting, rewarding, and satisfying.

It might help you to take a few moments before your first class to meditate about your reasons for teaching. This will do two things: it will encourage you to more clearly identify your personal goals and it will increase your confidence.

There may be students who question why someone with your expertise would spend their time teaching a college course. Be prepared. Have a few answers ready if students ask. If they don't ask, you might want to include it in your personal introduction. You certainly have good reasons. It might be to your advantage to communicate them. You may just enjoy teaching, like interaction with others, like the stimulation, enjoy being in front of a group, or feel it improves your own skills.

You should also give thought to your role in your institution. In short "what is an adjunct/part-time instructor?" Too often adjunct faculty, and thus their students, feel their place within the institution is a temporary and unimportant one. Nothing could be farther from the truth. Adjunct faculty in recent years have assumed a greater responsibility to the educational mission of their colleges and universities. Many institutions depend upon adjunct faculty for 50% or more of credit hours of instruction taught. Also in many institutions, adjunct and part-time faculty serve on committees and accept other non-instructional assignments. Finally, adjunct faculty often teach in specialized areas where specific qualifications and expertise is needed. Yes, whether you are a continuing adjunct or a last-minute part-time

replacement, yours is an important role and necessary to the integrity and success of your institution.

 As with their full-time colleagues, teaching is still a vocation for many adjunct instructors, a calling to those individuals who enjoy being with people and feel an intrinsic satisfaction in helping others to grow.

In your role as an adjunct/part-time instructor, you will realize many of the intrinsic rewards of the profession. You are repaying your profession for its contributions to your own personal and professional development. There is satisfaction in providing service to your community and you will find that teaching builds self esteem, offers personal rewards, and keeps you intellectually alive. Teaching can provide intellectual growth, community recognition and respect, and the development of new professional contacts. The satisfactions and rewards of being a good adjunct instructor are real and many.

Establishing a Teaching Environment

Over the past two decades, there has been a major movement in higher education called "the learning college" movement or community-centered learning. Quite simply, this means that learning has become student-centered rather than instructor-centered. This is especially important to adjunct faculty members, most of whom come from the surrounding community and thus are aware of community mores.

When establishing a student-centered learning environment, one should first examine the teacher-student relationship. The simple and most obvious way to develop a relationship with your students is be yourself and be honest, establishing communication in the classroom the same as you would in any other human endeavor. There are, however, additional specific steps that can be taken to establish a proper learning environment. Helen Burnstad describes four areas in

which the learning environment should be examined: teacher expectations, teaching behavior, physical space, and strategies for creating an environment for learning (Burnstad, 2000). Although it is impossible to describe these areas completely in this handbook, some of Burnstad's major points are examined below:

- *Teacher expectations.* It is important first, that each instructor have a clear picture of his or her own style and expectations. The expectations that you as an instructor have of yourself may differ considerably from those of the students in your class. This does not mean that you need to change your style. However, you need to examine the expectations of your students in terms of their position (rather than your position) on issues and principles that may arise in class. Also, it is important that you consider your own teaching goals. From this you can frame your philosophy and intent regarding the content of the course.

- *Teacher behaviors.* It is important that you examine your presence in the classroom. Students will sense whether you really love your subject matter or are teaching the course to reach some unrelated professional goal. A pleasant personality is important. Enthusiasm may be demonstrated through energy and engaging in activities with students. Remember, your feelings concerning the expectations of your students will unwittingly be reflected in the success or failure of your students.

- *Physical space.* Although in most cases you will have little control over the physical aspects of the classroom environment, there are several things that can be done by the instructor. If possible, you may physically move seats so that dialogue and eye contact are easier. You should monitor the attention span of your students; sense the need for reinforcement; calculate the time-on-task; and encourage students to move, interact and ask questions.

- *Environmental Strategies.* Some strategies that can improve the classroom environment include:

1. **Introducing yourself** to your students with some personal anecdotes.

2. **Being prepared** for students with diverse backgrounds.

3. **Using an activity for getting to know** your students, whether a game, a writing assignment, or reference card, etc.

4. **Learning each student's name** and providing ways for students to get to know one another.

5. **Preparing a complete and lively syllabus.** You can have your students from a previous class leave a legacy by asking them to write a letter for incoming students then sharing it.

6. **Using classroom assessment** techniques.

Finally, whether one is establishing a classroom environment or doing day-to-day activities, it is important that you be as positive in your student-teacher relationships as toward your subject matter. Make yourself available for student contact, either personally or electronically. Take a personal interest in each student and never judge or stereotype students.

Characteristics of Good Teaching

Using one's mind in the pursuit of knowledge and at the same time sharing it with others is very gratifying. The responsibility for a class and the potential influence on students can be very stimulating. It remains stimulating, however, only so long as the instructor continues to grow and remains dynamic.

The qualities of good teaching are quite simple:

- Know your subject content.

- Know and like your students.

- Understand our culture.

- Possess professional teaching skills and strategies.

Knowing your subject means simply that you have a command of your discipline and the capability of calling upon resources. Knowing students is part of the teaching process and is aided by formal and informal communication within and outside the classroom. Understanding our cultural milieu has become increasingly complex for today's instructor. Sensitivity to the diverse cultures in your classroom is necessary to succeed in teaching. Finally, it is necessary that you continue to develop and improve strategies and techniques for the delivery of instruction in the classroom.

Some characteristics that students look for in good teachers are:

- Being knowledgeable, organized, and in control.

- Getting students actively involved in their learning.

- Helping students understand the course objectives and goals.

- Being a facilitator, not a director.

- Knowing the latest trends and technology.

- Stimulating discussion utilizing ice breakers.

- Preparing professional materials and handouts.

The First Class

No matter how long you have been teaching you will always be faced with the another "first class". If it is your very first time teaching as an adjunct, the strategies you incorporate are not significantly different from those used on the first class of any future course you may teach. There will always be anxieties and some nervousness before the first class. For experienced faculty who have just completed a course where rapport and communication had been developed, you now face a new class where your students are strangers to you and you are a stranger to them. The anxieties of this returning class are

the same as those of the very first class that you will or have ever taught. It is often stated that you never get the second chance to make a first impression and this is certainly true in the world of teaching.

 In preparing for the first class, keep in mind that it is nearly impossible to anticipate all situations. The speed at which your first class presentation goes will vary from class to class. Many times student response is significantly greater or less than expected. Having excessive material prepared for the first class will allay this problem and is worth the extra effort in confidence gained.

Another stress reliever when facing your first class is knowing yourself as a teacher. Anyone mature enough to be teaching has some feeling of his or her own personal characteristics. Most of us are average in appearance; however, we usually have gone through life compensating for our variations from the average. There is no more need to be self-conscious in front of a class than there is in any social situation. However, minor compensations may help. If you have a tendency toward casual or even sloppy appearance, appearing neat and professional will pay off. If you have a light voice, practice in expression may be well worth the time spent. Generally speaking, students' first impression of you will include your appearance and actions. If you are timid — take charge. Being in control pays off not only in eliminating barriers to classroom communication, but in developing self-confidence in teaching.

Since the first class is a form of a social introduction, it will influence all successive meetings. You should have a detailed plan for the first class period which will diminish the threats and anxieties of expecting the unexpected. It might be helpful to speak with other teachers who have taught the class in an attempt to anticipate students' questions or concerns. It is a good idea to physically visit the classroom where you will be teaching before the first day. If possible, find out who your students are, their ages, their background, and any previous courses or prerequisites they may have taken.

Listed below are some suggestions that will help alleviate any anxieties and get your class off to a good start:

- **Plan an activity** that allows students to get involved immediately. It may simply be an information-gathering exercise.

- **Initiate casual conversation** with and among the students prior to presenting the specifics of the course.

- **Share anecdotes.** Students are interested in your background and some of your course-related experiences.

- **Introduce the following items** to your students: the name and number of the course, the objectives of the course, the text(s), syllabus, the dates of all exams, and your grading system. Finally take a roll call to establish that everyone there intends to be in your class.

- **Make certain you are early**, at least 20 minutes before the start of the first class. If possible, greet your students as they come in the door.

- **Identify course standards** including time required for outside work.

- **Use an icebreaker.** If possible, make it a question that is related to your course but without a specific answer.

- **Take care of housekeeping items** such as breaks and restroom locations.

- **Conduct a class with real course content.** It is important that students immediately understand that coming to class is a work situation with specific goals and purposes.

- Some successful instructors begin their first class by **asking students to write a short paragraph** about themselves and their concerns. Often students are willing to discuss their anxieties. This will help in understanding the class.

Setting the Tone

Education professionals and teacher trainers agree that creating positive feelings about the course is an important goal for any instructor. Often instructors assume that students know they intend to be pleasant, cooperative, and helpful. However, this should not be taken for granted. With differing personalities and types of students in the classroom, faculty members must realize that a positive comment or gesture to one student may in fact be negative to another student. Thus, you should make a concerted effort to be friendly. A smile, a pleasant comment, or a laugh with students who are attempting to be funny will pay great dividends.

In setting the tone of the classroom, permissiveness is sometimes a good strategy. We are all familiar with the old classroom where students were essentially "passive" learners. We are also familiar with situations where excessive permissiveness became a distraction to other students. Teachers of adults must realize that flexibility and permissiveness are important to a proper learning environment and that encouraging creativity and unexpected comments is part of the learning and teaching process. The instructor has ultimate authority so excessive distraction can always be controlled. Instructors need not exercise authority for its own sake. Remember, permissiveness and flexibility requires considerable skill to work. Authority comes with the title of instructor.

Teachers as Actors and Actresses

In reality, teachers are on stage; they are actors or actresses whether or not they recognize and admit it. A teacher in front of the classroom carries all of the responsibility for the success of the performance, and this requires all of the talents of anyone on the stage. Due to modern technology, unfortunately, students compare faculty to professionals they have seen in other roles. Thus, adjunct faculty must be alert to the ramifications of poor presentation. Faculty members have within themselves all of the emotions of stage performers but with greater audience interaction. There may occasionally be an emotional reaction in class and you should prepare for it. As an instruc-

tor, you will experience fear, joy, and feelings of tentativeness, but also feelings of extreme confidence and satisfaction. Handle fear with good preparation; confidence brought forward with good preparation is the easiest way to lessen fear. Remove anxieties from the classroom by developing communication systems. Some adjunct faculty members are effective at using humor.

As a general rule, however, humor should be used delicately. Jokes are completely out. Almost any joke that is told will offend someone.

Classroom Communication

Many kinds of communication exist in every classroom situation. You must be aware that facial expressions and eye contact with students as well as student interactions are all forms of communication. It is your responsibilty to ensure that classroom communication is structured in a positive manner. Communication starts the moment you enter the classroom for the first class session. The communication methods you use during the first class and the initial interaction with students are indicative of the types of communication that will exist throughout the course.

The amount of student participation as the course progresses is an indicator of the direction in which the communication is flowing; more is always better. Since many students today are adults, there is greater opportunity to call upon their experiences. The discussion of facts, events, examples, analogies, and anecdotes will often elicit an association for your adult students. This will encourage students to share experiences and anecdotes of their own.

Do not assume that classroom communication can only be between the instructor and students. Communication in the classroom can take any number of forms. It can mean a room full of small group activities where students are discussing and interacting with each other as the instructor stands silently by. It can also include animated and serious discussions and even disagreements while ad-

dressing a specific problem or issue presented in class. As the instructor, one of your major responsibilities is to provide a setting where students can communicate freely and provide an instructor-directed vehicle that maintains positive goal-oriented communication.

Some specific instructor-led communication activities include the use of open-ended questions, critical thinking techniques, anecdotes, and problem-solving activities. Communication activities among students include buzz groups, a partner system, student panels, collaborative learning activities, student group reports, brainstorming and group discussions. Remember, a good class is dynamic, participative, and interactive.

The Three R's of Teaching

Everyone remembers the three R's of learning. For any instructor, however, the three R's of teaching, are equally important.

The three R's of good teaching are: **repeat, respond,** and **reinforce**. Very simply, student comments and contributions, if worthy of being recognized in class, are worthy of being repeated. A simple **repeat**, however, is not sufficient. You should elicit an additional **response** either from the class or the student making the original statement. After the response, you should offer a **reinforcement** of the statement or add your own conclusions. These three simple rules improve class relationships by emphasizing the importance of student contributions, relationships between students, and the instructor's respect for all the students. This promotes two-way communication and represents the application of one of the basic tenets of learning—**reinforcement.**

Teaching Styles

Just as students have styles of learning, faculty have their own styles of teaching. Whether your style is one of planned preparation or a natural development, your style is important. For example, an instructor who emphasizes facts in teaching will have difficulty de-

veloping meaningful discussions with students who have progressed to the analysis stage of their learning. It is not important that part-time instructors modify their behavior to match that of students. It is important, however, that part-time faculty recognize their own teaching styles and adapt teaching processes, techniques, and strategies to enhance their most effective style. Some questions to assist you in determing your teaching style are:

- Do I tend to be authoritative, directional, semi-directional, or *laissez-faire* in my classroom leadership?

- Do I solicit communication with and between students easily or with difficulty?

- Am I well-organized and prepared?

- Am I meticulous in my professional appearance or do I have a tendency to put other priorities first and show up in class "as is"?

 A common mistake for many instructors is that they assume their students will learn in the same manner in which the instructor learned as a student.

Therefore, it would be wise to examine some of the basic learning styles of students, discussed in detail in Chapter 2. By understanding student learning styles, you can modify your teaching techniques to be certain that your presentation style does not turn off certain students.

For example, if you tended to learn best from a direct no-nonsense instructor, then chances are you will lean toward that type of behavior in your own teaching. This would satisfy students who learn in that manner; however, there will be students in your class who are more successful in a more *laissez-faire*-type environment that gives more freedom of expression. If you thrive on open communication and discussion in your learning process, expecting this from all of your students may be a false hope since many students are silent learners and may be intimidated by the need to verbally participate in class.

These are only a few examples of the types of teaching style adjustments that may be necessary to become an effective facilitator of learning. I have found that teaching styles are not static. Many of the techniques I used early in my career with younger students who appreciated humor and diversion were not as effective later with more mature students who felt they were there to learn, not to be entertained. I also noticed later in my career that although I was well-organized, had well-stated objectives, used good class communication, and observed the characteristics that I deemed important to good teaching, I had become too serious. For that reason I now occasionally mix in with my lesson plan an additional sheet that says to me, "smile, be friendly, smell the roses."

Also, I have found an evolution in the use of anecdotes. Strangely enough it was the reverse. Early in my career the use of anecdotes sometimes drew criticism from students as "too much story telling," or "more war stories." Later I began to put the question on my evaluation questionnaires: "Were the anecdotes and stories meaningful?" The overwhelming response from adult students was "yes." They were pertinent, they brought meaning to the class, and they were valuable because the adults were interested in real life experiences rather than rote lecturing.

One note of caution, however, the use of anecdotes should relate to the topic being discussed and not simply stories of other experiences. In general, however, most of today's students will approve of anecdotes and may have their own to contribute.

If you wish to do a quick analysis of your style, it can easily be done using the Internet. One such survey is "Gardner's Multiple Intelligences", available on most major search engines. This survey allows you to examine your strengths in eight categories, allowing you to analyze your own strengths and weaknesses in relation to your students. Although you need to be aware of copyright restrictions, many sites have surveys available with copyright permission granted so you can even use them in class.

A meaningful exercise might be to have your students complete the survey on their own (it is non-threatening) and discuss the composite results and what they mean in class.

Professional Ethics

Although the teaching profession has been slow (compared to other professions) to address ethical issues, developments of the past few decades have encouraged an examination of the ethical status of college faculty. Although the recent attention has been inspired by legal or public relations concerns, there has always existed an unwritten code of ethics for teachers based upon values that have evolved both within the teaching profession and our culture.

> *Wilbert McKeachie states, "Ethical standards are intended to guide us in carrying out the responsibilities we have to the different groups with whom we interact" (McKeachie, 1994).*

 Some institutions have adopted written standards of ethical behavior expected of all college faculty. A compilation of some of these standards is listed below as an example and all adjunct/part-time faculty should check with their department director or dean for information on their institution's standards. For clarity, the guidelines are presented in two categories: those pertaining to the profession of teaching and those pertaining to students.

Ethics and the Profession. This section is an attempt to emphasize the ethical expectations of the profession and the institution in which part-time faculty are employed.

Adjunct faculty:

- Will attend all assigned classes with adequately prepared materials and content as described in the course description.
- Will not attempt to teach a course for which they are not qualified and knowledgeable.

- Will present all sides on controversial issues.
- Will conduct a fair evaluation of students, applied equally to all.
- Will not promote outside entrepreneurial activities within the class setting.
- When reasonably possible, will attend college orientations and other development activities presented for the improvement of their role as an instructor.
- Will avoid behavior that may be interpreted as discriminatory based upon gender, age, social status or racial background.
- Will hold their colleagues and institution in highest respect in their actions and communication within and outside the institution.

Professional Ethics and Students. This section relates to ethical considerations concerning students.

Adjunct faculty:

- Will not discuss individual students and their problems outside of the professional structure of the institution.
- Will refer student personal problems to qualified staff.
- Will maintain and honor office hours and appointments with students.
- Will respect students' integrity and avoid social encounters with students which might suggest misuse of power.
- Will not attempt to influence students' philosophy or their positions concerning social and political issues.
- Will not ask students for personal information for research purposes.

These guidelines are quite general; however, they provide a vehicle for examining more closely the expectations of the institution in which you teach. Unfortunately, in today's world, there is sometimes a fine line between ethical issues and legal issues.

A more formal statement of professional standards is available from the National Education Association. For purposes of brevity, only the "Commitment to the Student" under the *Code of Ethics of the Education Profession* is presented here.

The educator strives to help each student realize his or her potential as a worthy and effective member of society. The educator therefore works to stimulate the spirit of inquiry, the acquisition of knowledge and understanding, and the thoughtful formulation of worthy goals.

In fulfillment of the obligation to the student, the educator—

- Shall not unreasonably restrain the student from independent action in the pursuit of learning.
- Shall not unreasonably deny the student's access to varying points of view.
- Shall not deliberately suppress or distort subject matter relevant to the student's progress.
- Shall make reasonable effort to protect the student from conditions harmful to learning or to health and safety.
- Shall not intentionally expose the student to embarrassment or disparagement.
- Shall not on the basis of race, color, creed, sex, national origin, marital status, political or religious beliefs, family, social or cultural background, or sexual orientation, unfairly:
  a. exclude any student from participation in any program.
  b. deny benefits to any student.
  c. grant any advantage to any student.
- Shall not use professional relationships with students for private advantage.
- Shall not disclose information about students obtained in the course of professional service unless disclosure serves a compelling professional purpose or is required by law (NEA, 1975).

Academic Dishonesty

Academic dishonesty usually appears in two forms: either outright cheating or plagiarism. The problem of cheating in college classrooms has probably become more common in the last few years due to the pressures on students to succeed. Adding to the problem is the fact that we offer student instruction in conducting research on the World Wide Web, which in turn leads to temptation to copy materials from the web rather than to conduct research.

To minimize cheating, some instructors place a significant percentage of the student evaluation in the form of shared or active student participation. These activities are evaluated for all members of the group, thus providing no incentive for individuals to attempt to cheat to better themselves. It is important also that in the classroom environment ethical responsibilities requiring trust and honesty are emphasized. Of course the traditional method of countering cheating is to develop multiple tests with different questions and to not repeat the same test or test questions term after term.

Regardless of the amount of trust built in a classroom situation all exams should be proctored and you should never leave the room in which an exam is being conducted. The instructor is ethically responsible for this commitment to the students who are striving honestly to achieve their goals and make their grade and to the institution. Obviously extra time spent by the instructor to devise an evaluation plan in which written tests are only part of the final grade is time well spent. Finally, on the final exam, students may be asked to write in their own words the two or three principles that affected them most in the course and what they feel they may gain in the future. This question could represent a significant part of the final grade.

If you suspect or encounter a student in the act of cheating or plagiarism, the student should be made aware of the situation. This should be done in confidence in a face-to-face meeting.

In the legalistic world we live in, there can only be one conclusive bit of advice: as an instructor, you must be aware of your institution's official procedures and the legal status of your position.

Suspecting someone of cheating or actually seeing it is not a pleasant experience; however, it will likely happen in your teaching experience sooner or later. Usually, reasonable rational procedures will adequately cover the situation without the destruction of the student's academic career or standing.

Checklist for Part-Time Faculty

There are many things that you need to know when receiving your teaching assignment. Each teaching situation may call for new information. There are, however, basic items that will almost assuredly be asked sometime during class. This section lists information you may wish to check before entering the first class.

(After reviewing this list, it is recommended that a personal timeline be developed including these and other important dates related to teaching the course.)

Figure 1.1—Faculty Checklist

FACULTY CHECKLIST

1. What are the names of the department chairperson, dean, director and other important officials?

2. Have I completed all of my paperwork for official employment? (It's demoralizing when an expected paycheck doesn't arrive.)

3. Is there a pre-term faculty meeting?
   Date_____Time_____

4. Is there a departmental course syllabus, course outline, or statement of goals and objectives available for the course?

5. Are there prepared departmental handouts?

6. Are there prepared departmental tests?

7. Where is and/or how do I get my copy of the text(s) and support materials for teaching the class?

8. Is there a department and/or college attendance or tardiness policy?

9. When are grades due? When do students receive grades?

10. Is there a college or departmental grading policy?

11. Where can I get instructional aid materials and equipment, films, videotapes, software? What is the lead time for ordering?

12. Is there a student evaluation of instruction form for this course? Do I have or can I get a sample copy?

13. Where can I collect background and demographic information about students and their expectations?

14. Who are some of the other faculty who have taught the course? Are they open to assisting adjuncts?

15. Where can I find information to develop a list of resources and references pertaining to outside student assignments?

16. Have the course objectives been reviewed to be certain they reflect changes in text materials or technology?

17. Do I have a variety of instructional strategies planned so that my course does not become repetitious?

18. Do I have a current academic calendar that lists the length of term, the end of quarter, semester, or inter-term for special assignment so everyone clearly understands the beginning and termination of the course?

CHAPTER

2

TEACHING ADULT STUDENTS

Although it is impossible to prepare a standard plan that fits all classes, there are some fundamental principles and activities for teaching adult students. Keeping in mind that even these activities must be constantly reassessed to meet changing institutional and cultural needs, this chapter provides a better understanding of today's students so that an appropriate classroom assessment can be made.

Student Characteristics

Today's students, whether they are older adults or just out of high school, possess some common expectations that effect classroom attitudes. These attitudes are based upon students viewing themselves as consumers of a product, rather than seekers of knowledge. As indicated earlier, they will expect well-planned and prepared course goals and objectives. Other recognizable characteristics include:

- Today's students are more self-directed than their earlier counterparts. In other words, they generally know what they want and where they are going.

- Today's students are highly demanding as consumers. They feel that, since they are paying for their education, they are entitled to a product. There have been legal cases in which colleges have been required to provide evidence of delivering advertised services (classes).

- Today's students often come to the classroom with rich life and educational experiences. They have read broadly and often have had interesting employment and/or travel experiences they may wish to share.

- Today's students expect to be treated as adults. They want to be treated as equals, not as students or "kids."

29

Although the students are more demanding, they are also more interesting, more challenging, and will contribute to a stimulating learning experience if given the opportunity. Most adult students are not in the classroom to compete. They are there to succeed and improve themselves. As a teacher of adults, you should minimize competition and increase cooperation to foster success. Above all, the age-old process of "x" number of A's, "x" number of B's, etc. based upon a bell curve, has been abandoned in the modern classroom.

The Modern Student

The modern student is sometimes described as "the generation X student" or "X-gens". Many say that such a label is no more definitive than trying to describe a teenager. Those that dwell on the "generation X" concept often describe the students as bored and unmotivated, and having an "attitude" toward college that is resistant to disciplined study. These critics feel that the basis for this behavior is the students' desire for immediate gratification rather than establishing long-term goals.

A differing argument maintains that this kind of student has always been present in the classroom. There is, however, a significant intervening factor. The X-gen students have grown up surrounded by the influences of media, experiencing an inappropriately large amount of fantasy driven by television, movies, videos, and music. Add to this the advent of the Internet and one realizes that today's young students have come of age in a cultural environment vastly different from the typical student of the past. This environment has encouraged attitudes that may surface in the classroom in the form of consumer expectations and a lack of respect of authority. In addition, many of these students are the first generation known as "latchkey kids", children who grew up with both parents working. And to a far greater extent than in the past, many were raised in single-parent homes and/or are the product of divorce.

In order for you as a part-time instructor to challenge these students, it will be necessary to develop teaching strategies and procedures that will co-opt these learners. These active strategies will include group work, role playing, cooperative learning and other techniques described later in Chapter 3. On the positive side, be aware that students today, although expecting a certain amount of autonomy, will respond to classroom activities in which they are involved and they see as meaningful. They will probably be interested in topics and work assignments that can be researched on the Internet rather than in print documents and periodicals from the library. To address their needs for immediate gratification, they will expect answers to their questions in class and comments and notes on their tests and quizzes.

 In planning your classroom strategies for the modern student, keep in mind that these students want *to do* something rather than *to know* something. Class presentation should incorporate a variety of format including charts, videos, graphics, computer projection and other technological visual aids.

Teaching With the Techniques of Andragogy

If you are the typical part-time instructor today, you were probably first introduced to teaching using the methods of pedagogy. Pedagogy is based upon the teaching of children and is synonymous with the word "leader" (Knowles, 1990). In the past several years, however, the role of the teacher has changed from being a leader or presenter of learning to being a *facilitator* of learning because the average age of the college student today is closer to 30 than to the 20 of a few years ago. This older and more diverse student body will come to class motivated to learn but with a different set of needs. They are likely goal-oriented problem solvers and bring with them a need to know why they are learning something.

Thus came the acceptance of the andragogical model pioneered by Knowles. The andragogical model is based upon:
- *The student's need to know,*
- *The learner's self concept,*
- *The role of the learner's experience,*
- *The readiness to learn,*
- *An orientation to learning, and*
- *Motivation.*

Andragogy has often been called the art and science of teaching adults because it places the student at the center of the learning process and emphasizes collaborative relationships among students and with the instructor—all techniques that work well with adult students. The andragogical model prescribes problem solving activities based upon the students' needs rather than on the goals of the discipline or the instructor.

Developing an andragogical teaching strategy requires a warm and friendly classroom environment to foster open communication. You must be aware that many adults have anxieties about their learning experience and lack confidence. Thus, plan activities that make students feel confident and secure with opportunities for students to share their experiences. It is important that this classroom environment be cultivated and nurtured in the first class session and that you establish yourself as a partner in learning and not an expert who has all the answers.

To incorporate the techniques of andragogy in your class, it is necessary that you become proficient in executing student-centered activities including: conducting a meaningful discussion, stimulating cooperative learning, developing good questions and critical thinking strategies, and involving all students in the learning process.

Student-Centered Learning

Student-centered learning is more than just implementation of adragogical strategies. As an adjunct faculty member, it would be wise for you to review your institution's mission statement or statement of philosophy. Many institutions in recent years have gravitated toward the concept of student- or client-centered learning. Institutionally, this may simply mean that the institution is striving to deliver their educational products to students anyplace at any time. Although the institution may be striving to meet the individual needs of the students, student-centered learning may or may not mean that the philosophy or purpose of the institution will change to adapt to all of the students' needs.

In the classroom, however, student-centered learning takes on a different meaning. Most contemporary institutions have adopted many educational delivery strategies to accommodate students in many ways in order to assist them in meeting their educational needs. In a learner-centered classroom, faculty are expected to implement strategies that allow students more self-determination in how they reach their goals. This objective is, however, tempered by the need of departments and disciplines to set explicit achievement standards that must be met to fulfill the goals of the academic discipline.

Some questions you may need to ask yourself to assess your goal of a student-centered learning environment are listed below.

- Do I have strategies to encourage **open communication** among students and between students and the teacher?
- Do I have appropriate **feedback mechanisms** in place so that the feelings and the needs of the students are communicated in a meaningful and timely manner?
- Do I have **collaborative learning strategies** in my lesson plans so students can work as teams, groups, or partners?
- Are the **needs of the students** being met along with the objectives of the course?
- Do I **recognize students as individuals** with diverse backgrounds and needs as well as classroom participants?

- Do I **vary my teaching strategie**s to accommodate a wide range of students?

Remember, a student-centered environment does not diminish the responsibility of the teacher nor give the students the power to determine course activities. Rather a student-centered environment requires skillful knowledge and use of cooperative and student-involved strategies implemented by the teacher.

Student Learning Styles

One can easily find many paradigms for student learning styles in educational literature. Faculty are not expected to master or study in detail all of these styles and then attempt to categorize their students. It is, however, useful for you to understand some of the different learning styles that may appear in your classroom so that you can give consideration to individual differences. One such learning style system is called the "4mat system." This system identifies four types of learners. They are: imaginative learners, analytic learners, common sense learners, and dynamic learners.

- **Imaginative learners** will expect the faculty member to produce authentic curricula, to present knowledge upon which to build, to involve them in group work, and to provide useful feedback. They care about fellow students and the instructor.
- **Analytic learners** are more interested in theory and what the experts think, they need details and data, and are uncomfortable with subjectiveness. They expect the class to enhance their knowledge and place factual knowledge over creativity.
- **Common sense learners** test theories and look for practical applications; they are problem solvers and are typically skill oriented. They expect to be taught skills and may not be flexible or good in teamwork situations.
- **Dynamic learners** believe in self-discovery. They like change and flexibility, are risk takers, and are at ease with people. They may, however, be pushy and manipulative. They respond to dynamic instructors who are constantly trying new things (McCarthy, 1987).

It is important to understand that all or some of these types of learners may be present in any given class. This makes it necessary for the instructor to possess the ability to use a variety of classroom activities.

I recall an experience while teaching that relates to this topic. Having for years been successful in teaching classes by encouraging open communication and maximizing student involvement, I found myself teaching a class in which an acquaintance was enrolled. This person simply would not respond or take part in discussions. Knowing the student to be social and bright, I was not completely surprised that when all the criteria for grades were considered, the individual easily earned an "A", contrary to my belief that all students must participate to learn! It was only later that I realized that the student's process for learning was not flawed, it was just different from the style that I, as the instructor, had perceived necessary for learning.

Closely reviewing the description of the student types will bring out another important factor. That is, just as students have learning styles, teachers have teaching styles. Thus, you should be able to identify your own teaching style from the learning style descriptions. Understanding your teaching style will allow you to modify your behavior to accommodate all learners.

After considering the learning styles above, it is just as important to keep in mind two major factors concerning adult learners. First, they have basically been trained to be cognitive learners so they will first seek to obtain the knowledge and information that they feel is necessary to complete the course work and receive a passing grade. Second, adults learn by doing. They want to take part in learning activities based upon their needs and application. When interacting with individual students in your classroom, you must continually recognize that all learners are not coming from the same set of circumstances.

Diversity in the Classroom

If there is any area of teaching that demands common sense, it is the diversity found in today's classrooms. Classes today are full of students of various age groups, ethnic backgrounds, cultural experiences, and educational abilities. This diversity can contribute to a more interesting classroom when interactive learning allows students to learn about different cultures and differing perspectives first hand through debate and discussion.

For the teacher, however, diversity poses significant challenges. While you must be aware of your students' diverse backgrounds, you must be equally cautious not to overcompensate or appear to give special attention to any one group or individual.

There are some specific teaching strategies that can be implemented and of which you should be aware. When contemplating the course content you should consider the age of the students and their experiences. For example, when older students contribute anecdotes, they usually use their own past experiences. While younger students may prefer topics that effect them immediately. In understanding student attitudes and behaviors, keep in mind that many older students were educated in structured classroom settings and are accustomed to formal lecture and discussion formats, while younger students will probably respond to a more active learning style. Older students also will have the confidence to share their experiences and backgrounds with the class whereas younger students may hesitate.

Above all avoid stereotyping any members of our culture. Solomon (1994) makes specific suggestions concerning diversity in the classroom. Some of his suggestions are:

- Do not address students by a preferred name. Learn to pronounce their correct name.

- Do not tell or tolerate racist, sexist, ethnic or age-related jokes.

- Do not imply negatives when addressing other ethnic groups or culturally different societies.

- Become aware of your own prejudices.

- Never allow your own personal values to be the sole basis for judgment.
- Constantly evaluate your cultural perceptions to be sure they are not based upon personal insecurities.

Generally keep in mind that the diverse classroom provides several opportunities. Diversity provides an enriching experience when students share with each other and with the instructor and may assist in reducing cultural barriers. The diverse class provides a forum for understanding the differences that exist between individuals and social classes. Through group interactive strategies, these differences can give students the chance to be full participants in their learning and development process. These group strategies can also provide opportunities for all students to become a part of their classroom community regardless of their background.

Bloom's Taxonomy of Educational Objectives

If there is a single paradigm that has stood the test of time in education it is Benjamin Bloom's Taxonomy of Educational Objectives (Bloom et al., 1956). Published nearly a half a century ago this taxonomy describes the learning process as three factors or domains. They are the cognitive domain, affective domain, and psychomotor domain.

Essentially, cognitive learning is learning that emphasizes knowledge and information and incorporates analysis of that knowledge. Affective learning centers on values and value systems, receiving stimuli, ideas and to some degree, organization. Psychomotor learning addresses hand/eye coordination, normally referred to as physical coordination.

The importance of these three domains is not so much the overall consideration of the categories as it is the breakdown provided by Bloom. For example, Bloom's cognitive domain is broken into several categories: knowledge, comprehension, application, analysis, synthesis, and evaluation. The affective domain is broken into receiving, responding, valuing, organizing and characterization of value com-

plex. A psychomotor domain essentially is that which provides for the development of physical skills.

The cognitive domain is usually emphasized in the classroom learning situation. However, when writing course objectives it is often expected that all three domains will be represented. This means that you should have objectives in the cognitive domain written not only at the knowledge level but also the evaluation, analysis, and synthesis levels. In the affective domain, you would have objectives covering responding, valuing and value complex. Many institutions require course objectives and activities in all three of the domains of Bloom's Taxonomy. It should be noted from examination of the descriptions rendered here that these domains effectively cover all areas of the learning process.

Motivation

Students are motivated for many reasons: individual improvement, intellectual curiosity, needed employment competencies, career change or advancement, employment requirement, or the completion of degree or certificate requirements. Although these motivational reasons are broad and varied, faculty must possess the skills to motivate students with a variety of activities including occasional risk-taking.

The following anecdote exemplifies such risk taking. After many years of teaching, I remember being faced with a class that would not respond or participate. Admittedly it was a Friday night class; however, you might expect that in such a class, highly motivated students would be enrolled. They were, however, very tired students and many of them were enrolled merely to pick up additional credits. After teaching the class about three weeks and experiencing very little student response, on the spur of the moment during the third evening, I simply stated, "We must start communicating. I would like each of you at this time to turn to a person near you, introduce yourself and tell them that you are going to help them get through the course, no matter how difficult it is, that you will be there to help them whenever they become confused, and that the two of you (by helping each

other) can be successful in this course." This seemingly simple technique worked wonders. The students became acquainted with someone they hadn't previously known, and in many cases, found someone who really could help them get through the course. For the remainder of the course, when it appeared that the class was experiencing difficulty, I simply needed to say "let's take a few minutes and get together with our partner." When chalkboard work was given, two students would voluntarily go to the board together. Thus a previously unused "risk" activity proved successful—and was my first experience with collaborative learning and the partner system. This is an example of trying a basic technique of motivation. In this case it worked. It may not work every time, but it was not a technique that I had in my repertoire prior to that time. So, when motivating adult students, remember that you must occasionally try techniques not necessarily found in the literature.; however, there are proven techniques that should be in the professional portfolio of all teachers, such as Maslow's Hierarchy of Needs.

Maslow's Hierarchy of Needs

It is virtually impossible to incorporate all theories of motivation for your students. It is appropriate, therefore, that we find refuge in a time-honored theory of learning called Maslow's Hierarchy of Needs. Maslow's hierarchy states that the basic needs of human beings fall into five categories:

- *PHYSIOLOGICAL—feeling good physically with appropriate food and shelter.*
- *SAFETY—the feeling of security in one's environment.*
- *LOVE AND BELONGING OR THE SOCIAL NEED—fulfilling the basic family and social role.*
- *ESTEEM—the status and respect of a positive self-image.*
- *SELF-ACTUALIZATION—growth of the individual.*

Physiological, Safety, Love and Belonging. The fact that Maslow's needs are in hierarchy form is a major problem for teachers of adults. For example, attempting to address the needs of esteem and self-actualization in the classroom, when physiological, safety, and love and belonging needs have not been met, is a difficult task. In fact, the lack of fulfillment of the basic needs may interfere with the learning process. This interference may manifest itself in anti-social behavior.

The challenge becomes, how does one in a short period of time, teaching on a part-time basis to mostly part-time students, over-come these barriers? The fact is that one may not overcome all of these barriers. If instructors attempt to take the time to analyze each of the unmet needs of each of their students, they will have little time to work toward the goals and objectives of the course.

There is, however, an important factor to support the instructor. It is that the need to achieve appears to be a basic need in human beings. The need to succeed, an intrinsic motivator that usually overcomes most of the other distractions to learning, is the factor upon which successful teachers capitalize.

There is little that faculty can do to help students to meet the physiological, safety, and love and belonging needs. The need for esteem and self-actualization, which are essentially achievement, are areas in which teaching strategies can be implemented.

Esteem. Esteem is the status and respect with which human beings are regarded by their peers and activities faculty members incorporate that assist students in achieving status and self-respect will support fulfillment of the esteem need. This is accomplished by providing an environment in which students can experience success in their learning endeavors. *Many learning theorists claim that success in itself is the solution to motivation and learning.*

One of the great fallacies of teaching is often stated by students who have succeeded in classes where other students have dropped out. That observation is: "That prof was tough, but he/she was really good." This may or may not be true. *The fact is that being tough has absolutely no relationship to being good.* Too often the reverse of this statement is perpetuated when some faculty emphasize toughness as a substitute for good teaching. There is no evidence to suggest that "tough teachers" are better teachers than those who are "not so tough". It is especially discouraging to marginal students who are working hard but find the chances for success negated by the instructor's desire to be tough.

Building esteem through success is accomplished in many ways. The following are some classroom instruction suggestions to assist students in achieving success:

- *Make certain that students are aware of course requirements.* Students should be provided with course objectives in written form that tell them what they are expected to accomplish.

- *Inform students precisely what is expected of them.* This means not only the work or the skills necessary for them to complete the course content, but also the time commitment.

- *Give students nonverbal encouragement whenever possible.* There are many ways this can be accomplished. Eye contact with students can very often elicit a positive response. Gestures are important. A smile, a nod of the head, just looking at students with the feeling that you find the classroom a pleasant environment is in itself effective nonverbal encouragement.

- *Give positive reinforcement at every opportunity.* Simple techniques such as quizzes for which grades are not taken, quizzes designed so most or all students will succeed, as

well as short tests as a supplement to grading are effective positive reinforcement strategies. Comments written on hand-in papers, tests, and projects are effective ways to provide positive feedback. Of course, the ideal form of positive reinforcement is provided through individual conferences and informal conversations with students at chance meetings.

- *Provide a structured situation in which the students feel comfortable.* The *laissez-faire* classroom is generally a lazy classroom. Most educators agree that a structured setting with students participating in activities is much better than an unstructured approach.

- *Provide opportunity for student discussion of outside experiences.* Some students in your class, who may not be particularly adept in the course content, may have significant contributions and accomplishments to share. One of the greatest builders of esteem is to allow students to share their success experiences with others.

Self-Actualization. Self-actualization, the highest of Maslow's hierarchy, is the realization of individual growth. Such growth is realized through achievement and success. Course planning for enhancement of student self-actualization is the ultimate in successful teaching. The suggestions listed here can assist in the student growth process.

- *Each class should offer a challenge to each student.* Challenges are presented in a variety of ways. If they are insurmountable challenges they become barriers; therefore, it is important that faculty plan activities appropriate for the course. Grades are challenges. However, grades must be achievable or they cause frustration. Achieving class credit is a challenge. Most students, even though they may not achieve the grade desired, will feel satisfied if they obtain the credit for which they are working. Assigning incompletes and allowing additional time for projects are techniques that will assist students in obtaining credit for

their work. Questions, if properly phrased, can become challenges.

- *Problem solving.* The ultimate challenge in the classroom is problem solving. Problem-solving techniques vary greatly depending upon the subject matter. Although it is impossible to discuss in detail the ramifications of problem solving, this challenge does not lend itself solely to scientific and mathematics classes. It can also be utilized in many other courses through discussion, professional journals and literature reports, outside projects, case studies, and group work.

- *Treat students as individuals.* Individual conferences and development of a system to promote interaction between students, their instructor, and other students are important. Many experienced faculty members do not hesitate to share with students their home or business phone number and/or e-mail address and are usually quite surprised at how seldom any are used.

- *Be cautious not to prejudge students.* Unfortunately, stereotyping still exists today. Faculty must make every effort not to "type" classes or students as "good" or "bad." Such stereotyping will affect grading and attitudes toward the students. Also, there is a good chance that the judgment may be incorrect. *There is no place for stereotypes in education.*

- *Treat students as adults.* Many of today's students hold powerful positions in business and industry. It is difficult for them to regard the teacher as someone superior. To adult students, the instructor is just someone in a different role. Above all, don't refer to them as "kids."

- *Give consideration to students' personal problems when possible.* Giving adult students personal consideration implies that rules concerning attendance, paper deadlines, tardiness, etc., may be flexible when faced with the realities of the lives of adult students. Practice flexibility whenever possible.

CHAPTER

3

CLASSROOM STRATEGIES
FOR TEACHING ADULTS

Teacher Behaviors

Adjunct faculty can assist student learning with tried and proven strategies. Some principles and strategies to remember are:

- **The teacher is a facilitator of learning.** Students do not expect teachers to know all there is to know about the subject. They do expect, however, the teacher to facilitate learning the facts and skills of the course.

- **Understand your teaching situation.** As an adjunct faculty member you may have a variety of assignments at different institutions. When making your class preparations, consider the following questions: Is this class part of a competitive program? Are the goals clarified for the student and the institution? Can student projects be developed to meet the students' needs?

- **Allow for individual differences.** Every classroom will contain a diverse group of individuals. Allow for this by giving individual help, knowing students' names, and being aware of differing backgrounds.

- **Vary teaching activities.** Use different activities in the classroom. Try new ideas. Some experts recommend changing activities every 20 minutes.

- **Develop a supportive climate.** Students should understand that you are there to support them in the learning process not to prove how tough the course is.

- **Be sensitive to barriers.** Some of the baggage students bring with them include: unsuccessful previous educational experience, time restraints, confusion concerning

college (procedures) in general, failure to understand their academic limitations, stress, physical and mental handicaps.

- **Be a learning partner.** Communicate to the students that you are a partner in their learning. You will develop and work with them on strategy, materials, and projects that will allow them to self direct their learning experience.

- **Emphasize experimentation.** Emphasize to the students that trying new learning techniques and making mistakes are often as valuable as reaching the right conclusion immediately.

- **Use technology to enhance learning.** Know about and be able to use the latest learning technologies such as computers and the Internet.

Most of all it is important that you be understanding and considerate. With dynamic changes in the educational field today, you need to keep up with these technological and cultural changes so that they become part of the teaching/learning process. Being alert to these changes will prevent the worst student criticism, "it isn't done that way anymore."

Student Behaviors

During your teaching tenure you will experience differing classroom behavior from students that may challenge your ability to maintain the class in a constructive and positive manner. Keep in mind that the following suggestions are simply observations of other teachers and may not apply to all situations.

- **The class expert.** This person has all or most of the answers and is more than willing to share them—and will argue if he or she is not right. Suggestion: Make eye contact with a different student in the class and ask for an opinion. Allow other students to react. Give respondent time to tell anecdotes and/or present position, then remind the "expert" and the class that they must get back to the objectives of the course.

- **The quiet class.** Give positive reinforcement to any response from any student. Change teaching strategies and request an answer to a simple question at the beginning of the next class session. Use questioning techniques, group work, partner system, current events, personal experiences, brainstorming, or icebreakers.

- **The talkative class.** Direct a question to a group or supportive individual. Quiet the class to recognize an individual to make their point or position known. Validate or invalidate the point and move to the next topic in the lesson plan. Allow time for conversation, specify time for class work to begin, exert your control.

- **The negative student.** Initially ignore! Invite the student to a conference, provide a success experience, determine an interest of student and cultivate it.

- **The off-the-subject student.** Allow some freedom for discussion and for the reaction of other students. Other students will usually provide incentive to get back on subject. Seize the opportunity and stress the need to get back to course objectives.

- **The unruly student.** Remain calm and polite. Above all keep your cool and your temper. Don't disagree. Try to determine the student's position and reason for concern. Listen intently and allow the student an opportunity to verbally withdraw from the situation.

If angry, try to determine the basis of the anger the student is expressing. Ask the individual to meet with you privately during the break and if necessary call an immediate break. As a last resort the class may be dismissed and institutional procedures for such a situation should be implemented. *Keep in mind that your primary responsibility is the safety of all students.* If procedures are not established, inquire of your institution why they are not.

Classroom Assessment

One of the most recent and dynamic classroom strategies is termed "classroom assessment". Basically, classroom assessment is an ongoing sophisticated feedback mechanism that carries with it specific implications in terms of learning and teaching. It can be used in large or small classes, in any type of class and at any level. Classroom assessment techniques can be used daily or periodically, at the beginning of the course or at the end. The techniques emphasize the principles of active learning as well as student-centered learning.

Specifically, classroom assessment techniques answer the questions: "what are students learning and how effectively am I teaching?"

Classroom assessment techniques are truly developmental, in that no credit should ever be granted for assessment activities. Using classroom assessment is closer to doing classroom research than to developing pedagogical or andragogical techniques. They are intended to provide teachers with a continuous flow of information on student learning and the quality of instruction in the classroom.

The recognized founders of classroom assessment movement, T.A. Angelo and K.P. Cross, discuss in significant detail assessment practices that can be implemented by the teacher. In *Classroom Assessments, A Handbook for College Teachers, second edition* (Angelo and Cross, 1993), they provide a detailed analysis of assessment as well as its philosophical and procedural background. For this brief description of classroom assessment, three of the most popular and common techniques presented by Angelo and Cross are outlined. They are called: the minute paper, the muddiest point, and the one-sentence summary.

The minute paper, sometimes known as the one-minute paper or the minute response, is a quick and effective way to collect written feedback from the students. It is simple to use, opens communication with students, and provides an active learning activity. To use the minute paper, the instructor merely stops the class two or three

minutes early and asks the students to respond to two questions: (1) what is the most important thing you learned in today's class? and (2) what is the most important thing that remains unanswered or leaves questions in your mind? Students write their responses on small sheets of paper or on cards and turn them in to the instructor as they leave the class.

The minute paper question, of course, can be worded in several different ways. If one is asking about the understanding of a problem-solving activity, it can be specified. The minute paper is then used at the introduction of the following class for either opening a discussion of the most noted minute paper responses or presenting the questions and answers that are most relevant. There is no need to ask students to identify themselves on the minute paper since the intent is to assess understanding.

The muddiest point. The muddiest point, unlike the minute paper, asks students to respond to a single question. The muddiest point asks the students to identify what they are *not* getting from the class or are *not understanding*. The instructor can specify whether the student is to respond to the lecture, a demonstration, or general problem-solving activity. Leaving the muddiest point unsigned and having them dropped in a box as the students leave the class relieves the student of any concerns about the relationship with the instructor and provides an efficient avenue of input to the instructor.

The one-sentence summary. The one-sentence summary requires students to provide additional information, actually reaching the synthesis level of Bloom's Taxonomy. The one-sentence summary asks students to answer the question "who does what to whom, when, where, how, and why" about the topic and then to analyze those answers in a simple long summary sentence. This technique should be used with important topics and principles, and works well in chronologically organized classes where students need to have some command of elementary principles and processes before moving on to a more advanced topic.

Use of classroom assessment techniques requires the instructor to first determine the goals and objectives of the course, the basic principles the students must learn to succeed in the course, and what types of examples students are required to complete or analyze.

Critical Thinking

Critical thinking can best be stimulated by raising questions and by offering challenges about a specific issue or statement. Many students still like the "right" answer from the instructor but critical thinking in instruction goes far beyond that. Critical thinking involves asking the right kinds of questions and goes so far as to let students develop assumptions and analyze (either in groups or individually) those assumptions. They can then examine alternatives to their assumptions.

Some types of questions to ask might be: "What is the source of your information and how reliable is it?" "What are your personal experiences in relation to the information?" "What are the different positions?" "What are your feelings on the topic?" "Why?" "Do you agree?" Allow students time to think and wait for some response. If students take a position on an issue, ask them for an alternate position.

Feedback

As has been indicated in other parts of this publication, obtaining student feedback is instrumental to good instruction. Most instructors rely upon student questions and responses in class for their feedback. Good feedback, however, is too important to leave to chance.

The faculty evaluation form that follows and the section on "Quality Circles" in this publication are examples of feedback. The institution in which you teach may have prepared instruments that can be of value. All such documents have weaknesses as well as strengths, whether they be open-ended or close-ended questions, rating forms or checklists. Given the time constraints facing most ad-

junct faculty, there are a few techniques that provide immediate and helpful feedback. They are:

- Prior to testing, give the class sample test questions which are not counted toward the grade, and ask them to write responses to the questions as well as the content.

- Maintain open and ongoing verbal communication, especially concerning clarity of assignments and deadlines.

- At the end of the course, have the students write a letter to "Aunt Millie" describing the course to her, then collect it.

- Do not confuse feedback with evaluation. Feedback is an opportunity for you to relate to your students and to enhance your class.

Some additional methods for obtaining feedback are:

class discussion	*study guides*
group discussions	*course post-mortem*
student conferences	*paper comments*
quizzes	*quality circles*

Faculty Self-Evaluation

Many colleges today have forms available for faculty who wish to conduct self-evaluations in addition to the official course evaluations for the institution or academic department. Whether voluntary or mandatory, keep in mind that most of these evaluation forms in fact capture student opinion and are not statistically valid. This does not, however, decrease the value of seeking student input to improve teaching. Whether you are an experienced faculty member or new to the profession, you will invariably find surprises while conducting such evaluations.

New faculty members will be astonished at the quality of some observations students make. I recall an acquaintance whose associates

thought he had an effective sense of humor. However, after conducting a classroom evaluation, he was surprised to find that the students not only rated him low, but many felt he did not possess a sense of humor.

Whether or not the results of student samplings of this type precipitate a change in faculty behavior is not always important. It is important, however, that faculty know how they are being perceived by the students.

There are two identifiable characteristics that are consistently valued by the students in relation to faculty behavior: a) demonstrating business-like behavior in the classroom, and b) being understanding and friendly.

Below is a form that you may use to conduct self-evaluation. Note that the form exists in two sections: classroom factors and personal factors.

The first section of the form (classroom evaluation) collects student insights into classroom behavior. The final section (personal factors) gives you an opportunity to select personal characteristics that you may wish to review and on which students may want to comment. Questions may be added or deleted to this form at will.

Remember that student perceptions are very often motivated by personal biases, rather than objective evaluation of the instructor; however, continued use of such a form helps to determine if there are characteristics that continue to surface that need attention. Many statistical techniques can be applied to evaluation forms such as this. A simple method of utilizing this form is to ask the students to assign numbers 1-5 to each of the categories and then weigh them on a number scale. It is not intended that this self-evaluation form have content validity; however, it will give faculty members insight into their teaching.

Figure 3.1—Faculty Evaluation Form

Faculty Evaluation Form

Class_____   Date_____

Instructions: Grade each factor on a scale of 1-5 your perception of the teacher's behavior or characteristics. (low=1; high=5, NA for not applicable).

Classroom Factors

Preparation for class _____

Communication of expectations to students _____

Command of subject matter _____

Course objectives clearly defined _____

Course content clearly reflects catalog description _____

Instructor encouraged student involvement _____

Instructor was professional and business-like _____

Instructor well prepared and organized _____

Tests reflected classroom presentation and objectives _____

Instructor utilized student-centered techniques _____

Instructor willing to give individual help _____

Instructor utilized technology and instructional aids _____

Instructor's Personal Factors

Considerate of differing opinions _____

Considerate of students with differing backgrounds _____

Personal appearance _____

Friendly and helpful to individual students _____

Overall rating _____

Greatest strengths_____

_____

Greatest weaknesses_____

_____

Suggestions to improve course_____

_____

(This form may be reproduced in its entirety if desired.)

PLANNING FOR INSTRUCTION

Of all the duties of part-time faculty, from lecturing to grading tests, the single most important is planning. Good planning is *essential* to successful teaching. Many of your students will come from structured backgrounds or employment situations where plans and performance objectives are expected. In addition, over the past several years, legal action has been taken against institutions that promised a high quality education in their product advertisement, accusing them of failure to provide this "product" to their student "customers." The best defense against this kind of action is a viable written plan.

Good planning requires a comprehensive approach, beginning with the course description and ending with the students' evaluation. Executing the plan for a course is much like a football game. Nearly everyone knows the standard plays and the standard procedures; the execution is what determines success.

Planning must take place prior to the first class. The preliminary steps include: becoming familiar with the text, organizing the material into content areas and topics, and prioritizing goals and objectives. Each of the major topics must be assigned class time and a plan designed for the activities associated with each topic. In addition, instructors should develop "fillers" for class sessions when additional material is needed.

> Good planning includes several documents. They include:
> - *Written Course Objectives*
> - *A Course Outline*
> - *A Course Syllabus*
> - *Lesson Plans*

Writing Course Objectives

Appropriate objectives for every college course based on the course description and institution-given goals, are not an option for any faculty. No longer is there dialogue about whether or not college courses will have objectives; all courses and classes must have them. Faculty success depends largely upon their ability to develop and implement course objectives. The flowchart below indicates the major components of the teaching/planning process.

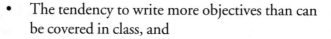

The most important activity in this process is developing appropriate course objectives.

Fortunately, the development of good course objectives is not as complex and difficult as one might expect.

There do exist, however, two remaining pitfalls:

- The tendency to write more objectives than can be covered in class, and

- The tendency to write objectives that are not clear to the student.

There are two very simple techniques to overcome these problems. First, in order to avoid writing objectives in a haphazard manner, simply develop the course goals and write the objectives for the goals rather than for the course. The course goals will be based on the course description the institution places in its catalog. Once you have written the goals, write objectives to support each goal. Don't worry about the ramifications of low priority objectives. A simple format is to write one goal at the top of a separate sheet of paper and then detail that goal's objectives underneath.

Avoiding the second pitfall, clarity of understanding, begins with using clearly understood descriptors when writing the objectives. Objectives should be few but concise. Begin developing appropriate objectives by verbalizing and writing your thoughts concerning the objective.

After writing down the objective statement, rewrite it and apply these appropriate descriptors:

write	solve
contrast	compare
compose	describe
compute	identify
list	attend

When writing objectives, remember that you must be able to measure whether or not the objective has been reached.

Conversely, descriptors that should not be used since they cannot be clearly measured include:

understand	appreciate
enjoy	believe
grasp	discuss

Conditional lead-ins, such as "at the completion of…" aren't necessary since these are understood. Some conditions may be included, for example, the achievement of a certain rating score or the completion of a certain activity in a given time. Make every effort, however, to be clear so students understand all conditions. Good objectives are essential to a good planning process.

> *You should evaluate and assign grades based on the completion of the course objectives.*

Robert Mager, one of the pioneers of the instructional objective movement, outlines several principles to be observed in writing objectives:

- *be explicit,*
- *communicate,*
- *tell what the learner will be doing,*
- *indicate conditions if there are any,*
- *include some recognition of successful completion* (Mager, 1962).

Examples of some well-written objectives are:

- The student *will recite* the Gettysburg Address.

- The student *will identify* the major components of a successful lesson plan.

- The student *will describe* the process involved in a bank approval of a consumer loan.

- The student *will write* a five-page news release on a selected topic with a minimum of two errors.

Some institutions may require the development of objectives based upon Bloom's Taxonomy of Educational Objectives. This taxonomy provides that instruction be organized around one or more of the hierarchy of objectives. They are: knowledge, comprehension, application, analysis, synthesis and evaluation (Bloom et al., 1956). If objectives are prepared across this hierarchy, you need to recognize that your objectives and the teaching strategies to achieve them can not be limited to the knowledge level where only information recall is required. You must develop instructional plans and activities that ensure students achieve competencies in the application, analysis, and synthesis domains. More active teaching styles will incorporate the higher order objectives that ensure students are able to reach the objectives described.

The Course Outline

While the course objectives give you the conceptual overview of the upcoming class, the course outline is much more comprehensive and allows you to flesh out the entire course by applying detail to the objectives.

The course outline usually uses the standard outline format to cover the topics from the course objectives. Generally, a topic should not be divided into more than three subtopics for a course outline. If there are more than three subtopics, place them in the daily lesson plan.

The purpose of the outline is very simple: to make certain that all major topics are recognized and addressed during the course.

The two types of outlines most commonly used in teaching are the chronological outline and the content outline. The chronological outline is used for courses that lend themselves to time or historic sequence. Sequential courses; such as mathematics, history, and science where previous knowledge is necessary to function at a higher level; require chronological outlines.

Content outlines are used with topics taught in a specified content order and are often called topical outlines. This allows considerable flexibility since you may arrange the course in the way that you consider most effective for presentation. For example, physical education faculty may allow students to actually perform an activity prior to its being taught so that the students can see a need for the techniques. Whereas, a chronological outline calls for the presentation of the basic information before students attempt to perform the operation. A course concerned with legislative, judicial, or community activities may not require that field trips to legislative bodies or courtrooms be conducted in sequence with other activities in the course.

Although in most institutions, there are course outlines available, generally they will not be maintained as formal documents.

Often, outlines are treated in the same manner as lesson plans—that is—something the instructor develops. (The formal document recognized at most institutions and approved by the college is the course syllabus). A sample course outline is shown in figure 4.1. Theoretically, a proper course outline is developed in conjunction with the course objectives. This assures direction and purpose of the outline.

Figure 4.1—Sample Course Outline

Achievement University
Basic Statistics 101 Course Outline

I. **Introduction**
    A. Basic statistics—use and purposes
    B. Data gathering
        1. Instruments
        2. Recorded data
        3. Machine utilization

II. **Presenting Data**
    A. Tables
        1. Summary tables
            a. Table elements
            b. Tables with averages
    B. Graphs
        1. Types of graphs
            a. Bar
            b. Pie chart
            c. Line graph
        2. Data presentation with graphs
    C. Frequency distributions
        1. Discrete and continuous
        2. Class intervals

III. **Descriptions and Comparison of Distributions**
    A. Percentiles
        1. Computation of percentile
        2. Inter-percentile range
        3. Percentile score
    B. Mean and standard deviations
        1. Computation of mean
            a. From grouped data
            b. From arbitrary origin
        2. Variance formulas

C. Frequency distributions
    1. Measures of central tendency
    2. Symmetry and skews
    3. Bimodal distributions
IV. Predictive or Estimate Techniques
  A. Regression
    1. Graphic application
    2. Assumption of linearity
  B. Correlation
    1. Computation of correlation coefficient
    2. Reliability of measurement
  C. Circumstances affecting regression and analysis
    1. Errors of measurement
    2. Effect of range
    3. Interpretation of size
V. The Normal Curve and Statistical Inference
  A. The normal distribution
    1. Mean
    2. Standard deviation
    3. Characteristics
  B. Statistical inference
    1. Employing samples
      a. Randomness
      b. Parameters
    2. Normal Distribution
      a. Standard errors
      b. Unbiased estimate
      c. Confidence interval
  C. Testing hypothesis
    1. Definition of statistical hypothesis
    2. Test of hypothesis
      a. Level of significance
      b. One-sided test
    3. Computing power of test

The Course Syllabus

A syllabus is defined in the dictionary as *"a concise statement of the main points of a course of study or subject."* Although this definition leaves room for interpretation, i.e. what constitutes "concise" and what constitutes "the main points", one thing is certain: *the syllabus is the official document of the course.*

> *As a permanent contribution to the institution's instructional archives, your syllabus is a contract between the institution and your students with the completion of the syllabus requirements determining their course grade. Thus, it is probably the most important document in the educational process.*

Confusion in academia concerning syllabi arises when faculty members interpret the word syllabus differently. For example, a concise statement to one faculty member may simply mean "Chapter V." Whereas to another faculty member the concise statement may mean enumerating the major points of Chapter V, describing each point, and writing a complete sentence for each. Often you will have access to other syllabi for the course you are teaching on which you can base your own course syllabus.

However, sometimes part-time faculty will encounter situations where a syllabus is not available. There are two reasons for this: course development and presentation have been left completely to an individual faculty member who is not required to provide this information to the institution, or part-time faculty may be teaching a new or recently revised course for which no syllabus has been developed. In either case, with or without sample syllabi, you must construct a syllabus for your course.

Development of the syllabus is a multi-step process. A good syllabus has several major parts:

- The complete name of the course, including the course number and catalog description

- The name and title by which the faculty member wishes to be addressed

- The faculty member's office hours

- The text(s) and other materials required

- The course objectives

- The student assignments and projects

- The course requirements and grading standards

- A complete listing of resources, outside readings, and field trips

- The evaluation plan

Items one through four are self-explanatory or should be available from the academic department staff. However, items five through nine require some explanation.

- **Course Objectives.** The first major part of the syllabus is the presentation of the course objectives. Listing the objectives for a course is often difficult for new faculty members. The tendency is to include everything you think is important to the course. This dilutes the objectives and often makes them too confusing or overwhelming for the student. As a rule, most courses can be adequately described by developing not more than ten to fourteen objectives.

> *One must be certain, however, that the objectives are reachable, teachable, and that student learning activities can be directed to each.*

- **Student Activities.** Following the course objectives, the syllabus should describe the student activities needed to meet the course requirements, including detailed specific activities, such as outside reading, laboratory activities, projects, and other assignments. Describe these activities in a way that relates directly to the objectives. Significant attention should be given to the reasons for the activities and how they relate to the course. This approach tells students that the class is all business and that there is a purpose for everything.

- **Course Requirements.** Next, the syllabus should include a detailed description of the course requirements and student responsibilities. This is one of the most important parts of the syllabus because it defines exactly what is expected to succeed in the class. It eliminates the possibility that students will claim ignorance of what was expected. In fact, it is useful in this section of the syllabus to list the class meetings by day and date as well as the reading and homework assignments and class topics to be addressed each meeting. Many experienced faculty members have felt that this detail was not necessary until they found themselves in an indefensible position concerning student accusations that the course content was not adequately covered. Sometimes this section of the syllabus is broken into two or more parts; the general rule is that excessive detail is better than too little detail.

- **Resources and References.** Finally, the syllabus should include a complete list of resources, outside readings, bibliographies, and other outside activities. Required outside readings and library reserve assignments should be specified. You need not be concerned if the syllabus eventually grows into a document of several pages. The students will appreciate your efforts, and you will be adequately protected if evidence of course content or teacher preparation is needed.

Distribute the syllabus the first day of class and take time to discuss the syllabus and any additional details. In fact, it is a good practice to review the syllabus on the second class meeting, noting the importance of the activities, assignments, and objectives, and address any student questions. The importance of the syllabus to students can best be exemplified by a recent experience of the author while teaching a summer class. Before the second class session I was approached by a student, who had missed the first session, with a request for a copy of my syllabus and course outline—a sign of the rising expectations of students.

A good syllabus requires considerable work initially but minimal time in subsequent updates. Work put into the development of the syllabus will pay dividends. A syllabus is a scientific document and a work of art, and it should be shown that respect in its development and use.

Figure 4.2 is one of numerous syllabi formats that may be used. In some institutions the syllabus format is rigid and faculty are expected to adhere to it. In other situations faculty are permitted the flexibility of developing their own format as long as it is complete and specifies student requirements. In some situations the course outline may be included as part of the syllabus rather than as a separate document. Other items that may be included are: required materials, assignments, course philosophy, and classroom assessment procedures (Bianco-Mathis, 1996).

Another style of syllabus construction emphasizes three major parts. They are: the general course and instructor information, the specific course requirements, and college policies. Specific course requirements may include a listing of all required materials, the course rationale, course learning outcomes, assessment, and a brief summary of instructional methods. Under "college policies," important information needs to be included such as registration policy, student withdrawal policy, inclement weather policy and fees and refunds and well as term calendar (Stephan, 2000).

Figure 4.2—Sample Course Syllabus

Achievement University
Syllabus
Name of Course: English 101-33241
Instructor: Dr. Dennis
Office: B151
Phone: 987-5037 (Office)
dgabrie@ ibm5060.ccc.edu (Internet address)
fax 987-5050
Office Hours: M-F 9:00 to 10:00
M,W, F: 12:00 to 2:00 (by appointment)
Lecture hours: 3
Lab hours: 0

Class requirements:
All papers must be typed or written on a word processor. Papers may be revised for a higher grade. Use the MLA format for all papers. Plan to spend three to four hours each week in the computer lab.

Course description (per catalog): Study and practice in the principles of good writing.

Performance objectives:
1. The student will organize and clarify the principles of basic written communication.
2. The student will complete critical readings as a basis for completion of his/her writing.
3. The student will develop and increase skills in expository and argumentative writing.

Essay patterns:
   Narrative
   Expository (analysis, contrast, cause-effect)
   Argument

Schedule:
January
10   Introduction to the course
     Diagnostic essay
     Homework: read chs. 1, 2. (handbook)
17   Discuss essay patterns, Ch. 2
     Return diagnostic essay w/ comments
     Discuss essay 1: narrative
     Hmwk: read Ch. 3
24   Discuss subordination, Ch. 3
     Discuss variety and details, Ch. 3
     assign essay 2
     Essay 1 due
     Hmwk: Ch. 4

31 Discuss writing the introduction, conclusion Ch. 4
    Crash Course in Phonics: Punctuation (handout)
    Discuss essay 2
    Hmwk: Ch. 5

February

7   Subject and verb agreement
    Usage problems
    Essay 2 due
    Hmwk: Ch. 6

14 Support paragraphs
    Developing topics
    Assign essay 3
    Hmwk: Ch. 7

21 Using the exact word
    Punctuation problems
    Essay 3 due

28 Pronoun and antecedent
    Usage problems
    Assign essay 4
    Hmwk: Ch. 9

March

7   Writing a paper for a literature class
    Essay 4 due
    Writing across the curriculum
    Hmwk: Ch. 10

14 Discuss topic for final exam
    Review course goals, objectives
    Hmwk: Outline final exam

Textbooks: *The Compact Handbook*
        American Heritage Dictionary, 3e
    Supplemental materials: 3.5" HD disk
    Suggested daily/weekly readings: *New York Times*
                        Newsweek magazine
                        Wall Street Journal

Last day to drop class: 4 March

Attendance policy: Attendance in class is important. To that end, quizzes may NOT be made up.

Final grade: Quizzes   20% (one per week)

Essay 1	10%	(due 1/24)
Essay 2	20%	(due 2/7)
Essay 3	20%	(due 2/21)
Essay 4	10%	(due 3/7)
Final exam	20%	(3/21, 8 to 10 AM)

The Lesson Plan

A lesson plan is a must for all teachers because it acts as a reference and guide for each class meeting. A flexible lesson plan allows for discussion of appropriate current events and provides a backup system if multimedia materials or equipment do not arrive or suffer a mechanical or electrical malfunction. The plan contains important questions and quotes from supplemental material not contained in the text, and should include definitions, comments on the purposes of the class, and student and teacher activities.

Make every effort to have lesson plans reflect your creative endeavors and unique abilities as a teacher. Often, the syllabus and to some extent the course outline are dictated to faculty. The demands for accountability and institutional goals sometimes restrict these two documents. Lesson plans, however, allow greater flexibility and permit techniques and strategies unique to the instructor, including appropriate personal experiences and anecdotes.

After determining your objectives, you then outline the major topics that will be covered, including definitions and references to sources not in the textbook, in your daily lesson plans. Your lesson plan may include everything you need to take to the classroom such as notes, handouts, computer disks, software references, etc. (Stephan, 2000). Shown in figures 4.3 and 4.4 are examples of a lesson plan and a sample form. An effective method of planning a course is to construct a plan for each class meeting, number the lessons, place them in a loose-leaf binder, and maintain them as a record and a guide for activities.

Figure 4.3—Sample Lesson Plan

Course # and Name: Algebra 101
Date_____
Session #9
Class Objectives:
1. To demonstrate equations through the use of various expressions of equality
2. To prove equality of expressions through technique of substitution
Definitions:
1. *Equation* is a statement that two expressions are equal
2. *Expression* is a mathematical statement
3. *Linear equation* is equation of 1st order
Student Activities:
1. Complete sample problems in class
2. Demonstrate competence of sample by board work
Instructor Activities:
1. Demonstrate validity of solution of equations
2. Assure student understanding by personal observations by seat and board work
Major Impact:
Understand the solution of basic linear equations.
Assignment: Problems—Exercise 8, pp. 41-42.

Figure 4.4—Suggested Lesson Plan Format

Course number and Name_____Date_____
(after first page simply number chronologically)
Session #_____
Definitions to be covered_____
_____
Class objective(s)_____
_____
Student activities or exercises_____
_____
Instructor activities_____
_____
Major impact or thought_____
Assignment_____
_____

TEACHING TECHNIQUES, INSTRUCTIONAL AIDS, TESTING

Once you have made the decision concerning your objectives for the course, the next step is to choose the instructional methods and strategies necessary to carry them out. In examining these teaching strategies and techniques, you should ask yourself the following questions:

- When should I teach by demonstration and when should I encourage students to try it themselves?

- When should I explain important topics and issues verbally and when should I prepare handouts for discussion?

- When should I lecture and when should I use question-and-answer strategies?

- When should I use audiovisual aids to support my points in discussion and lecture?

- When should I utilize multimedia technology and associated strategies to enhance my teaching?

In this chapter we will discuss some of the more common techniques, teaching aids, and evaluation procedures utilized in today's classrooms. These techniques, although not necessarily new or innovative, have proven valuable over the years to successful teachers. By utilizing a variety of teaching techniques, instructors can vary their students' learning experiences and generate excitement in the classroom.

Teaching Techniques

Successful teaching depends to a certain degree upon the initiative, creativity, and risk-taking prowess of the instructor. Even instructors with these characteristics, however, must use a variety of techniques and approaches to be successful. Some of the more common techniques used by successful teachers include:

Instructor-Based Techniques	Student-Based Techniques
Lectures	Active Learning
Class Discussions	Collaborative Learning
Question/Answer Sessions	Role Playing
Demonstrations	Buzz Groups
Guest Lecturers	Student Panels
Quality Control Circles	Oral Reports/Projects
	Lab Assignments
	Learning Cells

Out-of-Class Activities

Field Trips/Site Visits
Journal/Publication Readings
Term Papers/Research Projects
Outside Assignments
Case Studies
Internet Research

Traditional Instructional Aids	Technology-Driven Aids
Handouts	Videos/Films
Chalkboards/Whiteboards	Overhead Projection
Flipcharts	Computer Projection
Lecture Notes	Multimedia Presentations

These are but some of the possible activities to facilitate classroom instruction. You might start by checking off those techniques that you have used then go on to the more detailed descriptions of these classroom activities.

Instructor-Based Techniques
The Lecture

Extensive preparation and refinement are required to present a successful lecture. Although the lecture has long been recognized as one of the more appropriate ways to convey information, there is often a fine line between "telling" students and "presenting" a lecture. Historically, the lecture was intended for highly motivated and informed listeners who attended to hear a specific topic discussed. Today it has been adapted to nearly every classroom situation. The modern lecture frequently involves the integration of technology and other activities to form a total presentation.

A good lecture contributes the following to any teaching situation:

1. Lectures convey large amounts of information in a short period of time.
2. Lectures develop student interest in a subject.
3. Lectures maximize instructor control over the material and procedures.
4. Lectures present up-to-date facts not available in the text or other course materials.
5. Due to their passive nature, lectures cause minimum anxiety to students.

On the other hand, some of these advantages can lead to the disadvantages inherent in lecturing. They are:

1. Lectures place students in a passive and nonparticipative role.
2. Lectures assume that all students are learning and listening at the same pace and competency level.
3. Lectures do not normally contribute to higher levels of learning such as application, analysis, and synthesis.
4. Lectures can obstruct effective student feedback, especially in large classes.
5. Lecture material retention rates are significantly lower than other teaching techniques.

Listed below are several suggestions for building a successful lecture:

- Plan an expansive introduction of the lecture which encompasses: the purpose of the lecture, the statement or series of questions which will be addressed, possibly an anecdote concerning the purpose of the lecture, and problems to be addressed.

- Take a few moments to research and analyze your class prior to the introduction. With the diversity of ages and backgrounds of the students of today, it is important that the lecture considers the recipients' status.

- In addition to course objectives, have specific objectives identified to yourself for the lecture you are presenting.

- Do not read/refer to notes.

- Do not read from the text.

- Over-prepare. It will enhance your confidence.

- Use gestures. Remember a palm up is positive and down is negative.

- Encourage students to interrupt.

- Assist students in taking notes. Provide outlines and/or pause for note taking.

- Document references verbally, giving students time to write down the reference information and guide them to the reference documents.

- Prepare anecdotes and questions.

- Don't depend upon memory, write it down.

- Move around. Don't stand in one place or behind a lectern.

- Tell them what you are going to tell them, tell them, then tell them what you told them.

- Refer to examples or other topics.

- Tell them at the start what your intentions are and when you are changing topics.

- Summarize—it is important that the lecture be summarized, reviewing the main points and outlining the progress made from the beginning of the lecture to the end. Restate your expectations of what the students have gained from the day's session.

Lecture Techniques. Studies have shown that students retain more of the material presented in the early part of the lecture and less in the later phases. Thus, it is important that significant points are made early and then reinforced by activity later in the presentation. There are several methods to improve lectures. Adequate preparation with appropriate support of references, anecdotes, and handouts will enhance the effectiveness of the lecture. Depending upon memory for such support may prove ineffective; therefore, references, etc., should be written as part of the lecture notes. Physical appearance is also important, a business-like approach and dress will pay off while an unkempt appearance will negate hours of diligent preparation. Cue the class to the major points to be stressed in the presentation. Allow students time to take notes. Provide a complete summary with repetition and reinforcement of important points. It is important that vocabulary and definitions be explained. Avoid buzz words and jargon. Use the chalkboard and other visual techniques as necessary.

A lecture does not mean that only the instructor talks. It is important that time be allowed during the lecture for student feedback, questions, and discussions.

There are general guidelines to keep in mind when presenting the lecture. Although they are basic and well known, they are worth repeating here.

- Make certain your lecture is organized and presented in an orderly manner. Too often students are critical of instructors who appear to be rambling.

- Using illustrations throughout the lecture is an indication of a well organized lecture which the presenter is taking seriously.

- It is important that you remember to speak clearly and directly to the audience.

- Give mental breaks every ten minutes or so; that is, change the procedure by using an anecdote or activity so that the lecture is not a continuous one-way dialog.

- If you have a tendency to use distracters or mannerisms such as "you know" or "OK", be aware and avoid them.

- Use the chalk board, overhead, or any prop that you feel appropriate to enhance your lecture.

- Finally, do not hesitate to build "thinking pauses" into your lectures so your students have time mentally to catch their breath.

Discussion

Discussions are important to any interactive learning environment. They help students to formulate logic in understanding and lead to higher order learning. They allow students to identify problems and to use other members of the group as resources. This is especially important in today's diverse classroom, where older experienced adults and younger students will be sitting side by side in your class.

When stimulating class discussions, you quickly realize that this must be planned the same as any other classroom activity. Too often there is the tendency to "wait for the discussion to happen". This often leads to a lack of discussion or discussions that are not related

to the topic at hand. One discussion technique is to start with a common experience. The experience might be a current event, a common problem to be solved, or a controversial issue. It may be necessary to place students in small groups, give them a topic, and have them find a solution or develop a hypothesis. Then each group can interact and question each other's findings.

Preparation for a full-class discussion requires planning as well as review of the day's topics. If the topic has been discussed with your previous classes, draw from that experience or even give some of the previous classes' conclusions and have the present class react to them. When leading the discussion, give all students the opportunity to speak. If one or two students monopolize the discussion you may wish to take their comments and ask the rest of the class to respond to them.

If there is a lull in the discussion, sometimes it is best to let the silence continue for awhile; usually there are students in the class that will feel a need to break the silence.

Urge students to talk to each other and not to you, the instructor, and if there are students who do not participate, be cognizant of that and ask them to respond to other student's comments. In leading discussions, more than any other situation in the interactive classroom, you must remember that you are a facilitator of learning and not the director of learning.

Question/Answer

Questioning students is an important tool for stimulating classroom participation and motivating students. Experienced teachers make it a rule to question as many different students as possible during a class session. Besides encouraging student participation and arousing student curiosity, questioning students is an effective way to gauge their preparation for class as well as their progress and understanding of the class topic. Eliciting answers can develop student

confidence in self-expression. The right kinds of questions can also encourage higher orders of learning such as analysis, synthesis, and evaluation.

There is hardly a disadvantage associated with questioning if good judgment is exercised. Appropriate timing is important—pace questions so students have time to phrase their answers. For example, it would be unkind to continue to question a student who is embarrassed or is having difficulty responding. Such students need to be "brought along" in the classroom.

Good questioning involves several strategies:

- *Use open-ended questions when possible, that is, do not use questions that have a yes/no answer.*

- *Use questions that elicit a comment or additional queries from students, even to the point of saying to a student, "What do you think of that?"*

- *Questions should be part of the lesson plan. Prepare them ahead of time—don't wait for them to "happen."*

Different types of questions have different purposes. They are usually found in four categories: knowledge, content, discussion, and stimulation. For example,

- a **knowledge question** might be: "What is a spreadsheet?"

- a **content question** might be: "What are the functions of a spreadsheet?"

- a **discussion question** might be: "What are the advantages and disadvantages of using a spreadsheet?"

- a **stimulation question** might be: "How can spreadsheets enhance your job accuracy?" This may be followed with "Why do you think this?"

One would not normally pose questions as a form of graded evaluation because this intimidates students and typically negates the purpose of asking the question. Whenever possible, questions should be

addressed to individuals by name rather than to the whole class. If your class is giving you the silent treatment, a quick question and answer can bail you out.

Another benefit to using questions and answers is the way it encourages students to ask questions of their own. Skillful questioning stimulates students to respond with questions that show higher levels of thinking.

Encouraging student questioning means eliminating any threat to the questioner. Sometimes teachers, without knowing, discourage student questioning by moving so quickly through the course material that they don't appear to have time to consider a question. Some teachers may actually say "hold your questions until the end of class". This is not only discouraging; it also runs the risk that the student will forget a question valuable to the class discussion.

Some of the techniques involved in encouraging questions from students include:

- show complete respect for any questions or comments made by students,
- specifically ask students questions during the presentation,
- use probing questions with the students,
- ask students if they need clarification on any points or issues,
- ask students to give the pros and cons of a particular issue or point, and
- have other students ask questions concerning the response.

The Demonstration

For classes that lend themselves to this technique, a demonstration is an effective way to teach skills because it combines hearing with seeing. Research shows that nearly 90% of learning takes place

when both of these two senses are involved. Demonstration has other advantages:

- It is motivational.
- It attracts attention and can be presented to groups or to individual students.
- It is effective for large group instruction.

The demonstration is probably under-utilized as a teaching tool. To be successful, demonstration requires extensive preparation. To adequately prepare, you should simulate the demonstration prior to the class presentation. This allows you to examine the problems, be alert to possible difficulties, and even to forewarn the students that some steps are particularly difficult. Through this simple warning, the students will lend support and assist in making the demonstration successful.

Some guidelines for a successful demonstration include:

- Double-check that you have all materials and tools. (The most common flaw in classroom demonstrations is "something is missing.")
- Complete a checklist for materials and procedures as you perform the demonstration. Students can then "check" to assure correct procedure.
- State and distribute the objectives of the demonstration along with the expected outcomes.
- Have students write conclusions to the demonstration.

Although demonstrations carry the risk of failure; this is a small risk as compared to the benefits gained by showing as well as telling. Students normally will be less critical of teachers who are not successful when attempting complicated techniques. They are much more critical of boring repetitious classes.

The Guest Lecturer

In most college classrooms, guest lecturers are under-utilized. Most communities are rich with individuals who are willing, usually at no charge, to share their experiences and expertise. Our rapidly changing world makes it nearly impossible for faculty members to remain current on all issues. Inviting individuals who are on the cutting edge of changes in business, industry and community agencies to speak not only provides information but also a glimpse of the "real world" of work. Again, it is necessary to structure such a visitation so that students are aware of the objectives of the activity.

Beware of the danger that students will become a listening audience rather than questioning participants; students need to either prepare questions prior to the visit or be given time after the guest lecturer speaks to compose questions. You should also be sure to brief the guest lecturer on the objectives and intent of the visit and to act as mediator between students and lecturer.

Quality Control Circles

Quality control circles are one of the most dynamic and interesting concepts that has evolved in the past decade. It is a management technique generally credited to the Japanese (Weimer, 1990). This technique can be very effective with adult students because it requires the involvement of employees (students) in some of the class decision-making activities. It is a relatively simple process and is especially helpful for part-time teachers who do not have daily contact with students.

During the first class session, the instructor asks for five or six volunteers to join the quality circle. The group meets periodically with the instructor, possibly during a class break or after class, to provide feedback concerning the progress of the class. The feedback might include comments concerning lecture, discussion, homework, testing, or other class activities. This process provides an ongoing feedback mechanism that involves students. It will also provide stu-

dent support as you implement the circle's suggestions in the class presentation.

Student-Based Techniques
Active Learning

If you have recently read professional literature or attended faculty development workshops, you have heard the expression "active learning". You may wonder, is this strategy significantly different from learning strategies of the past? Basically, active student learning dictates that the personal learning needs of the students override the instructor/discipline-oriented learning of the past. In this scenario, the teacher develops a learning environment where students actively talk, listen and react to the course content through group activities, role playing, cooperative learning, and other student interaction techniques. The purpose of these activities is for students to apply what they are learning by sharing with other students.

In active learning, students are no longer passive participants but become responsible for their own learning. This provides students opportunities to collaborate and cooperate with others, rather than competing. Critical thinking skills are emphasized as well as an increased opportunity for students to express their values and understanding of their culture.

As you consider these interactive student-centered techniques, you may be tempted to ask, "don't all teachers do these things?" The answer is no; regardless of the emphasis placed upon varying teaching techniques and student involvement, studies still show that the teacher does over 60% of the talking in class.

Active learning techniques are applicable for all disciplines. In implementing these techniques it is important to recognize that the instructor's role is as a facilitator rather than as a director of learning. The instructor as a facilitator must establish rapport with the class and encourage and stimulate student discussion. Treating students with respect and showing a sense of humor and patience will help to establish this kind of environment. Students need to understand that

their questions and comments are valuable and that they will not be ridiculed for seemingly inappropriate observations or questions.

Very often nonverbal cues can be used by the instructor to relax the students. Talking directly to and walking toward the students who are raising questions or issues shows the entire class you respect them. A nod of the head or a concentrated look conveys a similar message that you are interested or understand. Moving around the room, looking relaxed and actually joining the class is another valuable nonverbal activity.

Cooperative/Collaborative Learning

Cooperative learning (also called collaborative learning), is one of the oldest educational techniques. In theory, cooperative learning brings students with differing abilities together into small groups where they teach each other the concepts of the class by reinforcing lecture and text materials. In practice, students either work on specific projects cooperatively or take selected quizzes and/or tests together. The process forces all students to become actively involved in classroom activities. Adult learners relate to cooperation in the classroom because of the cooperation required in most workplaces.

To effectively use cooperative learning techniques, you must spend considerable time structuring the situation so that students understand their roles as well as the objectives of the group.

A good cooperative learning group needs several conditions, that:

- all students must participate,

- a method to capture the individual member participation be used, and

- a written product must be the result.

For instructors, the two basic requirements for cooperative learning are thorough planning and a total commitment.

As a facilitator the instructor becomes an idea person, a resource person, a mediator (conflict resolution is as much an accomplishment in cooperative education as it is in the workplace or in life itself), and a supporter of students' efforts. Virtually all academic and technical disciplines can benefit from this technique.

Preliminary planning includes a discussion of classroom goals, specific activities that can be assigned cooperatively, and the balance sought between traditional and cooperative classroom activities. If grades are going to be assigned for group work the students must be made aware of this at the beginning of the term; the assignment of the same grade to each member of a group is the incentive needed to make cooperative learning work effectively.

The optimum size for a work group is four or five students; more students can be unwieldy while fewer opens the door to domineering students. Groups can be formed by:

- students themselves,

- the instructor assigning students to a group,

- random assignment, or

- selection based upon similar interests or specific criteria.

Typically, instructors should assign students, rather than allowing them to form their own groups.

Decided disadvantages of student-based selection are that students may choose to be with friends, thus excluding assimilation of new students into the mainstream of the class, and there may be stress in arranging groups if students do not know each other and have no basis for selection.

The benefits of cooperative learning include: adults have a vehicle to get to know others in class; attendance tends to be better (a result of a commitment to the group); improved grades due to an increased understanding of the subject matter; classroom groups lead to study groups outside of class; and students become participants in their own learning.

Instructors must regularly re-evaluate their classroom styles to accommodate changes in technology, abilities of students, and demands of students. Cooperative learning is but one of many viable strategies to encourage participation by students. Obstacles that might be encountered are: some students feel they have paid money to take the course, therefore the teacher is expected to stand in front of the class and lecture; groups may not take an assignment seriously; and some individuals may have difficulty working within a group. However, problems can be overcome by involving students in decisions regarding cooperative activities and adapting the assignments to the students in the class.

Adults are sensitive to how others view them and tend to be more candid when working in small groups; working with fellow students provides adults the opportunity to grow within the small group until they are ready to face larger groups (Sego, 1996).

The Student Panel

A student panel can be used as an alternative to lecturing by giving groups of students the opportunity to do the presenting. However, it must be structured so the specific objectives of the assignment are clearly defined prior to the panel presentation. Normally, a panel should consist of two to four members. Each member of the panel should be assigned specific topics or issues to be presented and/or defended. After the presentation, the rest of the class should be divided into discussion groups so these students can define their positions on the panel's topic. Instructors should remember to help students in developing open-ended questions for the rest of the class. A carefully structured panel is a valuable learning experience for the participants as well as the class.

The Learning Cell

In learning cells, students work in pairs to help each other learn; typically, the entire class is paired off for this activity. The pairs can work together in many different ways. It may involve an reading assignment in which the students share what they have read and then develop questions to present to one another. In this case they are demonstrating their reading comprehension and understanding of the issues while sharing their responses. Another possibility uses an open-question format where students can exercise their creativity in their responses or in a problem-solving situation. During the process the teacher moves about the room, going from pair to pair, seeking feedback and answering questions. Learning cells may be term-long assignments of students in pairs or may be assigned for a single class meeting.

Buzz Groups

As an in-class activity, the buzz group's purpose is to solve a specific problem or compare and contrast an issue. The instructor identifies the discussion topic or problem and allows students to form small groups, usually of three to five students. The students are given the freedom to develop their own discussion guidelines for reaching a solution to the issue. The solution is prepared for presentation, possibly on a flipchart or overhead transparency for the following class session. Occasionally the instructor may have a solution prepared and use it as a discussion of the differences between the student buzz group's and the instructor's conclusions.

Buzz groups should not be confused with small group projects. Buzz groups are as a quick conclusion activity that takes 10 to 15 minutes of class time.

Out-of-Class Activities

Outside Readings/Written Assignments

Outside readings and additional assignments can be used by part-time instructors in several ways. Since neither the instructor nor the student is on campus for extensive library use, outside readings and references should be listed in the syllabus. It will aid part-time students significantly if materials and periodicals selected are available in public libraries or on the Internet. The preparation of handouts with reference numbers will also assist students. This allows students to spend their time in the library actually using the materials rather than searching for them. Again, being specific in terms of the topic and objectives (and points counted toward the grade) are necessary for a successful outside reading assignment.

The Project

Student projects are one way students can get the opportunity to learn outside the classroom. Projects may consist of in-depth research into a class topic or a community-based activity such as agency visitations, interviews, or case studies. A properly developed project should allow students to choose from a variety of related activities within their own sphere of interest. After topics are selected, instructor expectations for completion of the project should be clarified. The project should weigh significantly in the final evaluation and assignment of a grade.

The Case Study

Traditionally case studies have been used mainly in sociology or psychology classes. The case study may, however, be used in many other disciplines. Students may be given case studies of individuals or processes in finance, investing, historic contrast, geology or other class situations. In a good case study, the instructor establishes the scenario, the objectives of the case, and the problem(s) that may be encountered. Students may then be given time to read and research the project and write their case paper or make an oral presentation

which can result in student discussions to reach consensus or a conclusion. Case studies are normally assigned to individual students and not to groups.

Field Trips

Field trips should be planned so that the entire session of the field trip is on location. The class activities and trip objectives should be outlined prior to the trip. Arrange the class in small groups, specify to the students what they are to observe. At the conclusion of the visit, meet to discuss the major points observed and any conclusions to be made. The most effective field trips include credit toward the grade and require a written or oral report.

Large Group Instruction

Although not a specific classroom technique, there are several strategies to improve large group instruction. Large classes are more impersonal and usually more difficult to teach. Successful large classes require greater preparation of materials, including more handouts and visual aids. The importance of a well-prepared lecture takes on added importance in large group instruction.

Some suggestions for easing the burden of teaching large classes include:

- **start out positively** by indicating that although large, the class is important and you are glad to be there;
- **keep a seating chart;**
- **try to learn a few student names each day,** walk around the large classroom and try to identify students with whom you have had discussions;
- **use techniques such as buzz groups, panels, collaborative learning**—don't assume that standard strategies do not work;

- **utilize the cell or partner format.** In a class of 100, utilizing cells reduces responses to 50; or utilize cooperative learning strategies. Again in a class of 100, using this technique will reduce the class to the equivalent of 20 students;

- **share your research, anecdotes, and background.** With a large class, chances are that someone in your class may have had similar experiences and might be willing to share them;

- **utilize the overhead projector, videos, and all types of technology** to vary the teaching activities;

- **use modern technology to communicate with your students.** Use your e-mail to share pertinent questions with all students. Or create a chatroom, bulletin board, or listserv. Be sure to share the responses with the rest of your class;

- **involve students** by asking for a show of hands or holding up colored cards (green for "I understand", red for "I don't understand");

- **have students write a brief response** paragraph to major questions and have them hand it in;

- **at the end of class ask students to drop a written question** to you on the way out, and at the beginning of the next class use the question to commence discussions;

- **keep students involved by giving short quizzes** (maybe ungraded) and use a show of hands to get feedback on the correct responses;

- **clearly identify major points and questions;**

- **arrange a 20-minute discussion group** before and/or after class for students who are having trouble in a large group setting; and

- **move around**—up the aisles and around the room as you lecture.

It is important that active techniques be utilized in large classes. Many teachers have a tendency to "give up" the interactive student responses, thinking that it is impossible in large group instruction.

Instructional Aids

Modern technology has opened a new vista of tools for use in the modern classroom. The comphrensive multimedia presentation requiring considerable training and support materials such as computer hardware and software is described in greater detail in Chapter 6. A brief review of the traditional instructional aids is contained herein.

Overhead Transparencies

The overhead projector has become one of the most popular support tools in education because it allows instructors to face the class while showing images on the screen using normal room lighting. Overhead projectors are inexpensive and are usually readily available from the academic division office or the audio-visual department. Some projectors are equipped with a roll that provides a continuous writing surface. This enables the retention of information on the roll in the event students later wish to discuss specific points and is especially useful in mathematics, engineering, etc. classes.

There is no limit to the artistic excellence that can be produced on a transparency. Many faculty members easily prepare their own transparencies. Transparencies may be typewritten, handwritten, computer-generated, or drawn on standard-size plain white paper and instantaneously produced on a standard copier. Many times it is worth the extra effort to make a professional-looking overhead transparency. They are easily maintained, durable, and thus can be a permanent part of future presentations.

Videotape

Probably the most effective modern instructional aid is the videotape. With the reduction in cost of camcorders and tape itself, the possibilities for expanded use are nearly endless. Most institutions now have equipment for instructors who wish to develop their own video clips as well as a library of tapes that may be applicable to your class. Videos are not only attention getters, but provide the opportunity for direct student involvement when students produce their own videos. However, instructors must indicate to the students the objectives behind any videos and combine the video with discussion, a written report, or other activity.

Flipchart

A commonly used visual aid for business seminars is a simple flipchart. When adapted to the classroom, the flipchart has many advantages over a chalkboard or overhead projector. The flipchart, a large tablet with pages that can be flipped vertically, is especially useful for small groups to record their discussions and conclusions. Instructors can record major points of a presentation and have room to add notes, descriptions, or comments. The information can then be retained by tearing off the page and taping it to the wall for future reference. A flipchart and felt-tip pen can be one of the most effective tools in the active classroom.

 NOTE: When planning on an instructional aid, be sure you have all the equipment you require before the class begins whether it's chalk, markers, flipchart easels, masking tape, or the TV/VCR to show your tape.

Handouts

Although sometimes overused in the past, handouts are still a valuable instrument for instructors. Modern copy technology along with computers and printers make preparing and updating easy. Handouts should be used for material that students will need for reference, such as important definitions, computations, or position statements for discussion. Handouts for lecture purposes should con-

tain only an outline of the material discussed with space for students to add their own comments.

 A serious note of caution: be careful of copyright violations! Your supervisor or department head should be able to provide you with the Fair Use guidelines you will need to follow.

Tests and Testing

There are multiple reasons for testing students. First and foremost is the evaluation to assist in the assignment for the total grade. In addition, however, tests serve multiple purposes. Testing communicates to the instructor if the course objectives are being met and to what degree. Of equal importance, tests are used as an instructional tool and a learning device for students. When tests are used for evaluation you must be careful to inform the students at the beginning of the class of the testing procedure, when they will be given, and the criteria upon which they will be based. Too often students are overheard criticizing their instructors with, "they didn't test over what they talked about in class."

Test/Question Types

The major types of tests used in college classes are: essay, multiple-choice, and recall. In special circumstances, performance, oral, and short answer tests may also be utilized.

Essay Tests/Questions. Essay tests are still one of the most popular of colleges tests. They are effective at any level of the learning hierarchy. Although essay tests require considerable time for students to respond, they do give an in-depth perspective of overall student ability. There are several factors to remember when writing test questions that require essay answers. Most important is that essay questions should be related to the written course objectives. They should incorporate a significant amount of content, including discussion, contrasting, comparing, etc. Finally, you must be certain that in terms of vocabulary, content, and subject covered, the student has sufficient

background to respond adequately to the question being asked and that the question is not ambiguous or deceptive.

Grading essay questions presents the greatest problem. You must keep in mind that essay questions are asking students to be objective, yet justify their answers. The appropriate way to judge an essay response is to list important items for the response and prioritize them, assigning more points to the highest priority. Assigning points to the prioritized criteria will then lead to a degree of grading objectivity.

 You must be cautious, however, that essay questions do not ask for student opinions since it's impossible to assign evaluation points to opinions.

Multiple-choice Tests/Questions. With the advent of computerized scoring and large classes, multiple-choice tests probably are the most used tests in college classrooms today. They not only are efficient in terms of time consumed, but with the use of item analysis, can determine question validity.

The development of multiple-choice questions is not a simple matter. The actual construction of the multiple-choice tests has several general guidelines, including:

- do not include answers that are obviously correct or incorrect, including impossible responses or distracters,
- be sure the correct answers are scattered throughout the response mechanism,
- provide four possible responses to minimize the guess factor,
- do not use "all of the above" or "none of the above,"
- do not use the terms never, always, likely, or similar adjectives that may divert the meaning for the student,
- be consistent with the format so that students are not confused with wording or punctuation changes, and
- keep choices approximately the same length since incorrect answers are frequently shorter than correct ones.

Disadvantages of multiple-choice tests are: they often test on only the knowledge level rather analysis and synthesis; they provide opportunity for guessing; and they depend primarily on recall and memory.

Recall and Completion Tests/Questions. Recall items may be posed as simple questions, completion, or brief response. Used too often, these tests tend to encourage students to memorize rather than understand. There are, however, advantages to recall tests. They are relatively simple to grade and construct; they can address a broad field of content; and they require specific recall rather than guessing or rationalization.

Some suggestions for developing recall questions are:
- Give information concerning the answer prior to the answer blank,
- Qualify information so students are clear about the response,
- Include responses at the analysis and synthesis level,
- Pose questions so that only one correct response is usable,
- Allow sufficient and equal space for the response,
- Avoid patterns of responses,
- Avoid direct quotes, and
- Avoid specific descriptors or adjectives.

 True/false questions are not commonly used at the college level any longer. Although they may have their place in a sampling of student responses or learning activity, they generally are not accepted as being objective or valid.

Assigning Grades
The Basics

Grading students is probably the most difficult task for faculty. All of the elements of teaching (preparation, presentation, and student activity) are reflected in the grading process. In addition, in an era of accountability, teachers are sometimes called upon to justify grades with documentation. Thus the establishment of firm criteria for grading is necessary. There are some general rules that are helpful in establishing the grading process. They are as follows:

- Communicate criteria clearly to the students.
- Include criteria other than test scores.
- Avoid irrelevant factors such as attendance and tardiness in the grading criteria.
- Place grading criteria carefully throughout the course.
- Weigh grading criteria carefully and always have a plan.
- Grade students on their achievement.

Many years ago, teachers used the technique of "grading on the curve." This placed students in competition with each other rather than cooperating in the learning experience. The practice has been abandoned in the modern classroom.

Evaluation Plan

In order to clearly delineate criteria for assignment of grades, it is helpful if you first develop an evaluation plan. An evaluation plan is a very simple device developed in a short worksheet form. The plan contains all of the factors that apply to the evaluation of the students. Across from these factors is listed a percentage of weight that will be assigned to various factors. A third column indicates the points received for each factor. A sample plan is shown in the figure 5.1.

Figure 5.1—Evaluation Chart

Grade Factors	Percentage of Final Grade	Possible Points	Points Received
Tests	60%	90	_____
Paper	20%	30	_____
Project	10%	10	_____
Class Participation	10%	15	_____
TOTALS	100%	150	_____

Note that this type of plan allows you the freedom to assign any number of points to any criteria or activity because the final percentage will always come out to 100%.

This documentation clearly indicates to the students the process by which evaluation is conducted in a businesslike and professional manner. Once the evaluation plan is completed, it is essential that it be included in the course syllabus since that is the official document of the course.

TEACHING AND LEARNING WITH TECHNOLOGY

This chapter is contributed by Gary Wheeler. We are grateful to him for sharing his expertise about educational technology and it applications for adjunct faculty. Gary Wheeler is the Associate Executive Director, Miami University, Middletown Campus, Ohio.

Introduction

Over the past decade educators have seen the increasing use of various kinds of technology in the college classroom with an accompanying challenge for appropriate and effective instruction. Technology that first was used in business and industry is now commonplace in the classroom. In much the way that overhead projectors were first used to great impact displaying individual scores in bowling alleys before being used to display text and charts to students during class, business productivity software is being adapted to the needs of education. Beyond word processing, commonly used computer software includes communication software (from simple e-mail to course management systems) and presentation software. There is so much data available via electronic networks that educators desperately need the ability to search for and find relevant information. The purpose of this chapter is to introduce instructors to what they need to know about these technologies and to provide tips on effective strategies to enhance student learning.

A widely used set of guidelines for classroom practice, "Seven Principles for Good Practice in Undergraduate Education," was published in the March 1987 issue of the *American Association for Higher Education Bulletin*. In 1997 authors Art Chickering and Steve

Ehrmann updated their seven principles with suggestions for using technology to enhance the original principles (Chickering & Ehrmann, 1997). Below are paraphrases of some of their arguments with particular application suggestions for the adjunct/part-time faculty member, following each of the seven principles:

1. **Good practice encourages contacts between students and faculty.**

    The use of electronic communications can provide an additional opportunity for students and faculty to contact each other. The opportunity to connect with and get to know a faculty member well helps a student make personal connections to the subject matter and make personal commitments for improved classroom behaviors and practices. Some students may find it easier to discuss individual responses to the academic material or to ask questions using a form of contact that is not face-to-face. Resources may be shared and distributed among the members of the class. Faculty may be able to offer additional assistance to students or provide a forum for discussion. Virtual office hours may be provided.

    The part-time faculty member is often one who does not have an office on campus or may not hold regular office hours beyond speaking with students immediately before or after classes. Their own time constraints make it difficult for them to spend much out-of-class time with students. Electronic communications technologies can provide a useful vehicle for part-time faculty to increase their contact with students effectively and efficiently.

2. **Good practice develops reciprocity and cooperation among students.**

    Student learning is improved and deepened when individuals work with and collaborate with others. Education is a social activity.

Among the skills most valued by business and industry is the ability to work as a member of a team. Similar to improved student/faculty contact leading to better student performance, it also is clear that student learning is improved and deepened by effective student interaction.

The use of technology, from groupware and e-mail to classroom management systems, provides a mechanism for increased interaction among students. Collaborative learning can be fostered by the use of existing technologies.

The issues for the part-time faculty regarding how to best promote student teamwork and collaboration center around having enough time in which to do team-based work and finding effective ways to encourage interaction while maintaining appropriate levels of classroom control. Technology provides effective solutions to both of these concerns.

3. **Good practice uses active learning techniques.**

   The commonly heard concern about the use of technology in the classroom—that it encourages passive learning by students—is more an issue related to the appropriate use of classroom strategies. There are many technologies that encourage active learning, from tools that feature learning by doing to real-time simulations to the incorporation of computer-based data in discovery science. The challenge is in helping faculty learn enough about the tools that encourage active learning and in encouraging them to employ active learning strategies in the classroom. Faculty teach by using a number of strategies, including lecture, use of textbooks and readings, discussions, practice exercises and activities, problem-solving and discovery-based work, field trips, and interactive opportunities. Technology can provide enrichment for each of these strategies.

Good active learning practice ensures that students have opportunities for putting into practice some of the ideas and concepts presented in class. Find ways to get students moving (intellectually) by giving them responsibility for finding information, for evaluating its relevance, for synthesizing disparate pieces of information, and for using the materials of the class to solve real-world problems. One strategy for part-time faculty to engage students in active learning is having students participate in organizing information that will be presented. While there are many ways to do this, one mechanism has students work in groups, organizing and deciding on which pieces of information will be presented in class, how it will be presented, and what problems are being addressed by this information. The in-class presentation can be made by the instructor or by the students themselves.

4. **Good practice gives prompt feedback.**

   Students need to recognize both what they know and what they do not—providing consistent and rapid feedback helps students by reinforcing correct knowledge and by pointing out where additional steps toward understanding need to be taken. There are many ways technology can provide appropriate feedback. These range from computer-based tutoring systems and simulations that give immediate responses to the use of e-mail to provide narrative feedback. Word processing programs can incorporate notations to student writing. Audio feedback can be sent as attachments e-mailed to students. Students can create electronic portfolios of their work, including their own self-assessments using text-based or audio/video systems and get feedback electronically from faculty and peers. Students can use e-mail to contact experts at distant sites for guidance and feedback.

   The effective part-time faculty member will encourage multiple mechanisms for providing feedback to students

throughout the course of study. Formative feedback can be enhanced by using technology to connect the student with peers, outside experts, and other faculty.

5. **Good practice emphasizes time-on-task.**

One of the more difficult tasks facing students today is time management. Making time to spend on class-related activities competes with time spent on employment, family responsibilities, commuting, recreation, and co-curricular or social activities among others. Technology enables students to work effectively whenever they choose using computer networks.

The time when students have the most energy for work does not always coincide with the time scheduled for classes. Students can work as a member of a team without spending the time coordinating schedules and meeting face-to-face. Time-on-task can be greater when the time expectations for students (and faculty) are adapted realistically to the schedules of modern life.

The part-time faculty member can establish specific guidelines for time-on-task as well as the qualitative time students spend with each other studying or interacting as a member of a group or team. Once guidelines are established and expected outcomes described, students can document their time-on-task as a part of their own development or to indicate the level of involvement with a project.

6. **Good practice communicates high expectations.**

High levels of achievement come from high levels of expectation. It is good practice to use technology for communicating and embodying high expectations. Significant work can be accomplished by incorporating compelling real-life problems, demonstrating the complexi-

ties of varying perspectives, and collecting information from a wide range of original sources and conflicting sets of data. The criteria for interacting with and interpreting data can be communicated effectively and widely among students throughout the course using technology and can include multiple examples and case studies via websites and models.

Part-time faculty members, whether teaching introductory or more advanced professional practice courses, should find ways to communicate their expectations and performance requirements using as many ways and modes of delivery as they do for course content. Simple declarations in class or in the syllabus are not enough. High expectations are communicated through how the classroom is managed, by the thoroughness of material presentation, and via the kinds of activities students are expected to accomplish. Technology provides a vehicle for regular reminders of expectations. It also can reinforce high expectations by enabling students to work with primary source materials and by providing a ready vehicle for demonstrating complex problems and solutions.

7. **Good practice respects diverse talents and ways of learning.**

    There is no one model for achieving excellence, based on modes of learning styles or personality types. Technology can enable self-paced learning; enriched projects for deeper understanding; multiple modes of expression that include data, audio, and video; and customized processes for student learning. While some percentage of students can do well while being instructed using the didactic model of the teacher lecturing, this model does not work for all—the typical lecture is not interactive nor does it encourage active learning or student reflection. It typically gives a single interpretation of materials and is more responsive to the perceived quality needs of the profession or discipline than the needs of the students who have diverse learning styles. Technology helps by enlarg-

ing the capabilities of all teachers by using presentation styles appropriate for the range of learning styles in today's classrooms.

Use the available technology to search for information on student learning styles and to find out more about the students in the class. Looking at the websites of area high schools and communities can provide useful insights into the kinds of places that have produced your students. Examine the demographics of the area. Find out the level of students' technology use and their level of comfort with technology. One lesson that is regularly learned by the faculty member who uses electronic communication (e-mail) with students is that those students who are less likely to speak up in class are likely to communicate more vigorously using e-mail. Another lesson is that students who had difficulty understanding complex concepts when these were presented orally, often learn these same concepts more easily and deeply when the presentation mode is visual, interactive, and employs active learning strategies.

Communicating with Students

Communicating with students goes beyond the expected in-class activity of the faculty member telling information and eliciting responses. Strategies for promoting student learning need to include multiple means for effectively communicating with students. This communication needs to be a two-way interaction, enabling the instructor and students to share information, discuss ideas, and to evaluate together the issues being examined in the course.

Technology-based strategies for improving communication include the use of e-mail, bulletin boards, instant messaging, and chatrooms including those provided as a part of a course management system such as WebCT, (http://www.Webct.com/), or Blackboard (http://www.blackboard.com/). Both of these are widely used at American colleges and universities.

Using e-mail

E-mail is used by virtually all students and faculty in higher education, although the particular software used by each institution may vary. Most operate similarly and begin with getting a user account (often including an e-mail address) on the institution's e-mail system, getting the appropriate software on office and home computers, and establishing the appropriate settings for communicating with others using this software. Some institutional e-mail systems use proprietary software while others have an open system, allowing anyone to interact with its members.

The best advice for faculty and students: learn the processes at your campus for access to campus networks and software and take advantage of any campus-provided workshops for using critical software, whether operating and network systems or e-mail.

Once the faculty and students can successfully log on, gaining access to the campus or external (AOL or other Internet Service Provider) network services, the class communication processes and activities may proceed. Strategies for successful use of e-mail include the use of one-to-one e-mail correspondence or one-to-many e-mail distribution using groups or listservs.

One-to-one contact involves the instructor and student exchanging information, usually something that is specific to that student only, with the instructor, for example, responding to a question by this student or the student commenting on material presented during class. One-to-many contact enables an instructor (or student) to send the same e-mail message to a larger group—the instructor sending general information such as study questions to the entire class or a student sending their input to a class discussion. Various files such as word processed documents, audio, video files, or spreadsheets may be attached to e-mail messages.

While attaching files is occasionally necessary, it is good practice to limit the use of attachments since attachments may be of a size and file type that make transmission and reading difficult.

One-to-many contact via e-mail is assisted by the creation of e-mail groups and listservs. Anyone may create within their e-mail software a group of people who together would receive particular e-mail messages. Usually this is done by creating a new named character or alias within the software's address book and, where the user would indicate the e-mail address of the person to whom the mail would be sent, including multiple e-mail addresses. The instructor might create an e-mail group that includes all of the members of the class. A student might create a group e-mail address that includes everyone in a study group or of several friends who get together for lunch on Wednesdays. The use of a group name with multiple e-mail addresses enable a single e-mail message to be sent easily to more than one person. When the number of people who could be a member of such an e-mail group gets fairly large—a good rule of thumb is any number larger than ten—a listserv would be helpful.

Listservs are created and maintained with software used by the institution's computer servers. The lists of people on a given server that automatically sends e-mail from one person to a whole group depends on how the lists are created. Lists may be created where individuals subscribe to the listserv (voluntary membership) or from a database of names and e-mails of individuals who are logically connected in some way (involuntary or automatic membership)—for example, everyone listed by the registrar as enrolled in a particular class.

Tips for getting the most out of using e-mail with students:

- **Make sure that all students have e-mail access and accounts before using e-mail as a primary mode of communication outside the classroom.** Many institutions automatically assign e-mail accounts when students register for classes, others require students to sign up for an account at some central location. Find out if your students have access to the Internet from home, dormitory/apartment, or some other location where they can receive e-mail messages. Also find out what the limita-

tions are for your students' e-mail—they may not be able to receive or decipher attachments, particularly attachments over a certain size or unusual file types.

- **Establish processes and expectations for e-mail use by your students that include guidelines regarding tone of language, frequency, educational purpose, and format.** As a part of the class syllabus, indicate the class expectations for using e-mail. A good practice is providing a welcome e-mail to all students in the class that provides a model for how the e-mail communication will be conducted. The structure of the model e-mail should include a subject line and a description linked to the educational purpose of the e-mail discussion to let everyone know what is being said along with any other issues. (See the Figure 6.1.)

- **Let students know how often they are expected to contribute to the discussion.** It is common practice to have students be expected to contribute one original e-mail commentary per week during the academic term and to also contribute one e-mail that responds to one or more received e-mails.

- **Encourage student e-mails for discussion purposes and monitor the discussion but realize that you do not need to evaluate all student e-mail.** Don't think you need to respond to everything in every student e-mail. If you've set up a strong system for encouraging e-mail discussion, you won't be able to keep up and you are likely to get in the way of your students communicating with each other. It may be important for you to monitor the tone of the discussion and contribute by setting an example, but open dialogue can be hindered by too much heavy-handed control. Do not allow anonymous e-mail discussion—it is too easy to make strong comments without the responsibility for being civil when the sender is anonymous.

A popular form of almost instantaneous communication, similar to e-mail, is instant messaging. Using specialized software, similar to e-mail and usually connected to the Internet web browser, instant messaging enables a user to write a note which almost immediately will appear in a window on the recipient user's computer. This immediacy is popular with many students because it provides an environment for "talking" to others that is similar to using the telephone. Because of its immediacy, instant messaging is difficult to control in an educational environment. On the other hand, it may provide exactly the right kind of contact between students who are studying for exams and who want the benefits of studying together despite being in two different places. Be clear about the circumstances in which instant messaging is encouraged, this is a powerful tool.

Figure 6.1—E-mail Guidelines for Format, Tone, Frequency, and Purpose

Sources include:
- E-mail netiquette guidelines from IEEE, http://eleccomm.ieee.org/email-netiquette.shtml
- "The Net: User Guidelines and Netiquette," by Arlene Rinaldi, Florida Atlantic University, http://wise.fau.edu/netiquette/net/elec.html
- " A Beginner's Guide to Effective E-mail," Revision 2.0 by Kaitlin Duck Sherwood, http://www.webfoot.com/advice/email.top.html
- Handouts available from the National Writing Center Association website: http://nwca.syr.edu/NWCA/WCHandouts.html

In using e-mail as a tool for communicating with others within the context of a scheduled class, the following issues should be pointed out, discussed, and enforced.

Format— Design the way the reader of e-mail sees information. The goal of the e-mail format is readability and effective communication. Be clear and straightfor-

ward, avoiding unnecessary verbiage. If there is a longer message that needs to be communicated, consider creating this as a word processed document that can be attached to a brief e-mail message. An attached document should be in a standard word processing format such as Microsoft Word™ or the sender takes the risk that the document can not be read by the intended reader.

Begin the communication by providing identification— who is writing the message? Also include a descriptive subject header that gives the reader enough information that they can decide when and under what circumstances to open and read the e-mail. Remember that the first indication of the e-mail for the intended reader (typically) is as a listing of e-mail that only shows the sender name, the date received, and the subject of the e-mail. Many e-mail readers will examine this e-mail table of contents and decide what to read and what to throw away without reading, based on who is sending the information and what is noted in the subject heading.

Tone— Tone refers to the overall emotional content of the language used for the e-mail. While email often feels like a private communication, it is not. E-mail is a relatively public activity, semi-private at best. Don't write things that you would not be concerned about having others read. E-mail is easily forwarded, either by the recipient to others or by the sender, often by accident. This being said, there are a few cautions to note about what you write in an e-mail and how you write it. These include:

- *Avoid inflammatory language.* E-mail text is often written without the usual drafting process that might weed out wording or use of phrases that can anger someone else. It is easy to write something that others may misinterpret because the text is written quickly.

- *Misunderstandings also may occur* because the informality of e-mail text, written in haste, will not adequately convey the correct inflection and subtle shading of meaning intended. The rapidity of e-mail text suggests the informality of spoken communication but does not have the same cues for meaning.

- In responding to the email of others, *be careful about quoting their e-mail, and about forwarding their e-mail to others. Taking wording out of context, especially the limited c*ontext of e-mail, can lead to major concerns by the people being quoted or by those receiving your e-mail.

- *Do not send email using all uppercase (capital) letters or all lowercase letters.* Messages in uppercase are interpreted as shouting. In either situation, the readability of the message is damaged and the likelihood of misunderstandings is increased.

Frequency and Purpose — Note to instructors: In a class environment, attention should be paid to the pedagogical rationale for using e-mail with students. Often this includes a trade-off of important options: regularity of frequent contact and communication on the one hand and in-depth writing on the other. Be clear about how often you expect students to e-mail and for what purposes. It may be more important that students e-mail each other (possibly with copies to you) than sending too-frequent e-mails to the instructor. The best advice is to be clear about the expectations. A good rule of thumb is that students should communicate with the instructor a minimum of once per week for traditional classes—courses that meet in person one, two, or three times per week. For classes that meet less often or not at all in person, the contact should be increased, particularly if this is a primary mode of contact and connection between the instructor and the student.

Presentation Software

Presentation software affords instructors many options for demonstrating class materials and for classroom instructional options. The instructor can use presentation software, such as Microsoft PowerPoint™, as a didactic aid during lectures. They also can incorporate presentation projects by students, as individuals or teams, to encourage active learning. The power of presentation software lies in its ability to incorporate a wide variety of media—text, audio, video, charts, links to websites and database files. In this way supporting materials of almost unimaginable variety may be used during a presentation. A further element provided by presentation software is timing; all of the items presented—each "page" is referred to as a "slide"—may be given a specific time signature and automated or made dependent on some action, such as a mouse click, by the presenter.

A good model for using presentation software as an aid to improve instructional quality involves looking at various component steps of a class presentation:

Step (1) **Attention and motivation**—Begin the class by gaining the attention of the students and proceed by moving the focus of their attention to the subject matter of the class. Among the common strategies for this are using rhetorical questions, introducing an example from current events that has strong general interest, or presenting a visual metaphor—some instructors use a cartoon or humorous anecdote. Good practice in this step recognizes that the attention of any audience is rather fleeting; move quickly to make connections between getting their attention and the ideas, approaches, or materials for the class. Once the attention of the class is engaged, move to personalize the context of the class opener while connecting it to the subject of the class. Let your enthusiasm for what you are teaching show.

For this step, presentation software can provide a wide range of suitable tools for gaining the attention of stu-

dents, including video clips of current news footage or an audio passage with accompanying text from a student presentation.

Step (2) Overview—Provide a general overview of what the class will be examining or discussing that day. This overview prepares the student and gives them a sense of how this material fits with what they already know. The overview includes a description of the various activities of the day's class, the broad topics, and a sense of what is expected of students—will they work in groups? Is there going to be a quiz at the end of class? Should they make sure they have their textbook at hand? The overview provides a road map for what is going to happen and helps to ensure that the students are prepared to meet expectations.

Step (3) Content—As the course material is offered to students, presentation software can help. Consider the kinds of content goals for the class.

- *Building a knowledge base.* The instructor presents information to students expecting that they are able to define, recall, identify, and remember. Building a basis for further work can be enhanced by additional reinforcing modes of media presentation. A good practice is providing this material, including the media presentation, to students on disk, via a website, or through an e-mail attachment.

- *Achieving a level of comprehension.* Students need to be able to paraphrase and summarize by explaining key concepts in their own words. A presentation slide can be used to cue this activity for the class as well as be used as a stimulator for student response.

- *Analyzing complex materials.* Student need to be able to break down presented materials into their component parts, make inferences and categorize and draw conclusions based on evidence. The use of presentation software can foster this activity by being a focal point for

displaying student work. As students demonstrate these skills, they can enter data and text and images that could be shown to the entire class for follow-up discussion.

- *Combining pieces into something new.* Students may be asked to take various elements of learned material and make predictions about what would come next, to be able to synthesize source materials or to rewrite and revise previous work in light of new or additional information. A good use of presentation software is asking students to create a class presentation that integrates a variety of material and demonstrates their ability to combine these into something new.

- *Assessing the quality of information.* Students need to be able to evaluate data, to appraise the value and relevance of particular elements to the class goals, to compare and contrast, and to come to some conclusions about the materials presented or discussed. Presentation software can be used to help pull source materials and critiques together for students to demonstrate their evaluative skills.

Step (4) **Summarize and reinforce**—This step is similar to the overview in that it presents a summary of presented content with a certain amount of "spin control", but it also reinforces the learning by letting students know what comes next. Connected to a repeat of the main points, this is the time to indicate what the students are expected to do with this information. Describe homework or other tasks that use the presented materials.

Note: this is *not* the time to introduce anything new; save it for the next class or a follow-up class e-mail. Use presentation software to show slides of key points and to make class assignments that follow-up and use the class materials.

Step (5) **Close**—An often ignored instructional step is making a definitive closing for the class. Make sure students know when the class is over. If students don't know what

to expect—including when the class ends—they are likely to decide it is over at a different point than the instructor. An appropriately understood ending helps ensure that all students stay until the end. Some instructors use a closing story or cartoon while others close by offering specific announcements that are of common interest.

A common ending (not recommended) is finishing a class by asking if there are any questions and when none are forthcoming, declare the class over. This makes it unlikely that students will ask questions—who wants to be the only thing standing in the way of being able to leave the room at the end of a long class?

A better ending (recommended) is to use the last few minutes to ask students to write down one question or comment on the class that the instructor then collects. Once the student completes this task, they can exit the classroom. This kind of ending provides a trigger to leave based on completing a task. The important thing is to ensure that students have a reason to stay until the end and that the ending is clear and consistently done.

The instructor can use presentation software to have a definitive and distinctive ending that is consistently performed each class. A slide can cue the students to write a "one-minute paper," by giving one question or comment to discuss.

Finding Information on the Internet

The rapid growth of data on the Internet has made finding something quickly and easily more challenging for the teacher and student. While there is a dizzying array of information available on virtually any topic, just try to find it. A simple search for a key word or name turns up far too many websites to be useful; "Martin Luther

King," for example, recently returned nearly two million results. Among the results were websites related to a range of items including the holiday, memorial library, and speeches devoted to Martin Luther King. While it might be possible that the first few results listed are the pages sought, the greater likelihood is that the search will result in more frustration than desired information. Instructors can and should address this problem while helping students learn better ways for doing Web-based research.

> *As with other kinds of information searches, Web-based research follows the usual processes of search and find, evaluate and verify, followed by appropriate use and citation.*

One search strategy uses well-established sites that have collected information resources into a kind of data warehouse of other previewed websites. These core sites may be owned and maintained by non-profit educational institutions (often a university), non-profit organizations (http://www.merlot.org, for example) or for-profit corporations (such as http://www.Bigchalk.com). One highly recommended site is the World Lecture Hall at the University of Texas: http://www.utexas.edu/world/lecture/index.html. As noted at their website, the "World Lecture Hall publishes links to pages created by faculty worldwide who are using the Web to deliver course materials in any language." A common feature of these warehouse sites is that they collect materials and websites, organize them into discrete categories and provide tools that enable users to locate resources within the site.

Another search strategy uses specialized search software or search engines. Whether proprietary or in the public domain, search engines try to find and index as many websites and Web pages as possible. Various search engines will boast about the number of sites in their indexing; others may claim an advantage based on their speed and search accuracy. The search indexing offered by the various search engines tends to be based on specific website characteristics, including unique key words, combinations of words, searching for particular fields of information, and limiting factors (boolean searches). No

single search engine is able to index a very large portion of the World Wide Web, and none can find specific kinds of information that are behind some kind of entry portal (sites which require a searcher to log in). The content of specially formatted documents, such as Adobe™ PDF documents, is not searched even when the document itself is available on the Web. Understanding the features of several search engines will help students learn to use each for particular purposes.

The more common search engines include:

> *Google*—www.google.com—a large index that includes the websites of many organizations; fast; uses – and/or OR boolean operators; can limit search by language and domain.
>
> *Fast*—www.alltheweb.com—a very large index; among the fastest; uses some boolean operators; can limit search by language and domain; searches for multimedia.
>
> *Northern Light*—www.northernlight.com—a large and growing index with powerful search features; fee-based access to online publications; specialized search domains; free personalized news and research e-mail updates.
>
> *AltaVista*—www.altavista.com—a very large index with powerful and unique searching capabilities; boolean searching with extensive language search limits.

Beyond these few, there are many other search engines and more are becoming available. Students and faculty need to be familiar with the search tools most pertinent to their area of study. For additional information on Internet search engines, see the websites of Greg Notess, http://www.notess.com.

Exercises in searching for information can provide a fun and useful way for instructors to include Internet researching into the context of a class. Instructors can develop elementary levels of familiarity by using exercises that ask students to find a variety of kinds of information and websites—a Web scavenger hunt. Students can work in small teams or individually and can report back on their success at finding certain kinds of data. In addition to easily found responses,

("At which website would you be most likely to find information related to federal oversight of water quality?"), students can be asked to make qualitative choices as a part of this assignment, ("At which websites would you find the most useful information related to the disputes over water quality in the Rio Grande water basin?")

One good search practice limits the search to specified URL domains. In this way the student can have some greater confidence that the material on population statistics, for example, from a website with the URL <.gov>, is probably reliable and based on governmental census data. Good practice extends the exercise of research skill from search to a level that asks students to make decisions about the quality of the information received.

Evaluating the quality of information and verifying the accuracy of the materials on the Web represents a major issue for teaching using the Web. Even if students can find information, the real question is whether the information is useful and/or valid. Anyone can put information out on the Web—and usually does; there is no requirement that it be validated in the same way information published in a reviewed journal. One-way to address this is to use sites that are reviewed, such as sites of major academic journals or full-text databases of various journals. These are often not searched when general purpose search engines look at the Web; for these the student may need to use the proprietary tools of the campus library or state library system.

Four criteria for evaluating Web pages and the information listed there, includes:

- **Who is the author?** Check the accuracy of Web documents by making sure that a name and affiliation is listed. Is there an e-mail address listed that can be used to follow up on the information? Is this person qualified to provide the information on the website? Why was this website created? Does it have an educational or commercial function?

- **What are the credentials of the author?** What is the authority of the website? What is the URL domain? Is the domain from an educational institution (.edu), governmental entity (.gov), organizational group (.org), or business (.com)? Are there citations for the data presented?

- **How objective is the material presented?** Try to determine if there is a hidden agenda or commercial purpose to the information. Ask why and for whom the Web page was created. One clue could be the detail of the information. What kinds of sources are cited for the data presented?

- **How current and up-to-date is the information presented?** Find out when the document was created or when it was last updated. Are there any dead links on the page? If so, this is a clue that the page has not changed recently and might indicate that the information on the page is outdated.

Additional websites that are useful when searching for information:

http://brainblitz.com Enables user to watch other searches on the Web. See how others search and what kinds of information is being searched.

http://unige.ch/meta-index.html W3 Search Engines; collection of many search engines and tools for finding information on the Web.

http://whyfiles.org The Why Files; the science behind the news.

http://edsitement.neh.fed.us Edsitement; National Endowment for the Humanities on the Web; many source materials available from this site.

http://www.researchpaper.com Source of topics and ideas for student research.

http://www.loc.gov Library of Congress homepage; key site for governmental data.

http://thomas.loc.gov Legislative information on the Internet.

http://www.emtech.net/learning_styles.html Bibliography and collection of URLs related to learning styles.

http://www.lib.uiowa.edu/proj/Webbuilder/ copyright.html Copyright and multimedia legal issues for website creators and authors.

http://www.du.org/cybercomp.html Composition in cyberspace; key source for information on writing and the Internet.

The appropriate use of Web information is specific to the course of study and the particular instructor (keyed to pedagogy). What is important here is that the instructor incorporate the use of search techniques with the class, instruct students in evaluation and verification of the information contained in the websites, and finally, ensure that students appropriately cite any information found on the Web.

References

Angelo T. & Cross K. (1993). *Classroom assessment techniques: A handbook for college teachers* (2nd ed.). San Francisco: Jossey-Bass.

Bianco-Mathis, V. et al. (1996). *The adjunct faculty handbook.* Thousand Oaks, CA: Sage Publications, Inc.

Bloom, B. et. al. (1956). *Taxonomy of educational objectives.* New York: David McKay.

Burnstad, H. (2000). Developing the environment for learning. In Greive D, (ed.). *Handbook II-Advanced teaching strategies for adjunct and part-time faculty.* Elyria. OH: Info-Tec.

Chickering, A. & Ehrmann, S. (1997). Seven principles for good practice in undergraduate education. *American Association for Higher Education Bulletin, 3-87.*

Greive, D. (Ed.). (2000). *Handbook II-Advanced teaching strategies for adjunct and part-time faculty.* Elyria OH: Info-Tec.

Knowles, M. (1990). *The adult learner-A neglected species.* Houston, TX: Gulf Publishing.

Mager, R. (1962). *Preparing instructional objectives.* Belmont, CA: Fearon Publishers.

McCarthy, B. (1987). *The 4-MAT system.* Barrington, IL: Excel, Inc.

McKeachie, W. et. al. (1994). *Teaching tips, strategies, research and theory for college and university teachers.* Lexington, MA: D. C. Heath and Co.

NEA, (1975). www.new.org/aboutnea/code.html.

Salmon, J. (1994). The diverse classroom. In Frye, B. (ed). *Teaching in college-A resource for college teachers.* Elyria OH: Info-Tec.

Sego, A. (1994). *Cooperative learning-A classroom guide.* Elyria, OH: Info-Tec.

Stephan, K., (2000). The syllabus and the lesson plan. In Greive, D. (ed). *Handbook II-Advanced teaching strategies for adjunct and part-time faculty.* Elyria, OH: Info-Tec.

Weimer, M. *Improving college teaching.* San Francisco: Jossey-Bass.

Index

K

Knowles, Malcolm 32

L

laissez-faire classroom 20, 42
large group instruction 80, 88, 89
learning cells 85
learning college 11
learning hierarchy 92
learning styles 20, 34, 35, 102, 103, 117
lecture 36, 49, 71, 73-76, 81, 83, 85, 88-91, 99, 102
legal issues 23, 55
lesson plans 33, 55, 60, 68
listservs 89, 105

M

Mager, Robert 58
Maslow, Abraham 39
Maslow's Hierarchy of Needs 39
McCarthy, B. 34
McKeachie, Wilbert 22
media, influences of 30
Microsoft PowerPoint 110
Microsoft Word 108
minute paper 48
motivation 38
muddiest point 49
multimedia 68, 71, 72, 90, 110-117
multiple choice 93
multiple-choice 92, 93

N

National Education Association 24
negative student (student type) 47
netiquette 107
networks 97, 104
non-verbal communication 41, 83
Northern Light (Search Engine) 115
Notess, Greg 115

If you found this book helpful, you'll want to check out these other Info-Tec titles:

Handbook II: Advanced Strategies for Adjunct and Part-time Faculty by Donald Greive

Handbook II carries on the tradition of practical and readable instructional guides that began with *A Handbook for Adjunct & Part-time Faculty* (new in a fourth edition!)

Intended for adjuncts who have already mastered the basics and for the managers of adjunct faculty, *Handbook II* offers in-depth coverage of some of the topics you just read about like andragogy, collaborative learning, syllabus construction, and testing. But this manual also goes beyond these topics to discuss specific teaching techniques for critical thinking, problem solving, large class instruction and distance learning assignments.

Brand-new in November, 2000, *Handbook II* gives you expert and current strategies to take your teaching to the next level. Available in paperback for $14.95 each.

Managing Adjunct & Part-time Faculty in the New Millennium edited by Donald Greive and Catherine Worden

New and exciting changes are taking place in higher education every day and one of the many tasks of an adjunct faculty manager is to keep up with these changes and communicate them back to their adjunct and part-time faculty.

In *Managing Adjunct & Part-time Faculty in the New Millennium,* noted author and educator Donald Greive has collected works from many experts in their fields. discussing topics like institutional quality, ethical and legal issues, faculty development, and distance education technology--all in a single volume.

Also new for 2000, *Managing Adjunct & Part-time Faculty* is available in hardcover for $34.95 and in paperback for $24.95.

FAQ's... for Info-Tec and its Products

How can I place an orders?

Orders can be placed **by mail** to Info-Tec, 1005 Abbe Road North, Elyria OH 44035, **by phone** at (440)366-4632 or 1(800)995-5222 x4632, **by fax** at (440)366-4113, and **via the Internet** at http://www.lorainccc.edu/campus/ and select Bookstore to be taken to the secure website.

How much do I pay if I want multiple copies?

Each of the Info-Tec products has a quantity discount schedule available. The schedule for the new Handbook is:

1-9 copies--$14.95 each   **10-24 copies**--$6.95each
25-49 copies--$5.95each   **50-99 copies**--$5.50each
100 or more copies--$4.95 each

Similiar discounts are available are listed in the Info-Tec catalog.

How can I pay for orders?

Orders can be placed on **a purchase order** or can be paid by **check** or **credit card** (Visa/Mastercard or Discover.)

How will my order be shipped?

Standard shipping to a continental U.S. street address is via **UPS-Ground Service**. Foreign shipments or U.S. post office box addresses go through the **U.S. Postal Service** and express shipments via **UPS-2nd Day**, **UPS-Next Day**, or **Fedex**. Shipping and handling charges are based on the dollar amount of the shipment and a fee schedule is shown on the next page.

What if you just want to look first?

Info-Tec offers a **30-day free examination period** on all our products. Request an exam copy and return it in good condition within thirty days at no charge. If you choose to keep the book, an invoice will be sent to you after the exam period.

What if I'm a reseller like a bookstore or wholesaler?

Resellers get a standard **20% discount** off of the single copy re-tail price. This discount structure allows resellers a **six-month return** period from the date of invoicing.

Info-Tec Instructional Products

Qty	Author:Title	Unit $$	Total
	NEW-Handbook for Adjunct/Part-Time Faculty (pb) $14.95		
	NEW-Handbook for Adjunct/Part-Time Faculty (hc) $24.95		
	Handbook II: Adv. Teaching Strategies (paperback) $14.95		
	Managing Adjunct/Part-Time Faculty (paperback) $24.95		
	Managing Adjunct/Part-Time Faculty (hardcover) $34.95		
	Teaching Strategies and Techniques (paperback) $4.95		
	Teaching in College: a Resource (paperback) $19.95		
	Total Quality Ed: T'ching Techniques for Tech Ed. (pb) $4.95		
	Cooperative Learning: A Classroom Guide (paperback) $4.95		
	Non-Credit Instruction (paperback) $4.95		
	Helpful Hints Bookmark 3-Pack (set) $1.00		
	Adjunct-Info: A Journal for Managers of Adjunct/ Part-Time Faculty (Single 1-yr. subscription) $40.00		
	Video: When Geroge Speaks: Resolving Conflict (each) $129.00		
		Subtotal	
		Shipping & Handling (See below)	
		Total	

Purchaser/Payment Information

☐ *Check (payable to Info-Tec)*

☐ *Credit Card #* _____ *Exp. Date* _____

☐ *Purchase Order #* _____

Name _____ *Title* _____

Institution _____

Address _____ *City/ST/Zip* _____

Phone: _____ *FAX:* _____ *E-mail:* _____

Shipping and Handling Fee Schedule:

$0-$30 purchase   *$5.00*

$31-$75 purchase   *$10.00*

Purchases over $75   *7% of purchase subtotal*

DATE DUE

DE 0 2 '03		
AP '04		

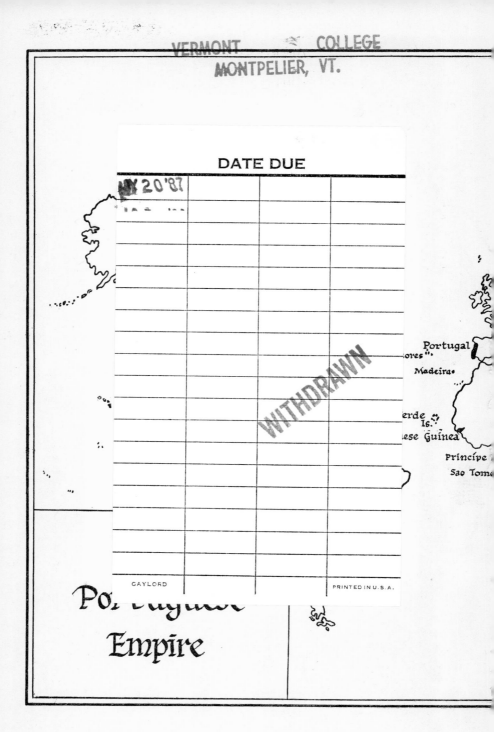

Portugal
ores ".
Madeira•

erde
Is.
ese Guinea

Principe
Sao Tome

Por tuguese

Empire

1

CULTURE TRUMPS VISION

Unless commitment is made, there are only
promises and hopes . . . but no plans.

—*Peter Drucker*

A church in the Midwest grew rapidly, but the growth curve gradually flattened. In recent years, they saw almost no growth at all. In the early days of explosive growth, the senior pastor taught seminars and spoke at national conferences to instruct other pastors in how to grow their churches, but in the past few years, he received very few invitations to speak. When the curve began to flatten, he took his senior staff to hear noted speakers. Surely, he thought, they could learn something new and overcome stagnation. When that didn't fix things, they hired consultants to analyze the situation and prescribe a solution. When this strategy didn't effect the change they wanted, the senior pastor began "cleaning house." He hired and fired so many people that the offices needed revolving doors. Still, the church didn't grow.

Out of frustration, the pastor left the church. He moved his family a few miles away and started another church with about two hundred people who followed him there. Some would call this a church plant; I think it was a glorified church split.

At the original church, a new pastor came into the office full of fresh ideas and a clear vision of where the church could go; that's exactly why he was selected. After a long, grueling first eighteen months with the new pastor on the job, however, the church's growth curve had barely budged. When he called me, he was frustrated and tired. In our first meeting, he told me sadly, "I don't understand. We spent time and money to reenergize the congregation. We took our top staff on a retreat to instill the new vision into them. We hired more staff, and we reformatted our worship experience. We started plenty of new programs. We redesigned our stage set. We created a killer Web site, reconfigured our offices, redecorated to create a fresh ambiance, and designed a new logo for the church. We even wrote a song about how great we are! But none of this has made a bit of difference. We haven't gone backward, and I'm glad of that, but I thought we'd be way ahead of where we are today." He paused for a second and then asked, "What am I missing?"

This senior pastor had done a lot of good things, but he failed to understand the impact of the existing organizational culture on his new, exciting vision for the church. It was like changing the engine on a sports car to make it faster, but it was spinning its wheels in the mud. Or to use a different metaphor, he tried to transplant a heart into a patient whose body rejected the foreign organ. No matter how perfect the new heart was, the patient had no chance at all unless the body accepted it.

Culture—not vision or strategy—is the most powerful factor in any organization. It determines the receptivity of staff and volunteers to new ideas, unleashes or dampens creativity, builds or erodes enthusiasm, and creates a sense of pride or deep discouragement about working or being involved there. Ultimately, the culture of an organization—particularly in churches and nonprofit organizations, but also in any organization—shapes individual morale, teamwork, effectiveness, and outcomes. In an article in the magazine *Executive Leadership*, Dick Clark explains how he took the pharmaceutical firm Merck to a higher level: "The fact is, culture eats strategy for lunch. You can have a good strategy in place, but if you don't have the culture and the enabling

Culture—not vision or strategy— is the most powerful factor in any organization.

systems, the [negative] culture of the organization will defeat the strategy."[1]

To help you uncover the nature of your existing culture and identify the steps of change, this book examines the full range of cultural health, from inspiring to toxic, and describes the seven keys of CULTURE:

1. Control
2. Understanding
3. Leadership
4. Trust
5. Unafraid
6. Responsive
7. Execution

Insight is the first—and crucial—step toward change.

Looking at the Landscape

In the past decade or so, dozens of books and countless articles have been written about the importance of corporate culture, but relatively few churches and nonprofit organizations have taken the arduous (but necessary) steps to assess, correct, and change their culture. First, we need to understand what we mean by the term *organizational culture*. It is the personality of the church or nonprofit. Like all personalities, it's not simple to define and describe. Organization development consultant, speaker, writer, and filmmaker Ellen Wallach observes, "Organizational culture is like pornography; it is hard to define, but you know it when you see it."

Organizational culture includes tangibles and intangibles. The things we can see are the way people dress and behave, the look of the corporate offices, and the messages of posters on the walls. The intangibles may be harder to grasp, but they give a better read on the organization's true personality. The organization's values (stated and unstated), beliefs, and assumptions; what and how success is celebrated; how problems are addressed; the manifestations of trust and respect at all levels of the organization—these are the intangible elements of culture. Every group in society—family, town, state, nation, company, church, civic group, team, and any other gathering of people—has a culture, sometimes clearly identified but often camouflaged.

Many leaders confuse culture with vision and strategy, but they are very different. Vision and strategy usually focus on products, services, and outcomes, but culture is about the people—the most valuable asset in the organization. The way people are treated, the way they treat their peers, and their response to their leaders is the air people breathe. If that air is clean and healthy, people thrive and the organization succeeds, but to the extent that it is toxic, energy subsides, creativity lags, conflicts multiply, and production declines. I'm not suggesting that churches and nonprofits drop their goals and spend their time holding hands and saying sweet things to each other. That would be a different kind of toxic environment! A strong, vibrant culture stimulates people to be and do their very best and reach the highest goals. Spiritual leaders point the way forward, but they invite meaningful participation from every person at all levels of the organization. Together, they work hard toward their common purpose, and they celebrate each other's accomplishments every step along the way. Trust is the glue that holds the organization together and gives it the strength it needs to excel.

Vision and strategy usually focus on products, services, and outcomes, but culture is about the people—the most valuable asset in the organization.

The inputs into the "cultural system" include the stories that surround the staff's experiences; shared goals and responsibilities; respect and care for people; balance between bold leadership and listening; and clear, regular communication. The outcomes include the reputation of the leader, the reputation of the organization, the attractiveness of the church or nonprofit to prospective new staff members, a measure of pride in being a part of the organization, and a positive impact on the entire community.

To see a few snapshots of a church's culture, we might ask these questions:

- Who are the heroes? What makes them heroes? Who determines who the heroes are?
- When someone inquires, "Tell me about your church or nonprofit," what stories are told?
- How much does the average staff member feel he or she has input into the direction and strategy of the church or nonprofit?
- Who has the ear of the top leaders? How did these people win a hearing with the leaders?
- What are the meaningful rituals? What message do they convey to those in the organization and those outside it?
- Who is rewarded, and for what accomplishments?
- What is the level of loyalty up and down the organizational chart? What factors build loyalty?
- What is the level of creativity and enthusiasm throughout the organization?
- When an objective observer spends an hour watching people interact in the offices, what mood does he or she pick up?
- How are decisions made, deferred, or delayed?
- Who are the nonpositional power brokers, the people who have authority based on the respect they've earned but who don't have authoritative titles?

- Where are control problems and power struggles most evident?
- How is "turf" defined and protected?

The shape of an organization's culture begins at the top level. The leader's integrity, competence, and care for staff members create the environment where people excel . . . or not. In his book *The Five Dysfunctions of a Team*, Patrick Lencioni observes that trust is the most powerful trait in shaping a positive culture, and trust thrives on honesty. He writes, "When there is an absence of trust, it stems from a leader's unwillingness to be vulnerable with the group," and "leaders who are not genuinely open with one another about their mistakes and weaknesses make it impossible to build a foundation of trust."[2]

I believe that the role of senior pastor is the most glorious and at the same time most difficult in the world. These leaders have the incredible privilege of representing the King of kings, imparting grace and life to people, and creating environments in which God's Spirit changes the eternal destiny—and the present relationships and direction—of men and women, boys and girls in the community. There is no higher calling. Yet senior pastors shoulder enormous burdens. They have to be "on" every time they speak, whether it's to the entire congregation or to an individual. They feel the pressure of finances, deadlines, new visions and missed opportunities, the mistakes and sins of their staff, and their own flaws. But even as they face those troubles, they are expected to be the source of hope, peace, and wisdom for every person in their world. Like the Apostle Paul, senior pastors report either metaphorically or actually, "I have labored and toiled and have often gone without sleep; I have known hunger and thirst and have often gone without food; I have been cold and naked. Besides everything else, I face daily the pressure of my concern for all the churches. Who is weak, and I do not feel weak? Who is led into sin, and I do not inwardly burn?" (2 Corinthians 11:27–29). Senior pastors are in a unique position to shape the culture of their teams and their churches, but they can't do it alone. They need the support, wisdom, and commitment of every person on the team.

Let me give a couple of examples of the impact of organizational culture. A senior pastor who understands the importance of creating an inspirational culture has a church with five sites and about a dozen daughter churches. Throughout the organization—from the first interview of a prospective employee to large staff meetings and every team's interaction—staff members remind each other that they come to work each day to make a difference in people's lives. It's not just a job, and they aren't just killing time each day. The pastoral staff has an open-door policy, and they welcome creative suggestions from every staff member. Treating each person in the community and each other with the utmost respect is a high value. The senior pastor regularly carves out time to roll up his sleeves and work alongside the most humble employee at the church.

In an atmosphere of mutual encouragement, top leaders at the mother church, the sites, and the daughter churches are devoted to each other's success, so power struggles are minimized. The senior pastor goes to great lengths to celebrate accomplishments, rewarding not only the vigorous effort to pull off all the work of ministry at the church but also the selfless service to the community. As you can imagine, staff loyalty is through the roof! Staff members express tremendous pride in being a part of such a caring, supportive organization that values them even more than their production.

The senior pastor explained his philosophy of leadership: "I make it a priority to say or do something each day to speak to people's hearts and affirm their commitment to serve God. They work hard, and I want to bring them joy and relieve some stress in their lives. With this as a priority, I find innumerable opportunities to accomplish this every single day. I think about the lives of our staff members and volunteers beyond the walls of our church. They have interests, homes, and families. How they are treated here has an impact on every relationship and every activity in their lives. They need to know I care—and that my expressions of love aren't just words; they're real." The staff at this church come to work each day excited about working as a team to solve problems and make a difference in people's lives. It all starts with the senior pastor's commitment to people and excellence.

The powerful, positive culture of this church is exactly what this book is about—but there are other examples, ones that aren't as inspiring. A friend of mine told me about his experience working at a large church. The senior pastor wore two faces. In public, he appeared to be the paragon of Christian virtue, referring often to Christ, brotherly love, and the Spirit's work in people's lives. In the halls of the church offices, however, he was a tyrant. Those around him observed that power and pride motivated him and shaped his relationships. Once when the pastor faced stiff opposition to a building campaign, my friend heard him snarl, "I don't care if people respect me. I just want them to fear me!" Machiavelli would be proud. Around the office, any semblance of Christian love was blown away by his ridicule of those who made a mistake, and rage at those who offered a suggestion that was different from his intentions. But nobody knew which suggestions would be accepted and which would be blasted. Everyone stayed on edge, fearful of offering an opinion about even the most trivial issue, and waiting for the ax to fall if the pastor disapproved.

The staff enjoyed working with their own teams in their areas of ministry, but they grew to despise the pastor and the circle of yes-men around him. The church lavishly celebrated when the denomination and other organizations gave the pastor accolades, but the staff rarely received even a pat on the back. "Your bonus," the fiercely loyal executive pastor told a competent but beleaguered staff member, "is continued employment. Don't ask for more." The executive pastor smiled as if he were joking, but the staff member knew he was serious.

In this culture, loyalty wasn't earned; it was demanded. When staff members or lay leaders left the church for any reason, they were severely criticized with vicious name-calling. Gradually, most of the competent and emotionally healthy people left the church, leaving behind only those who were afraid to suffer abuse for leaving, or even for considering leaving the church. One of the most alarming facets of this story is that the pastor was commended for several years by his denomination for his "integrity and exemplary leadership." I guess he wrote his own press releases, and enough people believed him. During those years, though, few people bothered to notice the pained expressions on the faces of his staff. Eventually, the diminishing quality of the staff took its toll. The church's numbers stagnated and then declined. Even today, the pastor blames others for every problem he and the church faced. He still doesn't get it.

A healthy culture inspires and stimulates all staff members—whether they're in the boardroom or the mailroom—to give their best because they are convinced their ideas will be valued. In a creative, supportive environment, people are less threatened by their own mistakes and by others' failures. Problems are viewed through a different lens: they become opportunities for growth, not causes for condemnation. Certainly, there has to be a balance between meeting immediate organizational goals and patient listening, but the vast majority of staff members are thrilled when anyone, especially the top exec, cares

> *In a creative, supportive environment, people are less threatened by their own mistakes and by others' failures.*

enough to listen at all. Employees who feel valued work harder, are more productive, and add value to the organization's purpose. A healthy culture works for everybody.

Key Principles

As we begin our examination of organizational culture, I want to communicate some important principles.

Culture Is the Most Powerful Factor in Any Organization

I travel quite a bit, and I've become a student of hotels around the world. In some cases, I've noticed a significant difference between hotels, even when the rooms actually cost about the same. The difference is in the quality of service. I've stayed in some very nice hotels where it seemed that my coming was a nuisance to the staff. No one opened the door for me or offered to lug my suitcase and boxes into the lobby. From the expression of the person behind the counter, I'm quite sure he would rather have been getting a root canal than checking me in. Sometimes, when I needed some assistance, no one came for a long time, and when they came, they weren't authorized to do what I needed them to do. So I waited even longer. Now don't get me wrong. I had a nice room with clean sheets and fluffy pillows, and I slept very well.

But I've also enjoyed very different experiences at some hotels. Not long ago, I stayed at a Ritz Carlton. When the car dropped me off, a man opened my door and greeted me by saying, "Welcome to the Ritz Carlton, Dr. Chand." I wondered, *Did I leave a nametag on?* No, but somehow he knew I was coming and went out of his way to greet me. The woman at the desk also knew my name (How did they do that?), and she gave me a key without hesitation. Instantly, another man came to help me with my luggage and escort me to my room. He was as kind and attentive as a favorite uncle. My stay was exceptionally pleasant, but a couple of days into it, I lost the key card to my room. As I stood in front of the door, I noticed a cleaning lady down the hall. I asked if she could help me. She instantly let me in and then called for the desk to send up a replacement key. In other hotels, the cleaning people may not be authorized to help in this way, so they have to call for someone else to take care of it. At the Ritz Carlton, though, every staff member has authority to do whatever it takes to care for a guest.

The slogan for the Ritz Carlton Hotels is "Ladies and gentlemen serving ladies and gentlemen." Can you see how this simple but profound statement reflects their inherent corporate culture? By treating each employee with dignity, the company fills his or her need for significance, and warmhearted service flows out of each one like a flood.

I can imagine that the other hotel chains had some kind of written statement to inform employees that they need to serve their guests, but its statement didn't create a culture of service like the one at the Ritz. In fact, it didn't seem to make even a dent. Vision statements, strategies, and goals are very good tools, but they can't compare in importance to the culture. The culture of an organization is the platform for building a strong church or nonprofit. It is the fertile soil for growing creativity and passion for excellence, and the rocket fuel for reaching new heights in excellence and accomplishments.

Culture Is Usually Unnoticed, Unspoken, and Unexamined

How often do we think about the air we breathe? It's so pervasive that we don't even give it a thought. It's absolutely essential for life, but only a few climatologists spend time analyzing it. Organizational culture is like the air; it's all around us, shaping every moment of every day, but we seldom notice it at all.

Sometimes, stepping into a very different culture gives us new insight about our own. When I came to America from India, I came face-to-face with a foreign, distinctly different culture. I had lived my whole life with the spoken and unspoken expectations of Indian life, and the moment I got off the plane in the United States, I knew I was a foreigner in a strange land. For years (and even still today), I've had to be a student of the American culture to know how to relate to people most positively. Sometimes a misunderstanding has led to some good laughs, but it has occasionally created heartache. My experiences in learning to live in a new country have made me aware of the importance of grasping the transforming power of culture.

Most leaders of churches and nonprofit organizations focus almost all their energies on the tangibles of growth and donations. Their means to fulfill their goals are a clear, compelling vision and a workable strategy. Those are important components, but they only succeed if the underlying culture stimulates creativity, passion, and productivity throughout the organization. Top leaders need to spend at least as much time analyzing their culture as they do crafting their new vision, strategy, and marketing plans.

Toxic culture is like carbon monoxide: you don't see or smell it, but you wake up dead!

Toxic culture is like carbon monoxide: you don't see or smell it, but you wake up dead!

Culture Determines How People Respond to Vision and Leadership

For one reason or another, some top leaders have an innate distrust of their staff. Their mode of leadership, then, is to tightly control everything their people do. They may smile while they're squeezing employees, but their people don't feel valued when they experience close scrutiny and micromanagement. On the other end of the continuum, a few leaders take a hands-off approach. They think their role is to push the ball and just let it roll wherever it goes. They don't give their staff members direction or feedback, so their people wander around confused and frustrated. Lack of clarity and pervasive ambiguity cannot become the long-term modus operandi. People are left to determine their own goals for their departments and their lives. And some leaders rule by ambivalence and ambiguity. They use the unknown to provoke anxiety and keep people off balance, and then they wonder why people are tentative, indecisive, and nonproductive. In these toxic cultures, people resent leaders instead of respecting them, their level of motivation wanes, they complain a lot to anyone who will listen (and some who don't want to), and they aren't very productive.

The intangibles of respect and trust transform a church culture into a beehive of thinking, creating, and working together to accomplish grand goals. When staff members feel valued, they far more readily embrace a leader's vision. Even if they disagree or don't understand, they are more willing to give the benefit of the doubt and pitch in.

The intangibles of respect and trust transform a church culture into a beehive of thinking, creating, and working together to accomplish grand goals.

The two examples earlier in the chapter typify the impact of culture on employees' response to vision and leadership. The staff at one church dreaded coming to work each day. They knew that if they were lucky, they'd avoid getting hammered. That's not much of a sense of purpose! In the other church, however, staff members felt tremendously valued—as people, not just as production units—and they were free to offer their opinions about every vision and strategy that came down from the leadership team. In this church, virtually every person loved coming to work each day. Many of them said something like "This environment is the best I could imagine. It's like a family to me. I love working here." And these people worked like crazy because they were convinced that what they did each day really mattered in the lives of people in the community and their fellow staff members, and in their own lives as well.

Whenever I uncover the culture of an organization, I instinctively ask two questions: Would I want someone in my family to work here? and Would I want to work here?

Culture Most Often Surfaces and Is Addressed in Negative Experiences

All of us would like to believe that we are incredibly perceptive and responsive, but the truth is that most of us stay stuck in the same ruts in our lives until something shakes us out of them. These pervasive patterns of behavior are too big for quick fixes. They force us to take a long, hard look at our organizations and ourselves. Only with deep reflection, accurate information, and courage can we take the necessary steps of change.

Make no mistake: most competent leaders rose to their positions because they are supremely confident in their abilities. They're convinced they know how to run the organization, and they've fixed enough problems to fill volumes of books. That's who they are and what they do. But sooner or later, they may run into difficulties that defy their attempts to fix them. Power struggles consume their top levels of leadership, complaints from staff members and church members sour the air each day, and their new vision for growth isn't getting any traction at all among volunteers and the people in the pews. The leaders try this or that, read this book and call that consultant, but nothing seems to work. When the difficulty revolves around people, it's probably a culture problem that won't be solved by any vision or strategy. The only solution is to change the culture.

One of the most important lessons in life is to embrace difficulties and learn from them instead of just trying to get them fixed as soon as possible. Culture problems, by their nature, are never solved quickly. They require a clear understanding of the problem, a commitment to systemic change, and patience and persistence to see change take root.

Culture problems, by their nature, are never solved quickly.

Almost always, the need to change the culture takes us by surprise. When I came to America in August of 1973 to attend a Bible college, I went to church the first Sunday after I arrived. I listened to the pastor's sermon, and after the service, I passed by him in the lobby of the church. He shook my hand, we talked for a few minutes, and then he graciously said, "If there's anything I can do for you, please let me know."

I responded, "Oh, hell, I'm fine, but thank you very much."

His face turned red, and I quickly realized that I had made my first serious intercultural faux pas. The people behind me moved me along, and one of them whispered to me, "Don't say that word . . . especially in church!"

"What word?" I answered.

He looked pained at my gross ignorance. He winced, "'Hell.' We don't say 'hell' here."

In India, we said "Oh, hell" the way Americans say, "My goodness." It's not offensive in the least. But in America, I had committed an almost unpardonable crime—in the lobby of a church while talking to a minister! The reactions of the pastor and the man in line behind me told me that I needed to learn something about the culture—and fast!

Far too often, we try to minimize difficulties and act as if they didn't matter, we excuse ourselves and say it's not our fault, or we point the accusatory finger at others. None of these responses leads to wisdom and change. A far more healthy and productive reaction is to stop, notice what happened, and ask, "Is there something more than meets the eye going on here?" That's how we uncover a flawed culture so that we can address it.

Culture Is Hard to Change, but Change Results in Multiplied Benefits

I don't want to minimize the mountain I'm asking leaders to climb. It's a steep and difficult journey, but those who have successfully negotiated it have never regretted a moment on the path. When they see staff members with a compelling sense of purpose, when they hear exciting stories that become part of the organization's history, when they see tears in people's eyes because they believe so much in what they're doing, and when they see them respond with joy and enthusiasm to make a good strategy even better, they know it's been worth it.

How do you know an organization's culture has changed? In his book *The Crazy-Making Workplace*, Christian psychologist Dr. Archibald Hart recounts a conversation with the CEO of a large company. He quotes him: "If you want to know what is really going on in most companies, you talk to the guy who sweeps the floors. Nine times out of ten, he knows more than the president. So I make a point of knowing what my floor sweepers know—even if it means sweeping the floors with them."[3] If you're a senior pastor, value the input of men and women who love you enough to tell you the truth. Talk to people far removed from the seat of power; ask them honest questions about what they see, think, and feel about the organization.

> *Talk to people far removed from the seat of power; ask them honest questions about what they see, think, and feel about the organization.*

Ask them how people are valued, what motivates them, and what is celebrated. And listen. You'll find out everything you want to know—and maybe more.

So, have you been investing your time and energies into crafting and articulating your organization's vision, only to find that people aren't as receptive as you hoped? When there's a disconnect between a leader's vision and the receptivity of the staff, the problem isn't with the vision; it's the culture. Most leaders don't invest much in their church's culture simply because they assume it's "just fine." I believe, though, that great leaders devote as many resources to building and shaping their organization's culture as they invest in vision and strategy. In fact, vision and strategy simply can't succeed without a positive, healthy culture.

This Book Is for You If . . .

I've written this book primarily for the top leadership teams in churches and nonprofits, but the principles also apply in the corporate world. The concepts apply to megachurches and small congregations, in every denomination and in independent churches. They work for large, multinational nonprofit organizations as well as mom-and-pop agencies in every sector of service. They apply to parachurch organizations, universities, charter schools, and hospitals.

The commitment to value people all along the organizational hierarchy must be implemented from the top down. The senior pastor and the executive team must lead this effort. When the top leadership team makes a commitment to change the culture, they can use this book to communicate the values and processes to their ministry leaders and other staff members so they are all on board.

As I've talked about these principles to leaders around the world, some have asked if ministry or department heads can implement the changes in this book even if their supervisors don't ever change. Yes, they can courageously take steps to change the culture in their worlds, but they'll always be fighting against the negative pressures from the executive suite. I've known many church ministry leaders and department heads who "protected" their people from the abuses of their bosses, but they often paid a high price. In most cases, they were glad to do that because they really cared for their people, but eventually, many of these dear, brave men and women were forced out, or they left simply because they couldn't take it anymore.

My Promise to You

If you'll read and reflect honestly on the principles in this book, I believe that you'll have a new appreciation for the impact of your organizational culture on every aspect of life. These insights will enable you to make a strong connection between culture and vision so that you always communicate vision *in light of* your culture. A positive culture will act as an accelerant for your vision. With a new appreciation for your culture, you'll empower your staff members to do their very best—and love doing it. You will create the context for vision to grow. When your people feel valued, their enthusiasm will electrify your church! To make all this happen, this book outlines a process to implement the changes necessary for you, your top leadership team, and all the rest of your leaders.

> *A positive culture will act as an accelerant for your vision.*

The principles and practices in this book are designed to equip you to be the leader you've always wanted to be. There's no magic formula—quite the contrary. Changing your organization's culture will be one of the most challenging processes you've ever implemented, but I guarantee you, you'll be glad you did.

In *Why America Doesn't Work*, Chuck Colson and Jack Eckerd observe, "It would be unrealistic to suggest that managers become personally involved in the lives of each worker. But a sense of intimacy and mutual trust can be instilled in the workplace when managers show genuine concern for individual employees."[4] A healthy culture begins at the top, but it eventually releases the creativity and energy of everyone in the organization.

The nature of the topic doesn't lend itself to a quick read and then never being looked at again. Changing the culture of an organization is hard, rewarding work. I've added some reflection questions at the end of each chapter for you and your team to consider, but I'm sure you'll go far beyond these discussions if you're really serious about implementing lasting change. One of the most helpful elements in this book (available on the Web site www.freeculturesurvey.com; see Appendix 1) is a free diagnostic tool to help you conduct a detailed assessment of your organization's culture. I'm sure you'll find it enlightening.

Think About It . . .

1. Do you agree or disagree with the premise of this chapter that culture trumps vision? Explain your answer.

2. Describe the most inspiring organizational culture you have experienced as a staff member or ministry leader. How did the senior leaders treat people? How did they impart vision and strategy? How did people respond?

3. Why did you pick up this book? What do you hope to get out of reading this book and implementing the steps of change?

2

CULTURE KILLERS

Few things help an individual more than to place
responsibility upon him, and to let him know that
you trust him.

—*Booker T. Washington*

On a few occasions when I walk into the offices of an organization where I've been asked to consult with the leadership team, I sense immediately that something's wrong. At that moment, it's too early to put my finger on the problem, but after meeting just a few people, I can sense a pervasive anxiety or confusion. If just one person is uncomfortable, I conclude that he or she is having a bad day. If, however, I pick up negative vibes from several people, I wonder if the culture has a systemic problem. The question I always ask myself when I sense a troubled culture is, *Why hasn't someone done something about it already? Don't they see it, too?* The answer is no. The dysfunction in the culture has become entirely normal. It's the way things have been and the way, people assume, they will always be.

Of course, cultures can change, but only when top leaders have the courage to take an objective appraisal of reality. When they don't recognize culture killers, toxic agents continue to infect every corner of the church or nonprofit organization. The first step, then, is to uncover and face the truth. I have the greatest admiration for senior pastors and other top leaders who have the courage and love to step back, take an honest look at their cultures, and take the necessary steps to change them.

Churches and nonprofits have a wide range of personalities. They may produce very different services, but a few common traits characterize healthy organizations, and a set of opposite traits characterizes those that aren't healthy. For our purposes, I want to plot the range of cultures on a five-point continuum:

**Inspiring . . . Accepting . . . Stagnant . . .
Discouraging . . . Toxic**

We'll use the metaphor of a race car to illustrate the differences. Think of a high-performance Indy car, finely tuned and built for speed. The car represents the organization's vision and strategy. The car, though, can go only as fast as the road allows, and the culture is the road. Are you ready? Let's take a ride.

Inspiring Cultures

Indy cars fly along the ground at amazing speeds on smooth, dry racetracks. That's the image of inspiring cultures. The spirit of the organization encourages people to bring their best to work each day, and together, they accomplish amazing things.

Characteristics of Inspiring Cultures

- The leaders of these organizations give clear direction, but they aren't authoritarian; they value the input of every person. Authority is decentralized.
- Leaders cultivate an atmosphere of trust and respect.
- People throughout the organization believe that what they do each day really matters—to themselves, to their teams, to the church or nonprofit, and to their constituents. They come to work each day with a compelling sense of purpose, a sense that they are involved in a cause much bigger than themselves.
- These organizations have high but realistic expectations. They set high goals, train people, give them the resources they need, stay connected throughout the process, and encourage them to succeed.

- Creativity is rewarded, and failures are viewed as stepping-stones of growth. In fact, failure is seen as an essential part of the process of innovation, not a fatal flaw.
- There are few if any turf battles, so communication flows up and down the organizational chart and between departments.
- Top leaders retrain or replace ministry leaders who can't provide a positive work environment for their teams.
- There is a powerful synergy between relationships and organizational goals.
- The organization invests significantly and systematically in creating and building a healthy culture.
- Leaders regularly celebrate success throughout the organization, and they even celebrate those who leave and find success elsewhere.
- These organizations are a magnet for job applicants. They have their pick of the best and brightest.

Case Study: A Blood Bank with Thirty-Two Branches Around the City

The first thing I noticed when I walked into the corporate offices of this blood bank was how happy the employees seemed to be. Soon I found out why. Jim and his partners had chartered the nonprofit in 1983 in conjunction with a major hospital in the city. From the beginning, they lived by the firm commitment "to serve the community differently." Jim told me, "I'd worked in several different nonprofit organizations in my career—some really good ones, some not so good—and when we began this organization, I had a very good idea of what I wanted it to become." Before he hired the first employee or opened the doors on the first day, Jim wrote out three lists of commitments he and his staff would make to themselves, their teams, and the people who would give a little of themselves to save others' lives. "These are the benchmarks of our attitudes, our relationships, and our commitment to excellence in everything we do," he explained. He had these three documents made into posters, and put them in every blood bank office and mobile station for everyone to see. "No secrets," he told me, "and no excuses."

At weekly staff meetings in their offices around the city, the branch managers begin by having someone read these three documents to be sure they remain the guiding lights for everything they do in the meeting and during the week. Then, before they get into information, strategies, and problem solving, they spend time sharing stories of how their work has touched people's lives. "For example," Jim related, "last week one of our assistant managers reported how a hospital's blood supply had been dangerously low, and our delivery came at the exact moment when victims of a car accident desperately needed units of blood. With a tear in his eye, he thanked his team for making that crucial, lifesaving moment a reality. Those stories take some time in our meetings, but I think they're the most important things we talk about each week. They light a fire under us!"

Jim learned a lot from his previous experiences in other non-profits, and he created an inspiring culture for people who work in branches throughout the city. After he told me a few more stories and introduced me to his immediate staff, he looked at me and sighed, "Man, I love these folks"—and they know it.

Accepting Cultures

The road for some churches and nonprofit organizations is fairly smooth, but a little bumpy with a few potholes here and there. On this track, the Indy car has to slow down a bit to be sure to miss the holes and navigate the rough spots. Still, the race car makes great progress. Accepting cultures are very good places to work, for staff, volunteers, and people in the community.

Characteristics of Accepting Cultures

- The overall atmosphere is very positive, but there are a few topics that are taboo, or there are a few incompetent leaders who remain in the job too long. These unresolved issues and problematic leaders are the bumps and potholes that create tension. In many cases, the difficulties remain isolated in the departments where those poor managers lead. For the people on these teams, the environment may be quite negative, while the rest of the organization thrives.

- Generally, most people in the organization are supportive of each other's roles and goals. Communication is a strength, and people don't feel the need to defend their turf.

- Some difficult decisions are avoided instead of addressed expeditiously. For instance, leaving a poor ministry leader in place too long erodes the trust and drive of those who serve in that office.

- Most people who work in these churches and nonprofits think they are the best ones they've ever experienced. They love the blend of clear goals and strong relationships, and they are highly motivated to do their best.

- The senior leaders in these organizations invest in developing people and the culture. If they were more assertive about taking care of problems in the culture, they could be even more successful.

- These organizations enjoy a strong reputation, so they attract a lot of applicants. However, the new hires who are placed under incompetent ministry leaders are deeply disappointed.

Case Study: A Large Church in the South

Every Sunday, almost five thousand people worship at this church in the suburbs of a major metropolitan area. A gifted leader orchestrates the music, and people love to hear the pastor's teaching. When I met with the staff, most of them had glowing things to say about the pastor and the executive leaders. I got a little more insight, though, from talking to a department director. After we talked for a while, I commented on the overwhelmingly positive atmosphere in the church and among team members. "Yeah," he began cautiously, "it's a little *too* positive if you ask me." I asked him to explain, and he said, "Don't get me wrong. I'm all about trusting God and being hopeful, but life isn't always consistently positive. I just wish we were a little more honest about the reality of pain and problems." I asked a few more questions, and he explained, "Oh, we talk openly about other people's problems, but not about our own. Or if we do, we talk about them only after they're resolved."

I asked about the mood of the staff, but he didn't really answer my question. Instead, he remarked, "I think staff members would have to commit a rape and murder to be fired from this church. To my knowledge, there's never been anybody fired, and I don't think there ever will be."

I assumed he was implying that the top leaders were somewhat incompetent in handling staff inefficiencies. "Are you unhappy here?" I asked.

His eyes lit up, "Oh no, Dr. Chand. I love it here. You should have seen the place I came from. It was a nightmare! There are some things here I don't like, but compared to where I've been, this is like heaven!"

Stagnant Cultures

Many organizations begin with a clear vision and great teamwork, but find that sooner or later, their culture loses energy and stagnates. The vision may still be as clear as it has ever been, but the atmosphere is like a humid summer day in Houston—so oppressive it makes you wilt! In these organizations, the Indy car finds itself on a dirt road full of ruts and holes, a road more suited to a pickup than a race car. To make much progress at all, the car moves slowly to avoid damage. At the end of each day, the driver is worn out but hasn't gone very far.

Characteristics of Stagnant Cultures

- The leadership team sees staff members as production units, not people. The staff members are valuable when—and only when—they produce. All praise is based on performance, very little if any on character.

- Staff members tolerate their leaders, but they don't trust or respect them. They still do their work, but only the most ambitious invest themselves in the success of the organization.

- The only heroes are the top executives, and the employees suspect that these top leaders are making a bundle, or at least receiving lots of accolades, at their expense. They resent it, too.

- Without trust, respect, and loyalty, people feel compelled to defend their turf, hang on to power, and limit communication. In this atmosphere, relatively small problems quickly escalate.

- Complaining becomes the staff members' pastime. Things aren't quite bad enough to prompt open rebellion, but a few disgruntled people are thinking about it!

- The leadership team isn't happy with the lack of enthusiasm and declining productivity, so they treat staff as if they were wayward teenagers. They try anything to control them: anger, pleading, threats, rewards, ignoring them, micromanaging them . . . but nothing works.

- With only a few exceptions, people become clock-watchers and check-cashers, caring little for the leader's vision. The whole organization lives in a status quo of lethargy.

- To correct the problem, the leaders may send people to seminars or hire consultants, but the top people aren't willing to take responsibility and make significant changes. It's always somebody else's fault.

- These organizations usually attract people with low expectations and low motivation, but they may attract a few who believe their personal mission is to bring life to the organization. These individuals usually give up after a few months.

Case Study: A Long-Established Church in the Midwest

When I met Sarah, she had been at the church as pastor of singles for about a year. She expressed exasperation with the lethargy and red tape at the church. "I know church work is difficult, and we need to be flexible," she related, "but a little planning by our leadership team would go a long way. I'm trying to make a difference in people's lives, but all I get from them is confusion and delays. The senior leaders say all the right things, but there's very little follow-through. Strange, isn't it?"

I asked if she had communicated her concerns to the people on the leadership team, and she bristled, "About a million times. Too many times, I guess, because now they're branding me as the problem. I used to love this work, but now I think I'm just going through the motions each day. We do some good work for the men and women in our ministry, but it's such a strain to work with the leadership team. I'm on the team, but I feel like I'm on the outside looking in."

I asked, "Sarah, how does your supervisor explain the situation as you talk to him about your vision and your need for support?"

She answered, "He says, 'Sarah, this church has been here for 150 years, and it'll be here long after you and I are gone. This is the way we've always done things, and it's worked pretty well. I think we should just keep doing the same things.'"

I met with several of her staff and key volunteers, and they all were very complimentary of Sarah's leadership. Some of them seemed hesitant to say much of anything to me, probably out of fear that I might talk to the senior pastor, but one of Sarah's administrative assistants volunteered, "Dr. Chand, I know the strain Sarah is under. She's the best thing that ever happened to this church, and she's the best thing that ever happened to me. She protects us the best she can, but she gets pretty discouraged. And let me tell you, if she leaves, I'm leaving, too."

Discouraging Cultures

A few organizations suck the life out of their employees, leaving them hurt, angry, and confused. Every church and nonprofit encounters problems, but good ones make a point of resolving difficulties so that they can rebuild trust and achieve their goals. Discouraging cultures, though, live with the ghosts of countless unresolved problems and unhealed wounds. These organizations may still have clear, bold visions and effective strategies, but their people spend most of their time protecting themselves instead of devoting their energies to the success of the organization. The church's vision and strategy are like an Indy car stuck in the mud. The energy of the engine is wasted in spinning tires.

Characteristics of Discouraging Cultures

- It's all about the top people: their prestige and their power. They act as though everybody else in the organization exists only to make them more successful, and most of the staff members deeply resent it.

- People spend as much time trying to survive the power struggles, protecting themselves from more hurt, and analyzing the top people's pathology as they spend doing the work of the ministry. Staff may become fiercely loyal to a supervisor who protects them, but they actively seek to undermine any perceived adversary.

- As the benchmarks of success decline, the top leaders become more authoritarian and threatening. They demand compliance and loyalty, and they defy anyone who disagrees with them or even offers another opinion. One man who worked in a nationally known church told me, "The ministry director told me that I had to work eighty hours a week or I could leave. I'm a salaried employee, so I don't get overtime. Basically, he was saying, 'We don't care about you at all. We *own* you.' That day, I started looking for another job."

- The leadership team often tries to remedy the problems, but with the wrong analysis and the wrong solutions. They seldom look in the mirror to find a culprit. Instead, the blame is always put on "incompetent" or "unmotivated" people throughout the organization, but these are the only ones who are willing to stay employed there! Leaders may ask staff members to go to seminars and workshops, and they may even hire consultants from time to time, but they seldom listen to any outside input.

- When these leaders communicate a new vision, nobody cares. They've heard it before, and they don't trust that anything will be different this time.

- These organizations attract malcontents, sycophants, and desperate people who can't find a job anywhere else.

Case Study: A Youth Ministry in the Middle Atlantic States

John is the director of twenty youth ministries in three states. About seventy-five staff members and volunteers report to him. He was hired because of his reputation for caring for staff. The previous director had been quite goal oriented, instituting a rigid set of performance expectations and reviews. The nature of people who are attracted to the staff of youth ministries, though, is highly relational. The local leaders chaffed under the former director's leadership, and he bruised a lot of them by insisting on their compliance "no matter what."

When John was hired, they said they wanted him to breathe fresh air into these staff members, but soon he realized that he was suffocating in the smog of the board's resentments and demands. He found himself in the middle of a power play among several powerful, wealthy men on the board. For over a year, he was caught between warring factions on the board; sky-high demands for staff performance (didn't they hire him to change the culture?); and misunderstandings by his local staff, who were upset that he wasn't able to implement change any faster. By the time I saw him, John was experiencing stress-related medical problems. He had come into his role full of confidence that he was a competent leader. "Now," he related with obvious sadness, "I don't know if I can do anything right anymore." He called me because he wanted my advice about dropping out of ministry.

Toxic Cultures

Strangely, some of the most toxic organizations have the most charming leaders. To people on the outside looking in, these senior leaders and nonprofit executives present themselves as gracious, gifted leaders, but those who see them every day are the victims of their fangs and venom! In these cultures, the Indy car is on the road, but the bridge is out! Disaster is waiting for those who stay on board.

Characteristics of Toxic Cultures

- Leaders create a "closed system," so any advice and creative ideas from the outside are suspect from the start. In his insightful book *Incest in the Organizational Family*, William White observes that these systems breed bad ideas, bad behaviors, and bad values into the organization over and over again. That's why he calls it incest.

- Individual rights and the dignity of staff members are surrendered to the powerful elite. People are expected to do as they are told—nothing less and nothing else. The organization's leaders believe they "own" every employee. They have exceptionally high expectations of workers, but they offer them little or no autonomy to make decisions.

- Fear becomes the dominating motivational factor of the organization, and those who choose to stay meekly comply—most of the time. Many, though, are too afraid to leave. They've noticed that when people even think about leaving, they're severely criticized for being "disloyal."

- Turf battles are the accepted sport of the organization, and open warfare becomes normal. Suspicion and resentment poison lines of communication, so even the simplest directive becomes a weapon.

- Leaders delegate responsibility but fail to give authority to people to fulfill their roles.

- Creativity and risk-taking have long vanished, and in fact, these traits threaten the status of the bosses as the only ones who know anything. In this environment, pathology is rewarded and health is punished.

- Ethical, financial, or sexual lapses may occur, but staff members are expected to turn a blind eye. The leaders may constantly look over their shoulders to see if they've been caught.

- These organizations run off good people, and they attract only the naïve or truly desperate.

Case Study: A Hospital

I talked with a woman who had been an administrator at a hospital in another city before she moved to her new position. "I had to get out of there," she told me. "It was a disaster." She related that her previous boss was a tyrant. "He was often asked to speak at civic functions around the city and even at churches from time to time, and he gave wonderful talks about our hospital being a place of hope and healing. But no one in the office trusted him. We had to warn any woman who came to work in our department that she might be a target of his sexual advances. Some of them listened; some didn't. One of them got pregnant and had an abortion."

I asked if she had talked to the hospital's human resources department. She laughed, "Oh, I tried several times. They talked to him, and he convinced them that I was blowing it all out of proportion." The damage, however, wasn't limited to the boss's sexual targets. "Everyone in the office suffered," she related. "Never did we feel safe and appreciated. I stayed as long as I could, but when I had the chance to leave, I took it." She explained that he was finally exposed, fired, and charged. "I hope they found a good person to take his place. Just think," she lamented, "all that happened in a place of healing. Very strange."

In my experience, the spectrum of cultures I've described falls along a bell curve. I've found relatively few truly inspiring organizations, but thankfully, I haven't encountered many that are genuinely toxic. Most churches and nonprofits fall in the middle three categories. Looking at the top end of the scale, we shouldn't assume that inspiring and accepting organizations simply don't have problems and that this is why they excel. Quite the contrary. They all experience difficulties, but the leaders of healthy organizations are steadfastly committed to resolving problems, not with a heavy hand to rigidly control people, but by treating everyone with respect. They work hard to continue to build their cultures, taking nothing for granted. An incestuous organization continually breeds bad genes back into the system, but healthy companies invite new ideas and creative input from every imaginable source. A significant element of their stimulating environment is their thirst for growth and development.

Potholes, Mud, Pits, and Collapsed Bridges

The most powerful features of an organizational culture are trust and respect. With them, almost any problem can be resolved, or at least people learn valuable lessons from difficult experiences, and in the process even learn to trust each other more. But without trust and respect, even the smallest molehill soon morphs into an Everest. The most common hazards we face are

The most powerful features of an organizational culture are trust and respect.

Unrealistic demands

Blaming others

Feeling threatened by others' success

Power struggles

Dishonesty

Creating an atmosphere of fear

Using people instead of valuing them

Unclear vision, strategy, goals, and values

A lack of authenticity

Let's look at some of the potholes, mud pits, and collapsed bridges that threaten to slow, stall, or crash our Indy car.

Unrealistic Demands

There's nothing in the world wrong with having high expectations of staff members, so long as there is always a healthy dose of realism in an atmosphere that welcomes give-and-take, creativity, and problem solving at all levels. Let's be honest. Leaders of churches and nonprofits shoulder enormous responsibilities. When times are tough, the easiest thing for them to do is pressure their staff to work harder and longer. These pressure points, though, are watershed moments for organizations. I've seen some leaders go to their staff, explain the difficult situation they're in, and say something like, "I know I'm asking for a lot, but here's what I need you to do. I'm in it with you, and together, we'll get through this." In these cases, the vast majority of staff members respond by rolling up their sleeves and working tirelessly, and the experience builds the bond between them and the leadership team. But too often, I've been called in after the leader damaged people and eroded their trust in him by simply demanding "more bricks with less straw"—a sure recipe for resentful staff!

Leaders may communicate unrealistic expectations in any area: deadlines, workload, skills, training, communication, or productivity. In dysfunctional cultures, however, any question from an employee is met by an angry response: "I don't care what it takes. Just get it done!"

Blaming Others

One of the most trust-building statements any leader can make is, "I'm sorry. I was wrong." Most of us have no idea how much it means to our staff when we take responsibility for our blunders. Almost nothing builds trust like a leader's accepting responsibility,

> *One of the most trust-building statements any leader can make is, "I'm sorry. I was wrong."*

and almost nothing destroys it as quickly as blaming others for one's mistakes. Some leaders try to wear Teflon, hoping nothing will stick to them when problems occur. They fail to realize that a responsible, heartfelt response to a single failure may do more for their culture than a hundred successes.

Feeling Threatened by Others' Success

Some leaders desperately want to appear supremely confident but actually are terribly insecure. They demand to be the center of attention, the go-to person for the organization, and they feel threatened when anyone else succeeds or receives applause. These leaders may occasionally smile and pat successful people on the back because they know it's expected of them, but perceptive staff can tell that their smile hides a grimace.

Power Struggles

When organizations don't enjoy an atmosphere of trust and respect, they quickly degenerate into a law of the jungle and survival of the fittest mind-set. Fitness, in toxic cultures, is measured not by competence but by cunning. Everyone longs for security and significance, but without trust, the only hope of achieving these goals lies in hiding to avoid trouble or in beating others to the top. In these organizations, people often form alliances—just as contestants do on the reality show *Survivor*. People secretly plot against each other, forming secret (or not so secret) alliances. Gossip, deception, lies, and sabotage become chess pieces in the game. In the end, everyone loses, even those who thought they won, because those who watched them as well as those who participated lost respect for people playing the game. People engage in these games at every level of corporate life, from the senior pastor's office to the loading dock. Without trust and honest communication, these games are inevitable . . . and destructive.

> *Fitness, in toxic cultures, is measured not by competence but by cunning.*

Dishonesty

Some leaders may be able to fool some of the people some of the time, but they can't fool all the people all the time. Sooner or later, their dishonesty will come back to bite them. To make themselves look good and others look bad, they may exaggerate just a bit, or they may outright lie to anyone who will listen. People treasure truth, fairness, and justice, so deceptive leaders shatter their reputations, breaking trust with those whom they need most to run a successful organization.

Creating an Atmosphere of Fear

Fear, I believe, is one of the most powerful motivators in the world—and one of the most destructive. The reason so many leaders use it is that it's very effective, and when these leaders see how it controls people's behavior, the effect is almost addictive. Outbursts of anger, cutting criticism, isolation, gossip, and a host of other painful actions may be directed at a single person, but the incident affects everyone who watches, listens, or even hears a rumor about it. Harsh words and deeds don't have to happen every day to destroy a ministry environment. Even occasional outbursts of anger and condemnation stick in the minds and hearts of the staff to create the fear that such outbursts could happen again—and could happen to them!

Angry leaders soon become convinced that fear works very well as a motivational tool, and they close their eyes to the damage they cause. Soon it becomes a normal part of the organization's culture. People learn to dance around it, hide from it, excuse it, and absorb the blame for others' misbehavior. Leaders who use fear to control people, however, need to remember that there are other, better ways to motivate people. Investment banker Charles Schwab commented, "I have yet to find the man, however exalted his station, who did not do better work and put forth greater effort under a spirit of approval than under a spirit of criticism."

Using People Instead of Valuing Them

Do you think people can tell if their leaders value them or are just using them for their own selfish ends? A few unperceptive staff members may not be able to tell, or they may be so happy to have a job that they're willing to put up with it, but most of them inherently resent being seen as things instead of people. They want to be more than cogs in someone's machine, more than a cipher on a spreadsheet of production, and more than a servant to respond to another's wishes. They long to be seen as people of value, and they do their best work when they feel appreciated. Australian entrepreneur John Ilhan observed, "If you treat staff as your equal, they'll roll their sleeves up to get the job done."

Unclear Vision, Strategy, Goals, and Values

People don't thrive in confusion. When a leader charts a clear course, the staff may ask a lot of questions before they get on board, and some may drag their feet for a long time before they embrace the skipper's map, but understanding is an essential element of a healthy work environment. Some leaders don't invite questions when they make their pronouncement of the future. Maybe they're not too sure about it themselves. And a few leaders believe that a slick presentation should wow people enough that they won't have any questions at all. A clear grasp of the direction of the organization, though, is essential for there to be alignment and teamwork in each area of ministry. Without it, people wander, complain, doubt their leaders, chart their own course, or leave to find better leaders. Unpredictable leaders produce tentative followers.

Unpredictable leaders produce tentative followers.

A Lack of Authenticity

People thrive on genuine appreciation, but they bristle when they sense that affirmations are less than sincere. A staff member of a megachurch told me, "I wish the ministry director wouldn't ever try to compliment me. Every time he does, it seems so contrived, forced, and insincere. I'd much rather hear nothing than that." It's not enough for leaders simply to say the right things; their people have to believe that in the depths of their hearts, the leaders mean them—and they shouldn't say them until and unless their words can be genuine. For some, this presents a problem: they simply can't seem to muster sincere appreciation for others. The difficulty, though, isn't in the leader's personality. I believe God made all of us with the capacity to show genuine thankfulness to him and to people. The problem is that some leaders resent the fact that they aren't getting as much praise as they're expected to give out. Their emotional tank is empty, and they hate filling up someone else's until theirs is filled.

People around us can sense when we're being sincere and when we're phony. They despise phoniness, but they thrive on sincere appreciation, even if it's not as frequent or as eloquent as they'd like it to be. A lack of authenticity in appreciation further erodes trust and creates doubt among the troops.

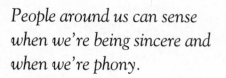

People around us can sense when we're being sincere and when we're phony.

Very few senior leaders of toxic environments read books like this. The last thing they want is an objective appraisal of the dysfunction in their organizations. However, a few find the courage to make drastic changes. And top leaders across the rest of the spectrum long for their churches and nonprofits to be strong, healthy places where people thrive, support each other, and celebrate each other's successes. That, they are convinced, is the key to genuine success for their organizations, their leadership teams, their staff members, and those they serve. They have learned to be wary of the culture killers and address them quickly when their ugly heads arise.

Think About This . . .

1. Think of the organizations where you've worked or, if you've worked only in one for a long time, think of the departments where you've worked. Where would you put each of these on the spectrum of cultural health?

   Inspiring . . . Accepting . . . Stagnant . . . Discouraging . . . Toxic

2. Pick one of those experiences and jot down the characteristics (positive and negative) from this chapter that describe it.

3. Review the list of potholes, mud, pits, and collapsed bridges in the second part of the chapter. For each one, rate on a scale of 0 (not in the least) to 10 (all day every day) the degree to which your leadership reflects these problems:

   _____ Unrealistic demands

   _____ Blaming others

   _____ Being threatened by others' success

   _____ Power struggles

   _____ Dishonesty

   _____ Creating an atmosphere of fear

   _____ Using people instead of valuing them

   _____ Unclear vision, strategy, goals, and values

   _____ Lack of authenticity

4. What does this exercise tell you about yourself? What does this exercise tell you about your organization?

3

SEVEN KEYS OF CULTURE

To look at something as though we had never seen
it before requires great courage.

—*Henri Matisse, painter*

Have you ever walked into an office and, after only a few casual,
brief conversations with people, sensed something was wrong?
Many of us have a sixth sense about the atmosphere and relationships on a team, but it's much easier to take a sniff test in
someone else's church, office, store, team, or home than our
own. Amazingly, some of us who are incredibly perceptive about
other cultures are clueless about the nature of relationships and
attitudes around us each day. To be objective, we need to step
back from time to time and take a good, long look in the mirror.
We might be surprised at what we see.

People have an almost limitless capacity for self-deception.
We don't know what we don't know and are therefore unconsciously incompetent. If we were aware of our deficits, we'd
ask questions and find
solutions, but because
we're not aware, we stay
stuck in the status quo
until something shakes
us awake.

> *We don't know what we don't know
> and are therefore unconsciously
> incompetent.*

Quite often, we need some help to see things clearly. We are
simply too close to the people and systems in our own environment to be objective. To change the metaphor: you wouldn't
ask a fish to tell you how water tastes because it doesn't have
objectivity. Only someone from the outside (or perhaps some

penetrating questions from an outside source) can help a fish analyze the purity of water—or assist us in taking an accurate read on the health of our culture.

Beyond Excuses

When I talk with leaders and teams about creating a new culture, many of them instantly realize the beauty and power of working together in an inspiring environment, and they commit themselves to do whatever it takes to achieve it. Others, however, find creative excuses for remaining stuck in the past. I've heard people say they can't take steps forward because

"I'm too new to the team. No one would listen to me."

"I only have three years left before I retire. It seems like it would take too much out of me to try to change our culture."

"The price is too high. I'm not willing to take those risks."

"I can't do everything. We're starting a building campaign, and I need to devote my energies to that."

"I've been trying to cast a vision for the future, but people just don't get it."

"Every time I try to talk about our culture, people get defensive. I've had it!"

Analyzing a team's culture is a lot like marriage counseling. The way people relate to each other and the way things get done are entrenched patterns that have been in place for years. These patterns frustrate people, but nobody talks about them until someone from the outside addresses the core issues of culture, connection, and communication. When I consult with pastors and teams, I often begin by asking, "Imagine your team is the U.S. Congress. How does a bill get passed here?" Quite often, people roll their eyes or laugh in a passive-aggressive way. They feel uncomfortable because I've asked a question that addresses more than surface issues. I've probed into the heart of their culture. I pause and let them realize that my question wasn't rhetorical, and then they really get nervous! After an awkward moment, one might say, "Well, we talk a lot, but not much gets done." Or someone might assert with a flash of anger, "We all have different

Imagine your team is the U.S. Congress. How does a bill get passed here?

ideas about how to do things, but we can't seem to come to a conclusion." Or more telling, a person might grumble, "I'm not sure if my input matters much, about this or anything else."

To help the team members uncover their needs and desires, I often ask, "If the meeting ended right now and you could make one suggestion to the pastor (or team leader) to improve the church or the team, what would it be? Anything goes. What would you suggest to him?" Recently, when I asked this question in a team, the responses included,

"Better strategic planning."

"Implement what we plan instead of just leaving the plans on a piece of paper."

"Clear communication and coordination."

"Empower people to do what they're asked to do."

"Simplify the strategy."

"Add strength and value to the present team."

"Relax more and enjoy what we do."

"Clear and simple opportunities to engage the vision."

"Hold people accountable."

"Plan ahead, and include us in the planning."

"Celebrate our achievements."

"Stop changing the goalposts."

Their answers told me volumes about their culture. These suggestions surfaced their perceptions of their current environment. Without saying, "Pastor, I don't feel valued by you, and I'm afraid you're going to replace me with someone else," the person communicated the same idea by suggesting that the pastor "value the present team." Words matter, and they often carry multiple meanings.

People might think that pastors become defensive and resistant when their people give these suggestions, but quite often, I've noticed a spirit of genuine openness. Pastors and team leaders genuinely want to be the best leaders they can be. Many of them spend thousands of dollars each year attending conferences to learn to fulfill their roles more effectively. When the issue of culture is raised, they simply haven't known the right questions to ask to get below the surface to talk about the team's environment. When I ask these questions and pastors hear their staff members' responses, they are often surprised, but they always want to talk more about their perceptions. Then, when we talk about culture, they often report, "I've never heard that before" or "I didn't know that." Leaders and team members need to start with a few questions that help them look in the mirror to see what's really going on. Insight provides choices, and these choices become steps in creating a vibrant culture.

Pastors and business leaders report that it's relatively easy to institute a new program or introduce a new product, but changing the culture is the hardest thing they've ever done. It requires wisdom, courage, and tenacity, but it begins with an understanding of the current condition. A few simple metaphors help them see the importance of addressing the culture of their organizations. I often explain that it doesn't make sense to serve a lovely dinner on a dirty plate, and a doctor can't perform a kidney transplant until the patient is free from infection. A stagnant, discouraging, or toxic culture is like the dirty plate and the infection. Very little progress can be made until the plate is washed and the disease is healed. But once they are, dramatic progress is possible. Leaders (and their team members) instinctively understand these metaphors. As I shared this concept with one pastor, he told me, "Dr. Chand, this is incredibly helpful. For a long time, I thought I needed to charge up my team by finding just the right program. When that didn't work, I tried to be more passionate about our vision, but the more intense I became, the more passive they got. I've tried all kinds of things. Some worked for a while, and of course, some worked better than others. But now I realize that I've been trying to serve a steak dinner on a dirty plate. No one wanted to receive what I was presenting. We have to clean the plate. Will you help me?"

> *It doesn't make sense to serve a lovely dinner on a dirty plate, and a doctor can't perform a kidney transplant until the patient is free from infection.*

A Glimpse of the Culture

I want to invite you and your team to look in the mirror to see the nature of your culture. The categories of "healthy" and "unhealthy" aren't very helpful because they aren't specific. To go deeper, we'll examine seven important factors that shape organizational culture, and for each of these, we'll identify particular attitudes and behaviors that point a culture toward either inspiration or toxicity. The seven keys of CULTURE are

1. Control
2. Understanding
3. Leadership
4. Trust
5. Unafraid

6. Responsive

7. Execution

As we examine these, don't focus on yourself. Instead, take the temperature of your whole team. Culture is about relationships, communication, and shared values, not just about an individual's perceptions and behavior.[1]

Control

People function most effectively if they are given control (or authority) with responsibility. If they are held accountable for a task without having the means to accomplish it, they'll fail, and they'll be terribly frustrated.

On the other end of the spectrum, if control is concentrated in one person who insists on making virtually all important decisions, the organization experiences a significant bottleneck. It should be a warning if everyone is expected to consult with one person about everything before moving on. Bottlenecks affect every person on the team, not just the one who is waiting for an answer. Isn't it odd (and thoroughly predictable) that when one lane of traffic is blocked on the interstate, all the lanes slow to a crawl? Teams thrive when there is a free flow of information and ready access to resources.

Contrary to the beliefs of some people, *control* isn't a dirty word. Delegating responsibility and maintaining accountability are essential for any organization to be effective. Strong, effective teams have a "Goldilocks approach" to control: not too much, not too little, but just the right amount of checks and balances. The leader gives clear direction, assigns tasks, delegates authority, provides resources, and then has a reasonable reporting procedure so the person can provide updates, coordinate with others, and stay on track until the task is finished.

The right control system for a team is like a conveyor belt of ideas and resources. It manages the flow of work—not to slow it down, but to make it flow smoothly and effectively.

Quite often, the real power broker on a team isn't the person at the head of the table. Good leaders involve everyone in the planning process, but sometimes an angry, sour, or demanding person can dominate a team. A sure sign of problems with control on a team are turf issues. When two or more people believe they have responsibility and authority for a task, they compete with each other for resources and, even

Turf battles are about personal pride and perceived power.

more, for supremacy over each other. Turf battles really aren't about the tasks people fight over; they are about personal pride and perceived power.

Team members need to see themselves as partners in a grand venture, not competing for control over others, not carving out territory to defend to the death, but using delegated authority for the common good.

Here and in the next sections, I want to ask a few questions to help you analyze each element of your culture.

Take a Look

- Are lines of authority and responsibility clear on your team? How can you tell?
- Do people know what is expected of them, or are they confused sometimes?
- What do turf wars look like on your team? What are they really about?
- Would you say there is too much control from the top on your team, too little, or just the right amount? Explain your answer.

Understanding

Every person on a team needs to have a clear grasp of the vision, his or her role, the gifts and contributions of the team members, and the way the team functions. Each person should be able to clearly articulate each of these vital aspects of the team's life.

The vision must be both global and specific—too big for anyone to accomplish without the power of God, but with handles on each person's specific role in fulfilling aspects of the overall vision. It breaks my heart when I talk to a staff member who says glumly, "I'm not really sure what I'm doing here."

Healthy, strong teams can point to one another and say things like, "Bill is really good at that," "Crystal understands this system really well," or "Kim has experience in helping people with that issue." Knowing one another and appreciating each person's contributions grease the wheels of progress on a team. How do we know what makes each other tick? By taking time to hear each other's stories. In staff meetings or during an hour over coffee, we can find out more about someone's heart and experiences than we could learn in years of sitting in meetings together. All it takes is a little time and a few caring questions.

Team communications are everybody's responsibility. Certainly the leader's task is to make sure each person clearly grasps the principles and delegated tasks, but good teams normalize the question everyone can ask: "Would you explain that again? I'm not sure I got it." In this way, misunderstanding is never an excuse for not getting the job done. Similarly, before a meeting is over, the leader can ask each person to share priorities, schedule, and coordination needed with other team members. This way, everyone is on the same page.

Understanding, though, isn't just about the *what* of ministry; it's also about the *why*. Again, grasping the underlying concepts is everybody's job. Leaders need to take time to explain how a new program fits into the plan, why it will make a difference in people's lives, and the important role each person will play in making it successful. Team members are encouraged to take initiative to ask questions so they understand these things, even if the leader forgets to explain them.

Take a Look

- Is the vision for your team both God-sized and specific? Explain your answer.
- Do people on the team feel understood, valued, and directed to give their best each day?
- Do most lines of communication on the team flow from the leader, or is there good cross-pollination? What's the result of this flow?
- How do people on the team respond when someone asks "Why?"?

Leadership

Healthy teams are pipelines of leadership development. They recognize that an organization is only as healthy as the pool of rising leaders, so they actively seek to *discover* those who show leadership potential, *develop* resources to equip and inspire leaders, and carefully *deploy*

> *Healthy teams are pipelines of leadership development.*

them in roles that enflame their hearts, challenge them to excel, and propel the organization to new heights.

We need to make a distinction between leadership and management. To develop people to become leaders, we focus on heart and character. Training is important, but it's a management issue, equipping people to perform a particular task. Both are significant, but developing people is far more essential in creating a healthy culture than training people in specific skills. Plenty of toxic and discouraging cultures have highly trained, efficient staff members. They know how to do their jobs very well, but their culture stinks.

Let me highlight the differences between leaders and managers:

Leaders	Managers
Conceptualize outcome by working from the FUTURE back to the PRESENT	Conceptualize plans by working from the PAST to the PRESENT
Embrace a MACRO—big picture—perspective	Embrace a MICRO—snapshot—perspective
Favor INNOVATIVE thinking	Favor ROUTINE thinking
Possess REVOLUTIONARY flair	Are PROTECTORS of the status quo
Emphasize the WHAT and WHY	Emphasize the HOW and WHEN
Are INSPIRING and motivating	Are CONTROLLING and directing
Are EXCITED by change	Are THREATENED by change
Move QUICKLY	Move SLOWLY
Identify OPPORTUNITIES	Identify OBSTACLES
Take RISKS	Avoid RISKS
Pursue acquisition of RESOURCES	Are bounded by AVAILABLE resources
Are PEOPLE centered	Are SYSTEM centered
Are IDEA centered	Are PLAN centered
Perceive people's approval as a WANT	Perceive people's approval as a NEED

Summary: Managers get the most out of themselves. Leaders get the most out of others.[2]

Many church teams focus on training people to accomplish tasks, but they neglect the essential role of developing leaders. In many cases, staff members are under enormous stress. They have a long list of jobs that need to be done—and done now!—and they're desperate for help. They are thrilled and relieved when someone steps into the gap to complete a task, but they don't even think about developing the person as a leader. We'll never have truly healthy cultures, however, if we don't identify and develop a host of strong, creative, passionate leaders.

Team leaders need to be perceptive about how rising leaders are assimilated into the group. Are old leaders threatened, or do they celebrate and mentor the new people? Great organizations enlist existing leaders to be part of the leadership pipeline, encouraging them to offer their insights and expertise and to help young leaders in every possible way.

Take a Look

- How would you describe the leadership pipeline in your organization?
- How well is the system working in identifying and developing rising leaders?
- What kinds of resources (time, money, personnel, and so on) are devoted to leadership development?
- When times are tough, what happens to leadership development in your organization?

Trust

Mutual trust among team members is the glue that makes everything good possible. Without it, a team quickly disintegrates into a gang of people protecting their turf and forming angry alliances. Trust is important up, down, and across the organizational structure. People need to have confidence that their supervisors mean what they say and say what they mean. When people trust each other, they make a strong connection between the vision, their own roles, the input of others, strategic planning, and the steps of implementation.

Trust may be freely given, but it is usually earned as people watch each other respond in good times and bad. Integrity and consistency provide a firm foundation for relationships to thrive. Trust is fluid. It takes time to be built, but it can be destroyed in an instant. Trust grows in an environment that is HOT: honest,

Trust grows in an environment that is HOT: honest, open, and transparent.

open, and transparent. People aren't expected to be perfect, but they are expected to own their failures as well as their successes. Confession, contrary to popular opinion, is good both for the soul *and* for the person's reputation.

Failure and times of difficulty are the windows people use to determine if others are genuinely trustworthy. It's easy to put on a happy face when times are good, but struggles reveal a person's true nature. In hard times for an individual, the team, or the church, the hearts of everyone on the team are exposed. When others fail in an important task, do the leader and team members delight in pouncing on the person who blew it, or do they use the failure as an opportunity for growth? And the person who failed isn't the only one who notices how he's being treated. Everyone on the team is watching; all members are living the experience vicariously, anticipating how they'll be treated when they fail.

Office gossip is one of the most prevalent—and one of the most destructive—behaviors for many teams. Gossip, I believe, isn't innocent fun. It's a form of undercover revenge designed to harm someone. In an article on workplace gossip, Shayla McKnight reports that she joined a company that had a no-gossip policy. She explains, "At the beginning of my employment interview two years ago, Marne Reed, the human resources manager who interviewed me, mentioned the company's no-gossip policy. She said something like this: 'There's no back-stabbing here, and no office politics. Gossiping and talking behind someone's back are not tolerated.' I remember thinking: 'Really? That's odd. How is that possible?' Everywhere I've worked people have gossiped." She says that the environment at this company is different because of the policy: "There's a greater sense of being part of a team here than in other jobs I've had.

If employees do violate the company policy, a manager speaks to them, and if they don't stop, they're let go. It might be human nature to think an unkind thought about a co-worker, but it's a choice whether or not to actually say it."[3]

Trust can be shattered in an instant by a dramatic event, or, more often, it is slowly eroded by countless relatively small but abrasive comments and actions. Every team is made up of flawed human beings, so on every team, trust will be an issue to some degree at some time with someone. Depending on the situation, it doesn't have to ruin a team. In fact, relationships that rebuild broken trust often are stronger and healthier than ever before because the people involved had to be ruthlessly honest, find forgiveness, and communicate better than before.

Take a Look

- In what ways is trust being built or eroded on your team?
- How does creating a HOT (honest, open, and transparent) environment build trust? In what ways does it threaten people?
- How is failure treated on your team? How does that response affect the level of trust?
- How does the team handle gossip? Are there clear guidelines? Should there be some? Why or why not?

Unafraid

Corporate courage is an incredibly appealing but slippery trait. I marvel at the bravery of soldiers who face withering enemy fire and mind-numbing conditions, but keep pressing forward until they win the battle. What is the source of their courage? It's not the absence of fear. They face a host of doubts and terrors, but soldiers report that two things keep them going: a clear conviction of the nobility of their cause and a commitment to the men fighting next to them. As I've watched church teams over the years, I've seen the same pattern. They aren't fighting a battle against flesh and blood, but men and women on staff teams face difficulties and challenges with courage if, and only if, they are convinced that what they are doing counts for all eternity and they believe in the people serving on their team.

Too often, I've met with teams who had a staff member or two who felt they had to walk on eggshells instead of speaking out boldly. For some reason (and it could be any of a host of issues, usually stemming from a painful past, but sometimes more recent wounds in the team environment), they feel insecure, and they believe they need to hide to avoid any risk. Being wrong or being asked a hard question, they assume, is the worst possible fate.

Healthy teams foster the perspective that failure isn't a tragedy and conflict isn't the end of the world. Great leaders welcome dissenting opinions, as long as they are offered in good will and with an eye toward a solution. These teams are willing to take great risks and even to fail miserably because they've gotten over the notion that failure is a personal flaw. They believe that God is worthy of noble efforts, and they trust that God smiles on them as they attempt great things for him. When they look at one another, they don't see competitors; they see friends who have their backs as they take big risks. Courage, support, and innovation go hand in hand in inspiring cultures.

Great leaders welcome dissenting opinions, as long as they are offered in good will and with an eye toward a solution.

Take a Look

- What are some examples of courage on your team in the past year or so?
- How does one person's courage affect a team? How do defensiveness and timidity affect it?

- Why is it important that wisdom direct a person's courage? What happens when a person is courageous without being wise?

- In what ways is courage "caught, not taught"?

Responsive

Teams with healthy cultures are alert to open doors and ones that are closing. An individual may not notice a particular threat or opportunity, but someone else on the team will. These teams develop the productive habit of keeping their eyes open so that they can handle every situation: on the team, in individuals' lives, in the church family, and in the community.

For teams to be responsive, they have to develop a consistent process for collaboration, with communication lines that are wide open. They value analysis and feedback, and they work on becoming and staying aligned with one another. Infighting and turf wars steal people's attention and keep them from noticing and responding to the needs around them. Effective teams, though, work hard to keep their minds and hearts focused on God's purposes. After decisions are made, team members fully support the team's decision. They understand that an individual's foot-dragging or resistance can hold up the entire process, so they learn the art of communication and finding common ground. They publicly support the team's decision instead of lobbying in the hallway for their contrarian's point of view for days or weeks.

Responsive teams don't just focus on big goals and sweeping strategies. They develop the habit of taking care of the little things, such as promptly returning phone calls, responding to e-mails, and communicating decisions to everyone who needs to know when he or she needs to know it.

Strong, vibrant cultures don't allow silos to close off communication between teams. In a somewhat whimsical but accurate definition of the term, a "business dictionary" says that silos in organizations are "non-communication between departments, incompatible goal-setting, intra-company snobbery, or out-right hostility. The term refers to the sealed-off nature of silos rather than to their utility in storing tomorrow's breakfast cereal. At its most extreme, siloing in the workplace leads to destructive competition among nominal allies while providing an opportunity to abuse agricultural metaphors."[4]

Leaders in healthy cultures work hard to disseminate information among the departments and get buy-in up and down the chain of command and between teams. Being responsive requires both a sensitive spirit and a workable system to make sure things don't fall through the cracks. The larger the organization grows, the greater the amount of energy that needs to be invested in being responsive to people inside and outside the team.

> *The larger the organization grows, the greater the amount of energy that needs to be invested in being responsive to people inside and outside the team.*

Take a Look

- How responsive is your team to threats and opportunities? What are the signs of responsiveness (or lack of it)?

- How do collaboration and communication affect a team's responsiveness?

- How often do "little things" like returning phone calls and e-mails fall through the cracks on your team? Is this a problem? Why or why not?

- Does your team's current organizational system (delegation, feedback, collaboration, and so on) foster responsiveness or hinder it? Explain your answer.

Execution

In my conversations with leaders and team members, one of their chief concerns is that teams often talk about decisions but fail to follow through on implementing them. When they don't see the fruit of their discussions, they lose faith in each other and become discouraged. It's not a big deal if something doesn't get done because someone was sick or there's another good excuse, but systemwide, consistent failure poisons the atmosphere. Executing decisions is a function of clarity, roles and responsibilities, and the system of accountability.

To be sure that follow-through becomes the norm, leaders need to define goals very clearly. Decisions should be articulated with precision, including who, what, why, when, where, and how. Obviously, some decisions require more thought and precision than others, but many teams err on the side of fogginess, and the team suffers.

Clear delegation is essential to execution. The person responsible needs to understand her authority and how to relate to everyone else involved. This person should walk out of the meeting with crystal-clear expectations, a plan to coordinate with others, deadlines, and any other requirements.

On some teams, accountability is haphazard at best, but this breeds complacency even among those who would normally be conscientious about following through with their commitments. People don't do what we expect; they do what we inspect. Plans are worthless unless they have target goals, deadlines, access to resources, and a budget. With those things in place, the leader needs to ask for regular updates on progress. She can ask in any way that works: e-mail, phone calls, personal appointments, or, even better, in the staff meetings. Asking for progress reports in meetings lets the whole team know how progress is being made and the role members might play in helping the person complete the plan. Some people mistakenly believe that deadlines aren't very important, but they are the benchmark that keeps a plan on track.

To help leaders plan and delegate more effectively, I suggest that they use a simple planning template and that they train their staff to use it too. (See the template in Appendix 2.)

Developing a culture of accountability takes the mystery and the sting out of giving reports. If everybody is asked to report, then nobody is singled out. If, however, someone consistently fails to follow through, the leader can recognize it more quickly if the system is in place, and she can help the person clarify the goals, develop skills, find resources, or overcome any other challenge that has prevented him from taking steps toward execution.

To facilitate clear, accurate reporting from team members on the tasks they've been assigned, I suggest that teams use a simple reporting grid. (See Appendix 3 for a sample.) In a culture that executes plans well, the leader is committed to ongoing training to equip team members to achieve the highest goals. Incompetent people are retrained, moved to roles that fit them better, or removed from the team. The organization is committed to ensuring that people are serving in roles that match their strengths. Leaders focus on these strengths, not on people's weaknesses, and they pursue excellence in every aspect of corporate life, including communication and team building. A relentless pursuit of excellence in execution is a catalyst—not a hindrance—for healthy relationships.

Take a Look

- At the end of each staff meeting, how clearly defined are the goals and responsibilities of each person? How do you know?
- How are people held accountable on your team?
- How do team members give feedback to each other about their performance and communication?
- How would you describe the blend of heart motivation and the pursuit of excellence on your team?

Getting Buy-in

One person can change the composition of a team. It's best if the leader grasps the importance of creating an inspiring culture and takes bold steps with the team, but a wise, tenacious team member can begin to create this kind of environment.

I've seen some leaders try to change their organizations by fiat, demanding that people trust each other, communicate freely, and be more responsive to those inside and outside the team. But as you can imagine, these efforts only further eroded the environment and created one more hurdle to overcome. Great leaders put cultural issues on the table and invite honest, open, and transparent conversations about changing the atmosphere. They know it's going to take time, and they are willing to lead the process. They understand, though, that a successful transition of a team's culture depends on the buy-in of each person on the team—and perhaps the replacement of those who prove unwilling to take steps of progress. Building a great team involves everybody, and in fact it works most effectively when team members feel empowered to give input, develop strategies, and take steps in shaping the culture. In an interview about his organizational culture, Steve Ellis, worldwide managing director of Bain & Company, explained, "If you're looking for a little management philosophy, then my advice is to keep cultural initiatives organic and driven by the employees, with a little support from management. . . . Top-down cultural mandates simply don't work." Developing a powerfully positive culture, though, isn't just about people feeling good about themselves and each other. Production matters. Ellis reports, "Results serve as the core of our culture. We are passionate about what we do, enjoy our work, laugh a lot, and celebrate success when we achieve it."[5]

Changing a culture requires tremendous patience. We can rearrange boxes on an organizational chart in a moment, but changing culture is heart surgery. Culture is not only *what* we do but also *why* and *how* we do it. Culture is about the heart and head, and then it shapes what we do with our hands. Leaders also need a healthy dose of creativity as they take their teams through cultural change. In an article on teamwork, Keith Sawyer, a researcher at Washington University in St. Louis, describes the impact of "group genius," the ability of a team to work together to apply creative insights. He says, "Innovation today isn't a sudden break with the past, a brilliant insight that one lone outsider pushes through to save the business. Just the opposite: innovation today is a continuous process of small and constant change, and it's built into the culture of successful businesses."[6]

Culture is about the heart and head, and then it shapes what we do with our hands.

Cultural transformation may begin when an individual has a fresh insight about the need to work together more effectively, but sooner or later, everyone on the team has to get involved in the process. Some jump on the wagon with enthusiasm; others are brought along more reluctantly—but everyone on the team has to become a willing partner in the venture. When people bring their best to the team, amazing things can happen. As the Japanese proverb says, "None of us is as smart as all of us."

Think About It . . .

1. As you looked at the keys of CULTURE in this chapter, in which area is your team doing well? What is the area that needs the most attention?

2. What is your role in changing and shaping your team's culture?

3. What will it take to get buy-in from the whole team? What will you have to overcome? What resources will you need?

Use the questions in each section of the CULTURE analysis with your team to open dialogue, stimulate discussion, and gain objectivity about the current culture of the team.

For a free CULTURE survey for you and your team, go to www.freeculturesurvey.com.

4

VOCABULARY DEFINES CULTURE

When you have healthy supervisors and good
working conditions, what more do workers look
for? . . . There is really only one answer to this
question: *Recognition*. Not just bonuses and plaques,
privileged parking spaces or "worker of the week"
announcements, though these are very important,
but the type of recognition that affirms the value of
your self at the deepest possible level.

—*Dr. Archibald Hart*

When I was in the first grade in India, I was a rambunctious
kid. I remember stepping from desk to desk across the room.
I'm sure I exasperated my teacher, Miss Boniface. One day,
she looked at me as I was walking across the desks and sighed,
"Samuel, you are just a *janvar*." In Hindi, the word means "animal." I'm sure she didn't mean any harm. She wasn't yelling or
clenching her teeth at me, but for the rest of my years in that
elementary school, the name stuck. From that day on, students
and teachers called me janvar, and I lived up to my moniker.
The word defined me and gave me an identity. I acted like an
animal because that's what people expected of me, and I spent
many hours in the principal's office. I didn't devote myself to
being a good scholar, and I didn't spend my energies on sports. I
picked fights every day. I never won a fight—not one. In fights,
I scraped, clawed, bit, and kicked. The fights really never ended
because I started them again the next day. In fact, I fought with
the same people day after day all year. My life revolved around
being as disruptive as I could be so that I could validate others'
opinion of me. Everybody wants to be known for something,

and acting like an animal immediately became my USP—my unique selling point.

But words can also have a wonderful, inspiring effect. Many years later, I had shed my identity as an animal to become an academician. I was president of Beulah Heights University, and I had learned to be effective at administration, vision casting, and building relationships. One day, however, a man I respected looked me in the eye and said, "Sam, you are a really good leader." To be honest, I was very surprised by his comment because I had never seen myself as a leader. My curriculum in Bible college and seminary didn't have a single course on leadership, and I wasn't even sure what a leader was. I knew, though, that this statement had the potential to change my life. This man's sincere affirmation meant the world to me, and the fact that he qualified the word "leader" with "really good" gave me a new standard to live up to. From that day, I saw my role in a different light. It wasn't that I changed directions or careers, but now I viewed myself and my role through a broader lens, and I had confidence that God could use me in bigger ways. My friend hadn't made an appointment that day to tell me how he saw me, and he wasn't playing the role of a life coach or mentor. He was just a trusted friend who held up a mirror to affirm what he saw in me, and he encouraged me deeply.

The words we use, and the way we use them, define organizational culture.

Words have the power to shape lives and organizations. Too often, however, leaders aren't aware of their vocabulary as they speak, and they don't realize how people are affected by their words. Even casually spoken statements can have profound effects. The words we use, and the way we use them, define organizational culture. Some leaders think that the vocabulary of culture is only about painting the biggest, most dramatic vision they can paint—the bigger the better. But that's not the case. Vision statements are only a small part of the vocabulary of a culture. Factors that are just as important include

- Avoiding terms that actually hinder us from fulfilling God's vision
- Using informal, compassionate conversations to show empathy and build trust
- Occasionally stopping in the middle of a meeting to talk about how the team is communicating
- Being honest with team members and avoiding "happy talk"
- Learning to listen with our hearts, eyes, and ears
- Speaking words of genuine affirmation
- Intentionally choosing vocabulary to shape the culture

For most of us, the words we use are second nature. We don't even think about them anymore, but we can't overestimate the power of vocabulary to define culture. To make changes, we need honest reflection, feedback from the stakeholders at every level, and the courage to change not only our words but also our hearts as we speak them.

Every Industry Has a Vocabulary

Every field of study, every industry, and every organization creates its own vocabulary to communicate to its constituents. Insiders instantly recognize the meaning of words that may sound like a foreign language to outsiders. And in some fields, such as technology, vocabulary is changing at a rapid pace. The Word of the Year in 2005 was *podcast*, a term that today seems as though it's been around for decades. Auto repair shops, restaurants, the medical field, the energy industry, churches, theology, and all branches of business have developed (and continue to develop) a language that connects with its constituents. Our choice of words creates a bond among those who understand the meanings and context, but it also builds walls that keep out those who don't understand.

Vocabulary makes a difference in communicating at every level of a church's life: one-on-one, in teams, in departments, churchwide, and to the community. Too often, our language becomes exclusive—and even offensive—to people in the community we are trying to reach with the message of Christ. Our vision statements proclaim that we want to communicate God's love and forgiveness to those outside the family of God, but Joseph Mattera, presiding bishop of Christ Covenant Coalition and overseeing bishop of Resurrection Church in New York, observes that many churches have adopted word choices that "make new visitors uncomfortable." Mattera has seen visitors cringe or roll their eyes when church members use terms like "praise the Lord," "amen," or "hallelujah" in casual conversations. He concludes, "Until our church members understand how unchurched people view our services and rid them of unnecessary religious behavior, the Sunday morning experience will never attract multitudes of the unchurched, no matter how much soul winning is part of the vision of the church."[1]

The existing vocabulary in a church is seldom analyzed—and even less often challenged—because the choice of terms is ritualized in an airtight tradition. The culture around us is changing rapidly, and the language we use for some aspects of life is morphing almost daily, but many churches still use the same vocabulary they used decades (and even generations) ago. As the culture changes around us, we sound increasingly irrelevant.

The Language of Trust

Trust is the glue of any relationship, and authenticity is essential. When people get too busy to care for one another, trust erodes and defenses go up. Even though we are trying to reach every person on the planet, we need to slow down to show interest in each individual. A few days after someone has shared about her mother's illness, we can stop her in the hall and ask, "How's your mom doing? Is she feeling better?" We don't have to remember the details of the diagnosis, but our simple questions show her that we remember and that we care—and touch the heart of a worried friend.

When ministry leaders forget that their staff members are flesh-and-blood human beings and treat them as "production units," these leaders lose their voice to speak vision, direction, and challenge into others' lives. Small talk about the things that matter to people on our teams isn't small at all—it's enormously important. Most pastors enter the ministry because they love people, and they are gifted at the art of chitchat. They can talk to almost anybody at almost any time about almost anything. As the pressures of ministry compound, however, they tend to focus more on the administrative load and looming deadlines. Then every interaction becomes an organizational transaction instead of a relational connection. When we become bulldogs about the tasks and fail to take time to ask about a family member, a vacation, an illness, or a new haircut, people feel used, no matter how many checks we see on our agenda at the end of a meeting.

Trust is built when we use inclusive instead of exclusive language: "I" instead of "you," "us" instead of "them," and "we" instead of "they." Obviously, sometimes we have to use words like "you," "them," and "they," but we need to watch the context and nuance of the message. For example, I've been in a staff meeting when someone said, "After *we* make this decision, *we* have to make sure that *they* understand what it means." The subtle implication was that the people in the room were the insiders and everyone else was an outsider. A better statement would be, "After this decision is made, we have to be sure that the whole team understands the implications." This wording implies that everyone is on the team, with equal value and equal status. This distinction matters to everyone. Those not in the meeting feel included as part of the team, and those in the meeting realize that there are no class divisions between insiders and outsiders. Does something so seemingly trivial really make a difference? Just ask people who feel excluded by the rest of their team.

When I was a university president, I discovered that the choice of words makes a big difference in attitudes and outcomes. At one point, we almost banned the word "problem" from our campus conversations because we noticed that it carried negative connotations. When people spoke of problems, they often had a sense of heaviness, even hopelessness, that was corrosive to the spirit of hope and faith. We consciously substituted the word "challenge," and we noticed that people instinctively sensed that people rise to meet challenges. Soon, the culture of our school changed from slightly negative to distinctly positive—all because we chose to use a different vocabulary.

As staff teams grow larger with multiple layers of leadership, I'm afraid that some churches are losing some of the magic of the vocabulary of volunteers. In the business community and with paid staff, we feel that we can demand compliance because people pick up a paycheck every couple of weeks. We can say, "The meeting tomorrow starts at 9:00 A.M. Don't be late." The subtle (or not so subtle) message is that the person will be in deep trouble if he doesn't show up on time. But with volunteers, we know we don't have that kind of leverage, so we appeal to "the better angels" of their natures. We take a little more time to explain the importance of the meeting and the contribution they'll make when they come. Then, when we say to the volunteer exactly the same thing we said to the paid staff member, "The meeting tomorrow starts at 9:00 A.M. Don't be late," the person hears it as an invitation to be part of something that will change people's lives! An honest analysis of the vocabulary of our church cultures involves looking at how we motivate our staff and volunteers. Sadly, too many churches treat volunteers like paid staff and demand compliance with precious little heart motivation. Instead, we need to treat staff like volunteers, always appealing to their hearts and their desire for God to use them to change lives. Some will ask, "But what about accountability?" If we're asking people to join us in touching lives and changing people's eternal destinies and they aren't excited about it, we may have one of two problems: we may have picked the wrong people, so we need to replace them, or we may not be connecting the vision with their hearts. When the right people are placed properly and invited to make a difference for the kingdom, accountability is seldom

We need to treat staff like volunteers, always appealing to their hearts and their desire for God to use them to change lives.

a problem—and it should never be a primary means of motivating people, whether they are staff or volunteers.

The culture of a team is shaped by the dominant person, who may not necessarily be the one with the title who sits at the head of the table. This person may be an enthusiastic, charismatic team member who expresses optimism that the team can accomplish even the most difficult challenge, but more often, it's a surly, opinionated person who feels compelled to voice every objection under the sun. The dominant person either demands to be the power broker or steps into a void left by an ineffective leader. Soon, the vocabulary used by the dominant person becomes the collective language of the team.

Quite often, people on a team have very different "hot button" issues they want to champion, so the dominant person may change from issue to issue. One person may feel strongly about the way printed material is presented to the congregation, so she lobbies with passion for excellence in these pieces. Another person couldn't care less about brochures and other handouts, but he wants the team to do something significant about the homeless in the community. The list of interests is almost endless, and for each one, team members may lobby for the team's participation and resources, sometimes with reason and eloquence; sometimes demanding compliance from others; and sometimes with joyful enthusiasm, inviting team members to join together in making a difference. Look for the language of each topic's champion. Notice how each person promotes his or her issue, and observe the response of the team members.

Starting Strong

The first thirty to forty-five seconds of a meeting are crucial. Most leaders, however, don't think much about how people are introduced to the meeting and the message of the day. When I have the remote control to my television in my hand and I'm flipping through channels to find something interesting to watch, I give each channel only two or three seconds to capture my interest. When we sit down at a conference table, the people in the room don't give us much more time than that. If we don't grab their hearts in those first few seconds, their minds will drift to other things they have quickly concluded are more important than our less-than-compelling agenda. And again, vocabulary is important. I've walked into a meeting when the leader announced, "I'm not sure what we need to do today," and the disinterest in the room was almost palpable. I've also heard a leader begin a meeting by saying, "A lot of people have told me that they disagreed with our decision." Immediately, I realized I had to guess who he was talking about, and I didn't want to play a guessing game. I wanted the cold, hard facts, with the issue stated as a challenge the team could overcome as they marshal their collective resources to meet it. A better way to begin the meeting is to say, "Last Thursday, I met with Larry (who, everyone knows, is a major donor), and he has some questions about the direction of the youth ministry." I may not agree with Larry's assessment of the situation, but I respect Larry as a key member of the church. The vocabulary used in this first sentence captures my attention and piques my interest.

As leaders we need to carefully plan the first couple of sentences for every meeting we lead. Very simply, a good beginning can say something like, "What we are talking about in this meeting has implications for the way the community perceives our church (or how we develop leaders, or anything else that's important to the team). This meeting is crucial, and we need everyone's help." Leaders have only a few seconds to connect with people in the room and enlist their participation in the discussion. Make the first statement positive instead of negative, in-

Make the first statement positive instead of negative, inclusive instead of exclusive, and hopeful instead of complaining about the past.

clusive instead of exclusive, and hopeful instead of complaining about the past. A few minutes of preparation equip us to begin well, and those first moments work wonders to grab people's hearts and set the tone for the rest of the meeting.

Asides

As we prepare for meetings and carefully choose our vocabulary for the first few sentences, we can anticipate who on the team will be the "yes, but" people and who will be the "yes, and" people. One of our jobs as leaders is to give some power to those who will carry the ball down the field and to gently nudge the negative people to see problems as challenges. Identifying these people doesn't take a doctorate in psychology. We've seen team members respond in dozens of meetings before, and we can accurately predict how they'll respond this time.

A leader's feedback about team members' contributions in a meeting is just as important as the discussion itself. These brief interludes and reflections are "asides" that guide group members' perceptions of how they are working together. In many meetings, I stop and reflect on a person who has made a valuable contribution. I may say something to the group like, "Did you notice what just happened in our discussion?" Then I'll turn to the individual and say, "Bill, you helped us move the conversation forward when you asked an insightful question, listened carefully, and then offered a solution. Could you tell how your contribution affected our meeting? I sure noticed, and I want you to know that I appreciate your impact today."

Asides aren't always glowingly positive. Sometimes, honest feedback can serve the dual purposes of correction and inspiration. When I noticed that Mary was always voicing concerns and shooting down constructive ideas, I stopped the meeting and said, "Mary, let me give you some feedback about how you influence the group. I've noticed that you have very good insights about the challenges we face, and you articulate them very well, but I haven't seen you offer many constructive solutions. That's important, too." Then I turn to the team and tell them, "Let's make this a standard for our team: let's be very frank about the challenges we face, but when we bring up something in the group, let's also offer at least three possible solutions to discuss. And now, let's get back to the point we were discussing." Mary knows that I haven't targeted her behavior alone for correction; we've made a commitment as a team to be rigorously honest and solution oriented. The message to the group is that the leader is aware not only of the issue being discussed but also of the way each group member is framing that issue. The process of the conversation is just as important (and ultimately, even more important) than the immediate topic of the conversation.

The process of the conversation is just as important (and ultimately, even more important) than the immediate topic of the conversation.

Leaders shouldn't use asides too often, or they will be accused of psychoanalyzing team members. A few times a year is enough, but those times leave a powerful impression on each person on the team. Sometimes I plan an aside before the meeting ever begins. For instance, I've walked into a meeting and told the group,

Before we get into our agenda for today, I want to give you some feedback about some patterns I've noticed in our discussions in the past few weeks. It seems that we talk about the issues, but I don't think we're putting 100 percent of our ideas and hearts on the table. The reason I say this is that in the past few weeks, several of you have told me things after we met that could have been shared in the meeting. And in fact, those comments would have changed our decisions in the meetings. I'm confused about why you don't feel like you can say those things when we meet as a team. Can you help me with this?

I may pause to see if anyone volunteers an answer. If no one does, I may say,

Of course, I don't know the answer, but here are some possible reasons. You may not trust one or more people in the group, or maybe you aren't sure how to handle it when people disagree. I want to assure you that it's perfectly okay for us to disagree as long as we do it agreeably. Maybe you aren't confident that you'll have all the answers if people ask you a question. That's fine, too. You can always say, "Good question. I'll get back to you on that." Here's the reason I'm bringing this up today: when you bring me additional information after we've made a collective decision, I second-guess our first decision, and I wonder if we're giving people everything we can. I don't want to do an 80 percent job for our people, and I know you don't want to either. Do any of these things ring a bell for you? Tell me what you're thinking.

And then I listen. Quite often, people voice personal inhibitions and surface things that happened long ago on other church staff teams. They've brought their fears to our team. Or maybe someone on the team has offended another, and trust has been strained. They don't want to take any risk of being vulnerable in front of the other, so they pull back and protect themselves. There may be any of dozens of reasons, but shining a light on the team's process of communication provides an opportunity to speak openly about our fears, hurts, and hopes so that trust can be rebuilt.

The Gift of Honesty

One of the most valuable things we can give people on our teams is the gift of honesty. People instinctively know if a leader is holding back information, shading the truth, or expressing blind optimism. Happy talk may be intended to look like genuine faith in God, but it comes across as phony, and a lack of authenticity poisons a team. The beginning point, though, isn't for the leader to simply analyze word choices. It's deeper than that. The first task is to take a long, hard look at the difference between respecting people and manipulating them. The two are polar opposites. When we respect someone, we value her as a person, and we honor her opinions even if we disagree with her. When a leader's agenda is to control people to get them to believe "the right way" and do "the right things," he's engaged in manipulation, not true leadership. In the article "How to Talk Straight in Hard Times," management consultants Maren and Jamie Showkeir observe, "One of the most powerful—and underutilized—ways to [engage employees] is through managing conversations instead of 'managing others.' How leaders talk to people matters, and authentic conversations create cultures where the survival, prosperity, and success of the organization is everybody's business."[2] The Showkeirs equate "managing others" with manipulating them. When people feel pressured to conform to our desires or direction, we may have slipped over into the realm of manipulation. Respecting people who have different opinions is essential if we want to create an inspiring culture.

The gift of honesty begins not with words but with the leader's perception and intentions. When we feel stressed, threatened, or out of control, our instinctive response is "fight or flight." We become defensive and demanding, and our goal changes from leading people to controlling them. In a flash or over a long period, we shift from treating them like adults to treating them like small children. When we play the role of "benevolent parents," we feel justified in telling them only part of the truth, and we protect our position as the keepers of reality. We may have seen people on our teams worry or explode when they learned painful information, and we want to avoid that response again at all costs—perhaps because we interpret their negative response as a reflection on our leadership. First, then, we need to be honest with ourselves about how we view people on our teams. Do we respect them as adults and thus can be honest with them, or do we believe we need to treat them like children and filter the information we share with them?

When we determine to treat people as adults, we then have some choices about our vocabulary. We can use the word "challenge" instead of "problem," but we need to be bluntly honest about the size of the hill that the team needs to climb. People may not like what they hear, but they respect leaders who speak the unvarnished truth.

Authenticity requires another step, however. If we want to create a culture of trust on our teams, leaders also need to acknowledge any personal faults in communicating with the team and the harm they have done. One ministry leader told his team, "During the last few months when we've been under a lot of stress with the reorganization, I realized I haven't been the leader you need me to be. Instead of treating you like adults and telling you the truth, I've hidden some things from you. I think you sensed that, and I can tell that you don't trust me as much as you used to. I take responsibility for that, and I'm sorry. I can give lots of excuses, but good intentions aren't good enough. Will you forgive me?" After they responded, he continued, "I promise I'll do whatever it takes for us to have healthy relationships, and I'll tell you the truth. I want you to be a part of the solution, and if I don't tell you the truth, you can't be. What do you think about what I've said today?"

His last question invited people on the team to share their frustration, anger, and disappointment. The leader may not want to hear these comments, but they are the path of healing and hope for the future of the team. When team members share their hearts, especially hurtful things, the leader needs to listen carefully without

When team members share their hearts, especially hurtful things, the leader needs to listen carefully without a shred of defensiveness.

a shred of defensiveness. One of the most important statements a leader can make during these conversations is actually a question: "Would you tell me more about that?" This simple question shows that he welcomes the team member's honest feedback.

When people have shared their frustrations and the tank of disappointment has run dry, the leader can express hope that the future will be different. His commitment is, "From now on, I'll treat you with respect. I promise. And if you ever feel that I'm trying to manipulate you, I give you permission to tell me. I assure you that I'll listen. Can we make that commitment to each other?" The leader's promise and invitation provide a strong foundation for the future of the team, but the original organizational challenge hasn't gone away. It's still a steep hill for the team to climb. The leader needs to state the challenge objectively, without promising "everything will work out just fine." That's just happy talk. A more accurate and more reassuring statement would be, "We face a tough challenge, but I'm sure God has some purposes in it for all of us. Let's tackle it together."

To make sure there are no hidden agendas and unaddressed emotional baggage, I developed a habit of ending meetings by going around the room and asking each person, "Is there anything you haven't said to me that you need to say or want to say?" Sometimes people seize the opportunity to say, "Yes, I have a concern that I want you to know about." And we take some time to address it there. This lets people know that I care about what they care about, but this practice has an additional value. It lets each person know that she has an open invitation to bring up her perspectives and concerns throughout the meeting, and if they don't come up in the course of conversation, she can voice them at the end. People's concerns are always important to me. Another benefit of this approach is that it normalizes honesty in the context of the group. Group members know that it's not acceptable to avoid important topics in the group and then talk to me later. If something is important to the group's process and decisions, members need to bring it up in the group.

The vocabulary of honesty can be spoken only by a leader who has made a commitment to respect people on the team. Manipulation, even with the best of intentions, may bring short-term gains of lowering tension for the moment, but it eventually causes people to feel devalued, and they conclude that the leader isn't a person they want to follow. Respect, honesty, responsibility, and hope are the language of a great team leader.

> *Respect, honesty, responsibility, and hope are the language of a great team leader.*

Questions and Slouching

Never in all of history has communication been so immediate and accessible, but I'm afraid the technological advances have had the unintended consequence of eroding the art of listening. The proliferation of devices has changed the way we relate. We expect to stay connected to everyone and everything through our cell phones, PDAs, text messaging, e-mail, and the Internet. Linda Stone, formerly of Apple and Microsoft, coined the term *continuous partial attention* to describe the constant distractions of our communication devices. She reports,

To pay continuous partial attention is to pay partial attention—CONTINUOUSLY. It is motivated by a desire to be a LIVE node on the network. Another way of saying this is that we want to connect and be connected. We want to effectively scan for opportunity and optimize for the best opportunities, activities, and contacts, in any given moment. To be busy, to be connected, is to be alive, to be recognized, and to matter. We pay continuous partial attention in an effort NOT TO MISS ANYTHING. It is an always-on, anywhere, anytime, any place behavior that involves an artificial sense of constant crisis. We are always in high alert when we pay continuous partial attention. This artificial sense of constant crisis is more typical of continuous partial attention than it is of multi-tasking.[3]

To change the way we communicate with people so that we genuinely connect with them instead of just passing on information, we can do two simple but profound things to enhance listening: ask pertinent questions and use the power of slouching. People get tired in meetings if they feel that they're being *talked to* but not invited to *talk with* the rest of the team. Let me share a few ideas that I've found effective:

• Attention spans are getting shorter and shorter, so we need to keep people engaged by asking for their input. A simple question, "What do you think?" can work wonders. It's become a staple in the way I lead meetings because I've seen a simple question stimulate people and keep them actively involved.

• I can tell if people are listening to me if they ask follow-up questions. If there are none, I assume they were just asking for my input because they have to, not because they are genuinely interested in what I have to say.

• When someone has shared a point of view, I often say, "That's a good point. Will you tell us more about that?" Or I invite him to be more explicit: "I've never seen it that way. Explain how it works in a little more detail."

- When I don't understand what someone is saying, I don't bark, "That makes absolutely no sense to me. What in the world are you talking about?" Instead, I sit back and explore: "That's an intriguing point of view. Help me understand what you're saying."

- Quite often, after listening to someone explain a point of view, I ask the group for their feedback, "Suzie told us her perspective. What do you think about what she told us?" Almost always, others in the group give valuable feedback to highlight the strong points and expose weaknesses. As the leader, I then don't have to fix every problem and answer every question. The group functions effectively as a team, and I'm not forced to function as a benevolent dictator.

Asking for additional input takes a little longer, but we have to understand the goal of our meetings. If the goal is to check off all the boxes on an arbitrary list of items, then by all means, press forward and charge through the list. But if the goal is to enflame the hearts of people and enlist their passionate involvement in the process, then we need to slow down and involve them more deeply in the conversation by asking for their contributions. Of course, taking time to ask for input, listen carefully, and value discussion about a finite list of topics doesn't leave time for other things that could have been discussed. The leader's role is then to be the CPO, the chief priority officer. Many times I've had to say, "We had some important things that we didn't get to talk about today, but we need to address these topics." If the issue is pertinent to only one or two of the group members, I sometimes ask them to meet with me between group meetings so that we can discuss it and move forward. If the topic concerns all of us, I usually ask everyone to think about it and bring some suggestions when we meet next time. They need to know that we will address important topics, but we need to be flexible and prepared so that we use our time wisely. When individuals and teams are confident, they feel free to fully engage the situation and each other. I call this "dancing in the moment."

Many of us feel that we have to settle every disagreement before we can move on, so we avoid disagreements—especially with people who have a history of being sour or demanding. An important principle of creating a healthy culture is becoming comfortable with some unresolved issues. A leader can say, "I can tell that we disagree about this, and I don't think we're going to resolve it now. Let's think about it and talk again next week. I want to ask each of you to bring a possible solution when we talk again." With this mind-set, we can ask for input without demanding universal agreement and instant compliance.

An important principle of creating a healthy culture is becoming comfortable with some unresolved issues.

Many oral communicators aren't good listeners, and people who feel pressured by deadlines and long to-do lists often are preoccupied with phone calls, texts, and e-mails during a meeting instead of making eye contact and listening to people with their hearts, eyes, and ears. These distracted behaviors communicate loudly and clearly: "You're not important to me!" Listening, though, isn't just about getting the facts. Nonverbal communication is very important, especially when we're listening. When I'm leading a team or meeting with an individual, I often employ "the power of slouching." I push my chair away from the table, sit back, cross my legs, and turn to face the person who is speaking so as to make eye contact. These actions send a powerful message: "I care about you and what you have to say, and I'm not in a hurry for you finish. Take your time and give me your best input." Giving people our undivided, relaxed attention lets them know that we are listening with our minds, our hearts, and our eyes, as well as with our ears. They feel that they are important and that we value them as people, not just as interchangeable cogs in the organizational machine.

"Some People"

One of the guidelines in building authentic relationships is to avoid vague accusations. Years ago, I spent far too much time chasing rabbits when someone in a group reported, "*Some people* have a problem with this or that." We tried to guess who it was, and we tried to address the problem even though the person who reported it was intentionally vague to protect his sources. Fairly soon, I realized this had to change, so I told the group, "We won't bring up any reports or complaints unless we identify the person who told us. If you don't have the person's permission to tell us, then don't make the report."

Years ago when I was a pastor in Michigan, a man in our church died, and we expected a lot of people to come to the funeral. In those days before e-mail and text messaging, we did the best we could to get the word out about the time and place of the funeral. At a board meeting about a week after the funeral, a member of our board announced, "Some people were upset that they didn't get the word about the funeral. They wanted to come, but they didn't hear about it in time."

I told him, "Joe, you know we don't talk about complaints unless we have the names of the people. If you'll tell us, we'll address it."

He didn't want to tell us who the person was (this was our first clue that it was an individual, not "some people"), so he remained quiet. I could tell, however, that he was agitated. At the end of the meeting, I asked if anyone had anything they wanted to tell me that hadn't come up, and Joe blurted out, "Okay, I'll tell you. It was Mr. Richardson. He was really upset that nobody told him about the funeral." Then, with genuine anger, he snorted, "And to be honest, I don't blame him."

As soon as the last word left Joe's lips, two board members told him that they had personally communicated with Mr. Richardson on the day of the death. One had seen him in the store, and the other left a message in his mailbox. If the accusation had remained nebulous and anonymous, the issue would have taken too much time in our discussions, and we almost certainly would have come to some wrong conclusions. This was an important cultural lesson for me, for our board, and especially for Joe.

I don't read anonymous letters. I tear them up and discard them. Anonymous people are cowards.

The principle of dealing with specifics instead of vague generalities also applies to how team members talk about the leader. People talk about their leaders—it's human nature—but they need to be taught that authenticity works both ways. They need to speak honestly with their leaders if they have concerns about their leadership. Years ago, I found out that a man on our board had been talking to several people to complain about my leadership. I saw this as an important moment to shape the atmosphere of our board, so at the next meeting, I addressed him in front of the group: "John, I understand that you said certain things to particular people about me. I'm not interested in finding out what you said or the list of people you talked to. That's not important to me. What I want to know is, what is it about our relationship and the context of our board meetings that prevented you from talking with me here? You had ample opportunity to do so, but you chose not to." I didn't want to become a detective to uncover what he said to whom. The only important issue was my relationship with him and the value of authenticity among us on the board. I could have talked to him outside the group, but I saw it as a cultural issue, not a personal one. And although my initial question was to the individual, my question was about the whole group: What is it about our relationships, our honesty, and our care for one another that needs attention?

The conversation among us that day was one of the richest and most significant we ever had as a board. If I had let John's gossiping go on, I would have given tacit permission to everyone to talk outside the group instead of in the group about the things that matter most: trust, respect, and honesty. To build a new culture, however, we first had to recognize and destroy the old one—not destroy the person, but destroy the culture of suspicion and secret alliances. Actually, the issue

> *To build a new culture, we first had to recognize and destroy the old one—not destroy the person, but destroy the culture of suspicion and secret alliances.*

of the man complaining to his friends only kick-started the conversation about our board's culture. After my initial statement, I didn't address him directly. He looked sheepish as the discussion developed, and he didn't add a lot to the give-and-take, but I'm sure he learned a valuable lesson that day.

Consistency

People on staff and volunteer teams watch their leaders like a hawk, and they want to see consistency between their words and their actions. A friend of mine told me about the leader of a national ministry who presented himself as a kind, wise, compassionate man of God, but behind closed doors, he was demanding and severely critical of anyone who dared voice a dissenting view. Soon his staff members were divided into the loyalists who turned a blind eye to his incongruent behavior, and the dissenters whose frustration and disrespect created enormous tension in their own lives and their relationships in the organization. I've also known a few leaders whose public and private personas were reversed. They were as kind and loving as a mother with the people in their offices and boardrooms, but when they spoke to the masses, they conveyed a raw anger that seemed far more than a righteous response to injustice.

As Abraham Lincoln famously said, "You can fool all of the people some of the time, and some of the people all of the time, but you can't fool all the people all the time." Followers notice the consistency of a leader's life. If his attitudes and behaviors in private match his public words of faith and nobility, they know they can trust him. If not, they first lose respect for the leader, then for their coworkers who remain loyal, and, finally, even for themselves for staying in such a toxic culture.

Thankfully, cases of significant inconsistency in churches and nonprofit organizations are fairly rare. The ones that make the news capture our attention, but for every one of those, there are thousands of churches with competent, consistent leaders. To some degree, all leaders struggle with consistency because they have to balance vision for the future with compassion today for hurting people, but most find a way to live successfully in that tension. It's a wonderful thing when people report, "He's the same person in the lobby that he is in the pulpit, and he's the same in the committee meeting as he is in the hardware store." People thrive under this kind of leadership. Loyalty earned is a beautiful thing, but loyalty demanded is toxic.

Loyalty earned is a beautiful thing, but loyalty demanded is toxic.

Authentic Affirmation

When my friend told me years ago that he saw me as a "really good leader," his message was powerful because I could tell he meant it. For words of affirmation to be meaningful, they need to be specific, personal, and timely. I've heard many leaders say to almost anyone within earshot, "You're great!" That's a lot better than "I hate your guts," but global comments seldom yield significant results. Affirming someone's character or abilities is a skill that requires preparation and practice. It's easy, especially for verbal communicators, to become lazy in their praise of people. Instead, they need to think carefully about the people they lead, and then notice, name, and nurture the characteristics they value. Instead of saying to a volunteer, "Man, you're terrific," it's much more meaningful for a leader to think about that person, the obstacles he has overcome, and how God is using him in specific ways—the more descriptive, the better. Then, in a private moment or in a meeting, the leader might say, "Sean, I've been watching you, and I'm really impressed with how you care for people. You consistently go out of your way. I saw you take extra time with Mrs. Adams when she couldn't get the answer she needed and she was getting frustrated. She really appreciated your help, and I want you to know that I appreciate you, too."

There's no magic formula for authentic affirmation. We can focus on a pattern of behavior or praise a single event we noticed. We might point out character qualities like compassion, courage, or persistence, or we can focus on skills of administration or leadership. The most important element of affirming someone is that she realizes we've been thinking about her, and our comments aren't "out of the blue." There's certainly nothing wrong with spontaneous praise for people we lead, but praise is even more powerful when they are convinced that we have been watching and admiring them for a while. If we say too much too often, people discount what we say, and if we don't say enough, they wonder what we really think about them. We need a balanced approach to words of affirmation: not too seldom, not too often, but just the right amount at the right time.

Mutual affirmation among team members is particularly powerful. I read a story about a math teacher who asked her students to list the names of everyone in the class on a piece of paper, and to write the nicest thing they could think of about each one of them. After the class was over, she gathered all

Mutual affirmation among team members is particularly powerful.

the papers. That night, she compiled all the statements for each student, and she presented the lists to each of them the next day in class. In a few minutes, everyone in the class was smiling. "Really?" one of them whispered to himself. "I didn't know I meant that much to anybody!" After that day, they never talked about the papers again.

Several years later, one of the students was killed in Vietnam. His body was brought back to his hometown, and the teacher attended the funeral. As she filed by the casket with the other mourners, a soldier serving as a pallbearer asked her, "Were you Mark's math teacher?" She nodded, and he replied, "Mark talked about you a lot."

At a luncheon after the funeral, Mark's mother and father came over to speak to the teacher. His father said, "We want to show you something." He took a carefully folded piece of paper out of a wallet, and then he told her, "They found this on Mark when he was killed. We thought you might recognize it." Instantly, she saw that it was the list of statements Mark's class-mates had written about him. His mother commented, "Thank you so much for doing that. As you can see, Mark treasured it." As they spoke, several other former students gathered around. One of them smiled and said, "I still have my list, too. It's in the top drawer of my desk at home." Others said they kept their list in a wedding album, in a diary, or in a purse. One of them spoke for the rest: "I think we all saved our lists." This dear teacher had invited students to affirm each other, and her simple assign-ment meant more to them than any subject they ever studied.

A Closer Look

How can we tell if our vocabulary is defining the culture we desire? We can pay attention to the signals we receive from the people around us, especially those closest to us. When their signals confuse us, we need to give ourselves permission to ask questions like, "What's going on? The people out there respond very well to my leadership, but those close to me look frustrated. Maybe I need to take a look at my words, my nonverbals, my congruence, and my authenticity." Feeling confused about our leadership isn't a bad thing. It's often the first step toward deeper analysis and change.

Good leaders regularly look at the culture of their teams and make necessary adjustments. They use asides to shine a light on the process of how the team relates to each other, and they inject affirmation, hope, and humor into the group at appropriate times. The discourse of a team tends to devolve to the lowest common denominator. If the range of people is from a Ph.D. to a high school graduate, the conversation tends to drift toward high school topics and a high school level of clarity. We need to be aware of that tendency so that we can intentionally direct the conversation to the middle level of the group. Then more people will stay engaged, and more will offer valuable input.

Changing culture always creates conflict. When we choose respect instead of manipulation, and honesty instead of avoidance of issues, most people will thrive, but a few resist even healthy changes. Don't be surprised when people on your team feel uncomfortable with honesty. Give them time to adjust, and keep loving

Changing culture always creates conflict.

them as you model a new vocabulary, but realize that some people may not want to participate in the new culture. They felt comfortable, and perhaps powerful, in the old one, and they prefer things to stay the way they were.

Our vocabulary, and especially the tone we use when we speak, powerfully defines and reflects culture. It's very easy to keep saying the same things in the same way over and over again, and expect different results—but that's a definition of insanity, not leadership. Unexamined vocabulary puts a ceiling on leadership.

Think About It . . .

1. What are some positive elements of your church's existing vocabulary? Which terms have you been using that hinder you from fulfilling God's vision?

2. Give an example of when you could use an aside with your team. How would you do it? What impact do you think it would have?

3. What are two specific principles or ideas from this chapter that you want to apply? How will you implement them?

5

CHANGE STARTS WITH ME

It's amazing how someone's IQ seems to double as
soon as you give them responsibility and indicate
that you trust them.

—*Timothy Ferriss*

Phillip heard me speak at a conference, and during a break, he
asked if I had time to meet with him. The next morning over
coffee, he poured out his frustrations. He told me that he was on
the executive team of a church of three thousand. "From your
description of cultures," he informed me, "I'd say our church's
culture is stagnant." I asked him to explain, and he told me
that his senior pastor is a wonderful man and a good teacher,
but Phillip has concluded that he has some serious flaws in his
leadership. "We seem to be drifting. We have a vision statement, of course, but we don't seem to be focusing our energies
and resources very well to achieve the vision." As we talked, I
realized that Phillip's chief concerns were in the area of leadership development.

I probed a bit: "Tell me, what was your previous experience
on a church staff?"

His eyes rolled and he shook his head, then said gravely, "It
was a disaster. From your description, I'd say it was genuinely
toxic."

"And you hoped this pastor, this staff, and this church would
be different."

Phillip's eyes lit up. "Exactly. And for the first couple of
years, it seemed like a dream come true. The problems have
surfaced more recently."

"So Phillip," I continued to probe, "what would you like to do that the senior pastor won't let you do?"

He looked surprised. "Well, nothing. He's happy for me to do whatever I think God wants me to do."

"Oh really," I mused. "Tell me, then, what do you think is your biggest frustration?"

He looked at me as if he couldn't believe I didn't understand already, and then he almost shouted, "Dr. Chand, I want to serve on a team that is inspiring, where the whole team is on the same page, and together we're trusting God and working hard to achieve God's incredible, compelling, challenging purpose for us!"

Without batting an eye, I asked, "Do you have the freedom to create that kind of culture on your own team in your ministry area?"

Again, he looked surprised, and he said, "Well, yeah. I do." He paused to reflect for a few seconds, and then he told me, "I guess I should be grateful for that, huh?"

Some of us have exceptionally high expectations of the leaders and the organization where we serve. Unrealistically high expectations cloud our perspective, create unwarranted disappointment, and steal our emotional energy. Certainly, some cultures are so toxic that the best course is to leave as quickly and as graciously as possible, but far more often, the best place to start a revolution of change is in our own hearts and minds. Instead of waiting for the top leader to change the culture and make everything smooth, pleasant, and easy, we need to begin with the one person we have the power to control: ourselves.

Unrealistically high expectations cloud our perspective, create unwarranted disappointment, and steal our emotional energy.

One person can make a tremendous difference on a team, even if that person isn't the leader. When I became president of Beulah Heights University in 1989, the janitor was a man named Benson Karanja. On my last day in 2003, he became president of the university. How could someone make this kind of leap in leadership? At every level and in every role—from janitor to library assistant to librarian to administrator to professor to director of student affairs to vice president to executive VP and finally to president—he always gladly accepted responsibility and never deflected blame for wrong decisions on anyone else. As he assumed more leadership, he was always willing to ask the tough questions, but he asked in a way that didn't threaten anyone. Whenever any challenge needed to be analyzed, he said, "Dr. Chand, I'll examine this issue and give a report at our next meeting." Whenever a task needed to be done, he volunteered. His humble spirit convinced people that he wasn't jockeying for position. He was simply serving God and the university with every fiber of his being. And everyone around him felt challenged to give more, do more, and care more for God's kingdom. The janitor inspired a university.

Replacing Disappointment

Christians, and especially those who serve in visionary churches, often have incredibly high expectations of their leaders. Like Phillip in the opening story in this chapter, they may have come from painful past situations in a family or church environment, and they hope, "This time, it'll be different!" They read glowing accounts of other churches, and they see how Jesus invited his followers to experience his love.

The number of "shoulds" in a person's mind and mouth is inversely proportional to his sense of peace, joy, and fulfillment.

They hope, pray, and expect—and too often demand—that this leader, this church, and this team will be heaven on earth.

(They need to read more of the New Testament to see how many problems most churches experienced, but that's a topic for another discussion.) Expectations surface in vocabulary. A word that appears in their conversations and thoughts is "should," as in, "The pastor should do this or that better," "He should lead this way or that way," "The board should give me more authority," and countless others. The number of "shoulds" in a person's mind and mouth is inversely proportional to his sense of peace, joy, and fulfillment.

To replace any nagging disappointment created by unrealistic expectations, let me suggest a few strategies:

- Focus on what you can control.
- Be tenaciously thankful.
- Resolve any role alignment issues.
- Invest creative capital.

Focus on What You Can Control

Many of us expend enormous amounts of energy worrying about and trying to manage things that are outside the realm of our control. To maintain mental and emotional health, and to be the kind of leaders and team members we can be, we have to realize that we aren't God. The scope of our responsibility and power is limited, and we need to devote our energies to those things that are inside our sandboxes. Thousands of recovery groups around the country use a German pastor and theologian's prayer to reframe their expectations. Most of us can quote the first part of Reinhold Niebuhr's "Serenity Prayer":

> God grant me the serenity
> to accept the things I cannot change;
> courage to change the things I can;
> and wisdom to know the difference.

The rest of the prayer, though, gives even more insight about trusting God instead of ourselves:

Living one day at a time;
Enjoying one moment at a time;
Accepting hardships as the pathway to peace;
Taking, as He did, this sinful world as it is, not as I would have it;
Trusting that He will make all things right if I surrender to His Will;
That I may be reasonably happy in this life
and supremely happy with Him Forever in the next. Amen.

The first step, then, is for each of us to realize that we can't control the universe, or even the smaller universe of our church environment. For now, we need clear-eyed objectivity and optimism, with a commitment to do all we can to create a positive culture around us. Accepting responsibility for what we can control—and making a steadfast commitment not to complain about what's outside our control—are crucial ingredients in spiritual, emotional, and relational health.

Accepting responsibility for what we can control—and making a steadfast commitment not to complain about what's outside our control—are crucial ingredients in spiritual, emotional, and relational health.

Be Tenaciously Thankful

Phillip had been missing out on much of the joy he could have been experiencing because his eyes had been riveted on the shortcomings of his senior pastor. It only took a few questions, though, for him to realize that God and his pastor had given him wonderful opportunities. His attitude almost immediately changed from griping to gratitude. From what I heard later, his thankful heart changed more than just his disposition. As the sludge of a critical spirit was washed away, he enjoyed his wife and family, his team, and every aspect of his ministry more than ever.

Resolve Any Role Alignment Issues

Sometimes a person's disappointment with a leader or a team runs deeper than attitude. When the job description doesn't fit the person's gifts and interests, confusion and heartache inevitably occur. The challenge of finding the best fit in a culture isn't always easy to resolve, but it's essential for each person to find, not the perfect fit, but a "good enough fit" so that the individual, the team, and the mission work well together.

Invest Creative Capital

In stagnant, discouraging, and toxic cultures, people spend their energies protecting themselves and creating alliances instead of creatively pursuing the mission. Even in accepting and inspiring cultures, individuals or pockets of people may live with deep disappointments caused by unrealistic expectations and shattered dreams. When people face these challenges with courage and hope, a new world opens up, and they can invest themselves in the cause that drew them there in the first place.

Characteristics of a Change Agent

Instead of waiting for the senior leaders or someone else to create a positive culture, each person on the team can take steps to be a change agent. Instead of waiting for someone to become trustworthy, each one can prove to be a trustworthy person; a man or woman of character, heart, and hope. There may be many different ways of describing people who, as leaders or team members, can shape organizational culture, but I want to offer my list of characteristics:

Heart motivation

Positive demeanor

Courage to ask tough questions

Honesty without limitations

Warmth and humor

Willingness to reflect reality

Heart Motivation

One of the first things to realize is that staff members and volunteers in the church world are motivated by meaning, not money. Dangling financial incentives to entice them to work harder proves to be counterproductive. They don't want to perceive that they are being treated unfairly in regard to salaries, but to touch their deepest motivations, leaders need to appeal to their desire for their lives to count.

Positive Demeanor

When the senior pastor says, "I believe God is calling us to trust him to pursue this vision," the atmosphere in the room is transformed if someone responds, "Pastor, we can trust God for that. Let's go for it." But a "can-do" spirit will only look like kissing up to the boss if another trait is missing . . .

Courage to Ask Tough Questions

Change agents need to be positive, but they need to be multidimensional: they must also possess the ability to ask penetrating questions to help the group discern God's will, to find the best alignment of roles and goals, and to develop the best plan for any challenge. In Benson Karanja, this rare and special combination of traits showed people that he was wise, humble, and optimistic. And as people spent more time around him, his attitude permeated every team on which he served.

Honesty About Limitations

People who claim to be able to do everything well lose the trust of those around them. Change agents are unfailingly optimistic, but they also have a good grasp of their strengths and limitations. They are willing to say, "I can't do that very well, but I know someone who can." Being honest about holes in our skill set shows people that we aren't power hungry or driven to win approval. We notice others' strengths and affirm their contributions, and we gladly defer to them when they can do a job better than we can. In this way, everybody on the team feels valued.

Being honest about holes in our skill set shows people that we aren't power hungry or driven to win approval.

Warmth and Humor

Every team needs someone who brings warmth to the relationships and can break the tension with humor from time to time. Remembering a birthday, a health concern, a child's struggle, or a joy in someone's life shows that we care about the people, not just the task they perform. Above all else, people want to know that others value them, and a word of warmth means everything to a team. And warmth is infectious. Just as one person's sour disposition can poison a team, an individual's sincere love for others can change the complexion of a meeting and a team.

Willingness to Reflect Reality

Unhealthy teams never talk about "the elephant in the room." They dance around uncomfortable topics, even though avoiding them further erodes trust among the people on the team. At that point, the refusal to talk about the issues is a bigger deal than the issues themselves. People who are cultural change agents are willing to say, "This is what I see going on with this issue," and even, "This is what I see going on with our team right now." Too often, leaders verbalize their perceptions only when they are so exasperated that they explode with their observations. That's not helpful. The first few times a leader practices healthy reflection, people on the team may feel uncomfortable simply

Talking about "the process of processing" is essential to a healthy team culture.

because it's so novel. After a few times, though, team members realize that talking about "the process of processing" is essential to a healthy team culture.

Practical Steps

For those of us who are serving in inspiring or accepting cultures, we simply want to sustain and enhance the quality of our relationships. Those who experience stagnant, discouraging, or toxic cultures, however, have more work to do to discover the right path forward. They may have been blasted for disagreeing with a leader, ignored and marginalized when they didn't measure up to the leader's expectations, or perhaps, even worse, patronized by insincere affirmations. In difficult cultures, people need to think clearly, avoid overreacting, and take wise steps. Let me offer a few suggestions:

- Go to the leader privately.
- Practice self-reflection.
- Make a commitment.
- Understand your equity and your risk tolerance.
- If you leave, go gracefully.

Go to the Leader Privately

Never ever confront a senior leader publicly. It's a lose-lose-lose proposition. The leader gets angry because she loses face, you lose respect (and perhaps your job), and the culture goes backward because of escalating tension. One of the greatest needs in churches today is someone who can offer the light of perception to leaders. No one likes to be told, "You're a bad leader" or "You're not doing that the right way." But most leaders will listen if a team member approaches them privately and with grace and wisdom, saying "I've been thinking about this, and I want to tell you my observations." After sharing her thoughts, she doesn't demand a response. Instead, she tells the leader, "You don't need to tell me what you think about that. I just wanted you to know."

On a team, a person may have noticed that the team isn't communicating honestly and respectfully with each other. In that case, the person might go to the leader and say, "I've noticed that our team seems to have some tension, and I think it's preventing us from accomplishing all we could do together. I'm guessing that if I notice it, others sense it, too. I'm not asking you to fix it, and I'm not complaining. I just wanted to share my observation. Thanks for listening." Simply surfacing the issue brings it to the leader's attention without demanding a particular reply or action plan to correct it.

If the issue is the team's communication, a team member may assume that the problem is his own when he talks to the leader. He may say, "In the past few months, I've noticed that I seem to be holding back in the meeting each week. I'm not sure what's going on with me, but I was hoping you could help me figure it out. What do you think might be happening?"

A friend told me that he used to experience significant tension in his relationship with his senior pastor. As the tension mounted, he planned more carefully how he would handle every conversation, but the problem only got worse. When he talked to a wise friend, the friend told him, "You're coming across as defiant and demanding. Instead, start each conversation with this phrase, 'Pastor, I need your help.' That will put him at ease and make him an ally instead of an adversary." My friend started using that technique, and he said it turned their relationship around 180 degrees.

The title of this chapter is "Change Starts with Me." We don't want to communicate with a leader in a tone and using words that demand that he or she change—or else! When we come across in a condescending or demanding tone, we are hoping that change will start (and end) with the leader. It's far healthier for everybody if each team member accepts responsibility for his own behavior and learns to communicate respectfully and wisely with the leader and the rest of the team.

It's far healthier for everybody if each team member accepts responsibility for his own behavior and learns to communicate respectfully and wisely with the leader and the rest of the team.

Practice Self-Reflection

Wise people notice dissonance in their emotions, thoughts, and relationships, and they take time to ask themselves, *What's that about?* As reflection becomes the habit of a lifetime, they are less surprised when they uncover selfish motives and harmful behaviors that may have been part of their lives since they were children.

Self-reflection is both planned and spontaneous. A question that I teach people to ask about themselves at regular intervals is, "What is it about *me* that keeps *me* from becoming the best *me* that God intended *me* to be?" This question invites us to take full responsibility for our growth and direction, and it rivets our purpose to God's plan for our lives. I'd encourage leaders and team members to take time to reflect on this question three or four times a year. But through the years, I've also learned to pay attention to little flashes of confusion, which are the first signs of insight. When I'm talking with someone and I say something that sounds odd, I may reflect, *I wonder why I said that.* Or as I'm preparing a message and working on a particular point that I've made hundreds of times in the past, I may feel some emotional disturbance and ask myself, *Why would I say it that way? There seems to be a demand in those words. What's that about?* Or if I find myself in a situation that used to bother me but doesn't any longer, I wonder, *What's changed? Is it a good thing or a bad thing that it doesn't bother me anymore?*

> *"What is it about me that keeps me from becoming the best me that God intended me to be?"*

For leaders and team members, confusion about their hearts and their roles isn't the biggest problem they face. I believe the dissonance that comes from being responsive to the Spirit's prompting may be unsettling for a while, but it opens a door to insight, growth, and better connections with the people we love.

All of us need honest feedback from a spouse and close friends, but we need to be careful that we are asking for the truth, not lobbying for allies to defend us. Try approaching a few very close friends and asking, "Do you see any patterns that have surfaced lately in my attitudes and actions with the staff team? I think I've turned into a jerk. I've responded with anger over even little things. Have you seen that in me?" And they'll tell you what they've seen.

Make a Commitment

Make a solemn commitment to be the best team member or leader you can be. Reflect on the attitude that has shaped your response, your skills in engaging your leader, and the impact you're having on others—and be honest with what you find. Think carefully about how to display the characteristics of a change agent, and take the risk to speak up, ask questions, offer encouragement, and be the kind of trustworthy person you want others to be.

If you're discouraged about your leader, step back and consider the pressures he's under. Leading people is very difficult, and even the best leaders aren't always successful. Just look at Jesus! Your leader may have suffered some losses that you haven't considered, or there may be family struggles, financial needs, health concerns, or other difficulties that rob him of stability.

Make a commitment to lead your own team with integrity, love, and skill. Be the kind of leader you want others to be. Even if you feel like a Lone Ranger, lead with passion and grace. As you lead your team, don't criticize your pastor or any other leaders in the church. And if your team members begin speaking negatively, stop them and explain how gossip ruins attitudes and relationships. God has a purpose for you as you lead your team. Look for him to lead you in every interaction with those you lead and with those on the team on which you serve as a member.

Be the kind of leader you want others to be.

Understand Your Equity and Your Risk Tolerance

I've watched some staff members become angry or righteously indignant (depending on who's telling the story) and leave their position without thought of the implications to their families. I'm not advocating that anyone stay in a toxic, abusive environment one day longer than necessary, but you need to be aware of the consequences and timing of your choices.

To understand the context of your decision more fully, consider these questions:

- "Could I have misunderstood my leader?"

I've known spouses who have misinterpreted each other's behavior for many years, so it's certainly possible that you could have misunderstood the leader's words, actions, and especially motives.

- "How long has the problem been going on?"

If the difficulty with the leader has occurred only in the past few weeks, you need to be more patient and see if the problem vanishes as quickly as it appeared. Look for established patterns. Don't be too concerned about isolated blips on the radar. Of course, if the problem is sexual harassment or another form of blatant disrespect, you don't need any additional time to look for patterns. The severity and nature of the issue determine how patient you should be in trying to resolve it, cope with it, or confront it.

- "Am I oversensitive about defending my role or my department?"

Is the issue you are so upset about systemwide, or is it possible that a decision is being made for the good of the whole that seems unfair or inconsiderate to your department? Sometimes leaders make global decisions, but they don't explain them so that each department leader understands why the choice was made.

- "Do I have anywhere to go?"

It's not appropriate to use office hours to look for a position at a different church, unless of course you have permission from your team leader or pastor. I've seen men and women resign "on principle" with nowhere to go. If they had waited a little longer, they may have been able to make an exit more gracefully for everyone involved.

- "How does my decision affect my family?"

Decisions to resign in the heat of the moment seldom consider a spouse's employment or children's school situations. Consider the broader implications of the decision, not just how it makes you feel in your role and work relationships.

If You Leave, Go Gracefully

At some point, some of us will come to the conclusion that we can't be effective in the culture where we serve, and it's time to leave. If we have learned to live and serve with integrity and wisdom in a difficult culture, we will experience deep sadness for our own loss and for those who remain, because we care for them. However, if we haven't learned the lessons of being change agents, we'll either explode in anger or slink away in shame (or perhaps a combination of those painful emotions).

A young man came up to me at a conference and told me, "Dr. Chand, my name is Jackson. I love being a youth pastor, and I'm thrilled to see God work in students' lives, but the struggle to serve at our church is killing me. The drama on our staff team is killing me. It's ridiculous. Everything is a huge hassle. I've tried to make it work. I've tried to do all the things you teach about having a great attitude, affirming others, approaching my senior pastor with wisdom . . . all of that, but it's just not working. I go home each night emotionally exhausted. When

I think about the student ministry, I can't wait to get up and get going each day, but then I think of the relationships on our staff team, and I want to run away. What should I do?"

I counseled Jackson to go back and give it one more shot, to talk with his pastor and try to find a way for it to work. I explained that he needed to know it was God's direction for him to leave or stay. It wasn't good enough to "go with his gut." I asked him to call me in a few months to let me know how it was going. Several months later, Jackson telephoned and told me, "Dr. Chand, I gave it my best shot, and I'm completely convinced that God wants me to leave. How can I do it gracefully?"

I gave Jackson a brief set of directions for a graceful exit:

- Meet with the pastor and thank him for the opportunity to serve at the church. Explain that you believe God is leading you to serve at another church. Tell him that you want to make the transition to the next person as smooth as possible. Ask him what he wants you to do to make that happen (for example, related to teams, contact information with students, schedules, commitments for camps, and so on).

- When the pastor or others ask why you are leaving (and they will), don't use the moment as an opportunity to "clear the air" and blast the pastor and other leaders. Keep it pleasant, thankful, and future centered.

- The hardest conversations are often with the top volunteers, many of whom know the struggles and have great compassion for the person leaving. Don't let these conversations devolve into angry blaming sessions. Thank people for their hearts and their service, and celebrate all the things God has done through you as you served together.

- Pave the way for the new person by leaving everything in great shape.

We need to remember that God calls his church to unity, not uniformity. We don't all have to be the same for the body to work well, but we have to be committed to a common purpose—loving one another in spite of our differences and resolving disagreements agreeably.

We don't all have to be the same for the body to work well, but we have to be committed to a common purpose—loving one another in spite of our differences and resolving disagreements agreeably.

The Process of Change

Most organizational consultants report that it takes about three years to change the culture of a team, a church, a nonprofit organization, or a business. I've seen this process as occurring in four stages, illustrated by this diagram:

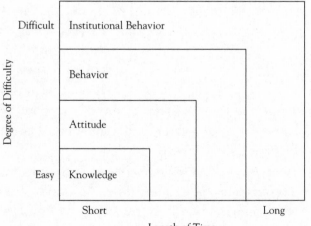

Originally developed by Sam Williams and adapted by Carol Childress, cited in "Levels of Change, Part 2," Leadership Network Champions Fax, Volume 3 Number 2, January 26, 1998.

Knowledge

The first level requires a change of mind resulting in increased knowledge. Facts that support the reasons for change need to be gathered and shared. Facts are far more persuasive than opinions, but facts alone don't produce culture change. In fact, they can precipitate conflict because everyone may not agree on what needs to be done or be ready to do it.

We gain knowledge by reading books and articles, attending seminars, and listening to friends who are learning important lessons about taking responsibility for their roles in the cultures of their churches or teams.

Attitude

The second level requires a change in attitudes about roles, goals, and relationships. In this stage, people may feel threatened because their rituals, expectations, and job descriptions are being examined. Quite often, leaders react by producing more information to support their views, but this is counterproductive. The issue now is emotional, not

The leader's role is to provide support, listen carefully, and help people steer through the emotional minefields that always accompany culture change.

intellectual, and the leader's role is to provide support, listen carefully, and help people steer through the emotional minefields that always accompany culture change.

At this level, our knowledge seeps into our hearts and produces convictions. We determine, "I don't want to act that way with Barbara anymore. I want to be kind and affirming, not short with her." As a team talks about the culture and its implications, don't be surprised when people become defensive. Turf issues surface very quickly at this point, but patiently listen. Let fears run their course. Answer questions, reassure people of their importance and their roles, and look to the future.

Behavior

The third level requires a change in behavior, and as those behaviors become habits, a new lifestyle becomes the norm in the culture. Each change may begin with incremental choices that feel relatively safe and offer the biggest chance for success. As those new behaviors come to feel natural, the leader and the team can move to the next, and perhaps more challenging, priority.

We may apply the principles of becoming a change agent in different ways, but all of us will take action in this level. Some of us instinctively remember a concern shared by someone in the last meeting, so we ask about it as the next meeting begins, but some of us need to write down those concerns to remind us to ask about them. If we realize that we talk to a particular team member only at the meetings, we may want to go to that person's office a few minutes before the next meeting to say something like, "Kim, I really appreciate the wisdom you share in our meetings. I wish we had more time together. I could learn a lot from you. Thanks for your contribution to the team."

We have different talents, different backgrounds, and different experiences, but everyone on the team plays an important role in shaping the culture of the team. During this stage of culture change, each person realizes his or her unique contribution, spoken by the person and affirmed by the team. The team leader may lead the culture, but it is sustained and deepened by the team members.

> *The team leader may lead the culture, but it is sustained and deepened by the team members.*

Institutional Behavior

The fourth level, which is the cumulative effect of knowledge, attitudes, and new habits, requires a change in the culture of the organization. Each person on the team has had time to think, plan, and experiment with new actions that, over time, take root and change the expectations and relationships.

Happiness and Effectiveness

In their thoughts and expectations, most people instinctively link happiness and effectiveness. They assume that the two are always mutually inclusive, but in observing people in hundreds of organizations, I can report that this isn't necessarily true. I've talked to people in stagnant and discouraging cultures, and even a few in toxic environments, who found a way to be effective in their work. They endured their team's passivity or pathology by putting their heads down and being the best they could be at the work God had given them to do. They weren't particularly happy, but they found a measure of satisfaction in "working heartily, as unto the Lord," and seeing lives changed. By contrast, I've not known anyone who was ineffective at the task she was commissioned to perform but found genuine joy on a team. God has made us so that we thrive emotionally at work only when we know we are contributing our knowledge and skills to accomplish something bigger

We thrive emotionally at work only when we know we are contributing our knowledge and skills to accomplish something bigger than ourselves.

than ourselves. Those who spend their lives complaining and dodging responsibility find neither happiness nor effectiveness.

Self-Analysis

To discover the kind of impact we're having on our teams, let me offer a few topics for self-analysis:

- Analyzing current relationships
- Clarifying expectations
- Living with ambiguity
- Gleaning the wisdom of new voices
- Monitoring deposits and withdrawals

Analyzing Current Relationships

When we examine our roles and our effectiveness, our first questions need to focus on relationships, not organizational issues or role competency. Our ability to connect with people, earn their trust, invite their opinions, and inspire them is the most important trait we bring—even more important than our experiences or skills. When we experience stress, we need to ask, "What patterns have shifted in my family, in my relationships with friends, and in my relationships with people on my team?" Quite often, significant shifts in key relationships show up as job stress. We internalize a deep sense of loss or the threat of loss, and we become defensive, demanding, or withdrawn. It's easy to see that what happens in the office affects how we relate to our spouse and children, but the reverse is also true: shifts in patterns of relationships at home can have a dramatic impact on relationships at work. Emotional health is primarily a function of relationships, not competence in our roles.

Clarifying Expectations

Idealism may be a good beginning, but it seldom serves leaders and team members well as they try to form a healthy atmosphere. "Shoulds" need to be replaced by an unvarnished grasp of reality—not at the expense of hope, but with the hope-filled expectation that God will use flawed people in often messy processes to accomplish his divine purposes. People who cling to idealism inevitably become disappointed and discouraged.

Living with Ambiguity

All of us need to gain the skill of living in ambiguity, knowing that we live between the *already* of God's fulfilled promises and the *not yet* of those that will be fulfilled only when we see him face-to-face. High-impact leaders and team members are like a car with three gears: forward, reverse, and neutral. People with only two gears, forward and reverse, have little capacity for careful reflection. They feel uncomfortable with ambiguity and the tension of waiting. Outstanding leaders and team members, however, don't feel pressured to make instant decisions.

Outstanding leaders and team members don't feel pressured to make instant decisions.

They can listen carefully to competing interests, ask penetrating questions, invite more dialogue, and say, "I don't know" until the answer eventually surfaces. Staying in neutral for a while enables them to listen, gain more insight, reflect, involve people, and gain God's wisdom on difficult matters.

Gleaning the Wisdom of New Voices

All of us need the challenge and the stimulation of hearing new concepts from new voices, but we need to be careful that we don't let those new voices poison our perspective. For example, a friend of mine listened to podcasts of a brilliant pastor teaching a doctoral course. He instinctively compared the pastor-prof to the pastor at his church, and his pastor suddenly dropped a few notches on his respect grid. One of the marks of a healthy person and a good team member is that we're always learning, absorbing new concepts and testing new strategies. But the urge to compare is often a tragic trait of human nature. If we're not careful, we'll use the new voices as a club to condemn others who don't measure up to our new standards. With a warning against graceless comparison, we need to ask ourselves,

- Who are the new voices that have recently inspired me?
- What are some books that have challenged my thinking in the past few weeks?
- What concepts, strategies, or visions have produced in me a sense of godly discontent?

These questions focus more on *being* than *doing*, more on the ontology of who we are than on what function we perform. Too often, we focus our development strategies on roles and skills instead of heart and character, but trust is primarily a response to the internal rather than the external characteristics of a person. God created Adam and Eve as perfect human beings, but after they sinned, the curse gave them arduous tasks to do. And still today, we define ourselves and describe each other by the things we do instead of by heart and character. In the Garden, mankind shifted from acceptance, grace, and love to blame, shame, and the compulsion to prove ourselves by our performance. To recapture God's design, we need new voices that penetrate our crusty defenses and speak to our souls, not only inspiring our actions but, even more, enflaming our hearts.

Monitoring Deposits and Withdrawals

There are two types of people in our lives, those who make deposits and those who make withdrawals. We can't orchestrate our lives to eliminate interactions with people who take more than they give to us, but if we are wise, we will do two crucial things: we'll limit our time with the takers, and we'll make sure we spend time with the ones who add to our emotional bank accounts. As we com-

There are two types of people in our lives, those who make deposits and those who make withdrawals.

prehend this principle, we'll be more understanding and patient with senior leaders. If we spent time with them each day, we'd see that 99 percent of their interactions are with people who make withdrawals. Almost every phone call they receive is someone saying, "Pastor, I need this," or "Pastor, I'm upset about that." When that pastor is less than perfectly gracious in a meeting, we might conclude that he has endured too many withdrawals and too few deposits lately. An accurate perception of the effect of givers and takers in his life encourages us to be compassionate instead of judgmental.

In stagnant, discouraging, and toxic cultures, people form alliances to provide self-protection and self-validation. The people involved might claim that these interactions are important deposits in their lives, especially compared to the passivity or abuse they experience in relationships with others in the culture. But people in these alliances need to take a long, hard look at the impact of these conversations. Do they bring truth, honor, and life, or do they perpetuate resentment and gossip? In negative cultures, even "supportive" relationships make withdrawals disguised as deposits.

The commitment of each of us is to be the best team member we can be and, on our own teams, to create an inspiring culture. When we look at the culture of any organization, we don't look only at the top leaders. It is the leaders' responsibility to shape the values and the environment, but culture percolates from every nook and cranny of the organization. As we've noted earlier, a toxic environment is like carbon monoxide; you can't see it, but it'll kill you. And an inspiring culture is like perfume, filling the air with the sweet aroma of love, encouragement, passion, and a commitment to excellence.

Perhaps the most important principle in this chapter is that each person is responsible for shaping the culture. It's not acceptable to sit back and complain about how we've been mistreated or how clueless our leaders are. Remaining passive and resentful, or being demanding and furious, certainly creates a culture, but not a good one. On the spectrum of smells, we can all make the commitment to bring an aroma of life instead of carrying around the smell of cultural death.

Think About It . . .

1. How can a person have a thankful, positive attitude no matter how difficult the culture may be?

2. Look at the characteristics of a change agent. On a scale of 0 (not at all) to 10 (exceptionally well), give yourself a grade on how you're doing with each one right now.

   ____ Heart motivation

   ____ Positive demeanor

   ____ Ability to ask tough questions

   ____ Honesty about limitations

   ____ Warmth and humor

   ____ Willingness to reflect reality

3. Write down the names of people with whom you have your most important relationships at home, socially, and at work. Next to each one write "deposit" if that person's net impact on you fills you with encouragement, hope, and love, and write "withdrawal" next to those whose net impact drains you. Finally, reflect on the pattern of deposits and withdrawals in your life and complete this sentence:

   No wonder I feel . . .

4. Look at the list again, and for each person answer this question: In her relationship with you, would she say you are making a net deposit or a withdrawal in her life? When you are finished marking "deposit" or "withdrawal" for each one, consider this question: What needs to happen for you to make deposits in more people's lives?

5. What are some specific steps you can take today or in your next meeting to be the best team member you can be and to lead your team in creating an inspiring culture?

6

THE CATALYST OF CHAOS

If you have a job without aggravations, you don't have a job.

—*Malcolm Forbes*

To create a new culture, you have to destroy the old one. Half measures won't do. If we try to ease our way into a new culture with as little pain as possible, we'll probably fail to make the necessary adjustments, and any change we make will be incomplete or nonexistent. Expect blood on the floor. To galvanize people's resolve to kill the old and raise up a new culture, every growing organization has to make friends with an odd ally: chaos. The commitment to change a culture is always learned from negative experiences that look like chaos but are actually open doors to a new world of creativity and growth. These experiences often take the form of failure, conflict, and power struggles, but chaos also is the result of imple-menting bold new plans

> *To create a new culture, you have to destroy the old one.*

when other people want to rest on past success. In the crucible of chaos, God forms our character, creates a new culture, and determines our destiny.

Stakes in the Ground

All organizations experience change. Even churches that treasure their ancient traditions have to find ways to connect with people in a high-speed, postmodern world. Some people feel threatened by the speed of change even more than by the actual changes, and some resist change because they feel uncomfortable during the awkward time of uncertainty between the old normal and the new normal. The pace of change in our society is so fast today that leaders in every field desperately try to find ways to keep up. Most leaders try to anticipate the changes that will occur in the next five to ten years. (Who would have dreamed that the technology that gave us "mobile phones" we carried like suitcases twenty years ago would produce the Internet-connected smart phones we use today? And what will we use twenty years from now?) But Jeff Bezos, founder and president of Amazon.com, has a different perspective. He focuses on the things that will remain the same "because you can really spin up flywheels around those things," he observes. "All the energy you invest in them today will still be paying dividends 10 years from now." This perspective encourages leaders and their teams to value a few things that won't change, but it has the positive result of putting everything else on the table for evaluation and change. What does Bezos say won't change? In his world, it's selection, low prices, and fast delivery.[1]

In the church world, many things have changed since the Ascension, but we can count on a few constants: God's word is the source of truth, his Spirit changes lives, people value authentic leadership, and they thrive in close-knit communities of faith. These things are the stakes in the ground we can always count on. Many people who feel threatened by change are secretly (and perhaps unconsciously) wondering if their bedrock values are going to be thrown out along with the changes to worship songs, choir robes, small group content, and service times. If they are convinced that the church's core values will always be respected, they may be more willing to embrace changes in other areas.

All cultures are shifting, but thankfully, not everything in those cultures is changing, or we'd suffer from an overload of dislocation. In our family, Brenda and I still live in the same house we've enjoyed for many years, she teaches at the same school, and

I do the same work with the same kind of pastors, but even in our stable world, we experience pleasant surprises, unanticipated challenges, nagging difficulties, and wonderful new opportunities. All of these demand our attention and call for us to change.

As we examine chaos as the catalyst of change, we need to remember that our people have varying capacities to embrace change. Some are terrified by it, and a few thrive in it, but they all ask a fundamental question at every step: "How does it affect me?" The way a leader navigates change may do more to define the organization's culture than any purpose statement. The path charted through threats and opportunities demonstrates the actual values of the leader, the team, and the organization. The response to chaos, then, is both a reflection of the existing culture and an open door to cultural change.

The way a leader navigates change may do more to define the organization's culture than any purpose statement.

I've seen leaders experience chaos in countless ways, but three of those ways stand out as unique challenges: redefining failure, creating a sense of urgency to take advantage of opportunities, and managing conflict. Let's look at each of these.

Redefining Failure

Today, innovation is a key component of growing churches, but fresh approaches carry an inherently higher risk of failure than safer paths. Truly innovative leaders and their teams not only encourage people to dream new ideas and find new solutions but also have found a way to transform the inevitable failures into platforms for future success. They recognize the nature of risk and are realistic about the possibility—and even the probability—of failure. They know that Magellan hit scores of dead ends before he found the passage around the tip of South America to the Pacific, Edison experimented with hundreds of materials before he found the carbon filament for the light bulb, medical researchers work for years to find a single drug to fight a disease, and many authors are turned down by dozens of publishers before they find one who will put their work in print. If these men and women had quit after the first (or fiftieth) failure, the world wouldn't have the benefit of their discoveries and insights. In a similar way, Christians need to ask,

> What are we willing to risk for God's kingdom?
>
> What is the point when we give up hope and quit trying to implement change?
>
> How do we treat others when they fail?

I encourage pastors to create a culture of experimentation in which creativity is celebrated and failure isn't a tragedy. By its nature, innovation breeds a form of chaos because each day people say to themselves and each other, "I wonder if this will work." In these environments, we see versions of the "happy warrior," but here it's the "happy innovator" who is willing to risk his time, money, and reputation to see if God might bless a new way of doing things. Of course, creativity has to be guided by wisdom,

I encourage pastors to create a culture of experimentation in which creativity is celebrated and failure isn't a tragedy.

but excessive caution shouldn't rule our lives. There are always far more people who say, "Don't" or "Wait" than those who eagerly say, "Let's go for it!"

Pastors and team leaders certainly don't enjoy falling on their faces, but instead of spending their emotional capital pointing fingers and defending themselves, they can develop a culture that redefines failure and replaces condemnation with tenacious hope. To create this kind of culture, leaders need to apply a few simple but important principles:

- Look in the mirror to see how you respond to failure.
- Develop a vocabulary of risk.
- Respond positively to success.
- Respond graciously to failure.

Look in the Mirror to See How You Respond to Failure

Some of us try to be positive when others fail, but we harshly condemn ourselves for our own failures. It's very difficult to offer patience, hope, and wisdom to others when we don't experience it personally. We have to draw water from a full (or at least a filling) well.

Develop a Vocabulary of Risk

People long to follow a leader who blends vision and wisdom, but they soon become skeptical of a wild-eyed visionary or, on the other end of the spectrum, a leader who is too cautious to take any risks at all. Think about the leaders you admire, the ones who are thoughtful, caring, and willing to attempt great things for God. How do they communicate at every level: with their top leaders, all their staff, the church, and the community? What kinds of words and phrases do they use? What are the nonverbal signals they send to those who are watching and listening? The goal isn't to take wild and crazy risks but to bring people along to trust God to accomplish his purposes—and his purposes are always big enough to enflame the hearts of his people.

Respond Positively to Success

The way leaders respond to success is a predictor of how they'll respond to failure. A healthy culture celebrates success, but it always takes time to reflect on what went right and what could

A healthy culture celebrates success. be better next time. And it's important to give credit where credit is due: to the Lord and to the hard work of men and women who trusted God to use them. Leaders who take too much credit for themselves erode trust, discourage followers, and drip toxins into the culture.

Some leaders have exceptionally high expectations of success, and they are devastated by anything less. I knew a pastor whose standard for success was that his church would grow by 18 percent each year. When it grew at that rate or higher, he walked into meetings with confidence and joy, full of emotional deposits to share with others. But when his church grew only 16 percent one year, he saw it as a personal failure and a failure of his staff. He grumbled to express his displeasure, and he thought about firing several staff members. Instead of making deposits in others' lives, he took out hefty withdrawals. Couldn't he celebrate 16 percent growth? Apparently not.

Success means different things to different people at different times in their lives. To this pastor, the measure of success was the rate of growth—in fact, a consistently high rate of growth of his church. At one point, success for me was determined by how much money I made. Today, I measure it by how much impact God gives me in the lives of leaders. Bob Buford, the founder of Leadership Network, has written eloquently about the need to shift our attention from success to significance. I believe there is a category after that: fulfillment, the sweet spot at the intersection of God's gifting in our lives, people's needs, and our joy at seeing lives changed.

Respond Graciously to Failure

Many people come from families and church cultures where failure was condemned in one way or another. There may not have been name-calling and raised voices, but the one responsible got "that look" that spoke a thousand words of blame and disappointment. Attempting great things for God always results in a mixed bag of success and failure. Expect it, and don't come unglued when failure happens. Look people in the eye, reassure them with an affirmation that they went for it with boldness and faith, and make a point of asking two forward-looking questions:

1. What did you learn?
2. What will you do next time?

Ironically, some Christians feel particularly threatened by failure because they believe that God's involvement should guarantee success. They forget that responding to failure with faith is the cornerstone of the Christian life, and the examples in the scriptures are almost limitless. Peter denied Christ three times after proudly professing that he was willing to die for him, Paul lists many times when he faced brutal opposition to his efforts to tell people about Jesus, and it seemed to the whole world that Christ himself had failed miserably when he died that Friday afternoon to the jeers of his enemies. But in all these cases, apparent failure became the launching pad for a demonstration of God's amazing work of grace and power. As sinners saved by grace, we face our own failures time after time, but we, too, find new opportunities to experience light in each moment of darkness.

Failure can be the platform to learn life's greatest lessons so that we can continue to think the unimaginable, dream the impossible, and attempt incredible things for God.

Failure isn't the end of the world. In fact, if we develop an optimistic, forward-thinking culture of experimentation, failure can be the platform to learn life's greatest lessons so that we can continue to think the unimaginable, dream the impossible, and attempt incredible things for God. Redefining failure for your team and your church is a vital part of creating a strong, inspiring culture. Stop playing not to lose, and start playing to win.

Anticipate Opportunities

Every organization experiences natural cycles of growth and decline. British author Charles Handy has popularized the Sigmoid Curve to encourage leaders of change. The cycle begins with an energizing vision and moves into a growth mode. If momentum isn't sustained, energy gradually subsides, and passion erodes into empty regimentation and lifeless institutionalization. Finally, decline leads to stagnation and death. At that point, people remember the "good old days" when the vision was fresh and strong. In the diagram, point A marks the period when the vision begins to fade, but decline doesn't occur until later, at point B.

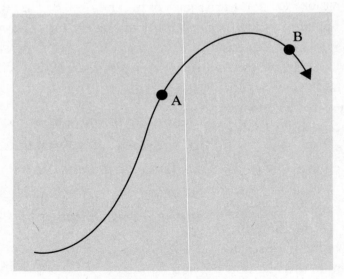

Vision, Growth, Decline, Stagnation, and Death

Churches may be at point A when a successful building campaign has been completed, a new small group emphasis has doubled the size of that ministry, a bold outreach has seen hundreds come to Christ and join the church, a new discipleship philosophy and strategy has profoundly shaped people's lives, or any other major emphasis in the church has been successful. At that moment, leaders and followers are tempted to take a deep breath and conclude, "Wow, that was great. Let's take a break for a while." They don't realize that the failure to capitalize on the momentum is the beginning point of decline. In fact, most leaders don't recognize the need for change until point B, when decline has already become a reality.

Great leaders have the foresight to predict the need at point A for a fresh vision and change, before decline sets in at point B. Communicating this perspective is a difficult task because very few people, if anyone, in the organization sees a need to "fix" what isn't broken. At this pivotal moment, visionary leaders need to infuse a successful system with a sense of urgency that change is necessary—right now before it's too late! But this attempt carries a risk. Communicating a fresh vision for change during a time of peace is seen by some as a power trip on the part of the leader. They question his motives—and perhaps his sanity. Great leaders,

Great leaders are often misunderstood, especially when they create chaos when everyone expects a time of tranquility.

though, are often misunderstood, especially when they create chaos when everyone expects a time of tranquility.

If a leadership team takes action at point A and infuses the church with a new vision, strategy, and heart, they can change the shape of the curve and experience another growth cycle. The time between the envisioning of the new wave at point A and the upward movement after a period of preparation (often two or three years) is full of doubt, fear, and questions—a time of chaos.

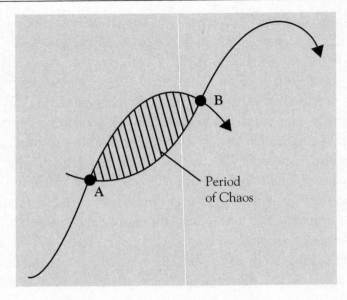

Period
of Chaos

When the leader makes the change at point A, he will inevitably incur misunderstanding from many and resistance from some. In the season of chaos between point A and point B, people are in a state of flux, routines have been disturbed, and the security of the familiar is absent. This chaos can certainly be avoided, but only if the leader waits until it's obvious the change is needed at point B. At this point, however, it's too late to stay on top of the game. We must change before the need to change is obvious. Constant growth means consistent chaos. Consequently, if an organization wants to continue to grow, the leaders must invite chaos to be their constant companion. At every recurring point A, they recognize the need for more change, a new vision—and chaos!

If the leader and the organization are secure enough to endure it, this chaotic, flexible mode of operation will provide a path to the future. The blunt truth is that all of us experience change. The question is this: Will we change too late? Church consultant Thomas G. Bandy looked into the hearts of leaders who antici- pate opportunities and predicted, "The future of the church in the 21st century will not be determined by planning. It will be

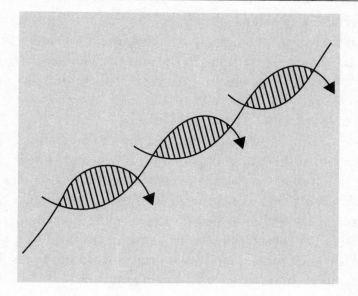

determined by leadership development. These leaders may be clergy or laity, and they will probably not care about the designation. They will be risk takers and adventurers. They will always be wondering what opportunity lies over the next cultural hill. They will be explorers of the unknown. They will be you."

The following are important diagnostic questions for leaders to consider:

Questions About Chaos

In the last ten to fifteen years, when were the times when your church experienced significant momentum?

What created the momentum?

How did you respond when you had momentum? Did you capitalize on it, or did you let it drift away?

When I spoke to a group of pastors to explain the importance of capturing momentum at point A, Rick came up to me at the next break. He blurted out, "Oh my gosh, Dr. Chand. I get it! I didn't get it until now, but now I get it."

I had no doubt he was going to share his story with me, but I asked anyway: "What is it that you now get?"

"When you talked about looking back to see how we responded when our church had momentum, I suddenly realized what happened. Three times in the past twelve years we experienced a tremendous surge of new people when God blessed us. We were clearly at point A."

"And how did you respond?" I asked.

"We blew it," Rick said with more joy for finding insight than sorrow for missing those opportunities. "We just blew it. Each time, we coasted. Oh, we were very thankful for God's blessings, and we worked hard to incorporate all those people into the life of the church, but within six months to a year, the momentum began to subside." His eyes widened with a fresh insight, and he told me, "And you know something? It's a lot easier to capture and build on existing momentum than to generate it from scratch."

We continued to talk, and he shared his current situation. His church was completing a new worship center. It was scheduled to open in five months, and they expected to grow by 30 percent in the first few weeks after the grand opening. Rick observed, "Dr. Chand, I've focused our staff on those first few months after we get into our new building. That's when we'll have incredible momentum. But I haven't even thought about how to capture that momentum and plan for the next three years. Today we're going to start our next phase of chaos!"

I kept up with Rick over the next few months. He went back from the pastors' conference and explained the concept of capturing momentum at point A to his senior staff and board. I asked him how those conversations went, and he told me, "Most of the people looked at me like they believed an alien had taken over their pastor's body. They couldn't imagine planning another big surge a few years down the road when we hadn't even gotten into our new building. But by the time the first meeting was over, a few of my staff realized the importance of taking advantage of the momentum God was going to give us. In a few weeks of many, many conversations and explanations, most of the others on our team finally came on board."

"Did you have any that simply refused to sign on to the vision God has given you?" I asked.

Rick smiled in a sad way and told me, "We have a couple of openings I'd like to fill."

"I understand," I nodded.

"Dr. Chand, I'm so excited about the future. I finally understand how we failed to capitalize on momentum in the past, and I don't plan to make that mistake ever again. I feel like I have a whole new way to think about our church and plan more strategically. Thank you so much for turning on the lights for me."

When leaders understand the importance of anticipating and implementing change at point A instead of waiting until decline happens at point B, they can infuse their culture with optimism and urgency. Award-winning author John Kotter observes, "Central to a continuous change culture is a continuously high sense of urgency. It does not follow a pattern of recognizing we have a problem, solving the problem, and going back to a sense of complacency. It's a culture that constantly reinforces the behaviors of being alert, of being curious, of doing it now, of leading no matter where you are in the organization."[2] Most leaders, Kotter asserts, think they are doing a great job of injecting urgency into their cultures, but a few conversations with people on their teams suggest otherwise. Organizations naturally drift toward complacency instead of urgency, fear rather than optimism, and blaming others instead of taking responsibility. To overcome this drift, leaders can invite fresh, challenging ideas to stimulate creative thinking, tell stories to capture people's hearts, and be models of urgency for their team members.

When leaders understand the importance of anticipating and implementing change at point A instead of waiting until decline happens at point B, they can infuse their culture with optimism and urgency.

In his insightful book *The Incestuous Workplace*, William White observes that the sickest cultures are those that close their doors to new ideas. Closed organizations thrive on "rigid, unchallengeable organizational belief systems" and "progressive isolation" from the outside world. The absence of fresh thinking robs the organization of creativity and the stimulation of new ideas, and soon, people turn inward, creating institutional stagnation.[3] The options for opening the system to fresh ideas are almost endless. Leadership teams have used consultants, seminars, and books to challenge their thinking and their strategies. Some have invited people in the community to visit a staff meeting to share their impressions of the church. New hires can bring a fresh perspective to a team and shake up the old order in a healthy way. Almost anything can help if the leader invites new thinking to challenge the status quo. The goal isn't to throw everything out the window and start over every few months, but to be always open to new ideas and fresh ways of fulfilling the vision God has given the church. Teams that are open to new concepts continually ask, "What can we do better?" and "What can we learn from others?" These questions raise the intellectual antennae, heighten awareness, and infuse the team with enthusiasm.

Urgency rarely comes from graphs on a presentation. Power-Point slides and charts on paper may communicate important truths, but stories capture people's hearts. That's why we love novels, biographies, and movies. When I'm in a meeting and someone tells a gripping story about a danger someone courageously faced or a life God changed, people put down their PDAs, stop texting, and sit on the edge of their chairs. It takes time to find and organize a story, but it's preparation time well spent. The leader, though, doesn't have to be the only person to tell stories. In fact, it's often more powerful when team members share stories of God at work to transform individuals and families.

One of Kotter's chief concerns about leaders who want to create a sense of urgency is that they often fail to model it in their own lives. They talk a good game, but there's no fire in their eyes or spring in their steps. Kotter reports, "It is astonishing how many leaders I have seen who say they now 'get it' about urgency, say they understand they must move the troops out of their complacency, and can talk about it correctly, but when you watch them go into their next meeting, their own behavior screams 'everything's fine, no need to worry.' I am amazed at how rare it is for leaders to act with urgency in their own conduct throughout the day. It's as if urgency is just for other people."[4]

Strategy and a commitment to excellence are important, but they can't overcome the daunting obstacle of complacency in a leader's life. Leaders may be able to fake urgency for a while, but not for long. For it to be real and for it to last, urgency has to come from a heart gripped by people's needs and God's grace to meet those needs. Bill Hybels of Willow Creek Community Church talks about the need for God to give leaders a strong sense of "holy discontent" that causes them to be dissatisfied with the status quo and drives them to attempt great things for God. Bob Pierce, the founder of World Vision and Samaritan's Purse, lived with a compelling sense of urgency that came from the heart of God. He famously pleaded, "Let my heart be broken by the things that break the heart of God." Urgency can be modeled only by leaders who are in touch with God's heart.

Managing Conflict

In my conversations with leaders over the decades, perhaps nothing has robbed them of joy, urgency, and vision as much or as often as enduring conflicts on their staff teams. These challenges threaten to rip the heart out of compassionate leaders, and they create an inordinate share of chaos for a leadership team.

I'm convinced that many church leaders put up with far too much mediocrity and resistance among their staff members.

Most of these leaders are compassionate and don't want to upset people by correcting them or demanding compliance with spoken and unspoken norms on the team, but failure to address nagging staff problems creates a stagnant culture at best, and at worst, a toxic one. Actually, I've never consulted with a pastor who didn't need to fire at least one of his staff members. I've heard all the reasons and excuses for keeping resistant, negative people on a team, but I don't buy them. When I hear leaders protest my advice to fire someone, I tell them, "You'll pay a price either way; either a brief and relatively small price by replacing the person, or a much bigger and long-term price if you let the person continue to sour the team and do a poor job in an important ministry area at the church. It's your choice which price you'll pay."

When chaos occurs on a staff team, the first thing the leader should do is look at herself and ask some questions: "What am I doing that might be causing this difficulty?" and "What is the pattern here? Is it a long-term, pervasive issue, or an isolated event with a single individual on the team?" The leader may not have given clear directions, defined roles, or facilitated communication among team members. If the conflict or resistance is a single flare-up, the issue is usually resolved fairly easily with good listening, soothed feelings, and clear directions. But too often, conflict on a team is systemic and needs a firm hand. When leaders avoid the hard work of correction, an individual with a negative attitude can cloud the team's ability to communicate effectively and hinder creative ways to touch more people's lives. Living with mediocrity (or worse) on a staff team normalizes ineffectiveness and runs off the best people who want to serve on a team committed to excellence.

Living with mediocrity (or worse) on a staff team normalizes ineffectiveness and runs off the best people who want to serve on a team committed to excellence.

To identify mediocre staff members, Paul Idzik, COO of Barclay's Bank, suggests that leaders look for signs of someone who

Is stubborn and resistant to change

Is reactive rather than proactive

Is lazy and unprepared

Makes promises but seldom delivers

Shirks responsibility and blames others

Identifies problems without offering solutions[5]

By all means, do everything you can to help struggling staff members find success and fulfillment. Conduct a performance review, be honest about the person's work and attitude, and do everything possible to create a workable, productive situation. There is a wealth of information available on managing staff, so I won't take time to articulate those principles here. There comes a point, however, when we've done all we can do to redeem a staff member, and it hasn't worked. Now it's time to help that person transition as graciously as possible. Provide assistance in helping him find a suitable placement, but don't let your team suffer and God's vision languish any longer.

Having the right staff members and top volunteers is crucial to fulfill a church's vision. Eric O. Long, general manager of the Waldorf Astoria in New York, observes that finding, recruiting, selecting, and placing outstanding staff are becoming more difficult in our society, but good selection yields amazing results. In an interview for *Leaders* magazine, Long observed, "Our organizational-development team recently made a presentation to our executive staff, sharing the results of several well-documented studies. It revealed that one great team member has the impact of multiple [mediocre] team members, and in some cases, the ratio was as high as 8:1."[6]

In selecting outstanding staff members, look for more than positive references and experience in certain skills. Dig deeper to uncover the person's passions and commitments. Linda Hudson, president of BAE Systems, offers some pointed suggestions in hiring: "I approach interviews a little differently. The first thing I always ask someone is: 'O.K., I've got your resume. I've been over all the details. Just tell me about your life. Start wherever you want to, from the beginning or the end, but talk to me about you, what you've done, and then walk me through what you've done with your career.' And I found that the way people talk about what matters to them tells me an awful lot about how engaging they are, their energy level, their passion." Hudson is looking for passion, a commitment to excellence, and a good fit. She notes, "I'm looking for the chemistry that would fit well in our environment and how articulate they are. Can they communicate effectively? Do they have that extra something and the passion and people connection that sets them apart from others? What gets you excited? What do you look forward to? Those are the kinds of questions I ask."[7]

When I consult with church leaders about hiring or promoting staff, I suggest they ask four questions:

1. Competence: Can you do the job?
2. Character: Can I trust you?
3. Chemistry: Can you fit in our culture?
4. Capacity: Can you grow with us?

Two crucial mistakes I've seen in the composition of church leadership teams are keeping mediocre people too long and hiring people too quickly without doing all the homework needed to make a good decision. A good rule to follow is, *make people decisions slowly*. If you rush to hire someone to fill a slot, you may spend countless hours trying to make the person fit, or working through the pain (for everyone) of replacing the person who didn't fit.

Embracing the Chaos of Change

Every team leader knows that some people on the team are more eager to jump on the train of a new idea than others, and there's always someone who drags his feet yelling, "No, it won't work!" up to the day the team celebrates the success of the venture. Leaders need to recognize that people have different degrees of capability to embrace the chaos of change. Perceptive leaders develop the ability to anticipate the response of each person to a challenge or a new opportunity.

To understand people and their responses to change, we need to remember that all of us instinctively ask, "What's in it for me?" Perceptive leaders also learn to ask themselves and their team members two other questions:

1. What about me embraces or resists this particular change?
2. What about the culture of our team embraces or resists this change?

An individual may embrace or resist change for any number of reasons: a simple preference, a core value, peer pressure, groupthink, or the need to defend staked-out turf. As I've observed people in times of change, I've noticed that the change itself is often a minor issue in a person's response. The more important factors that shape team members' responses are the way the change is presented, the level of respect for the person who presents it, the rate of change, and the clarity of the team member's role in the process of change. For instance, one team member will gladly embrace any new idea if Susan suggests it because she trusts Susan. If Bill had suggested exactly the same concept, she would have shot it down with a vengeance! Those factors give confidence (or erode it) in the crucial time when people are internalizing the new reality of a changing world.

The Diffusion of Innovations model (popularized by Everett Rogers) helps us understand the terrain of our teams and our churches as we propose change. According to this theory, people adopt one of five roles in their response to change. In my book *What's Shakin' Your Ladder?* I identify these as excited embracers, early embracers, middlers, late embracers, and never embracers. The distribution of these roles in a group forms a bell curve.

- *Excited embracers* make up 2 percent of a population. They are the dreamers and visionaries who are usually recognized as leaders or policymakers.
- *Early embracers* are 18 percent of a group. They are respected and influential, and they eagerly get on board when the concept is explained. Leaders treasure these people on their teams.
- *Middlers* are the largest part of the population, about 60 percent of people in the group. They feel more comfortable with the status quo, and they listen very carefully to anyone who resists change. They are willing to get on board only when they are convinced that everybody else will, too.
- *Late embracers* make up 18 percent of the people in a large group. They resist change as long as possible, offering objections all along the way. Eventually, they will go along with the majority, but with a large measure of skepticism and without any enthusiasm at all.
- *Never embracers* are 2 percent of the group. They are steadfastly committed to the past, and they continue to resist change long after the rest of the team is working hard to achieve success.

If you can convince the majority of middlers to support the initiative, you are on your way.

In most cases, the battle is to win the middlers. You won't need to work hard to convince excited embracers and early embracers of the value of your new idea. Late embracers won't be convinced until the idea becomes reality, and the never embracers are a lost cause. But if you can convince the majority of middlers to support the initiative, you are on your way.

Most middlers prefer the known to the unknown, the present's certainty to the future's uncertainty. This doesn't mean that middlers are closed to reason or can't catch the excitement of a new vision, but they tend to support the status quo unless they are given a good reason to change. They need to be assured that change won't result in loss of quality and won't cause them to lose their important role on the team.

Make early embracers your allies. Usually they are respected members of the team and the church, so their opinions are given serious consideration, and their leadership is usually followed. Make a list of the early embracers and solicit their active support. Ask them to endorse the new proposal in formal meetings and informal discussions, and enlist their help with the middlers. Explain that hallway and parking lot conversations often influence middlers more than anything else, and let them know that in every meeting, they will make the difference between failure and success.

Church leaders don't have any choice about the range of people who attend the church and show up at business meetings. Invariably, late embracers drag their feet and never embracers object to anything and everything. But leaders certainly have the authority and responsibility to select staff members and top volunteers. Careful selection is not an option but a necessity—it makes all the difference in how the team functions, as well as in how (or even if) God's purposes are fulfilled. Look for patterns in people's responses to the chaos of failure or the chaos created by a fresh vision. Some are resistant to only one or two items on the agenda, but others display a pervasive pattern of negativity.

Let me be clear: *know your people.* Give chronically resistant people every opportunity to change, but if they don't change their attitudes in a reasonable amount of time (you'll know), you can't afford to have an anchor on the team holding you back.

I don't subscribe to the "convoy theory" that a team moves only as fast as the slowest person. Good leaders have the ability to pull people along more quickly than they would normally move.

> *Good leaders have the ability to pull people along more quickly than they would normally move.*

But leaders shouldn't have anyone on a team who is slower and more resistant than a middler. Of course, we certainly respect people who ask penetrating questions. That's incredibly valuable to a team! But we need people who ask those questions with an eye toward solutions and a commitment to take bold action when the team has charted a course. Don't settle for anything less.

In times of chaos, leaders need to be observant about the types of responses they can expect from team members, and they need to marshal their primary resources in the organization—the early embracers—to help get others on board with the new plan. Change may be thrust upon the team or the church by outside forces, such as a downturn in the economy or demographic shifts in the community, or high-impact leaders may infuse change into the system by anticipating an opportunity for growth at point A. The leader's response to the chaos of change reflects the current culture, but more important, the experience of chaos offers a perfect classroom to impart a new culture to the team and the body of believers. No matter how well a leader anticipates change and communicates with others, resistance is inevitable. Author and humorist Robert Orben quipped, "Sometimes I get the feeling that the whole world is against me, but deep down I know that's not true. Some of the smaller countries are neutral."

The Value of Honest Feedback

In an open culture that values experimentation and learning, we treasure people who help us reflect more deeply. That's the role Benson Karanja played in my life when I was president of Beulah Heights University. Benson trusted me enough to challenge my thinking, disagree with me, and help me think more clearly than ever before. He was always willing to ask hard questions, often questions no one else was willing to ask out loud, but he didn't ask difficult questions because he wanted to throw up roadblocks. He asked so we could find the very best solutions to the challenges we faced. In our relationship, disagreement wasn't a threat. It only created a context for us to explore and experiment together. All leaders need someone like Benson who is ruthlessly honest, thoroughly good-hearted, willing to patiently probe the depths of an issue, eager to pursue workable solutions, and supportive of the team at every point in the process. I wouldn't be doing what I'm doing today if it weren't for Benson. He is a great gift to me.

People don't bring the same level of insight, skill, and passion to every subject. Some may be passionate about children's ministry, but they couldn't care less about music. In meetings, I've learned to discover what each person brings to the table so that I can appropriately value her for her area of expertise and enthusiasm. In a similar way, some people on the team have more relational and emotional authenticity than others. When perceptive, caring people speak about others' emotional responses to a service or a program, I listen intently

Good leaders are observant. They notice what makes people tick, the resources they bring to each issue, and their level of integrity.

to what they have to say. But if the topic of conversation is the budget, I pay close attention to the accountant who has a clear grasp of the numbers, even if he's not relationally perceptive. Good leaders are observant. They notice what makes people tick, the resources they bring to each issue, and their level of integrity.

Chaos—no matter what the cause might be—is a test that shows what people and organizations are really made of. Experiencing times of chaos is like squeezing a sponge: whatever was lurking there before comes out. But seasons of chaos are only tragic if leaders fail to take advantage of them. If we respond with insight, courage, and hope, they become catalysts for incredible growth—for the church and for each person on the team.

Think About It . . .

1. How do you typically respond to failure? How can you help people on your team redefine failure so that it becomes a stepping-stone for growth?

2. Describe the importance of crafting a new vision at point A on the curve instead of waiting until point B. Where are you now in your church or team's life? Do you need to infuse new vision and strategies into your church now? Explain your answer.

3. Who are the early embracers on your team you count on? How can you enlist them more fully to influence the middlers?

7

CHANGING VEHICLES

Reinvent yourself every three years . . . so that
you can remain relevant and able to make new
contributions in a world of constant change. . . .
Reinvention is the key to longevity.

—*Stephen R. Covey*

We've seen that changing the culture of a team or a church doesn't happen by magic, and it doesn't happen quickly. It's relatively easy to change a program, but it's more difficult to change the ministry philosophy and strategy that shapes the implementation of a program. But these are relatively easy compared to changing the culture, because culture reflects our most sacred values of integrity, trust, and heart, as well as how we implement our values in every relationship and program. Changing a culture requires clear thinking, concerted effort, enormous courage, and tenacious consistency. But first, we need to recognize what needs to change.

Vision and Vehicle

If I wanted to travel to London from my home in Atlanta, it wouldn't matter if I had a Lamborghini or a Rolls Royce—a car wouldn't get me to Piccadilly. A car could get me to the airport or to a port where I could get on a ship, but a car simply isn't designed to travel across the ocean. No amount of wishing or claiming promises will make the car a suitable vehicle to reach the destination I desire. Now there's absolutely nothing wrong with a car to get me to anywhere on the contiguous land mass. It's perfect for that purpose, but not for ocean travel. If London is my vision, I have to abandon the vehicle I'm using and find another to get me there.

This analogy fits the situation for many church leaders. We may have a very good vehicle (our organizational structure and personnel) to achieve a limited vision, but the one we are currently using may not be able to take us to the place God wants us to go. Like the traveler, no amount of wishing or tinkering with the engine will solve the problem. We can try to put wings on a car, but it still won't fly. We can attach a sail or a rudder to the car, but it won't make the ocean voyage. We need a new vehicle, often a radically new one, if we're going to achieve all that God has for our team and our church. This doesn't make the current vehicle "bad." There's a difference between *bad* and *wrong*. The vehicle we've been using isn't morally deficient or evil in any way. It simply can't produce the results we need. It's the wrong vehicle to take us where we want to go.

When I talk to pastors and explain this principle, they almost always instantly get it. The lights come on in their eyes, and they suddenly realize that they've been trying to drive a car to London! No wonder they've experienced so much frustration. After a few minutes, I often ask, "Now that you see that the vehicle of your organization can't get you to the destination of your vision, which one needs to change—the vehicle or the destination?" This may seem like a simplistic, rhetorical question, but actually, it's crucial. When leaders keep butting their heads against a wall day after day—or, using our metaphor, they keep driving up to the beach on the East Coast and realizing they can't go any farther toward

> *"Now that you see that the vehicle of your organization can't get you to the destination of your vision, which one needs to change—the vehicle or the destination?"*

London—many of them scale back their vision to match the capabilities of their organizational vehicle. That's precisely the wrong solution! When they finally realize how their existing structure and personnel aren't capable of achieving their vision, their frustration melts into a firm conviction to do the only reasonable thing: change the vehicle.

When I meet with pastors and discuss the principle of creating an organizational vehicle to fulfill their vision, I want to find out if their vision is clear and strong, and I want to help them see if their organizational structure and people can take them to reach that vision. Dr. Gerald Brooks (www.growingothers.com) has helped me think through this issue by using a series of test questions.

1. The heart test: Is the vision burning brightly in the heart of the leader, both in public descriptions of where God is leading him and passionately in his heart?

2. The leadership test: Do the top leaders in the church share this vision, or are they apathetic or resistant? Are these the people who can take the church to the vision's destination?

3. The organization test: How well does the current organizational structure work to achieve the vision? What are the bottlenecks? Which aspects are cars that can't take you there? Which ones are planes or ships?

4. The recruiting test: Are new hires and volunteers on board with the vision, or are they still a work in progress?

5. The message test: Is the vocabulary of the vision consistent and strong in every part of the church? Is the message of the vision reflected in sermons, written materials, the budget, signs, and conversations about the priorities of the church?

6. The planning test: Is the church's vision your staff's benchmark for strategic planning in every area?

7. The facility test: Do facilities, including their layout, design, and decor, reflect the vision?

8. The money test: Does the budget demonstrate the vision's priorities?

9. The pragmatism test: Does the vision make sense? Is it both God-sized and workable? Can you see it happening? Is it so global that it doesn't capture anyone's heart, or is it appropriately targeted?

10. The capacity test: How well does the capacity of the current organizational structure and personnel match the vision?

11. The clarity test: Can people throughout the organization articulate the vision clearly and with passion? If you ask people who come out the door after the service on Sunday morning to articulate the vision of the church, could they share it clearly and with enthusiasm?

12. The counsel test: Who are the outside voices that are helping to shape the vision and the vehicle to fulfill it?

13. The growth test: How do the ministries of the church need to be organized to capitalize on the next two stages of growth?

How do we know if a vision is from God? One of the measures is that it has to be something so big that it requires God's wisdom and power to pull it off. Anything less is just a good idea. God's vision is to redeem not only individuals but the entire creation. He's not just making new men and women; he's going to re-create the entire universe in the New Heaven and New Earth. That's a big vision! Small visions don't enflame people's hearts—yours or those who follow you. Don't dumb down your vision to be something that isn't threatening. If your vision is from God, it will blow your socks off and keep you awake at night! People

If your vision is from God, it will blow your socks off and keep you awake at night!

instinctively understand the power of a big, compelling vision. When he was an old man, English sculptor Henry Moore was asked, "Now that you are 80, you must know the secret of life. What is it?"

Moore smiled and answered, "The secret of life is to have a task, something you do your entire life, something you bring everything to, every minute of the day for your whole life. And the most important thing is: It must be something you cannot possibly do."[1] That's a good benchmark for our visions, too.

Some churches are rocking along pretty well. They have a bold, clear vision, and they enjoy a culture of creativity and experimentation, so their people are conditioned to embrace new ideas. Many churches, though, have been doing the same things so long that they don't even know other vehicles exist. To change the metaphor, these leaders need to heal the infection before they can perform a heart transplant. If they attempt surgery before they've dealt with the infection, the patient—their team and their church—will suffer and die. The first step for them is to get the body as healthy as possible, and then take bold steps to change the culture.

Clarity, Congruence, and Courage

When Raymond heard me speak at a conference, he asked to meet with me for breakfast the next morning. After we got to know each other for a few minutes, he began to pour out his frustrations. "Dr. Chand, I have no idea how our church got to this point, but I feel like I'm spending most of my time on things that weren't the reason we began the church eight years ago. Can you help me sort this out?"

"I'll certainly try," I assured him.

Raymond's eyes lit up as he described how the church began. He and his team believed that God called them to reach unchurched people in the suburbs of New York. "We didn't have to look very far to find unbelievers," he said with a smile.

I asked, "How did things go the first few years?"

He sat back in his chair and shook his head with a big grin. "It was incredible. We saw so many people saved, so many families reunited. I loved every minute of it."

"What happened?" I asked him. "What has caused your disappointment since then?"

"Somewhere along the way, we started doing good things instead of the best things." I knew exactly what he meant, but I asked him to continue. "As more people came to Christ, we began discipling them. Soon, people wanted us to have a family life center, and before long, we had a bowling alley and a coffee shop."

"These weren't part of the vision God gave you?" I probed.

Raymond shook his head again, but this time without a smile. "I thought they were, and people assured me they were, but in the past few years, we've invested far more time, money, and people into things like the bowling alley than reaching people for Christ." He paused, then told me, "I'm not sure what to do now. I feel like we've missed what God called us to do, but there seems to be no turning back."

"You can always do what God called you to do, Raymond. But you're right. You're going to have to unravel some good things so you can devote yourself to the best. It'll be hard, but God will give you the wisdom to do it."

You're going to have to unravel some good things so you can devote yourself to the best.

Many leaders have faced similar circumstances. They joined a church with a passionate vision, but over time, the vision atrophied or shifted to something else. Let me explain the difference between the dining area of a fine restaurant and the restaurant's kitchen. When I take my wife to a lovely restaurant, we enjoy the nice tablecloth, flowers, soft music, gentle lighting, courteous service, and wonderful meal. But a few inches beyond that idyllic setting is a very different environment: the kitchen. That's where people are running around cooking, preparing plates, and fussing with each other so that they can provide the perfect dinner for my wife and me. In the same way, when people come to a church's worship service, they enjoy the best and the most beautiful setting we can provide. Sometimes they say to each other, "Wow, I'd love to work in a place like this. It's wonderful!" But they have no idea that the real work of the church is much more like the kitchen, and they are shocked to find that making a delicious entree is a messy process. Leading a church isn't much different from being a chef in a busy, chaotic kitchen.

Quite often, ministry leaders and board members have offered ideas, suggestions, and plans that sounded great, but may not have been in alignment with the original vision. The leader didn't want to discourage the creativity of those people, so he smiled and went along. "It can't hurt anything, can it?" he wondered. But eventually the leader wakes up and realizes that too many compromises have been made and that the organization's vision is significantly different from his own. To remedy the conflict, too many leaders conclude that it's easier to adjust their own sense of God's calling and vision than to expend all the energy it would require to bring the entire leadership team, plans, and programs back into alignment with the original vision.

Maybe he's tired. Maybe he's discouraged. Maybe he's tired of fighting and feeling alone, and maybe he realizes all too well that it will be a colossal struggle to turn the team around. But if he continues to give in and support a vision he doesn't really believe in, he's not being true to himself, to God, or to his people. The leader has subordinated his God-given vision to a group of people who are taking the church to a different place. The conflict probably isn't between good and evil. Their vision and their destination are probably noble and worthy, too, but the pastor has to own a vision, not acquiesce to someone else's. We're not talking about a dictatorship or a heavy-handed style. We're talking about the importance—the necessity—of visionary leadership. The members of the team must be in line with the leader's vision and core values. If they aren't, he can't lead them. A pastor can't chart a course, plan effectively, and motivate his troops if his people aren't on board with his vision and core values.

A pastor can't chart a course, plan effectively, and motivate his troops if his people aren't on board with his vision and core values.

Organizational congruence is necessary if staff members are going to achieve God's vision and work effectively as a team. Without it, there's only confusion and conflict.

When a leader's vision and values are aligned with the organization's goals and the hearts of the team members, the congruence will be reflected in everything they do. For example, a local Atlanta church states that one of its core values is missions. This value is demonstrated in planning, budgeting, personnel, and even in prayer. The budget shows a large percentage of the church's income going to mission projects, and the missions department has more staff members and volunteers than any other department in the church. A glance at the church calendar shows that it's peppered with missions-related activities. Missionaries, mission trips, and mission funding and prayer are high priorities on the pastor's schedule, too. This focus demonstrates organizational congruence at the church around a compelling vision.

As I've worked with church leaders, I've observed them moving through the following phases as they've implemented new strategies, especially in changing their cultures:

1. Entrepreneurial, or the *discovery* phase, when the strategy is seen as viable: it can be done!

2. Emerging, or the *growth* phase, when credibility is crucial: the leader can be trusted.

3. Established, or the *maintenance* phase, when stability is achieved: the systems are in place and functioning well.

4. Eroding, or the *survival* phase, when the church is vulnerable: signs of decline are obvious.

5. Enterprising, or the *reinvention* phase, when leaders adapt to a fresh vision and new strategies: they adjust so they can grow again.

The only way to avoid eroding is to keep going back to being entrepreneurial. When leaders rest on their past successes, they become organizationally flabby—soft and passive. In fact, the more successful an organization has been in the past, the more likely it is to fail in the future. Without the constant infusion of entrepreneurial spirit, flourishing can lead to floundering!

Churches must "re-dream" the dream or discover a new compelling vision for their existence. For a leadership team and those they lead to continue developing and growing, they must focus on the organizing principles of the stages ahead. Leadership styles and the key issues to be addressed are different for each stage of the cycle. Effective leaders understand the cycle and are able to adapt their leadership to the corresponding needs of each stage.

> *Churches must "re-dream" the dream or discover a new compelling vision for their existence.*

The danger is that the old mental models will remain in place and that the desire for the security and familiarity of the past will win out over the opportunity of the moment to embrace and live out a new dream. Your thoughts will create your attitude, which leads to action. The Chinese characters that form the word *crisis* are a combination of *danger* and *opportunity*. Every crisis calls us to face danger, but we need to redefine it as opportunity. Olan Hendrix, author of *Three Dimensions of Leadership*, observed, "Generally, religious organizations start out with a goal orientation . . . deteriorate to a task orientation . . . and finally degenerate to a bottom-line control organization." Don't let that happen to you!

Your effectiveness will always depend on your ability to see the future. To be an effective leader, you must understand the difference between *change* and *transition*. *Change* is the event (for example, the first vision is realized, the founding pastor is gone, the community demographics have changed), and *transition* is the emotional, psychological, and social response to that change. In most situations, not enough attention is paid to the transition side, and leaders often move forward without realizing that the congregation, staff, or both are not processing the change at the same level they are.

Your future can be bright if

- You have a compelling vision.
- You have aligned the resources and ministries of the church to the vision.
- You understand the process of change and transition.
- You have the blessing of the Lord.

Strategic planning needs to be written in pencil because in a dynamic, changing environment, strategic planning needs constant evaluation and adjustment.

Congruence is a key component of an effective organizational vehicle. It is clear focus that organizes people, plans, and funding, and it flows from the church's vision, mission, and core values, permeating every department of the church. Of course, some churches do a better job than others, but the fact is, most leadership teams never even

The organization can't fulfill a God-sized vision, even in its local market, without the alignment of people, plans, and funding around a common purpose.

consider the importance of congruence. They just think, talk, and plan the way they've always done. The results are pockets of wonderful success, with some department leaders competing with others for resources, and some apathetic about what happens in other parts of the church. The absence of congruence is like a plane with one wing missing, a ship without a rudder, or a car with a flat tire. The organization can't fulfill a God-sized vision, even in its local market, without the alignment of people, plans, and funding around a common purpose.

Congruence and Strategic Planning

An old adage says that the devil is in the details, but actually, I believe that the fulfillment of a vision is in the details. Global statements have a place, but they need to be backed up with specific, strategic plans to fulfill the vision. Developing a healthy culture is the "soft side" of leadership, but strategic planning, the "hard side" of leadership, is also essential. The two complement each other. When staff members and church attenders hear concrete plans designed to accomplish the church's purpose, they trust their leaders, and the culture takes a step forward. If, however, they always hear glowing vision statements without seeing how the vision is going to be realized, they become skeptical of their leaders. Stagnant, discouraging, and toxic cultures usually aren't short on vision. In fact, their leaders often communicate grand and glorious pictures of the future. Many of these cultures are unhealthy because their leaders don't back up their lofty words with specific plans. Their people soon learn that they are full of hot air.

Strategic planning enables a team and every department in the church to work together for a common goal. It's the hallmark of congruence, and it's essential to healthy church cultures. For example, a pastor explained to me that he wanted to grow the children's ministry at his church. The church's vision statement is "Bringing families to the church." The pastor and his staff didn't just hope people would come to their church so that their families could experience God's grace. They did their homework to study the specific demographics of their community, and they began formulating their plans around the opportunities they found. They learned that a lot of children lived in apartments near the church. Many of these children lived in single-parent homes. The pastor and his staff talked about the emotional, relational, financial, and spiritual needs of these parents and their kids. One of the staff members in the children's ministry had coordinated a program for this demographic group at a church a few years before. Another person called a friend who served at a church across the country, a church that had a large and successful ministry to single parents and their kids.

The pastor and his team didn't rush to create a program. They carefully studied the demographics, talked to people with successful ministries, and read books and articles on the subject. After several weeks of study, reflection, and conversation, they were ready to dive into the planning process. They began with the existing vision and discussed how this idea of reaching families was congruent with this vision. As they dug down deeper, their questions became increasingly specific. The process they used included these elements:

Crucial Questions

- What is our church's vision?
- What is the need we see in people's lives? How does meeting this need relate to our vision and core values? (Is there congruence with the vision?)
- Who will be responsible for this plan and this ministry? How will the implementation of the plans enhance or detract from existing activities and priorities? Is this price worth paying? Why or why not? Do the responsible people have a passion to meet these needs?

- What are the specific elements of the plan to accomplish this goal?
- What are the due dates for specific tasks, and who will accomplish them? What are the benchmarks of progress in the next month, six months, year, and two years?
- How much will the plan cost, including people, materials, facilities, funding, and other resources?
- Do we have the capacity to undertake this right now? If not, what needs to happen to increase capacity? What is the threshold for taking the plan from the conceptual stage to implementation?
- How will we measure success?

After the team walked through the planning process (which took three weeks to complete), they reviewed their plans to be sure that all team members were on the same page. The pastor reiterated the church's vision statement, shared the results of the team's research, and stated the overall plan to reach families in the community with a new strategy. Then he asked the group, "Just to be crystal clear about our plans, why are we doing this?"

The children's ministry coordinator responded, "Because over 70 percent of the local families have children, and if we can reach the children, we can reach the rest of their families."

"Who is going to do it?"

An associate pastor looked across the table and nodded, "Annette is our children's coordinator, and she'll be responsible for it."

"How will she do it?"

Annette replied, "After looking at all the options, our team is going to use a programming plan that worked at a church in Oregon."

"How much will it cost?" the pastor asked.

Annette answered, "Each program will have a deadline and a budget associated with it."

"Annette, who will you be accountable to?"

Everyone laughed and pointed back at the pastor. He smiled and responded, "You're right. She'll report directly to me. We will evaluate her progress monthly and base it on the growth in the number of children enrolled in church school, children's church, and special activities, and we'll track to see if the new people who attend are from our target area. We also plan to have an annual review, and we will attach separate goals for that review."

> *When a team learns the principles of strategic planning and gains some experience, it becomes second nature for them to value the congruence of vision, people, and resources.*

Strategic planning is an acquired skill. When a team learns the principles of strategic planning and gains some experience, it becomes second nature for them to value the congruence of vision, people, and resources. A healthy, powerful culture moves a team and a church body toward the ultimate objectives God has given them.

I've noticed that many leaders don't have a framework for decision making. They just do whatever looks best at the moment. Perhaps the simplest and clearest template for planning is to follow the acronym SMART. Plans need to be specific, measurable, accountable, reasonable, and timely.

When presented with a complicated decision that could change the direction of the organization and shape the culture, we need to ask four questions; and it is important that we ask them in this order.

1. *Is the program in line with our vision, mission, and core values?* No matter how great an idea or opportunity, if the program isn't in line with the vision, we must say no to it. Most church leaders use their vision statements to say yes, but they rarely use it to say no and eliminate options. If everything imaginable fits

under the umbrella of the vision, perhaps the vision statement is too broad and needs to be refined and clarified.

2. *Do we have the organizational and human capacity—and the heart—to do this?* The program may be so large that it creates enormous stress for the entire team, or perhaps we don't have the right people on the team to accomplish the objective, our facilities and volunteer manpower are not be adequate to achieve the goals, or it's just not the right time.

3. *How will God be glorified?* Most leaders will ask, "Will God be glorified?" and the answer is almost always yes. When the answer is always yes, we are probably asking the wrong question. Instead, ask, "How?" This question will help us understand the true impact the decision will have on God's kingdom.

4. *How much will it cost?* This must be the last question asked. Understand the true nature of this question, and then consider it carefully. It's not "Can we afford it?" Most churches and nonprofit organizations don't have piles of money sitting around waiting to be used. The initial answer to the question of affordability is usually no. But the answer to "How much will it cost?" is different. The cost includes not only dollars but also people, resources, time, and energy pulled from other projects and programs. Most churches didn't come this far in their history because they had plenty of resources, but because their leaders were resourceful. It's not about resources; it's about being resourceful. A program that is immediately blocked by the question "Can we afford it?" might get a different response after asking all four questions. If the vision is big enough, if the people have a heart for doing it, if God will be glorified in a specific way, then the money will come.

Answering these specific questions *in this order* helps us grasp the nature of the opportunity in front of us. Then we can make principled decisions based on a larger organizational context, not on a situation, such as the amount of cash in the bank account. Using these four questions to train leaders and teams in decision making has proven to be tremendously helpful.

The discussion enabled them to know why they made a particular decision, why they rejected a course of action, and why they deferred a choice until later. The four-question grid gives teams direction and confidence as they consider any decision, from the largest to the smallest issues they face.

Passengers in the Vehicle

When things aren't working, leaders often prefer to change the structure of an organization because it is the easiest area to tackle. Moving boxes around on an organizational chart, reassigning who reports to whom, and handing out new titles don't rock many boats. Restructuring is a clean process, and it seems to offer the biggest gain at the least cost. In most organizations, however, reorganizing the structure doesn't make people work better or harder. This reminds me of the man who needs to clean out his garage but decides to organize his bedroom closet because it's easier. He may get finished more quickly and he may not get as dirty, but he won't have a clean garage.

Changing the organizational structure doesn't change an individual's motivation, behavior, values, or way of relating to others. Changing the culture—the way people relate to each other and their commitments—or changing the people are the only ways to see real progress. To change things in an organization, it's far more important to make adjustments to the informal connections, not the formal structure. These informal processes are the ways people communicate, make decisions, and support or hinder each other. These are far harder to identify and address than moving a box on an organizational chart, but they promise far greater rewards. We need to set the standard very high for our staff members. The stakes are far too high for us to settle for less. God has called us to partner with him to redeem the world, and like Jesus, we are willing to work with anyone who responds. As we consider our leadership teams, however, we need to continually raise the bar. Staff members who can't or won't become part of a supportive, reflective, visionary culture shouldn't be allowed to poison it. Larry Bossidy, chairman and CEO of Honeywell, remarked, "People have told me I spend too much time on people, but I know that if I get the best people, I am going to walk away with the prize. In this day and age, organizations that don't have the best people don't win." People must take priority over structure.

> *Changing the organizational structure doesn't change an individual's motivation, behavior, values, or way of relating to others.*

Jim Baker is executive pastor of Brentwood Baptist Church in Brentwood, Tennessee. He notes, "In the midst of rapid growth, we have learned that organizational clarity, alignment, and collaboration are everything. In fact, we have learned that our effectiveness is ultimately the result of how well we execute these three critical processes. [These have] helped create a culture of shared purpose and achieve consistent levels of peak performance." Baker and his team have worked hard to make sure they have congruence among the staff's roles, the church's vision, and their strategic plans. "Establishing this culture is not easy," he relates, "and every church and organization must find its own way. But the outcome is worth the effort. Supervisors will spend less time fretting over what their [staff members] are doing and more time focusing on the future of the ministry. Employees and volunteers will know what to do and feel empowered to do it. And everyone will be excited, surprised and delighted with extraordinary results."[2]

Changing from one vehicle to another always creates chaos for a team. It's inevitable. The patterns of roles, expectations, reporting, and lines of communication that have been so familiar are now analyzed, and many are changed. Sometimes pastors realize they need to change vehicles at the moment when their church experiences a huge growth spurt. I consulted with a pastor who moved his church from a three-thousand-seat auditorium to one that holds over seven thousand. In the months leading up to the move, he assured me that he had prepared his staff and everything was under control. A month after the move, he told me, "The moment we moved into the new building, 80 percent of my staff proved to be inadequate for their new roles. We simply hadn't prepared them. We've had to scramble to equip them for the new expectations. Some are going to do fine, but a few aren't going to make the change. I thought I could just put new tires on the old vehicle and we'd reach our vision's destination that way, but now I realize that I was thinking way too small." Over the next few months, this pastor led his team in demolishing the old vehicle and creating one that promised to take them where God was leading them.

Steps of Transition

People often say they "are afraid of" change or they "don't like" change, but in my observation, most people are far more afraid of the process of the transition from one team to another, one plan to another, or one leader to another than they are afraid of the actual change itself. Many leaders focus on changing the external in their church world, but changing a culture rivets our attention on the deeper internal issues: relationships, values, and other matters of the heart. To be a good pastor or team leader, it isn't enough only to think through what you're going to do. You must also take time to consider all of the contingencies and write a comprehensive transitional plan.

Many leaders focus on changing the external in their church world, but changing a culture rivets our attention on the deeper internal issues: relationships, values, and other matters of the heart.

In the previous example of the pastor and his leadership team developing a strategic plan for the children's ministry, the next step in the planning process would be to make a list of all possible challenges and changes. For example, how would Annette's priorities change? Would some of her responsibilities shift to someone else, or would the church suspend those programs?

New plans always have a ripple effect in altering priorities, schedules, budgets, and, perhaps, reporting relationships in several levels of the organization. Even if only the children's ministry is directly affected by major transitions in the new strategy, the people in every other component of the church's life need to understand how the change will affect them. To minimize surprises, the team, and especially the team most involved with the changes, needs to anticipate these ripples and consider possible contingencies. If the new plan isn't carefully thought through, people in the organization may be confused and wonder about the credibility of the decision makers. Credibility is a people problem, but it's not the only relational problem to consider during a transition. The main question is, How does a leader position each team member for success?

After thinking about this question, the leader can create a written plan and then make decisions based on the plan. For example, she can ask herself these questions:

How will I approach each person?

How will I communicate the details of changes in priorities, budget, schedule, and reporting to this individual?

What information will that person need to understand this change?

You can be sure that different people will have very different perceptions of every new direction, and even if you explain things very carefully, some of them will disagree. That's especially true when you need to remove someone from a high-profile position. I talked to a pastor who told me that his worship leader confessed to viewing pornography. He didn't confess, though, until someone saw explicit images on his computer in his church office. The pastor wanted to save this man's reputation and protect his wife's feelings as much as possible, so he let him quietly resign. When staff members found out how the pastor handled the situation, they were polarized: the women were furious because they believed that the pastor should have publicly rebuked the worship leader as an example to the flock, but most of the men felt that the pastor had been too hard on him. It was, after all, the first time he'd been caught viewing porn. When some of the students learned what was going on, they wondered what the big deal was about. Some of the older people in the church wanted to lynch him!

This was a classic transitional challenge. Moving him out of his role as worship leader was a simple, straightforward change, but the transitional issues of communication and community understanding proved to be very difficult. In my experience, transitional difficulties are quite predictable when staff are fired.

In every major transition in a church, leaders need to be alert, and they must anticipate all the contingencies and make plans to deal with each one of them—knowing that some of these plans will be implemented, but most won't be needed.

William Bridges, a noted expert on change and transition, explains in his most recent book, *Managing Transitions: Making the Most of Change*, that the reason change agents fail is that they focus on the solution instead of the problem. This may seem counterintuitive to forward-thinking, visionary leaders, but Bridges teaches that people need to be gripped by the need before they will embrace the solution. In fact, he believes that 90 percent of a leader's efforts should be spent on selling the problem and helping people understand what is *not* working. He rightly claims that people don't perceive the need for a solution if they don't fully grasp the problem.

I've listened to countless pastors explain their vision to me, to a group of pastors, or to their congregations. Most of them focus their attention on the benefits they will enjoy when God fulfills a particular objective in their church and community. Comparatively few of them take time to paint the picture of people's needs so that hearts are stirred. When people are touched by pain, heartache, and lostness in others' lives, they'll eagerly embrace solutions to meet those needs. That's the power of organizations like World Vision and Compassion International. They don't just ask people for money for kids. Before they mention money, they show the faces of children who live in poverty and ignorance, and only then do they show how a person's contribution can effectively change a child's life. Is this manipulative? Not in the least. It's simply the most effective way to move the hearts of people so that they want to participate in meeting the needs of hurting people.

When people are touched by pain, heartache, and lostness in others' lives, they'll eagerly embrace solutions to meet those needs.

Good planning is essential in creating a positive culture, and it works at all times with all people. When I resigned from Beulah Heights University, I traveled all over the country to meet with board members and tell them what I was going to do and why. I was recommending Benson Karanja as my successor. In making that change, I had a transition plan. I knew the people I was going to talk to, when I was going to talk to them, and what I was going to say. The time spent thinking and planning for this transition made what could have been a painful time for me and the school into a very positive learning experience for everyone involved.

The responsibility for a successful transition is in the hands of the leader making the change. In one of my seminars, a young woman named Regina said she was moved from a minor role in the children's department to a larger responsibility as minister of Christian education. Regina did everything she could to prepare her people for a change. She found and trained her successor and helped transition her old team to their new leader. But no one helped pave the way for Regina's transition to her new role. The pastor failed to make an announcement to the church that Regina was given this new responsibility. And even worse, the former Christian education minister wasn't informed that he was now out of a job, so he continued in his position as if nothing had changed. This was a change without a transition. Regina had made the change, but without her pastor helping with the transition, she was now impotent in her new responsibility.

Some might wonder why a pastor would be so neglectful. I have a little more information that brings light to the situation. Regina is the pastor's daughter, and he was worried about how people would react to his giving her such an important role. He believed that she was the best person for the job, and she felt that she was ready, but his poor communication of the transition kept the church from having confidence in her. As you can imagine, this pastor created quite a mess. He had to deal with both a personal conflict—after all, she's his daughter—and professional challenges: he needed to resolve conflict on two teams and between two staff members who had been assigned the same role. But the pastor wasn't very quick to resolve these problems. When I first heard about the situation, Regina had been in her job for three months!

My recommendation to the pastor was to make a clear pronouncement to his people: "My daughter, Regina, is going to provide great leadership to the Christian education ministry department at our church. Actually, she should have been functioning in this position for the last three months, but I have been remiss in not making that announcement. I'm correcting that today. Come on up here, Regina, and tell them about your vision. What's God going to do through you and your team?"

Assimilating people into leadership roles is one of the most difficult challenges we face. However, if we properly prepare and execute a transition plan, and if

Assimilating people into leadership roles is one of the most difficult challenges we face.

we take responsibility for the changes we institute, we'll build trust, provide clear direction, and reinforce a positive culture.

Transitions in a Team's Culture

Some of us look at the size of our church and conclude that it's impossible to make any difference in its culture. The vehicle of organizational structure and personnel is, we're convinced, what it is, and it will always be the same. We've been to conferences, prayed, and talked to other leaders until our tongues hang out, but nothing has changed. Before we give up completely and fade into passive resentment of leaders or followers (depending on our position), we need to understand that our role in implementing change should be focused only on those immediately around us. We don't need to fret about everybody, but we can take bold steps to make a difference in the culture of our own teams. In an article in *Leader to Leader*, Dave Logan, John King, and Halee Fisher-Wright identify smaller clusters of people they call "tribes." A small organization may have only one tribe, but large churches and other corporate entities might contain hundreds or even thousands of tribes. The authors observe that changing a tribe's culture from toxic to inspiring follows five distinct stages. Change doesn't happen by trying to jump two or three stages at once, but instead by slowly and carefully building trust and authenticity to move up one stage at a time.[3]

Using the language of our scale of five types of culture, the authors report:

- About 2 percent of tribes are toxic. They create and perpetuate a poisonous environment like a street gang. Life, they are convinced, is totally unfair, and each person is left to dominate or to defend himself at all costs.
- Following a bell curve, 25 percent of tribes are discouraging. People perceive themselves at hopeless victims who have no power (and no responsibility) to change the atmosphere.
- Approximately half of all organizations are composed of stagnant tribes. Here, effort is expended on achieving personal success, personal advancement, and personal gain. In these tribes, people are divided into the "haves" who are beating the system and the "have-nots" who aren't making the progress they desire. The words "I," "me," and "my" dominate conversations.
- Accepting tribes are found in 22 percent of organizations. In these productive and supportive environments, shared values and teamwork focus attention on the common goals of the group.
- Only 2 percent of tribal cultures inspire people to devote their shared energies to creative solutions aimed at achieving the seemingly impossible. This kind of culture is rare, and it is also quite vulnerable to slipping back to a state of reduced creativity, confused values, and selfish ambitions.

Senior pastors can work hard to take all the tribes in their churches on a journey from where they are to become inspiring communities, but the first step is to work on their own leadership team. And the rest of the staff members need to realize that they can't change the whole culture of the organization, but can take their own teams on a journey from one stage to the next. There is no magic bullet to transform a team into an inspiring culture overnight. Those who try to make that happen frustrate themselves and disappoint their teams. To see change in a team's culture, the first step is to take a good, hard look at our own perceptions, attitudes, and behaviors. Change begins with us.

Healthy cultures thrive because the right people are in the right roles sharing a common vision and working with congruent plans, priorities, and resources. All these elements are essential. As we've seen, too many leaders put up with less than healthy cultures because they aren't willing to pay the price to destroy the old and create the new. Changing an unhealthy culture to a strong, vibrant one requires both a sledgehammer and a potter's wheel. We have to be ruthless to attack systems (not people) that block us from achieving our new objectives, but we also need to carefully mold a new culture with gentleness, wisdom, and strength—like a skilled potter making a beautiful vase.

> *Too many leaders put up with less than healthy cultures because they aren't willing to pay the price to destroy the old and create the new.*

Good leaders ruthlessly wield sledgehammers to destroy inadequate organizational vehicles, but they pull out a wider range of tools to use with people. Team members are closely tied to the old structures, so it's wise to use the right tool to communicate effectively with each staff member. I've known some who needed only a light tap to shatter old thinking and get them into the new vehicle, but I've also had to use a twenty-pound sledgehammer to make a dent with a few people. My goal in all cases isn't to hurt them, but to help them make the transition from the old to the new. And all along, I've painted pictures as clearly as possible to show them what we're missing, capture their hearts by showing them the needs of people, and show how they play a crucial role in the new vehicle. Communicating clearly and powerfully is my responsibility. I explain that each of us "has to give up a little to go up a lot." If I've observed them very well, I can anticipate how each one will respond, and I know how big a tap I need to make to help that individual let go of the old way of doing things and take steps toward a new, stronger, more effective vehicle.

One of the most interesting questions to ask leaders is, Who are the real power brokers in your meetings? At first, most of them will say, "Well, I am." They have the title and the role, but quite often, the informal power is owned by a sour person who fills the room with doubts, or a person who sees every decision through the grid of money instead of God's calling, or someone who demands that everyone agree with him on any subject. When these people (and these are just a few examples) are given informal power in a meeting, moving forward is as hard as pushing a rope uphill. This kind of culture has to be crushed so that a positive one can be created.

In these times of transition, people often become territorial—precisely at the time we want them to be more open to working as a team. In a meeting, for example, if a ministry leader insists on clinging to a room assignment because that's where and when one of her groups has met for years, but I've asked her to make an adjustment, I first go to that person privately and say something like this: "Beth, I know that group is important to you and it's inconvenient to ask them to meet at another time, but I need you to help me think and plan for the whole church, not just for your department. Can you do that for me?" Usually, that's enough, just a light tap, and she gets on board. But if she still resists my direction in the next meeting, I turn to her with a heavier hammer and say, "Beth, I've noticed that every time we have conversations about making the transitions we've been discussing, you want to protect your department from any changes. Your department is very important to all of us, but we are all making some trade-offs to make this work. I need for you to work with the rest of us. We've talked about this privately. Resistance to change bogs us down and takes our attention away from where we need to go. Can I count on you from this point forward?" Then I turn to the rest of the group and say, "Now, where were we?" And we continue our meeting.

When leaders face transitions like those described in this chapter, they often instinctively ask, "How much am I going to bleed when I go through this?" But that's the wrong question. A better question is, "I know I'm going to bleed. How can I help my team get healthy as quickly as possible?" When a surgeon has to amputate a man's leg, does the man want her to use a scalpel or a butter knife? If she uses the butter knife, she'll eventually get the leg off, but the process will be very messy. The biggest risk for a patient with a diseased leg is to avoid surgery, and if you wait until you're 100 percent sure that surgery is necessary, it's probably too late and the patient will die. If surgery is needed, the patient will do best if a skilled surgeon uses the sharpest scalpel she can find. That's the way to get the operation over as quickly as possible and protect the health of the patient. If you have to fire three people on your team, you and the rest of your team will bleed far more if you fire them one at a time over several months.

In healthy cultures where skilled, caring leaders communicate often and well with their teams and value their input, risks are minimized because people feel affirmed, have clear roles and goals, and don't become embroiled in turf wars.

In healthy cultures where skilled, caring leaders communicate often and well with their teams and value their input, risks are minimized because people feel affirmed, have clear roles and goals, and don't become embroiled in turf wars. But in unhealthy cultures, almost every interaction carries the risk of increasing levels of misunderstanding and distrust.

Don't put up with a deficient vehicle any longer. Destroy what you need to destroy, and create something beautiful in its place. The sledgehammer, though, has to be used with precision. Destroy possessive turf wars on your team; take the hammer to decisions that are based solely on money instead of vision; hit the spirit of blaming others and being exclusive; and obliterate the spirit of secret alliances, suspicion, and distrust. The free CULTURE survey (www.freeculturesurvey.com) will surface elements that need attention in your environment. When you see them, take a deep breath, think carefully, and pray deeply, then pick up your sledgehammer and begin destroying any unhealthy segments as you create a new culture for your team and your church.

Think About It . . .

1. Will your current vehicle (organizational structure and personnel) take you to the destination of your church's vision? Why or why not?

2. Describe the level of congruence of your church in the areas of a shared vision, a common ministry philosophy and strategy, and the use of resources. In what areas is there conflict or passive acceptance instead of eager support for one another?

3. What's the role of strategic planning in creating a new vehicle that will get you where you believe God wants you to go?

4. How does (or will) the process of thinking through the contingencies help you navigate the transitional issues as you develop a new vehicle?

8

YES, YOU CAN!

> I've missed more than 9000 shots in my career. I've
> lost almost 300 games. Twenty-six times I've been
> trusted to take the winning shot and missed. I've
> failed over and over again in my life. And that is
> why I succeed.
>
> —*Michael Jordan*

Is it possible to transform a culture? Some of us think that it seems almost too good to be true. But yes, it's not only possible but also the most productive work we can do because it has a dramatic, multiplied impact—on the team, in the church, and throughout the community.

If Scott Can . . .

If Scott Wilson can change his culture, anyone can. Scott joined the staff of his father's church in South Dallas as the youth pastor, and God used him in marvelous ways. Before long, the board and his father asked him to be the co-pastor of the church. This arrangement was an honor, but it proved to be quite awkward for everyone involved.

Years before, Scott's father, Tom, had come to the church as the pastor and as the superintendent of the church's private school. The church had been one of the most prestigious in the denomination, but it had declined in recent years, and the school was in financial trouble. It had borrowed $75,000 to pay overdue utility bills to keep the lights on and the doors open, but it ran a $100,000 deficit each year. Tom is a gifted leader, but he had walked into a hornet's nest. The church and school didn't have clear delineation. They shared finances and shared staff, which initially sounded like a good idea, but soon led to enormous headaches. The future looked grim for both the church and the school. Something had to be done, and done quickly. Tom and his board closed the school, but a large number of families were incensed at the decision and left the church. The remnant could barely support the church and the now almost empty worship center. In fact, things got so bad that they considered closing not only the school but the church, too.

Adding Scott as the youth pastor gave the ministry a shot in the arm. South Dallas is a rough area with rampant gang violence and related crimes. Under Scott's leadership, however, gang members came to Christ, attendance grew, and hundreds of lives were changed. But the specter of the past haunted Tom, Scott, and the church. Several board members were still bitterly disappointed that the school had been closed, and they blamed Tom. He spent those first years trying to rebuild the board and the trust with those who stayed.

Heartache, though, wasn't relegated to turf wars on the board. The youth ministry was strong and growing, but tragedy threatened to derail it. Many students in that part of the city were involved in gangs, including some students who were part of Scott's ministry. One night, a young man was killed in a drive-by shooting. Two of his friends were young men who had joined rival gangs, and one of them wanted revenge. He invited the other to watch television at his house. As his friend sat in the living room, he went to another room, picked up a pistol, came back in and shot him. He took a picture to show his gang what he had done. That was the price of loyalty. The incident shook the whole community of faith, and it set the stage for a change of direction for Tom Wilson. He wanted to do something to help these kids stay out of gangs and find meaning in their lives, and God led him to launch a charter school under the auspices of the state, not the church. That's when he asked Scott to join him as co-pastor.

During those years, the church grew to about nine hundred three different times, but each time, it lost momentum and dropped back to about six hundred people. Scott went to a conference, and he realized that his vehicle simply wasn't capable of taking him to the destination of his vision. In his book *Steering Through Chaos*, he explains, "Instantly, I realized that the way we hired staff, designed our programs, and trained leaders worked really well up to about 900 people, but if we continued to follow our present methods, we'd keep hitting the same ceiling again and again. Change, I was convinced, was absolutely necessary, but as I sat in that conference room . . . , my vision for the future was tempered by the stunning reality that change required hard decisions that would create tremendous pain for me, my family, our staff, and the lay leaders of our church."[1]

Scott and his father realized that they were serving in an antiquated organizational system with inherent role confusion between the two of them and between the church and the new charter school. They began to carefully but boldly destroy the old in order to build something new. Tom left the pastorate to devote his energies to establishing charter schools around the nation, and God is using him in incredible ways.[2] Scott became the senior pastor. God led him to begin a new church several miles south of Dallas in Red Oak, while keeping the previous campus as a satellite.

Over the past several years, Scott has worked hard to create a strong, healthy, inspiring culture for his board and his staff, and the results are amazing. They currently have five campuses in the Dallas area with several thousand in attendance. But that's just what people see on the surface. As we've noticed throughout this book, culture is what flows in the organizational bloodstream, not just what's skin deep.

I've been consulting with Scott for several years. He's a remarkable leader. He is always open to new ideas; in fact, he's a sponge. He's more than a problem solver. In every situation, he wants to dig deeper to uncover hidden truths. He seldom (if ever) jumps to conclusions. Instead, he asks questions, pursues insights, and involves people in the process all along the way. Then, when they come to a decision, he has the buy-in of his team and the confirmation that he is on the right track. As I've talked to Scott about the importance of culture, he immediately grasped the principles I've shared in this book, even before they were ever committed to paper or shared at events. People on his staff are convinced that he loves them and values their contribution to the vision of the church. His affirmations come from his heart, so people don't have to wonder if his praise is genuine. He has created a culture of experimentation in which he and his team challenge each other to attempt great things for God—without fear that failure will be condemned. They certainly strive for excellence, but they never neglect the spice of creativity in all they do. Scott's blend of vision, creativity, and authentic relationships lowers walls of resistance and builds trust with his staff, his board, people who attend the church, and those in the community. The culture of this church is so inspiring that people can't wait to get involved there!

Scott has created a culture of experimentation in which he and his team challenge each other to attempt great things for God—without fear that failure will be condemned.

Some leaders put on a good face in public, but they aren't very good at capturing the hearts and winning the loyalty of those closest to them. That's not the case with Scott. He has learned to be a shrewd judge of character and skills. One of his best hires is Justin Lathrop, whose leadership style is the perfect complement to Scott's. Justin works tirelessly behind the scenes to put all the pieces in place in the grand design of the church's vision and strategy. These two men are both better leaders because they found each other, and they aren't threatened in the least by the other's consummate abilities.

Over time, Scott transformed the culture of the church board. Years ago, they were tasked, like most church boards, with handling mounds of minutia. Gradually, Scott gave them more authority to have input in the larger issues of vision and strategy. Board members now feel empowered and valued because they know they are part of the top leadership team of the church. Any turf wars from the past have been drowned in the tidal wave of caring about God's kingdom instead of the price of copy paper.

Scott is an outstanding leader because he is an excellent learner. When he began the process of change, he was as lost in the woods as anyone else. But he wasn't content to let things stay the way they had always been. He believed God wanted something better in his church's culture, and he was open to learning how to make the necessary changes. That's what it takes: a little insight, a little creativity, a little courage, and a lot of love.

A Question About Music Style

William is the pastor of a church in Tennessee. He heard me explain the importance of creating an inspiring culture on his team and in his church, and went home ready to take bold steps forward. He patiently explained to his leadership team the principles of capturing momentum at point A, and he helped them understand the necessity of changing the vehicle so that they could fulfill their vision. As the months went by, the team implemented new ways of relating to each other, valuing those who ask hard questions, and creating new feedback loops to be sure everyone was on board. They also began to craft a new vehicle. As always, some members of his team adopted the new concepts very early, but some needed a few more questions answered.

As they talked about changing the style of music, the pastor realized that the people in the congregation—and especially those who didn't yet know Christ—responded more positively to more contemporary songs. The praise and worship leaders,

Joel and his wife, Liz, had been with the church for over eight years. The band, the choir, and the congregation loved them, but when William talked to them about changing music styles, they were adamant that they shouldn't change. During a month of weekly staff meetings, William shared his heart and his vision for the church, and he patiently explained how he believed the new worship style would have a powerful impact on people. But Joel dug in his heels. His intensity had been rising in each meeting, and now he leaned forward and glared at William. "If we change our style of music, I won't be true to my calling from God. I can't and I won't do that!"

Suddenly William realized that the issue for Joel (and, he assumed, for Liz too) was not about the preference for a particular music style, but about personal integrity. I'm not sure what Joel saw in William's face at that moment, but he must have thought he held all the cards. He growled at William, "And if you insist on changing direction with the music, then you're abandoning God's calling, and *you* have a problem with integrity!" Joel had raised the stakes, and he pushed all his chips to the center of the table.

Joel had raised the stakes, and he pushed all his chips to the center of the table. He called William's bet, but he lost.

He called William's bet, but he lost. William calmly replied, "Joel, I'm sorry you feel that way. I don't see it as a matter of integrity. I just want to reach people with the love of Christ, and music is an important part in our efforts. I had hoped you would see the heart of this change and gladly be part of the team. If you can't, then it's best for you to leave."

Joel stormed out in a huff. As it turns out, Liz had prompted Joel to frame their resistance as an integrity issue. They were both furious with William, and they felt betrayed by the rest of the leadership team because they supported him. As soon as the dust cleared, William met with Rich, the associate praise and worship leader, to find out where he stood. Rich had listened to both sides of the debate (which is what the discussion had become), but he came to a different conclusion. He told William, "Pastor, I'd prefer the music style we've been using since I've been here, but if you believe God is leading us to touch more people just by changing our worship, I'm for it."

William was pleasantly surprised, and it must have shown on his face, because Rich continued, "Pastor, it's not really about the music. It's about the kingdom. I want to honor God and reach people. That's what I understand you want to do. God gave you a vision, and I'm here to serve. I'll be glad to help any way I can."

Rich became the praise and worship leader, and he's doing a great job in his new position. The new music style seems to be having a positive effect. It's hard to tell why more unbelievers and new believers are coming, but they say they love the music!

William and his team experienced chaos when they took steps to change their culture. It's inevitable. He understood the risks, and he anticipated that people on his team would respond all along the Diffusion of Innovations bell curve. He had a good idea whom he could count on to be the early embracers, but he was surprised that Joel and Liz proved to be never embracers. He thought it might be Rich or someone else, but he was ready for every possible response.

Asking the Right Questions

To take a team through the labyrinth of changing the culture, we need to engage their hearts and minds. Gifted teachers know that asking a great question is often more valuable than an hour of brilliant lecture. Questions challenge a person's thinking and draw her into the process of exploring solutions.

Gifted teachers know that asking a great question is often more valuable than an hour of brilliant lecture.

The best ones are open questions that don't have simple, quick answers. They ask why and how, not just what and who. Sometimes, though, a simple question (and its answer) provides the foundation for a richer, deeper, more thought-provoking open question that follows it.

First, ask poignant questions to yourself. I'd suggest the following:

Personal Reflection

- Who am I? Where does my identity come from?
- What matters most to me?
- How well does my daily schedule relate to what matters most to me?
- Beyond roles and paychecks, what is my deepest, most compelling motivation? Really?
- How do I define success?
- Where am I in the process of learning, growing, and changing as a person and as a leader?

Don't rush your answers. Carve out some time alone, away from the hectic pace of the office, so you can genuinely ponder these things. Ask God to give insight into your heart, your desires, and your values—and listen to his Spirit as you think and pray. Leaders report that some answers come easily, but when they are committed to being ruthlessly honest with God, some questions challenge them to the core. Don't feel that you have to have all the answers tied up with a nice bow. Give yourself room to keep thinking, praying, and reflecting on your deepest motivations.

In a series of conversations with your team, ask them some penetrating questions. Listen carefully to their answers without correcting them or defending your positions. You'll know you're really listening if, when someone says something you don't agree with, you reply, "That's a very interesting point. Tell me more." I suggest you ask these questions:

Questions About the Team's Perception of the Leader

- What are three things you'd like to change about our team?
- What are three things you want to be sure we don't change?
- What do you want me to do for you?
- What are you afraid I'm going to do?
- What helps you serve with a full heart? What hinders or clouds your motivation?
- Is there anything lingering in your mind or on your heart that you want to talk about? Nothing is off-limits; anything goes.

These questions are open enough to encompass the full range of challenges, relationships, systems, and motivations on a team. In fact, if the conversation doesn't go deeper than the level of job descriptions, it hasn't touched people's hearts. I'd also recommend that you use the questions in each section of the CULTURE analysis in Chapter Three. There's no time limit or deadline for completing these conversations. The process of discovery and disclosure is at least as important as the topics your team discusses. Opening lines of communication to talk about the things people have longed to discuss builds trust for the future.

Opening lines of communication to talk about the things people have longed to discuss builds trust for the future.

Many pastors and teams also invite input about the culture from a wider range of midlevel leaders. They may ask each ministry director to schedule times to involve her staff and top volunteers, or the pastor may want to hold a town hall meeting.

Large meetings are expedient, but they aren't conducive to the kinds of interactions needed to talk openly about the culture of the ministry team. I'd recommend that the ministry leaders follow the example of the pastor and lead their teams in open dialogue about the things that matter to them. The following are some questions for these teams:

Questions About the Team's Planning and Process

- How well do people on our team understand how our work fits into the overall vision of the church?
- In what ways are we celebrating success and affirming people for their contributions?
- Do people on the team and the volunteers under them feel empowered and appreciated? Why or why not?
- In what ways does our operating system (delegation, meetings, reporting, follow up, and so on) provide a forum for honest dialogue among team members and the ministry leader? How does the system hinder this kind of dialogue?
- Do we have the tools and resources we need to fulfill God's vision for our team? If not, what do we need?
- How well do we cultivate a culture of experimentation that celebrates taking risks to accomplish great things for God?
- How well are we identifying, selecting, and developing rising leaders in our pipeline?

Be aware that asking these questions (and others from the CULTURE analysis in Chapter Three) often surfaces perceptions that can be inflammatory. Leading a team through the chaos of culture change is challenging work, but don't let the left hand of dread and the right hand of fear squeeze hope from the hearts of your team. Invite open dialogue, but always communicate that you and the team will trust God together to find solutions. Leaders rise to meet challenges, and as Napoleon remarked, "Leaders are dealers in hope."

Don't let your team get stuck in the past. Invite team members to be honest in their assessment and creative in finding answers. In all these discussions,

Leading a team through the chaos of culture change is challenging work, but don't let the left hand of dread and the right hand of fear squeeze hope from the hearts of your team.

teams have four needs (much like a family that is going through a significant change). These are

1. The need for clarity
2. The need for the leader to model steady emotions, avoiding extreme highs and lows
3. The need to take action after decisions are made and the new direction is set
4. The need for security in unsettling times

In holding all these important discussions, realize that leaders are abstract communicators, but most team members think more concretely. Abstract communicators can add concrete points and illustrations to make sure they connect with people, but the vast majority of concrete thinkers have difficulty internalizing abstract thoughts. Those concepts bore them; they want specifics. For example, the pastor shares his vision: "God wants us to reach this community with the Good News of Christ." As Sally listens with the rest of the team, she wonders, "When he says 'community,' does he mean the people who live in a one-mile radius of the church, or five miles out?" But that's not her only concrete question. She also wants to know, "What kind of training will they provide for us? I'll tell you, if they have the training on Thursday night, I can't come because I have to take my daughter to piano practice. And if Jim is leading the training, I'm not going to go whenever it's offered. I don't like him at all."

Sally's thinking process isn't wrong. It's just concrete. Pastors need to understand that the vast majority of people on their teams and in their churches don't separate vision from strategy, which includes specific plans, meetings, roles, and schedules. It's a mistake for abstract-thinking pastors to share their vision one week and their strategy the next. They'll lose people that way. When pastors realize that their people's minds are quick-set concrete, they'll make sure to simultaneously share specific plans and details of their global vision.

The leader's example of honesty and faith sets the tone for the team's future. If everyone feels like an integral part, everyone will contribute her best. Honesty invites long-buried emotions to come to the surface, so conflict is inevitable. Don't be surprised, but don't let conflict cloud the team's future. Welcome honest dialogue and seek resolution for each issue. Keep pointing people to God, his provision for the future, and his purpose for the team and the church. The way your team learns to relate to each other sets the tone for the culture of the church.

Change with Grace

All change is a critique of the past. If we're not careful, we can step on the toes of those we're trying to lead as we destroy the old vehicle and create a new one. Leaders need to understand what's at stake in the hearts of those who treasure the past. They may not be thrilled to change vehicles! We can't improve anything without

The conundrum of leadership is this: people want improvement, but they resist change.

changing it. The conundrum of leadership is this: people want improvement, but they resist change. Our task is helping them learn to embrace change.

The vocabulary of change is very important. As we lead people to capture momentum at point A and change vehicles, we need to avoid labeling the current systems as "bad" or "ineffective," or using any other language that devalues the hard work and dedication of those who have come before us. To help people take steps into the future, we need to celebrate the past. When they feel that we truly value the past, they will be willing to let go of it and take steps forward.

When I was a pastor of a church in Michigan years ago, we realized that we needed to replace the old single-pane windows that were scant protection against the frigid winter winds. We raised enough money to have top-quality, triple-paned windows installed. When the man from the window company came to get measurements of our eight windows, he called me over and said, "Pastor, there's a problem. The windows aren't all the same size, and they aren't all a standard size. We're going to have to customize some of the windows. I'm afraid the price is going to be significantly higher. Do you want to proceed?"

I called a board member, Brother Bolen, to come to the church to talk about this problem. As we inspected the building more carefully and took precise measurements, we found that one wall was 18 inches longer than the other—an additional block had been added to that wall during construction many years before I arrived. As Brother Bolen and I took measurements, I began to complain about the shoddy construction of the church. "Why in the world," I said in disgust, "would anyone build a building this way? Didn't they know better?"

Brother Bolen shuffled his feet and said in a quiet voice, "Brother Sam, we did the best we could in those days." He paused, then continued. "We worked in the oil fields during the day, and we came to the church at night to build it. This area was a swamp, but we filled it in with wheelbarrow loads of dirt trucked in. The light wasn't very good, and some of us had never built anything before. I'm sorry. We did the best we could."

I hoped that Jesus would come back in that instant or, better yet, that the earth would open and swallow me so I'd never have to see Brother Bolen again. I had hurt the feelings of a man I loved. I had focused only on the change necessary for the future without a thought about the values and commitment of men and women in the past.

I learned a valuable lesson that day. Sometime later, I wanted to change the paneling in the church. It was the best they could afford when the church was built, but it was ugly—incredibly ugly. This time, though, I realized that I needed to honor the past in order to change it. I preached a four-message series called "If the Walls Could Talk." I interviewed people who had been at the church for many years, and I told their stories: this person was saved here, that couple got married, this student was baptized, and God changed that family forever. To prepare for the third Sunday, I asked people to bring their old family Bibles that contained their spiritual histories, and I asked them to bring markers so they could write on the walls. That Sunday, they shared pictures of loved ones, told stories and cried happy tears, and asked for prayer for people who were still lost without Christ. They wrote cherished names and personal notes on the paneling during that service, and we poured out our hearts to celebrate all God had done within those walls. They knew that the next day, the workmen were coming to put sheet-rock over the old paneling and paint it a beautiful color. They weren't going to rip it out and replace it. As a testimony of the past, we left the paneling and the names written on it for as long as that building would stand.

In their minds (or maybe on paper), leaders need to keep a ledger during times of change. On one side of the ledger are gains, and on the other, losses. The leader casting the vision for change can list many things under gains. She sees the future, and she is convinced that the changes she proposes will propel the church to fulfill God's vision. A few other visionaries are in that column, too, but virtually everyone else, about 95 percent of the people, feels a genuine sense of loss because of the proposed change. Even small changes to a church threaten people's stability and their sense of history. Someone might grumble, "I don't want to meet in the new building because my husband and I were married in our worship center. It means the world to me." Losses always carry emotional weight.

As we stand in the pulpit or meeting room to extol the wonderful benefits of the change we are inaugurating, we feel excited about the glorious possibilities, but the vast majority of people listening to us feel only sadness. No wonder they are resistant. If we don't connect with their hearts and win them, they start to question our motives and our wisdom to lead them. To bring them along, we have to recognize their losses, celebrate the past, grieve with them, and lead them gently into the future. If we don't take these compassionate steps, we effectively communicate that we don't care about their feelings or their history. In our communication about change, we want them to be convinced, "He understands what's meaningful to me. He wants to move us forward, but he celebrates the past. I can follow a leader like that."

My walk with Brother Bolen that day at the church gave me valuable insight about change. It was a hard lesson, but one I'll never forget. All change is a critique of the past, and we need to be sensitive and wise as we talk about the past our people treasure. We simply can't take them forward unless they are convinced that we treasure their past, too.

> *All change is a critique of the past, and we need to be sensitive and wise as we talk about the past our people treasure.*

Quo Vadis

Now, at the end of the book, which way will you go? This is not the kind of book that you breeze through, picking up a principle or two and moving on to something else. Either you embrace the process of transforming a culture and devote yourself to the hard but rewarding work, or you put the book down and go back to business as usual. There's not much middle ground. Those who take up the challenge are in for the ride of their lives. Very few tasks are as stimulating and difficult, but seeing a culture change in front of our eyes is a glorious thing to behold. The early stage is often the most difficult. Misunderstandings and resistance threaten to stop us in our tracks, but if we have the courage to keep moving forward, people begin to get it, and they become allies. Changing the culture of a team or a church forces us to delve below the surface and confront our motives and our systems. It's not for the fainthearted, but it's worth it. I hope you're in—all in.

Think About It . . .

1. How might the questions listed in this chapter help you and your team begin the process of changing your culture?

2. How have you seen leaders implement change with grace? Why is it crucial to identify with people's losses about the past as you help them take steps into the future?

3. What's the next step for you? How will you take it? What do you expect in the next month as you take that step with your team?

Appendix 1

OVERVIEW OF THE FREE CULTURE SURVEY

www.freeculturesurvey.com

This survey was developed by Dr. Samuel R. Chand, Mr. Pat Springle, Professor Tom Snider, and Mrs. Melinda R. Keeney to help senior leaders and their organizations obtain an accurate assessment of the culture of their organizations and teams. Each factor of the team's life and health will be graded and reported as

Inspiring . . . Accepting . . . Stagnant . . . Discouraging . . . Toxic

The survey measures individual perceptions of the **seven** key components of **CULTURE:** Control, Understanding, Leadership, Trust, Unafraid, Responsive, and Execution.

This survey can be used by teams as small as three members or as large as two hundred.

To complete the survey, go to http://www.freeculturesurvey .com and sign up the senior leader and the team. Enter the name and e-mail address of each person on the team to be surveyed. An e-mail will be sent to team members to invite him or her to come to the site and fill out the survey. If team members haven't come to the site in a reasonable period of time, they'll receive an e-mail to remind them.

When all surveys have been completed, an e-mail will be sent to the senior leader notifying him or her that the results are available for viewing. The report will include a rating of the team on each of the seven CULTURE components, along with a written summary of the results and suggestions for enhancing the team culture.

To build a more positive, productive culture, teams may benefit from reading and discussing this book.

www.freeculturesurvey.com

Appendix 2

STRATEGIC PLANNING GRID

What	Why	Who	How	When	Where	How Much	Accountable to Whom	Evaluation Process

© Dr. Samuel R. Chand

Appendix 3

TO-DO LIST AND STATUS REPORT FOR *MAJOR* ITEMS

Department:
Responsible Person:
Date:

	Item	Date Item Received	Status	Projected Completion Date	Actual Completion Date
1.					
2.					
3.					
4.					

All people making reports should do the following four things:

1. Report *data*.
2. Create meaning by providing *implications* of the data.
3. *Recommend* actions for the implications.
4. Be ready with *strategies* once recommendation(s) have been confirmed.

© Dr. Samuel R. Chand

Notes

Chapter 1: Culture Trumps Vision

1. Dick Clark quoted in "Corporate Culture Is the Game," *Executive Leadership*, Nov. 2008, p. 3.
2. Patrick Lencioni, *The Five Dysfunctions of a Team* (San Francisco: Jossey-Bass, 2002), pp. 188–189.
3. Archibald Hart, *The Crazy-Making Workplace* (Ann Arbor, Mich.: Vine Books, 1993), p. 67.
4. Chuck Colson and Jack Eckerd, *Why America Doesn't Work* (New York: Random House, 1994).

Chapter 3: Seven Keys of Culture

1. Note: Most assessment tools used in organizations measure an individual's temperament or aptitude. Teams can use some of the best tools to show how each person tends to respond to others. The free CULTURE survey is available online. To sign up for your team, go to www.freeculturesurvey.org.
2. Samuel R. Chand, *Who's Holding Your Ladder?* (Niles, Ill.: Mall Publishing, 2003), p. 62.
3. Shayla McKnight, "Workplace Gossip? Keep It to Yourself," *New York Times*, Nov. 14, 2009, http://www.nytimes.com/2009/11/15/jobs/15pre.html?_r=2.
4. "Spirit Lexicon," *Spirit*, Dec. 2009, p. 56.
5. "Bain & Company" (interview with Steve Ellis), *Consulting*, Sept.-Oct. 2008, p. 19.

6. Keith Sawyer quoted in Janet Rae-Dupree, "Teamwork, the True Mother of Invention," *New York Times*, Dec. 7, 2008, p. B3.

Chapter 4: Vocabulary Defines Culture

1. Joseph Mattera, "Why a Church's Culture Always Trumps Its Vision," 2007, http://josephmattera.org/index.php?option= com_content&task=view&id=474&Itemid=1.
2. Maren and Jamie Showkeir, "How to Talk Straight in Hard Times," *Leader to Leader*, Summer 2009, p. 15.
3. Stone offers this definition in the Q&A section of her Web site, http://lindastone.net/qa.

Chapter 6: The Catalyst of Chaos

1. Adapted from Julia Kirby and Thomas A. Stewart, "The Institutional Yes," *Harvard Business Review*, Oct. 2007.
2. "Developing a Change-Friendly Culture" (interview with John P. Kotter), *Leader to Leader*, Spring 2008, pp. 33–38.
3. William L. White, *The Incestuous Workplace* (Center City, Minn.: Hazeldon, 1997), p. 51.
4. "Developing a Change-Friendly Culture," p. 36.
5. Adapted from "Drop the Ax on Mediocrity," *Executive Leadership*, May 2008, 23(5), 1.
6. "The Really New Waldorf" (interview with Eric O. Long), *Leaders*, Jan. 2004, 27, 80.
7. Linda Hudson quoted in "Fitting In, and Rising to the Top," *New York Times*, Sept. 20, 2009, http://www.nytimes .com/2009/09/20/business/20corner.html.

Chapter 7: Changing Vehicles

1. Henry Moore quoted in John A. Byrne, "Celebrating the Ordinary," *Fast Company*, Jan. 2005, p. 14.

2. Jim Baker, "Achieve Peak Performance with a Leadership Culture of Shared Purpose," *Church Executive*, July 2008, pp. 76–78.

3. Dave Logan, John King, and Halee Fisher-Wright, "Corporate Tribes: The Heart of Effective Leadership," *Leader to Leader*, Summer 2008, pp. 25–29.

Chapter 8: Yes, You Can!

1. Scott Wilson, *Steering Through Chaos* (Grand Rapids, Mich.: Zondervan, 2009).

2. To find out more about Dr. Wilson, charter schools, and consulting to help communities launch effective charter schools, go to www.nationalcharterconsultants.com.

The Author

Dr. Samuel R. Chand, having been raised in a pastor's home in India, is uniquely equipped to share his passion to mentor, develop, and inspire leaders in ministry and the marketplace. Dr. Chand has served as senior pastor, college president, chancellor, and president emeritus of Beulah Heights University, the country's largest predominantly African American Bible College.

Dr. Chand speaks regularly at leadership conferences, churches, corporations, ministerial conferences, seminars, and other leadership development opportunities. He was named one of the top thirty global leadership gurus by www.leadershipgurus .net. Dr. Chand serves on the board of EQUIP (Dr. John Maxwell's ministry), working with five million leaders worldwide, and assists Bishop Eddie L. Long's leadership development team. Dr. Chand works with leaders through leadership consultations and resources, including books and CDs, online mentoring, and speaking. Some of the books he has written are *Who's Holding Your Ladder?*, *LadderShifts*, and *Planning Your Succession*.

His educational background includes an honorary doctor of divinity degree from Heritage Bible College, a master of arts in biblical counseling from Grace Theological Seminary, and a bachelor of arts in biblical education from Beulah Heights University. Dr. Chand and his wife, Brenda, live in McDonough, Georgia, with their two daughters, Rachel and Deborah, and granddaughter, Adeline. You can learn more about Dr. Chand's ministry by visiting www.samchand.com.

Other Books by
Dr. Samuel R. Chand

Failure: The Womb of Success

Futuring: Leading Your Church into Tomorrow

Who's Holding Your Ladder? Selecting Your Leaders—Your Most Crucial Decision

Who Moved Your Ladder? Your Next Bold Move

What's Shakin' Your Ladder? 15 Challenges All Leaders Face

LadderShifts: New Realities—Rapid Change—Your Destiny

Ladder Focus: Creating, Sustaining, and Enlarging Your Big Picture

Planning Your Succession: Preparing for Your Future

ReChurch: When Change Is No Longer an Option

Master Leaders—a Collaborative Book with George Barna

Weathering the Storm: Leading in Uncertain Times

www.samchand.com

Index

The Services of
Dr. Samuel R. Chand Consulting

Dr. Chand has only one product—LEADERSHIP. However, he delivers the product through three distinct systems:

1. Consultations: Every consultation is totally customized with four distinct components—Assess→Articulate→Align→Advance leading to culture formation, vision fulfillment, capacity enhancement, and leadership development.

2. Speaking at leadership conferences and training events: Dr. Chand's busy speaking schedule covers a broad spectrum of churches, corporations, nonprofits, and other organizations.

3. Resources—books, CDs, DVDs, and online resources: Dr. Chand's resources continue to be used as reference guides by leaders globally. Among his many books, *Who's Holding Your Ladder? LadderShifts, ReChurch,* and *Futuring* continue to engage and challenge leaders at all levels.

www.samchand.com

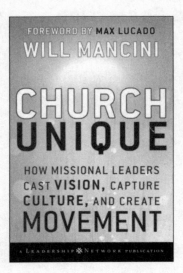

Church Unique

How Missional Leaders Cast Vision, Capture Culture, and Create Movement

Will Mancini

ISBN: 978-0-470-58039-4

Paperback | 304 pp.

"Will Mancini's vision for vision is contagious. Church Unique *doesn't hold back—challenging existing paradigms, yes, but also providing new maps for churches to engage in God's mission."*

—Ed Stetzer, director, LifeWay Research;
coauthor, *Comeback Churches* and *Compelled by Love*

Church Unique is written by church consultant Will Mancini—an expert on a new kind of visioning process to help churches develop a stunningly unique model of ministry that leads to redemptive movement. He guides churches away from an internal focus to emphasize participation in their community and surrounding culture. In this important book, Mancini offers an approach for rethinking what it means to lead with clarity as a visionary. Mancini explains that each church has a culture that reflects its particular values, thoughts, attitudes, and actions, and shows how church leaders can unlock their church's individual DNA and unleash their congregation's one-of-a-kind potential.

Mancini explores the pitfalls churches often fall into in their attempt to grow, such as adding more programs, using outdated forms of strategic planning, or adopting the latest conference technique. He explores a new model for vision casting and church growth that has been tested with leaders in all kinds of congregations, including mainline, evangelical, small, and large. The practices and ideas outlined in *Church Unique* will help leaders develop missional teams, articulate unique strategies, unpack the baggage of institutionalism, and live fully into their vision.

Whether leading a megachurch or church plant, a multisite or mainline, a ministry or parachurch, *Church Unique* will provide inspiration as a practical guide for leading into the future. There is a better way.

Church Turned Inside Out

A Guide for Designers, Refiners, and Re-Aligners

Linda Bergquist | Allan Karr

ISBN: 978-0-470-38317-8

Hardback | 240 pp.

"What an extremely hopeful, heart-lifting, and practical book for anyone who loves the church. We must never be afraid to look at our church from the inside out as that is where true change will happen."

—Dan Kimball author, *They Like Jesus but Not the Church*

In *Church Turned Inside Out*, Linda Bergquist and Allan Karr push back on the one-size-fits-all approach. They invite leaders of all kinds of churches—new and existing, megachurches and microchurches—to walk through an inside-out design process. Instead of starting with models and methods, they insist that every sphere of church life resonates with and communicates what you really believe.

As the book unfolds, it moves from abstract concepts toward concrete suggestions. It considers the uniqueness of individual leaders, their teams, and their particular communities, cultures, and contexts while taking seriously both spiritual and practical dimensions. This process results in more potent and effectively organized churches. Perhaps more important, it helps church leaders discover ways to live and work more wholly and faithfully, according to how God created them. It really is possible for a church to be so beautifully designed that every structure, program, and relationship reflects what it intends. Sometimes this requires a whole new design, and other times it only takes re-aligning or refining what already exists. This thoughtful and systemic approach opens a wider array of possible church paradigms than most people ever imagine, but the real goal is not innovation but transformation.

Other Books of Interest

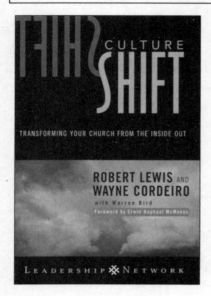

Culture Shift

Transforming Your Church

from the Inside Out

Robert Lewis | Wayne Cordeiro

with warren bird

ISBN: 978-0-7879-7530-2

Hardback | 256 pp.

"Like snowflakes and fingerprints, every church's culture is unique. Learning the art of cultural analysis and cultural formation shown in Culture Shift *is indispensable for church leaders."*

—John Ortberg, teaching pastor, Menlo Park Presbyterian Church; author, *If You Want to Walk on Water, You've Got to Get Out of the Boat,* and *The Life You've Always Wanted*

Would you describe your church's culture as thriving and irresistible? Are your church's members confidently using their gifts, talents, passions, and energy to serve and advance the Kingdom of God? If you hesitated in answering, *Culture Shift* is the hands-on resource that can help your church release its full potential as a force for good.

Culture Shift, written for church leaders, ministers, pastors, ministry teams, and lay leaders, leads you through the process of identifying your church's distinctive culture, gives you practical tools to change it from the inside-out, and provides steps to keep your new culture aligned with your church's mission. Real transformation is not about working harder at what you're already doing or even copying another church's approach but about changing church culture at a foundational level.

The good news is that you already have everything you need—but you must look within for radical, transformational power. Your job is to develop a healthy atmosphere and let the Holy Spirit do the work through you. Once this fundamental shift has occurred and the new habits and values become central to everything your church does, a healthy, energetic, God-honoring church will be unleashed into a world that is desperately crying out for it.

Other Books of Interest

Hybrid Church

The Fusion of Intimacy and Impact

Dave Browning

ISBN: 978-0-470-57230-6

Hardback | 160 pp.

"Dave Browning gives a really well articulated, organizationally insightful, insider's view of what happens when missional meets mega and when movemental forms engage best practice in contemporary church leadership and organization. Hybrid Church is clear evidence that God is doing something fundamental in our day."

—Alan Hirsch, author, *The Forgotten Ways*

"Hybrid Church has something important to say to leaders of the emerging house church, as well as the largest megachurches in the world. You will appreciate the spirit of this book as much as its content."

—Steve Kim, president, Ministry Direct

A hands-on resource for both large and small churches. It has been predicted that in the twenty-first century extremely large churches would emerge in America that resemble neither an elephant nor a field of mice. Which is better? At one time the answer would have been either/or. Now it's both/and. We want both the intimacy of smallness and the impact of bigness—we want a hybrid of the two. *Hybrid Church* is a practical guide for clergy and leaders who want to have the best of both church worlds: the intimacy of small "house church" groups and the impact of very large megachurches.

Baby Boomers and Beyond

Tapping the Ministry Talents and Passions of Adults over 50

Amy Hanson

ISBN: 978-0-470-50079-8

Hardback | 224 pp.

"Amy Hanson does a brilliant job of reminding us that the most powerful and under-utilized source of Kingdom impact is the fifty-plus generation. I have seen firsthand how the mission of Jesus offers them more fulfillment than retirement, golf, or the next sight-seeing trip ever could."

—Dave Ferguson, lead pastor, COMMUNITY/Movement Leader, NewThing

Baby boomers—arguably the largest segment of the population—are entering their retirement years at an unprecedented rate. With more discretionary time and increased longevity, this group is searching for a way to make a meaningful impact with their lives.

Baby Boomers and Beyond explores the opportunities and challenges that the older adult population presents for the Christian community. Author Amy Hanson dares church leaders to let go of stereotypes about aging and embrace a new paradigm, that older adults are for the most part active, healthy, and capable of making significant contributions for the Kingdom of God.

Hanson offers a realistic view of the boomers and reveals what matters most to this age group: staying young, juggling multiple relationships, and redefining retirement. By tapping into their needs, pastors can engage this burgeoning group and unleash the power of the boomer generation to enhance and strengthen the mission of the church.